DATE DUE

THOSE WERE THE

☞ A HAPPY LOOK AT

GOOD OLD DAYS

AMERICAN ADVERTISING, 1880-1950

BY EDGAR R. JONES

Published by SIMON AND SCHUSTER

PUBLISHED BY SIMON AND SCHUSTER
A DIVISION OF GULF & WESTERN CORPORATION

SIMON & SCHUSTER BUILDING
ROCKEFELLER CENTER
1230 AVENUE OF THE AMERICAS
NEW YORK, NEW YORK 10020

Library of Congress Cataloging in Publication Data

Jones, Edgar Robert, 1911-
  Those were the good old days.

  1. Advertising—Specimens.   2. Advertising—
United States—History—Sources. I. Title.
HF5813.U6J6 1979   659.13′2   78-16669
ISBN 0-671-24718-2
ISBN 0-671-24598-8 Pbk.

CONTENTS

Hello

...a corsetmaker putting a jingle in Queen Victoria's mouth
...a shaving-soap maker taking six separate liberties with Barnum's face
...the Reverend Henry Ward Beecher endorsing a toilet soap
...new cars at $260 f.o.b.

... these are some of the things you'll find in this book, a 70-year collection of advertisements from the magazines of 1880–1950.

☞ Some of the ads were chosen for their pictures, some for their words, some for their prices. Some because they were good ads, some because they were bad ads. Some are here because the products were ahead of their time, others because the ads themselves were ahead of their time. Some because they are straightforward, others because they are misleading. And, of course, some of the most entertaining are those that urge you to buy for fear you will lose wife, friends and fortune if you don't.

☞ A few show that national publications used to print material that would now be felt to be in bad taste. Many illustrate the beginning and the growth of products of wide interest.

☞ All of these ads prove again and again that people are people, no matter when.

☞ The date you see is the date the ad appeared. It may or may not be the date of the product's appearance. If any of the dates are wrong, I am sorry. In the business of selecting, clipping, trimming, sorting and pasting it is easy for errors to creep in. The whole thing stops in 1950 because that date marks the end of the period of nostalgia for most of us. The last quarter of a century or so is still too close to seem old-fashioned.

☞ That is all I have to say. I hope you enjoy this chance to reminisce and explore the past, completely free from any heavy-handed intrusion or social commentary by the editor. Naturally, I would have liked to have cluttered up the book with deductions, conclusions and profound comments, but good sense won out.

Look at the pictures, read the ads, have a good time!

EDGAR R. JONES

HARPER'S BAZAR.

SATURDAY, JANUARY 26, 1884.

WITH A PATTERN-SHEET SUPPLEMENT.

BLOWN IN THE BOTTLE.

IT would seem as if it were impossible for us as a people to complete the half of our great undertakings, to carry on the farming of our continent, make our railways, dig our canals, tunnel our mountains, rule our cities, write our books, make our inventions, without a tolerably fair supply of good health to support us through so huge a sum of work, and such a constant exhaustion of our physical and mental resources. Yet who that reads, for the first time, the advertisements in our daily papers by the proprietors of patent medicines, filling columns and pages with their big letters and their atrocious pictures, who that sees every fence and board along the lines of our railroads lettered over with the same thing, who that sees rock and river and meadow disfigured throughout the whole course of summer travel by solicitations to buy this nostrum and assurances of the worth of that compound—who that sees these gigantic and broadcast advertisements would think our public was anything but a mass of disease, paying immense tithes to be healed of its leprosies, meeting the cost, as it does, of all these placards, and seeing without complaint, as it does also, the fairest landscapes of the country-side ruined?

One well may ask, although the question remain unanswered, if we are sick, how do we accomplish our tremendous work, and if we are not sick, who buys these patent medicines, and if we use the patent medicines, why do they not destroy us, and is it possible there is any balm or virtue in them, and is it a part of our national ailment that we are contented to see our choicest scenery daubed over and spoiled without registering a vow never to buy one drop or one pill of that particular element of destruction whose name confronts us, and is it altogether a fact that we are an ailing, dyspeptic people, given up by the doctors, and given over to the quacks, really bowing down before the patent draught, purchasing it, swallowing it, and having vitality and vigor enough left to survive it, and feel no sense of wrong and outrage as we look up and see the proprietors roll by in their coaches, and their wives flash in their diamonds?

What strange names have these compounds which have so acquired the upper hand of the good old drugs by which our fathers and mothers lived and died, and what absurd little romances are printed in the wrappers of the boxes and bottles, and believed in by those who are eager to be deceived! These, indeed, do but bear the label of "Old Dr. So-and-so's Bitters," carrying conviction of an ancient and established reputation for well-doing; and those are the "Only Original Pill," as if the world were full of imitations of an invaluable article; but others carry statements which are saturated with the incredible to that audacious point which is supposed to compel belief. Here is one recommended by legislators and soldiers: a physician travelling in Russia falls in with a band of mounted gypsies, and admires the wondrous feats of horsemanship of the son of their chief, who ends by breaking a leg, which the physician sets, and the grateful chieftain presents him with this recipe, which when compounded is little less than spray from the fountain of perpetual youth. In another, the author of the precious prescription becomes, under the shadow of the Himalayas, a pet of the Brahmins, is led by them through all the mazes of their lore, taught what herbs answer the moon with their sacred juices, and at what time of the moon to cut them with a golden knife, and is intrusted at last with the century-kept secret, which he brings over the seas, and peddles out at so much the parcel. And in the third, a life spent in the lodge of the red man has resulted in acquaintance with this invaluable drug, whose use will do away with all the cure-passing fevers that "come shaking down into the joints of miserable men." And there are people enough who believe these remarkable stories, and buy the "alterative," or the "cure," or the "remedy," at rates and in quantities which allow the vender to feed his horse on Malaga grapes in the morning; and when the horses are seen shining and prancing along the avenues, there are other people who think it not amiss to find out what is in the stuff that produces such golden results to its owner, and they buy too, till it seems as if the only sure road to wealth were, not in building railroads, in running steam-ship lines, in opening mines, in operating in stocks, in whitening the sea with commerce, but in owning a proprietary medicine in vogue. In fact, one is inclined to say that everybody buys the things: the professor recommends them with the large-minded air of one who does not keep in a rut; the minister quietly acknowledges having been helped by them, as he fancies; the physician himself tries them in secret; the fashionable lady resorts to them in her closet; the Puritan maiden finds comfort in some one of the host. "John, how could you be so unfriendly as to have this without notifying me?" is cried by one young man to another on going into John's room, and finding that John had the start of him in a new medicine which he had not seen himself.

To go into the place of manufacture of certain of these medicines is an experience that opens one's eyes with wonder if not alarm, on seeing the ledgers devoted to the different States, to Europe, to Australia, the countless clerks absorbed in their duties, the great shipments ready for South America and the East, the order, the business, the dispatch, the wealth, of the concern; and it occasions one to marvel if there is not, on the whole, in the greater part of the compounds, with their innocent names blown in the bottle, some one prevailing tonic or stimulating draught that under any other name would be as sweet to tired nerves and stomachs, or else either to blush for the credulity and ignorance of the buying race, or to sigh for the sorrows that science can not heal, and that turn for help and find it only in the patent lotion, pill, or powder.

10

11

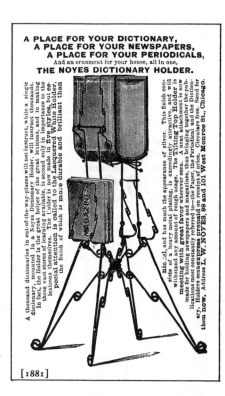

12

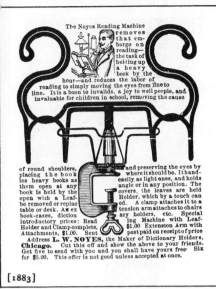

The Noyes Reading Machine removes that embargo on reading—the task of holding up a heavy book by the hour—and reduces the labor of reading to simply moving the eyes from line to line. It is a boon to invalids, a joy to well people, and invaluable for children in school, removing the cause of round shoulders, placing the books as them open at any book is held with a Leaf-be removed or replaced table or desk. An ex book-cases, diction introductory prices: Read Holder and Clamp complete, Attachments, $1.00. Sent post paid on receipt of price Address **L. W. NOYES**, the Maker of Dictionary Holders, **Chicago.** Cut this off and show the above to your friends. Get five to send with you and you shall have yours free Six for $5.00. This offer is not good unless accepted at once.

and preserving the eyes by where it should be. It handles easily, as light ones, and holds angle or in any position. The covers, the leaves are held Holder, which by a touch can ary holders, etc. Special ing Machine with Leaf-$1.00 Extension Arm with

[1883]

COLUMBIA BICYCLES

The Art of wheelmanship is a gentlemanly and fascinating one, once acquired never forgotten, which no young man should neglect to acquire.

The Bicycle is practical everywhere that a buggy is, and enables you to dispense with the horse and the care and cost of keeping him. It is destined to be the prevailing light, quick, ready conveyance in country towns.

The Youth take to bicycles like ducks to water. They ride it quickly, easily, safely and gracefully. They can get more pleasure out of it than out of a horse, a boat, and a tennis or cricket outfit all together.

Parents should favor bicycle riding by their boys, because it gives them so much enjoyment, makes them lithe and strong, keeps them from evil associations, and increases their knowledge and their self-reliance. There is no out-door game or amusement so safe and wholesome.

The above paragraphs are but fragmentary suggestions; ask those who have ridden: read "The American Bicycler" (50 cts.), the "Bicycling World" (7 cts. a copy), our illustrated catalogue (3-ct. stamp).

The Columbia bicycles are of elegant design, best construction, fine finish, and are warranted. They may be had with best ball-bearings, finest nickel plate, and other specialties of construction and finish, according to choice.

The Mustang is a less expensive, plain and serviceable style of bicycle made by us for boys and youths.

Physicians, clergymen, lawyers, business men of every class, are riding our Columbias in nearly every State and Territory to-day, with profit in pocket, with benefit in health, and with delightful recreation. The L.A. W. Meet at Boston brought 800 men together on bicycles; but the **boys,** who outnumber them, and who have their own clubs and associations in so many places, were at school and at home. Why don't every boy have a bicycle?

Send 3-cent stamp for our 24-page illustrated catalogue and price-list, with full information.

THE POPE M'F'G CO.,
598 Washington Street,
BOSTON MASS.

[1881]

THE WATERBURY.

THIS IS THE BEST WATCH FOR BICYCLERS

The Cheapest! The Most Reliable! The Most Simple! The least liable to get out of order! The easiest repaired is the **WATERBURY WATCH.**

All in Nickel-Silver Case. Every Watch Warranted. ASK YOUR JEWELER FOR IT.

[1884]

BICYCLES AND TRICYCLES.
Our Two Descriptive
ILLUSTRATED CATALOGUES
for 1884 are now ready.

Send a two-cent stamp and a note stating which Catalogue (whether Bicycle or Tricycle) you require, to

THE CUNNINGHAM COMP'NY,
(Established 1877.)
510 Tremont Street, Boston, Mass.

[1884]

POPULAR—PLEASANT—PROFITABLE.

Amateur Photography in Easy Lessons. Read "How to make Pictures." Price 50 cents per copy.
OUTFITS FROM $10 UPWARD.

DESCRIPTIVE PRICE LISTS SENT FREE UPON APPLICATION.

GUARANTEED TO PRODUCE PICTURES OF HIGHEST EXCELLENCE.

Amateur Outfits and Photographic Supplies.
SCOVILL MANUFACTURING CO., 419 and 421 Broome Street, New York.
(Established in 1802.) W. IRVING ADAMS, Agent.

[1882]

13

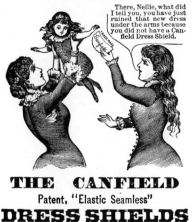

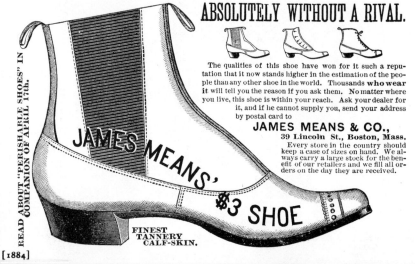

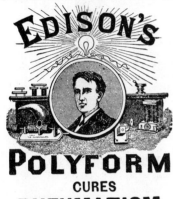
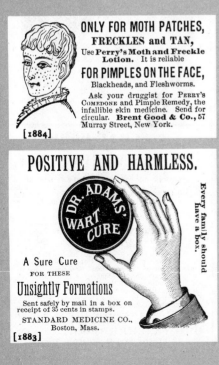

17

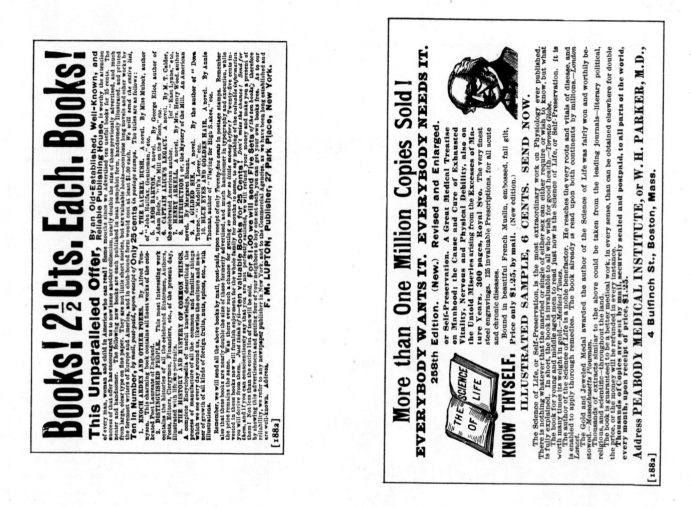

19

[1883]

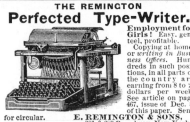

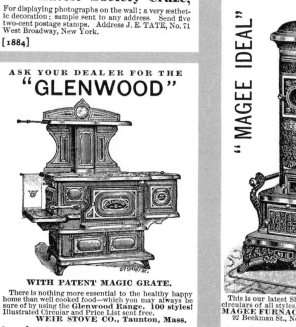

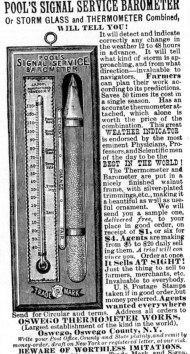

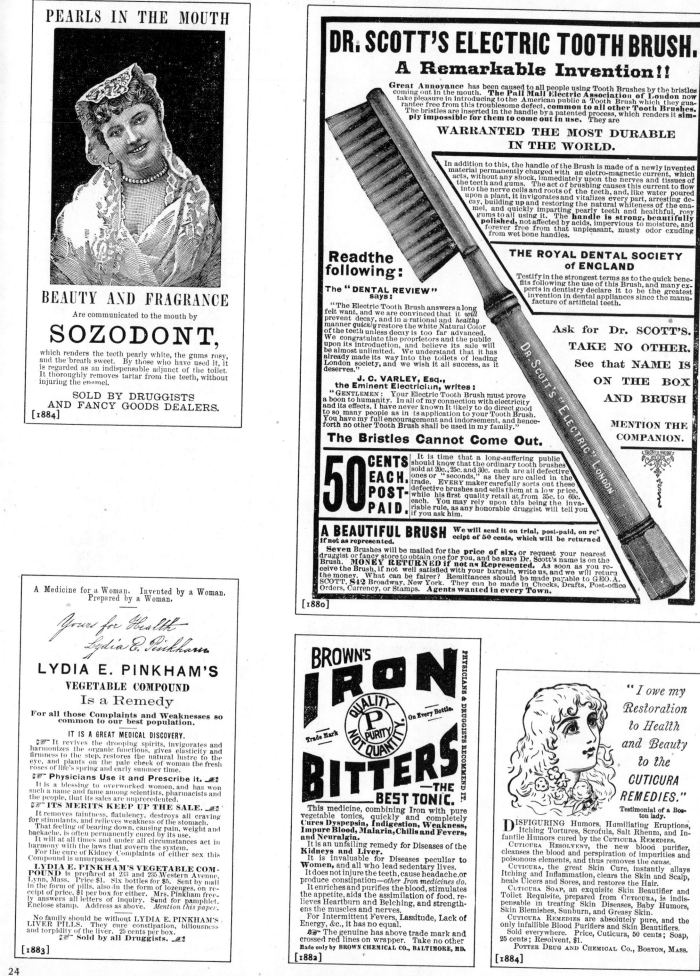
24

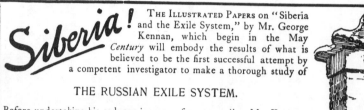

Siberia!

THE ILLUSTRATED PAPERS on "Siberia and the Exile System," by Mr. George Kennan, which begin in the May *Century* will embody the results of what is believed to be the first successful attempt by a competent investigator to make a thorough study of

THE RUSSIAN EXILE SYSTEM.

Before undertaking his arduous journey of 15,000 miles, Mr. Kennan, author of *Tent Life in Siberia*, etc., had spent 4 years in Russia and Siberia, was thoroughly conversant with the people and the language, and had reached the conclusion that the Russian Government had been misrepresented, and that the exile system of Siberia was not so terrible as was supposed. Knowing that Mr. Kennan held these views, the Russian Government gave him every facility for a thorough inspection —the most thorough that had ever been made by a traveler—of the mines and prisons of Siberia. Armed with letters from the Russian Minister of the Interior and other high officials, Mr. Kennan went everywhere, inspecting mines and prisons, convict barges and hospitals, and traveling with chained exiles along the great Siberian road. He made the intimate personal acquaintance of more than 300 exiled "liberals" and nihilists, many of whom wrote out their histories for his use. The actual facts, as revealed by this searching investigation, were far removed from Mr. Kennan's preconceived ideas, as the thrilling narrative of fifteen months' privation and adventure will show.

As is already known, the publication of Mr. Kennan's preliminary papers has resulted in his being placed on the blacklist by the Government, and copies of *The Century* are not allowed to enter Russia. Nor will he be permitted to cross the border again.

Mr. G. A. Frost, artist and photographer, accompanied Mr. Kennan, and the results

THE BOUNDARY POST BETWEEN RUSSIA AND SIBERIA.

of his work will form the most interesting series of pictures of Russian and Siberian life and scenery ever made.

THE MAY CENTURY

is a great issue. It contains, besides the first Siberian paper, an interesting illustrated article on ranch life; first chapters of "The Liar," a novelette by Henry James; the exciting narrative, "A Locomotive Chase in Georgia"; a suggestive paper on "The Chances of Being Hit in Battle"; an essay on Milton by Matthew Arnold; "A Love Story Reversed," by Edward Bellamy; a full-page portrait of Pope Leo XIII., etc. All dealers sell it; 35 cents. *This number begins a volume.*

[1882]

THE CENTURY CO., N. Y.

HARPER'S BAZAR.

New York, January 19, 1889.

TERMS: 10 CENTS A COPY.—$4 00 A YEAR, IN ADVANCE.

MRS. BURNETT'S NEW STORY.

The next number of Harper's Bazar *will contain the first instalment of a charming new novelette, entitled*

"THE PRETTY SISTER OF JOSÉ,"

by the popular novelist Mrs. Frances Hodgson Burnett, *author of "Little Lord Fauntleroy," "That Lass o' Lowrie's," etc. This story, which is brilliantly illustrated by* C. S. Reinhart, *is full of interest, and promises to be one of the literary sensations of the season.*

Our next number will contain a Pattern-sheet Supplement, *with a variety of patterns, illustrations, and descriptions of* Winter House *and* Street Toilettes; *a superb double-page illustration of* Evening *and* Ball Dresses; Tailor Gowns; Russian Costumes; Morning Gowns; Girls' Frocks; *Aprons, Neck-Wear, etc., etc.; together with numerous literary and artistic attractions.*

A MATERNAL OUTRAGE.

WE are often irresistibly drawn to wonder what sort of nerves a certain class of mothers can have—mothers who sit down quietly and allow their children to make themselves nuisances to every one else about them, while they themselves pursue life with placidity, and chat and sew and read and eat and amuse themselves as if they had not the least responsibility in the case, and whomsoever else the children's behavior annoyed, it did not annoy them. The child of any of these mothers in question is of an inquiring disposition; it handles every small article that it is able to lift, and leaves its finger-marks in bold relief on embroidered book-cover or delicate table scarf, on polished furniture, on the piano keys, and on all the dainty bric-à-brac impartially; and the owner, or even the chance beholder, lives in constant fear of seeing brittle glass smashed to atoms, china cracked, lamps overturned, books made unreadable, fans ruined, boxes broken, unable in politeness either to express anxiety beforehand, or reproof or condemnation or regret afterward, and all this while the tranquil mother, content that the child amuses itself, never observes that anything out of the way at all is taking place. Moreover, the child's inquiring turn of mind does not stop short at handling and fingering and soiling; it calls in allies of the voice and of a pertinacity equal to a wasp's; it queries and wonders and argues and discusses and contradicts, and becomes a living interrogation point, and makes its victims feel that their innermost secrets are not safe from the cross-examination of the prying little tongue, which may at any moment turn up an unexpected treasure, and which all the time, as the Irishman said of his corn, is a perfect thorn in the side.

At the table this easy-going mother pursues the same easy path; the child speaks up unrepressed, and expresses its preferences and commands its own dishes, and keeps the waiter running, and consumes time in making selection, spills the salt, spills the gravy, upsets glasses of water, makes a mess all around its plate, monopolizes conversation, and renders rational enjoyment out of the question; and the mother, used to it, never considers that the repast is being injured, the appetite destroyed, and the pleasure taken away from every one else at the board who likes some peace and quietness with the meal.

Perhaps the child is one whose lessons are carried on at home, and the mother, finding them a weariness to hear, does not undertake to separate them from the pleasant thread of her morning life downstairs and among other people, but attends to them in pauses of gossip, in which gossip the child joins on occasion, in the intervals of crochet and arrasene, and instruction and scolding and iteration, and crying, and possibly violent scenes, and possibly gentle but equally pitiful ones, make a misery of the morning for every one else as well as for the child whose mother has so poor sense and so little decency.

Or perhaps this child is musical. Then woe betide every one having daily intercourse with that child's mother, and may the undulatory theory of sound have mercy on the keys and strings of the piano! In season and out of season the thrumming and strumming and drumming go on, with masters or without them, by the ear or in spite of the ear, and without the least concern regarding the rasping torture to uninterested hearers. Who would interfere with a child's musical development, which may be that of a genius? Who would despoil a child of pleasure? How can any one be so trifling as to be annoyed by a thing like that? And whang-bang goes the poor instrument, with chords, with discords, with fragments of tune broken off in the middle, with no tune at all, with a torrent of never-ending sound, and with a relief and joy when there comes a simple gush of scales in all their grinding monotony.

We are not saying anything at present about the injury wrought upon the poor child by this extreme unwisdom, nor of the fact that it causes the little creature to be generally detested, and to receive the avoidance and harshness of which well-brought-up children know nothing. But is it not an outrage on the rest of the household, and does it not inflict harm on every member of it who has any auditory nerves, or, indeed, any nerves at all—harm that makes the sufferer feel like a candidate for an insane asylum, and if not quite mad enough for that, mad enough, at any rate, if the child must be let alone, to shake the mother?

No mother has any right to take the feelings of other people so for granted, to inflict the disagreeable portion of her child upon them, as if it were something of the common circumstances of the place, the atmosphere, the walls, and as if it were one's part and lot and duty, being totally without responsibility, to endure it all. If the child were put under bonds of self-restraint and respect for others commensurate with its capacity, it would be different, no one would resent its behavior, even when the petulance or the fatigues of childhood had got the better of it; every one of proper feeling would rejoice in its sunshiny presence, and try to increase the reason for sunshine. Were it ill, no one would refuse to help and care; were it sorry, every one would hasten to soothe its little sorrows, and every one would be glad to assist the mother in looking after its well-being. It is not the child's behavior, after all, that is in question; it is the mother's, in her desire to get through life in the easiest way possible, combined with a total disregard of the desires of every one else to get through it with no more vexations than naturally and inevitably belong to that one's share. She has no right to allow a child to finger and handle the things that are not hers; she has no right to allow the child to ask personal and impertinent and wearying questions; she has no right to allow it to annoy and disgust others at the table; she has no right to hear its lessons in public; she has hardly the right to allow practising, but no shadow of right to allow drumming on the piano, where it can disturb a mortal or immortal soul. We do not dwell on the child's part of it, as, of tender years, it has little or no real accountability yet. But one of the duties of motherhood is to rear one's children so that they shall not be in peril of making themselves disliked, and may have the chance of carrying through life all the liking it is possible for them to gather on the way, and without which they will find life itself a very heavy burden to carry.

What's all this Fuss about a Nail?

Because every man who owns a horse knows that the animal is of no value or use unless it has sound feet, and soundness depends very largely on the nail used in shoeing. Some nails SPLIT when driven into the hard hoof, one point coming out where it should, to be clenched, the other going into the tender part of the foot, causing either permanent lameness or lockjaw, followed by death. Such cases are frequent and can be easily referred to. THE PUTNAM NAIL cannot SPLIT, SLIVER or BREAK. It is Hot-Forged and Hammer-Pointed, and is the only Horse-Shoe Nail made by machinery that is exactly like an old-fashioned hand-made nail. When your horse is shod do not let the blacksmith use a CHEAP NAIL; it may RUIN YOUR HORSE. Insist on the PUTNAM.

THE PUTNAM NAILS are made in various sizes to meet every requirement:—The **Government Standard**—Regular Nail; **Turf Nail**—A light Nail for race-horses; **City Head**—For hand-made shoes; **Counters**—Long heads for railroad and special shoes.

For sale by all dealers in Horse-Shoe Nails. Samples free by mail. *Mention The Youth's Companion.*

THE PUTNAM NAIL CO., Neponset P. O., Boston, Mass.

[1889]

All Ocean Travel by the famous Cunard Steamers.

All Travel by Rail and Hotel Accommodations first class.

SIXTY-FIVE DAYS' TRIP.
Visiting the capitals, great cities, and places of interest in **England, Scotland, Belgium, Germany, Savoy, The Rhine, Switzerland** and **France**. Nine days in **Paris** during the great exposition. Nine days in **London**. The cost of guides, interpreters, carriage drives, care of baggage, transfers, steamer, railway and hotel fares included. A skilful physician and competent conductors in charge of the company the entire route. Ladies and young people can travel unattended in our care. Refer you to the Publishers of THE YOUTH'S COMPANION. For daily itinerary and cost of trip, address, **Hartshorn & Cheney**, 50 Bromfield St., Boston, Mass.

THE WORLD'S SUNDAY SCHOOL CONVENTION to be held in Memorial Hall, London, England, from July 2d to 5th inclusive. This will be the most important gathering of Sunday School workers the world has ever seen. The Cunard Steamer "Bothnia" has been secured for the exclusive use of the delegates. Send for illustrated announcement. **W. N. HARTSHORN,** Chairman Transportation, 50 Bromfield St., Boston, Mass.

[1889]

The "TASKER" Skating Shoe.

Sent to any part of the United States For $3.00

Manufactured by

H. & F. H. TASKER

991 AND 993 Fulton Street,

Near St. James Place,

BROOKLYN, N. Y.

Send for Descriptive Catalogue.

[1885]

THE BRADLEY

TWO-WHEELER. Perry's patent. The only Two-Wheeler that is absolutely free from Horse Motion. Illus. Price List *Free. Bradley & Co.,* Syracuse, N. Y. 22 College Pl., N. Y.

[1885]

ONLY $3.95

STEM-WIND STEM-SET

AMERICAN WARRANTED

This is not a Key-Wind WATCH.

Both Case and Movement of American Manufacture, therefore guaranteed and warranted in every respect. Remember this as evidence: We will give you at any time within a year from date of purchase, a new watch or refund money paid, if you do not find this watch exactly as we represent it in every particular, and we put our registered guarantee to this effect in every watch. The case is solid silver nickel, and will wear longer, keep brighter, and be of more service than any coin or sterling silver case made: also that the movement is a genuine American movement, and guaranteed to keep perfect time, for it is thoroughly inspected and adjusted before leaving the factory. This is not a Swiss imitation American watch. *We offer the first genuine All American Watch ever produced and warranted for such a low price, $3.95.* Send for our Catalogue; it contains a large variety of Watches, Clocks, Silverware, Rings, Chains, Charms, etc., etc. Mail us 50 cents in cash or stamps, and we will send this watch by express for examination, for we are positive you will hand the agent $3.45 immediately and take the watch, for remember, it is stem-wind and stem-set, guaranteed to keep perfect time, and we will *refund your money* if not as represented. If you do not know us, write the *American Exchange National Bank, Chicago.* Address, **Fort Dearborn Watch & Clock Co., 139-141 State St., Chicago. D. A. WILKINS, Secretary and Manager.** *Don't buy an old-fashioned key-wind watch. Our watch is a stem-wind and stem-set American Warranted Watch.*

[1889]

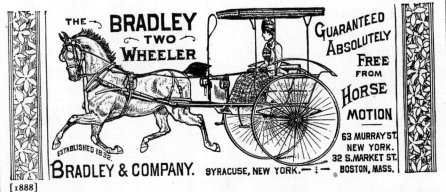

31

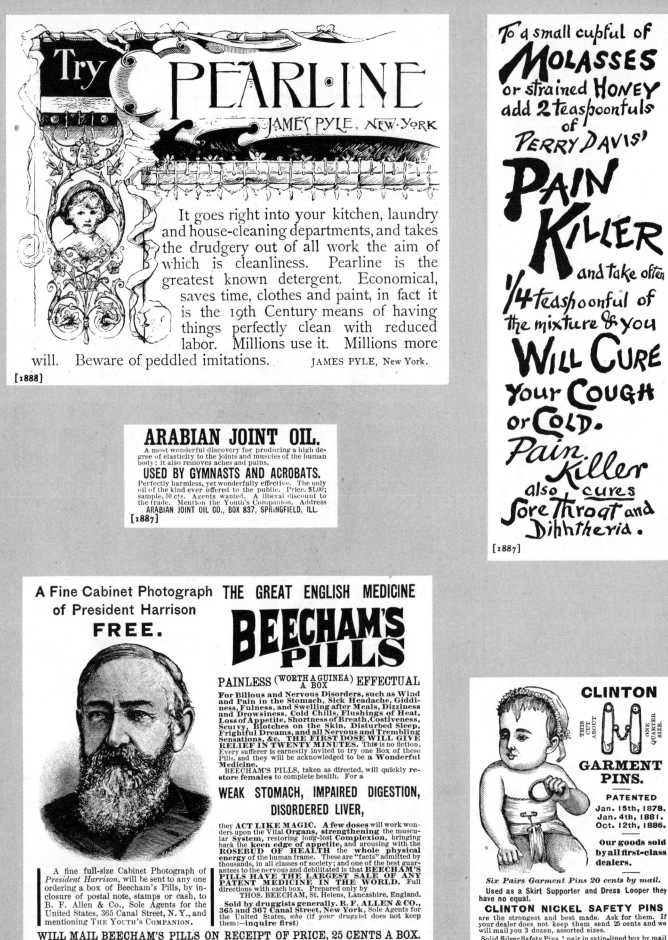

A COFFEE PLANTATION

RUSSELL & RICHARDSON SC

SCENE ON A COFFEE PLANTATION —CONTROLLED BY— **CHASE & SANBORN.**

OUR COFFEES HAVE A NATIONAL REPUTATION REPRESENTING THE FINEST GROWN.

SEAL BRAND COFFEE JAVA and MOCHA, surpassing all others in its richness and delicacy of flavor. Justly called **The Aristocratic Coffee of America.** Always packed whole roasted (unground), in 2 lb. air-tight tin cans.

CRUSADE BLEND A skilful blending of strong, flavory and aromatic high-grade coffees. Warranted not to contain a single Rio bean, and guaranteed to suit your taste as no other coffee will, at a moderate price. Always packed whole roasted (unground), in 1 lb. air-tight parchment packages.

TEST FREE We are exclusively an importing house, selling only to dealers. But to give consumers an opportunity of testing our famous coffee before buying, we will, upon receipt of 6 cents in stamps to cover the cost of can and postage, send *free by mail a 1-4 pound of Seal Brand Coffee.* Address

CHASE & SANBORN, 85 Broad Street, Boston, Mass.

[1888]

MARK TWAIN'S NEW WORK,
"ADVENTURES OF HUCKLEBERRY FINN"
(Tom Sawyer's Comrade.)

APPEARS FEBRUARY 18th
Prospectuses now ready.

Fine Heliotype of the author in each book.

Agents wanted.   Splendid Terms!

CHARLES L. WEBSTER & CO.,
Publishers,
658 BROADWAY, NEW YORK CITY.

[1885]

"I was caught in a python's folds and saw fierce eyes glaring down into mine. If that tremendous coil were tightened around me, I knew that I might at once check my luggage for the undiscovered bourne. In this crisis of my fate I saw the great python's tail in close proximity to his mouth. I grasped the snake's tail and pushed a yard or two down his yawning jaws. Serpents seldom bite their prey; they lubricate it and suck it down. With such a long and cold-blooded creature, I calculated that it would take over a half a minute before the sensations of his tail could be conveyed to his head, and render him aware that he was committing suicide,"

**NEW BOOK FOR BOYS,
EXCITING AS MUNCHAUSEN.
Hairbreadth Escapes of
MAJOR MENDAX.**

BY F. BLAKE CROFTON. His perilous encounters, startling adventures and daring exploits with Indians, Cannibals, Wild Beast, Serpents, Balloons, Geysers, etc., all over the World, in the bowels of the earth and above the Clouds, *a personal narrative. Spirited Illustrations* by Bennett. 225 pages. **Cloth, elegant, $2.00.** Press critics say: "*Irresistibly comic.*"—CHRISTIAN WORLD. "*Bold but humorous.*"—PUBLIC OPINION. "*Munchausen never imagined greater marvels.*"—NEWS. "*Beats everything of its kind.*"—GAZETTE. For sale by all Booksellers, or mailed on receipt of price. HUBBARD BROS., Pubs., 723 Chestnut St., Philada.

[1889]

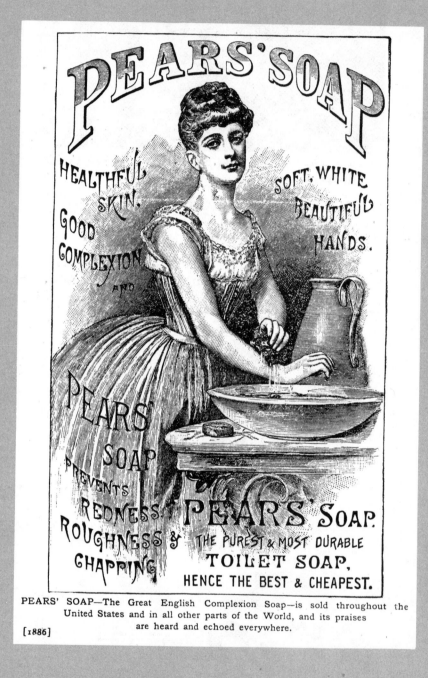

PEARS' SOAP—The Great English Complexion Soap—is sold throughout the
United States and in all other parts of the World, and its praises
are heard and echoed everywhere.

[1886]

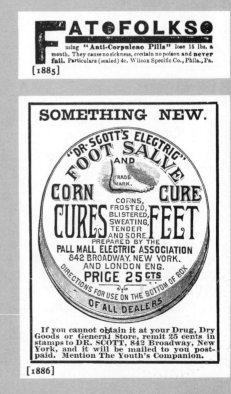

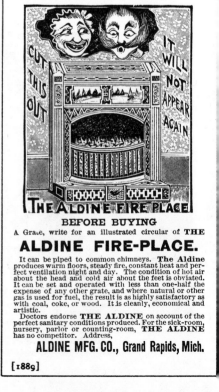
36

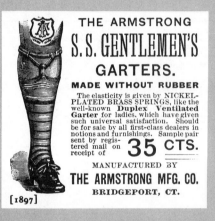

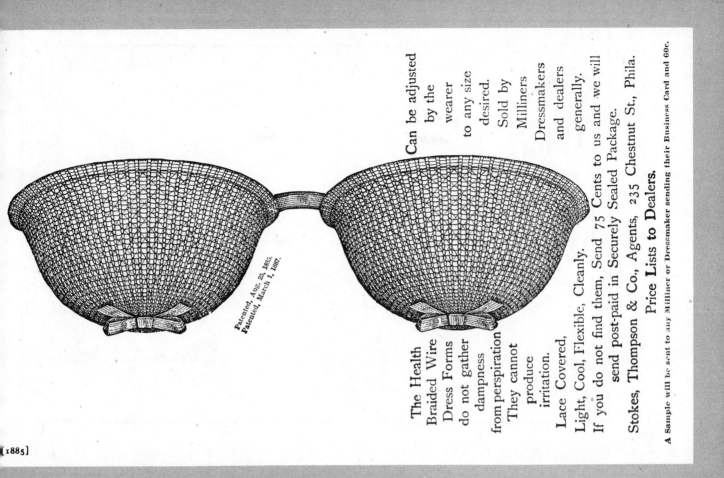

The Health Braided Wire Dress Forms do not gather dampness from perspiration. They cannot produce irritation. Lace Covered, Light, Cool, Flexible, Cleanly. If you do not find them, Send 75 Cents to us and we will send post-paid in Securely Sealed Package.

Stokes, Thompson & Co., Agents, 235 Chestnut St., Phila.

Price Lists to Dealers.

Can be adjusted by the wearer to any size desired. Sold by Milliners Dressmakers and dealers generally.

A Sample will be sent to any Milliner or Dressmaker sending their Business Card and 60c.

Patented Aug. 25 1885.
Patented March 1, 1887.

[1885]

[1886]

[1885]

He wont be happy till he gets it!

[1888]

MADAME ROWLEY'S TOILET MASK.

TOILET MASK

OR

FACE GLOVE.

The following are the claims made for Madame Rowley's Toilet Mask, and the grounds on which it is recommended to ladies for Beautifying, Bleaching, and Preserving the Complexion:

TOILET MASK

OR

FACE GLOVE.

First—The **Mask** is **Soft** and **Flexible** in form, and can be **Easily Applied** and **Worn** without **Discomfort** or **Inconvenience.**

Second—It is durable, and does not dissolve or come asunder, but holds its original mask shape.

Third—It has been **Analyzed** by **Eminent Scientists** and **Chemical Experts**, and pronounced **Perfectly Pure** and **Harmless.**

Fourth—With ordinary care the **Mask** will **last for years**, and its **VALUABLE PROPERTIES Never Become Impaired.**

Fifth—The **Mask** is protected by letters patent, and is the **only Genuine** article of the kind.

Sixth—It is **Recommended** by **Eminent Physicians** and **Scientific Men** as a **SUBSTITUTE FOR INJURIOUS COSMETICS.**

Seventh—The **Mask** is a **Natural Beautifier**, for **Bleaching** and **Preserving** the **Skin** and **Removing Complexional Imperfections.**

The Toilet Mask (or Face Glove) in position to the face.

TO BE WORN THREE TIMES IN THE WEEK

Eighth—Its use cannot be detected by the closest scrutiny, and it may be worn with **perfect privacy**, if desired.

Ninth—The **Mask** is sold at a moderate price, and is to be PURCHASED BUT ONCE.

Tenth—Hundreds of dollars uselessly expended for cosmetics, lotions, and like preparations, may be saved its possessor.

Eleventh—**Ladies** in every section of the country are using the **Mask** with gratifying results.

Twelfth—It is safe, simple, cleanly, and effective for beautifying purposes, and never injures the most delicate skin.

Thirteenth—While it is intended that the **Mask** should be **Worn During Sleep**, it may be applied WITH EQUALLY GOOD RESULTS at any time to suit the convenience of the wearer.

Fourteenth—The **Mask** has received the testimony of well-known society and professional ladies, who proclaim it to be the greatest discovery for beautifying purposes ever vouchsafed to womankind.

COMPLEXION BLEMISHES

May be hidden imperfectly by cosmetics and powders, but can only be removed permanently by the Toilet Mask. By its use every kind of spots, impurities, roughness, etc., vanish from the skin, leaving it soft, clear, brilliant, and beautiful. It is harmless, costs little, and saves its user money. It prevents and removes wrinkles, and is both a complexion preserver and beautifier. Famous Society Ladies, actresses, belles, etc., use it.

VALUABLE ILLUSTRATED TREATISE, WITH PROOFS AND PARTICULARS.

—MAILED FREE BY—

TOILET MASK

OR

FACE GLOVE.

Send for Descriptive Treatise.} 1164 BROADWAY, {Send for Descriptive Treatise.

THE TOILET MASK COMPANY,

NEW YORK.

Mention this paper when you Write.

TOILET MASK

OR

FACE GLOVE.

[1887]

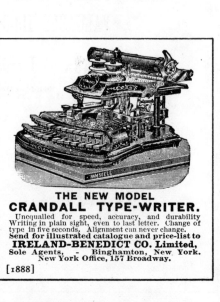

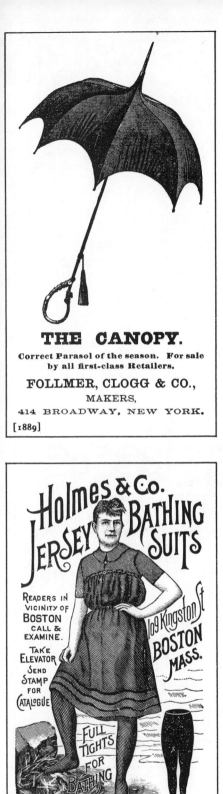

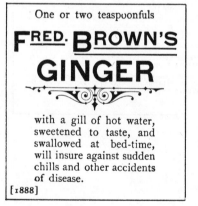

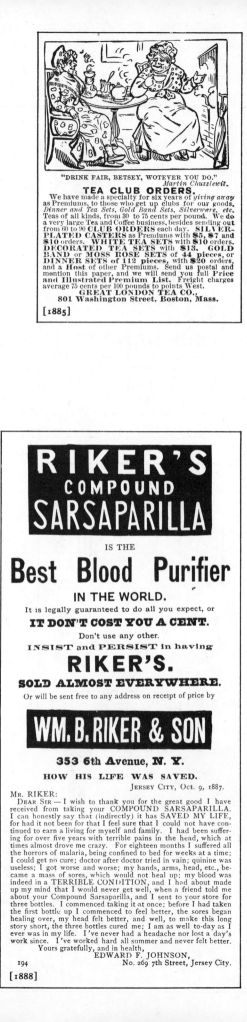

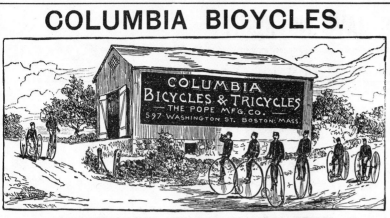

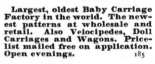

THE LADIES' HOME JOURNAL

An Illustrated Family Journal with the Largest Circulation of any Magazine in the World.

Published Monthly by

THE CURTIS PUBLISHING COMPANY,

At 433-435 Arch Street, Philadelphia, Pa.

With Press-Rooms at 401-415 Appletree Street.

Edited by

EDWARD W. BOK

In association with

MRS. LYMAN ABBOTT
MISS RUTH ASHMORE
MARGARET BOTTOME
KATE UPSON CLARK
MAUDE HAYWOOD
EMMA M. HOOPER
MRS. LOUISA KNAPP
MARY F. KNAPP
ISABEL A. MALLON
EBEN E. REXFORD
ELIZABETH ROBINSON SCOVIL
REV. T. DE WITT TALMAGE, D.D.
KATE TANNATT WOODS

Advisory and Contributing Editors.

With editorial representatives at London and Paris.

Subscription Rates	One dollar per year, payable in advance. Single copies ten cents.
Advertising Rates	Three dollars per Agate line each insertion before (this) editorial page; two dollars and fifty cents per Agate line on succeeding pages. Reading Notices, five dollars per Nonpareil line.

BRANCH OFFICES:

New York: Potter Building, 38 Park Row
Boston: 7 Temple Place, Cor. Tremont St.
Chicago: Chickering Hall Building
San Francisco: Chronicle Building

Philadelphia, August, 1891

WE never fully appreciate a thing until it is taken from us, and we never think half so much of America until we go away from it for awhile. I notice that while our tourists are willing to take a slow outgoing steamer, there is always a desire to select the fastest home-bound ship afloat. This country seems astonishingly attractive to the American when he is away from it; and the dearest sight that comes to the traveler is the first view of American land upon his return. He will watch for the English Needles with curiosity; but for Fire Island Light he looks with an affectionate longing. The same man who lazily turned over in his berth last year when he was told the ship was off The Needles, sprang on deck with boyish glee when Fire Island was sighted. There were home, family, friends and interests. And where, on God's green earth, can those influences seem so beautiful, where do they mean so much, as on the North American continent?

LESLIE'S WEEKLY.

W. J. ARKELL............................Publisher.

NEW YORK, DECEMBER 29, 1892.

TERMS TO SUBSCRIBERS.

UNITED STATES AND CANADA, IN ADVANCE.

One copy, one year, or 52 numbers	- - -	$4.00
One copy, six months, or 23 numbers	- - -	2.00
One copy, for 13 weeks	- - -	1.00

Cable address: "Judgeark."

A SUGGESTIVE INCIDENT.

THE New York *Sun* mentions an incident of recent occurrence at the national capital which well illustrates the simplicity of our national life, and how truly we are dominated by the spirit of democracy. A young Maryland girl, going on a bright Sabbath morning to the church attended by the President, found the edifice crowded, and in her perplexity appealed to the usher for a seat. This personage, finding none in the rear of the church, led the embarrassed maiden to the pew of President Harrison, into which she was at once courteously ushered by the President, where she was as courteously welcomed by the two lady members of his family who accompanied him. It was said that the young lady was overwhelmed to find herself in such a presence, but that her surprise was, if anything, increased when she was permitted to share in the singing from a hymn-book in the hands of the President's daughter.

The incident is a trivial one, but it presents in a marked way the contrast between American social conditions and those which obtain abroad. Our British cousins are very fond of criticising American manners, and they do not hesitate to make the most of anything *outre* which they may discover in our social life, but we suspect that not in this century has any British newspaper been able to record an incident so full as this one of all graceful courtesy and so illustrative of that spirit which makes all the world akin. The President of the United States matches in point of power and responsibility the kingliest of rulers. He represents and stands for a people whose influence has become largely determinative in the political and commercial policies of the world. But, while the petty royalties of Europe, the dukelings and lordlings who hedge themselves about with artificial barriers, too often imagine themselves exempt from the performance of the civilities of life to ordinary folk, the President of this great republic, remembering that he is of the people, and that the vast power lodged in his hands is the trust of the hour, counts it no less a duty, because of his exalted station, to practice toward all with whom he comes in contact the "small, sweet courtesies of life." It is just because, under our political system, the people are kept in constant touch with their rulers, that the nation possesses a solidity and strength which are impossible in countries where the chief executive stands in remote isolation, and forgets that he is brother to the weakest and the humblest.

BEECHAM'S PILLS

(Vegetable)

What They Are For

Biliousness	jaundice	hot skin	fluttering of the heart (palpitation)
indigestion (dyspepsia)	bellyache	ringing in the ears	irritability
sour stomach	cramps	dizziness (vertigo)	nervousness
sickness at the stomach (nausea)	colic	sick headache (megrim or hemicrania)	depression of spirits
vomiting	piles (hemorrhoids)	nervous headache	great mental depression
heartburn	backache	dull headache	general debility
water brash	pain in the side	neuralgias	faintness
loss of appetite (anorexia)	drowsiness	fulness of the stomach (distention)	exhaustion
coated tongue	heaviness		listlessness
bad taste in the mouth	disturbed sleep	shortness of breath (dyspnoea)	weakness
wind on the stomach (flatulence)	sleeplessness (insomnia)	pain or oppression around the heart	poverty of the blood (anaemia)
torpid liver	nightmare		pallor
	hot and throbbing head		
	coldness of hands and feet		

when these conditions are caused by constipation; and constipation is the most frequent cause of most of them.

One of the most important things for everybody to learn is that constipation causes more than half the sickness in the world, especially in women; and it can all be prevented. They who call the cure for constipation a cure-all, are only half-wrong after all.

Write to B. F. Allen Company, 365 Canal Street, New York, for a little book on CONSTIPATION (its causes consequences and correction); sent free. If you are not within reach of a druggist, the pills will be sent by mail, 25 cents a box.

HOW TO TAKE THEM

First night, take one at bedtime. If this does not empty the bowels freely, e second night take two. If this fails, ie third night take three, and so on; or a child old enough to swallow a pill, one pill is the dose.

The object, in the beginning, is to empty the bowels freely.

The dose to go on with is generally one or two pills; but a person very hard to move may require as many as eight for several nights in succession.

The nightly dose should be diminished gradually until a night can be skipped without missing the stool next morning.

The object now is to keep the bowels regular. The pills do that, if enough and not too many are taken. They do more. See that list at the top of the page.

LIEBIG COMPANY'S

EXTRACT OF BEEF

"IN DARKEST AFRICA,"

By HENRY M. STANLEY.

"One Madi managed to crawl near my tent. . . . He was at once borne to a fire and laid within a few inches of it, and with the addition of a pint of hot broth made from the Liebig Company's Extract of Beef, we restored him to his senses."—*Vol. II, page 58.*

"The Liebig Company's Extract was of the choicest."—*Page 39, Vol. I.*

"Liebig and meat soups had to be prepared in sufficient quantities to serve out cupfuls to each weakened man as he staggered in."—*Page 89, Vol. I.*

[1894]

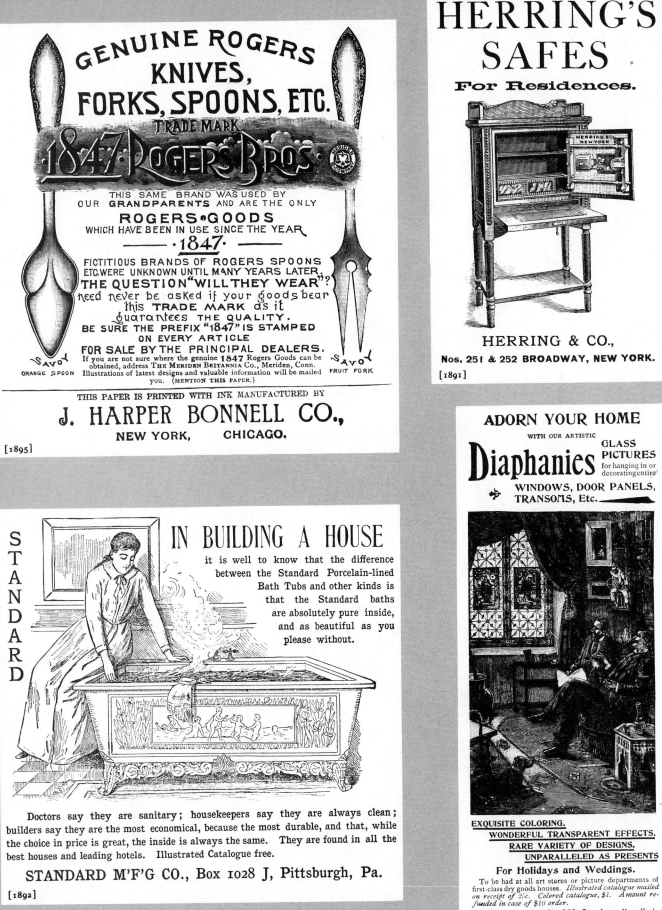

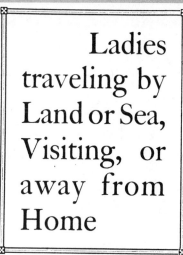

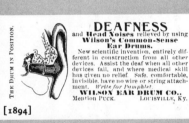

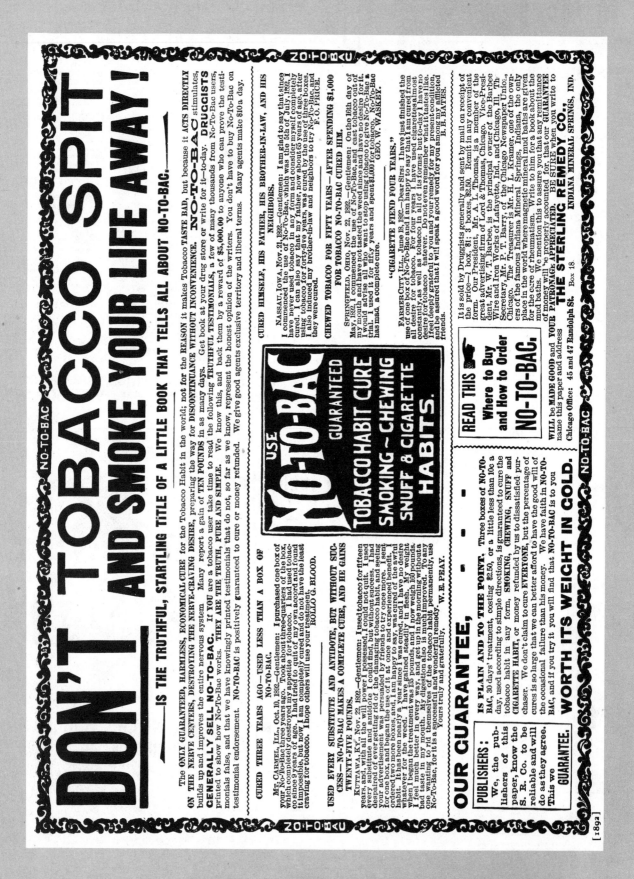

58

WILLIAMS' SHAVING SOAPS have enjoyed an unblemished reputation for excellence—for over HALF A HUNDRED YEARS—and are to-day the *only* shaving soaps—of absolute purity, with well-established claims for healing and antiseptic properties.

"CHEAP" and impure Shaving Soaps—are composed largely of refuse animal fats—abound in scrofulous and other disease germs—and if used—are almost sure to impregnate the pores of the skin—resulting in torturing cutaneous eruptions and other forms of blood-poisoning.

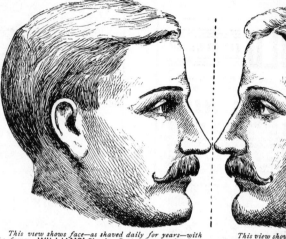

This view shows face—as shaved daily for years—with the famous WILLIAMS' Shaving Soap—always soft—fresh—bright and healthy. Not a sore or pimple in over 20 years of Shaving Experience.

This view shows the effect of being shaved ONCE with an impure—so-called "Cheap" Shaving Soap. Blood-poison—caused by applying impure animal fats to the tender cuticle of the face.

MR. CHAS. A. FOSTER,

34 SAVIN STREET,

BOSTON, MASS., writes:

[1893]

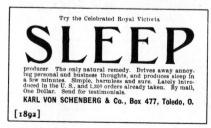

61

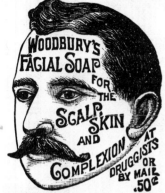

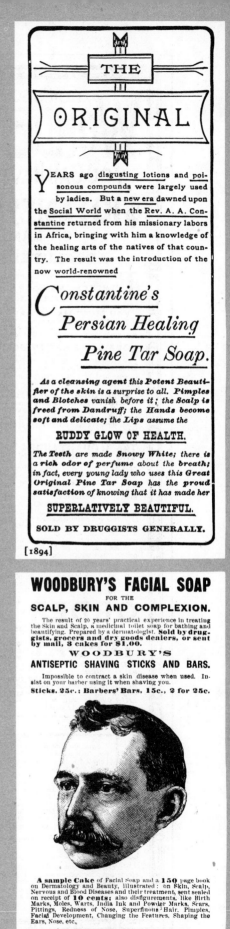

LESLIE'S WEEKLY.

ARKELL WEEKLY COMPANY, Publishers and Proprietors,
No. 110 Fifth Avenue, New York.

APRIL 25, 1895.

TERMS TO SUBSCRIBERS.

UNITED STATES AND CANADA, IN ADVANCE.

One copy, one year, or 52 numbers	$4.00
One copy, six months, or 26 numbers	2.00
One copy, for thirteen weeks	1.00

Sky Scrapers.

IT not many years ago when a traveler coming across the bay or the river at the southern end of Manhattan Island saw only solid blocks of low buildings, with here and there one that projected a trifle above the general roof-level. These notable buildings, in the time alluded to, fifteen or sixteen years ago, were the *Evening Post* building, the Western Union building, and the Equitable building. And above all of these, as though they pierced the sky, were the graceful and historic spires of St. Paul's and Trinity churches. Then came the era of taller buildings, and in the course of ten years that level was entirely broken, and from a ferry-boat on the bay or river, or from the Brooklyn bridge, an observer with a memory might note the greatest possible changes. The Produce Exchange and the Washington building were erected at the foot of the island, and they made the other tall fellows of the past era look small and almost insignificant, so far as altitude was concerned. Then the Union Trust Company building, just below Wall Street and almost opposite Trinity Church, was put up, and it towered above the great buildings farther south, while the cornice was higher than the beginning of the Trinity spire.

The completion of this building created much comment, and there was a tolerably free expression of opinion to the effect that the limit in altitude had been reached. There was talk, indeed, that the time had come when, in the interest of life and of art, the Legislature should take a hand and, by statutory enactment, indicate how far builders would be permitted to go with their sky-scraping structures. Nothing beyond discussion came of this, and indeed nothing is likely to be done in that way, even now, when the Union Trust Company building, tall though it is, is not by any means any longer remarkable by reason of its altitude. A little farther down the street the Manhattan Life Insurance building was erected, and it towered above the Union Trust some fifty feet or so, while the flag-staff on the tower was actually higher than the cross on Trinity steeple. For a long time the United States weather office had been on top of the Equitable building, which within a few years past had been raised many stories until it was again one of the high buildings in Broadway. The erection of these much taller buildings farther down the street now cut off the view to the south almost entirely, so the weather observers were moved to the top of the Manhattan Life building, which was now the tallest building in Broadway, and one of the tallest in the world. But the end was not yet. There appeared to be a rivalry between these rich corporations as to which could house itself in the most altitudinous edifice. And so the American Surety Company—to borrow a phrase from the card-table—saw the raise of the Manhattan Life, and went some fifty feet better.

When this company concluded to do this thing on the small plot of ground at Pine Street and Broadway, invitations were extended to the architects to attack the difficult problem of putting up a twenty-story building, three hundred and six feet from sidewalk to cornice, on a plot of ground seventy feet by ninety feet. Mr. Richard M. Hunt, the most distinguished architect in America, and one in whom all other architects have entire confidence, was selected for umpire of the competition. Plans were submitted by the best men in the profession, but the award was given to Bruce Price for the plan of a building which carried out in its design the idea of an ornamented and decorated column. This is the building which is now nearing completion, and on which, in the picture printed herewith, the men are seen at work. It towers above the Trinity steeple across the street, and the weather observers on the Manhattan Life building, farther down the street, will not be able to see to the north any better than they could see to the south from their old location on the Equitable.

Mr. Price had a very serious engineering problem to solve in constructing this immense tower of steel and stone. It was absolutely necessary for him to get to the bed-rock for his foundations. Otherwise his structure would be unstable, and, however stiffly it was braced, it would not withstand the vibrations when the winds blew at sixty miles an hour. The bed-rock at that point is seventy feet below the sidewalk. Of course water is reached long before that depth is secured. He concluded to establish his foundations on piers carried to the bed-rock through the water by means of caissons, and to unite these piers with cantalever trusses. This was well and comparatively easy. But here was a more difficult thing. The houses on the property adjoining that on which Mr. Price was to build were erected on foundations which did not go lower than twenty feet or so. If he went on the property line to the depth he wished with these piers he would undermine these houses and they would topple over. To get around this he set his piers inside the line, and then, when they were up to the level of the sub-cellar floor, he placed a cantalever over the pier to the property line, and on this projecting truss the steel frame and the stone masonry have been erected. This was bold, but it is as secure as it is ingenious, and both engineers and architects have viewed it with admiration.

As a rule these tall buildings are only imposing on account of their height. This tallest of all the tall buildings is generally regarded as a thoroughly successful and artistic treatment of a problem long looked upon as quite hopeless. Naturally the work reflects great credit upon the designer, Mr. Bruce Price, who hitherto has been esteemed chiefly for his success in building country and suburban residences.

It is likely, however, that the limit in tall buildings has been reached. This is not because they are unsafe, not because they are inartistic ; but it is questionable whether or not they will pay. When a tall building is opened the owner finds that his four or five top stories rent quickly, but those below go off very slowly, even though the rent on all the floors is the same. Managers of estates say that everything points in the direction of lower buildings because they will pay better.

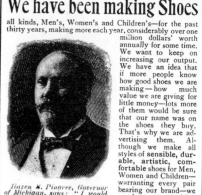

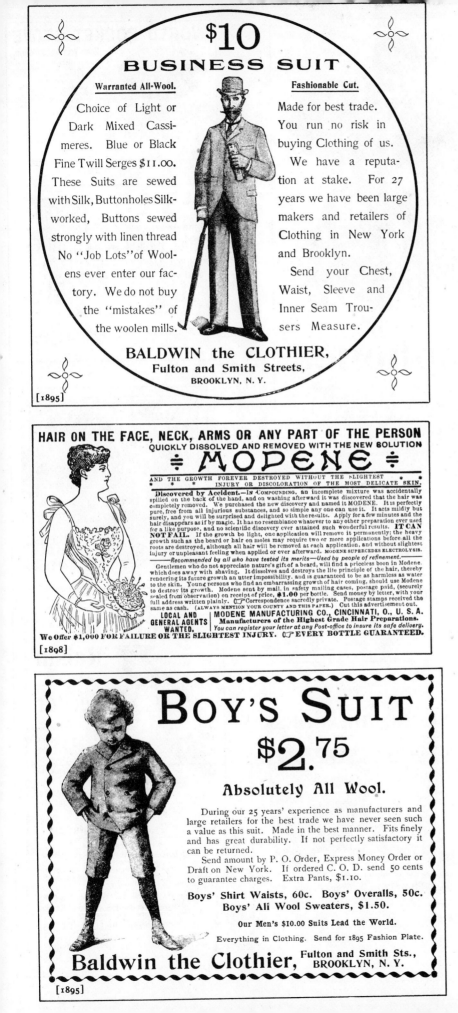

68

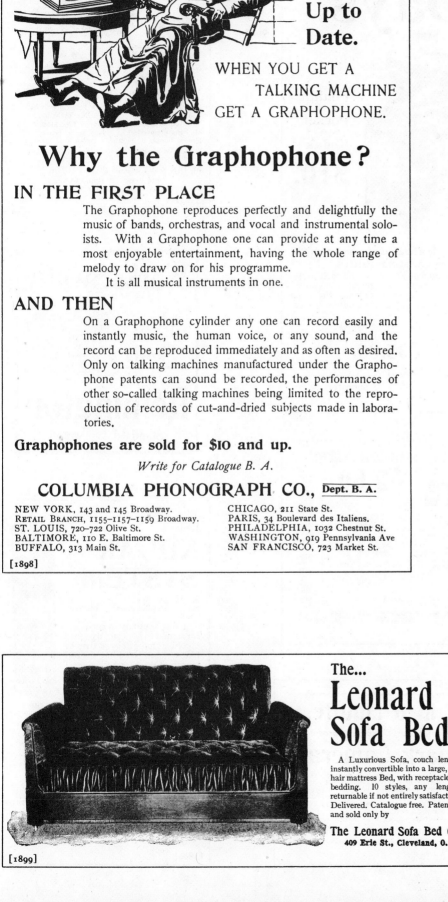

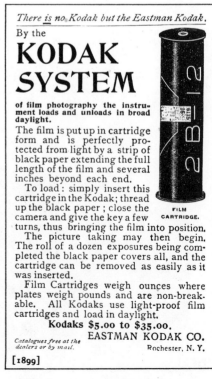
70

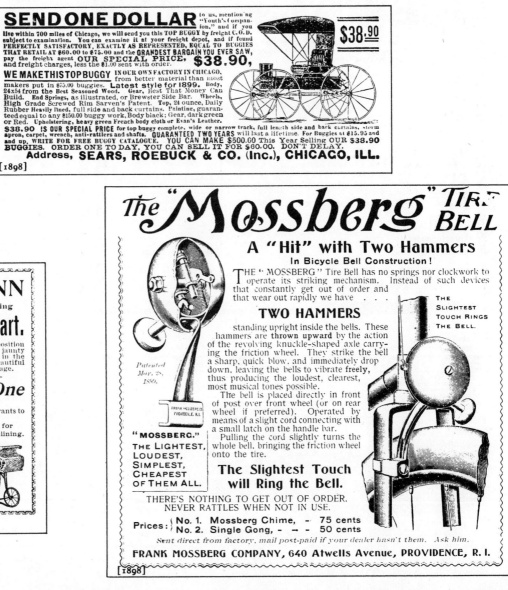

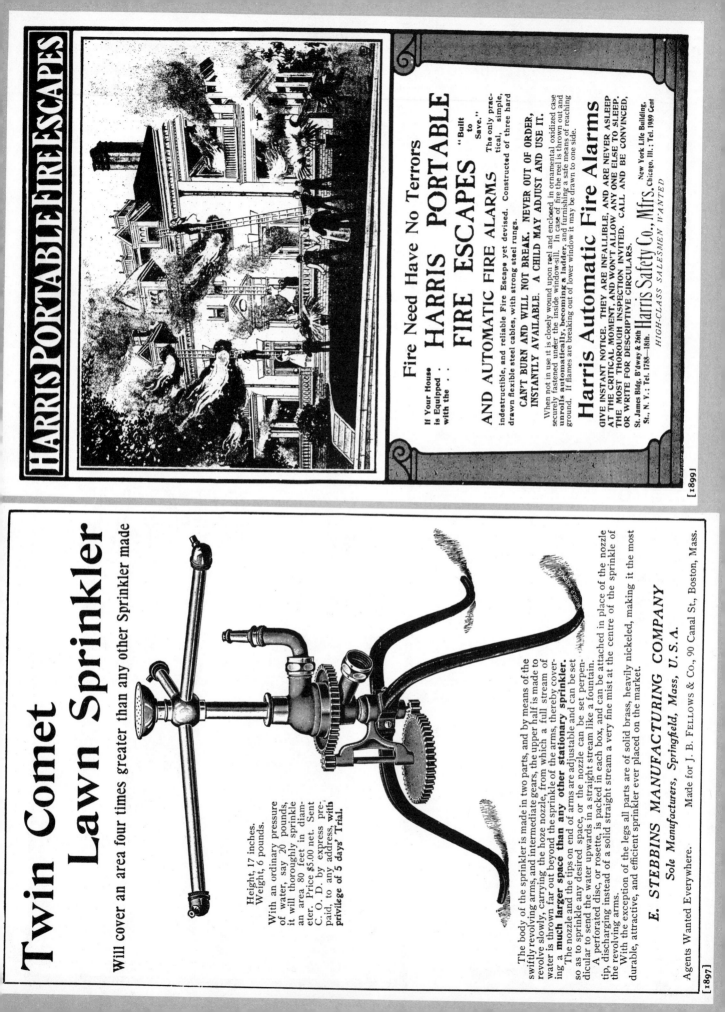

A Sun Bath
after a shampoo with
Packer's Tar Soap.

Lincoln

[1898]

"****Long ago distanced all competitors."—*Medical Standard.*

PACKER'S TAR SOAP

is almost a necessity in summer. Children especially enjoy it. It quickly relieves irritated conditions of the skin due to perspiration, chafing, rashes, stings, etc. Bathing and shampooing with this soap are delightfully refreshing; while its antiseptic and soothing qualities make it invaluable for the footsore and weary athlete or traveler.

THE PACKER MANUFACTURING CO., NEW YORK

[1898]

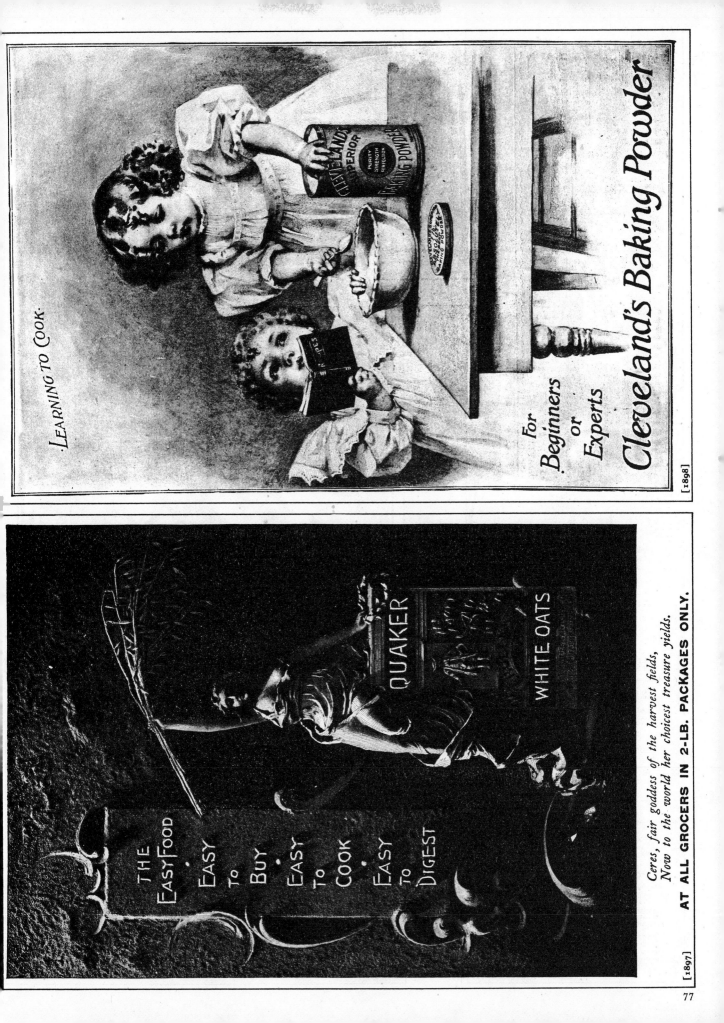

LEARNING TO COOK.

For Beginners or Experts

Cleveland's Baking Powder

[1898]

Ceres, fair goddess of the harvest fields,
Now to the world her choicest treasure yields.

AT ALL GROCERS IN 2-LB. PACKAGES ONLY.

QUAKER

WHITE OATS

THE EASY FOOD
EASY TO BUY
EASY TO COOK
EASY TO DIGEST

[1897]

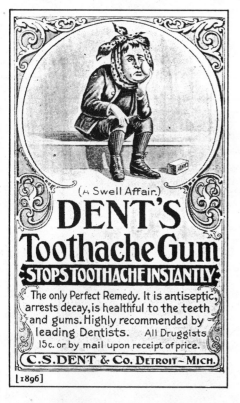
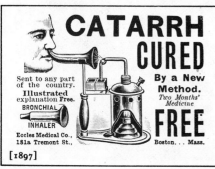

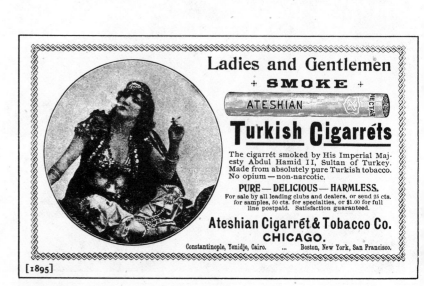

A LITTLE TREASURE

of a baby needs to be nursed with a Silver Nipple when its mother cannot nurse it.

No colic. No sickness. No trouble.

All mothers know just how disagreeable rubber nipples are. Just think how sweet and healthful a *silver* nipple might be. We make one and believe it perfect. Rubber nipples are both unclean and unhealthful, and, at 5 cents each, a baby will use about $5.00 worth. We will send the

King Silver Nipple

in *sterling* silver to any mother for $1.00; after using it thirty days she may return it to us and get her dollar back if she wants it.

Providence Lying-In Hospital, 96 State St.,
Providence, R. I., June 5, 1896.

Dear Sirs—The King Silver Nipple has been in constant use in the Providence Lying-In Hospital for more than two years. We consider it superior to any other nipple ever used by us. It is non-collapsible, non-absorbitive, is easily cleaned, and does not irritate the mouth. We have no hesitation in recommending the Silver Nipple for general use. Respectfully,
Miss A. B. PIKE, Matron.

R. I. Agricultural Experiment Station, Chemical Division.
H. J. Wheeler, Ph.D., Chemist.
Kingston, R. I., Dec. 3, 1896.

In reference to King's Silver Nipple, I will say that we have used it with much satisfaction for nearly nine months. It can be easily and effectually cleaned, and it is of great advantage, owing to the uniform delivery of the milk, which cannot be accomplished with a rubber nipple. By its use a nipple of uniform size is always on hand, and the difficulties met with in changing from a nipple which has become enlarged by use, to a new one of smaller size, are never encountered. We can, therefore, most heartily recommend it. Very truly yours, H. D. WHEELER.

Our references—any bank in Providence

HALL & LYON CO., Providence, R. I.

[1897]

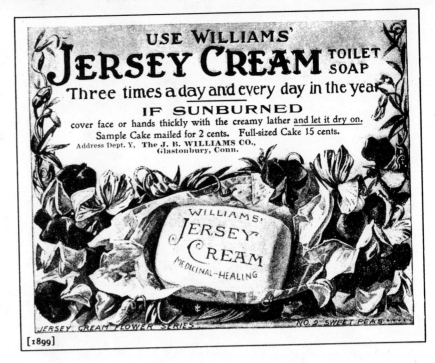

For EASTER GOWNS that bouffant and stylish effect in sleeves and skirt will be secured by the use of FIBRE CHAMOIS INTERLINING. Nothing else so fully meets the demands of lightness, keeping the garment in its original shape and style, and in giving body to the thinnest material. ❧ ❧

REDFERN Uses It — LILLIAN RUSSELL Wears It — JENNESS MILLER Recommends It.

Three weights: No. 10, Light; No. 20, Medium; No. 30, Heavy. Width 64 inches.

Beware of worthless imitations.
See that what you buy is stamped
[1896]

Fibre Chamois.

To be had at the Lining Counter
of all Dry Goods Stores.

"Our Combination" Suit

For Boys Ages 6 to 15.

Extra Pants and Cap.

$3.50 AND $5.00

New Styles, Better Values than ever. Strictly all-wool. Sample pieces sent *free*. Combinations shipped C. O. D., privilege of examining before paying. Or send us the money with **60 cents** additional for postage and registering and we will forward Suit to any address.

Money cheerfully returned if the goods are not perfectly satisfactory. More than 10,000 YOUTH'S COMPANION readers are our customers.

Ask for Samples of Men's Semi-Dress Suits, $11.50.

Enclose 2 cents and we will send our "Great Wonder" Puzzle and Spring Catalogue.

PUTNAM CLOTHING HOUSE, 135 Clark Street, Chicago, Ill.

[1895]

This Neatly Laundered
SHIRT WAIST

made of cool summery materials together with **Three Collars**, one of the same material and two white; one new "Marlborough," high turn-over; one "Dutchess," the popular high standing collar, and an elegant **Shirt Waist Set**

complete, gold or silver plated, assorted designs, consisting of collar button, three studs and pair sleeve links,

ALL FOR $1.00, And we Pay the Express.

Made of the choicest materials. Colors guaranteed fast. Stripes, Checks and Waves in Green, Pink, Blue and Black and White. Sleeves large and stylish. Made by lock-stitch, therefore NO RIP. Make and finish perfect. Sizes 32 to 46. Give size and color explicitly when ordering.

WE MAKE GARMENTS

at less than usual cost of materials, and our **NEW SUMMER CATALOGUE** from which this waist is selected and which contains all the new and desirable styles — some illustrated in colors, will be sent to every one who writes and mentions the *Youth's Companion*. We also send you more than

FIFTY SAMPLES FREE,

tape measure and measurement diagram (which insures a perfect fit), to all who write to us. We make every garment to order and we **Guarantee Perfection of Fit.**

Millinery, Silks, Dress Goods and Cloths by the yard at wholesale prices.

We pay express charges to any part of the United States. 58 West 23d St., New York.

Richard

[1896]

FEDER'S Pompadour Skirt Protector

When Buying
ready-made suits and skirts,
insist on having them bound with

Feder's Pompadour Skirt Protector

The best stores sell them.
Each skirt so finished bears this
label sewn thereon.
Every dry goods merchant in
the country will tell you that this
guarantee is absolutely good.

J. W. GODDARD & SONS
(Est. 1847)   98-100 Bleecker St., N. Y.

THIS SKIRT IS FINISHED WITH
FEDER'S POMPADOUR
SKIRT PROTECTOR
GUARANTEED to wear
as long as the skirt.

[1899]

Good Nature

good health, good looks,
and good style come
to the woman who
breaks away
from corsets
and revels
in the
comfort
of a Ferris
Waist. Perfect
in form and
style, adding sym-
metry to the figure
while it supports and
strengthens,—the

FERRIS' GOOD SENSE CORSET WAIST

should be in every woman's wardrobe. Made
in short or extra long waist, high or low bust.
Children's, 25c. to 50c.   Misses', 50c. to $1.   Ladies', $1 to $2.
For sale by all retailers.

[1896]

"The ONEITA"
PAT. APR. 25TH 1893.

Elastic Ribbed Union Suits
Are complete undergarments, covering the entire body.
Perfectly elastic, fitting like a glove.

No Buttons Down the Front

Made especially for Women and Misses. Convenient to
put on, being entered at the top and drawn on like trousers.
With no other kind of underwear can ladies obtain such perfect
fit for dresses, or wear comfortably so small a corset.

Send for Illustrated Booklet 2

Oneita Knitting Mills, No. 9 Greene St., New York   OFFICE:

[1899]

Your Arm

can be enlarged **1 inch** and strengthened 50 per cent.
in **one month** by using the **Hercules Graduated
Gymnastic Club and Strength Tester 5 minutes each day.** It will develop and strengthen the
arms, chest, back and waist in less than one-half the
time required by any other apparatus known. The
busiest man may become strong and healthy by its use.

Write for descriptive pamphlet and price-list to

HERCULES, Box 3559Y, Boston, Mass.

[1899]

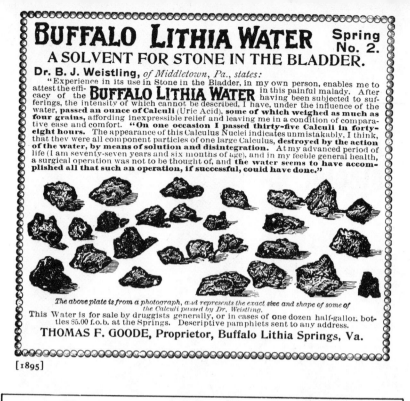

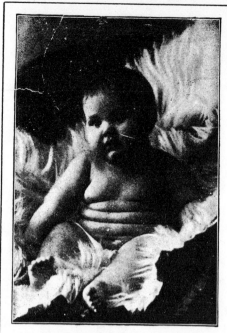

84

THE INTERRUPTION

(CLEVELAND BAKING POWDER CO., NEW YORK)

[1899]

COPYRIGHT 1899 E. DONALD ROBERTS.

A Delightful Dream ... A Delicious Reality.

A Dream

"LOWNEY" ON EVERY PIECE

LOWNEY'S Chocolate Bonbons

"LOWNEY" ON EVERY PIECE.

A Trial Package of our Finest Goods for 10c. in stamps. When not to be had of dealers, we will send on receipt of price: 1-lb. box, 60c.; 2-lb. box, $1.20; 3-lb. box, $1.80; 5-lb. box, $3.00. Delivered free in the U. S. Address all correspondence to

THE WALTER M. LOWNEY CO., 120 HIGH STREET, BOSTON, MASS.

BOSTON RETAIL STORE, 416 WASHINGTON STREET (BELOW SUMMER).

NEW YORK RETAIL STORE, 1123 BROADWAY (25TH STREET).

[1897]

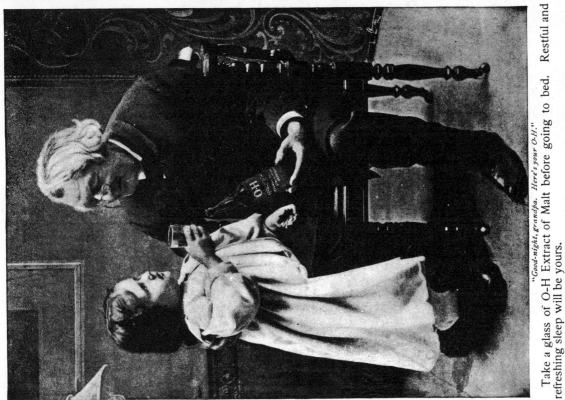

Highest Tribute Ever Paid to a Bicycle!

New York, March 25th, 1896.

Mr. W. C. Pawley,
Sec. Jersey City Y. M. C. A.

The National Board of Trade of Cycle Manufacturers hereby sanctions a public exhibition of cycles, accessories and sundries, at the Y. M. C. A., March 27th and 28th. This sanction is granted on the express understanding that no exhibition of VICTOR BICYCLES will be permitted.

Yours truly,   R. L. Coleman, President.

WHY are the members of the National Bicycle Board of Trade

AFRAID to exhibit their wheels with

VICTORS?

BECAUSE VICTORS

Cost more to build,
Are made of better material,
Show better workmanship,
Run easier and wear longer,
Are worth more than other bicycles.

Why Not Ride the Best?

OVERMAN WHEEL CO.,

New York.   Boston.   Detroit.   Denver.
San Francisco.   Los Angeles.   Portland, Ore.

[1896]

Bicycle Riders
Make No Mistake in Equipping their Wheels with

The "American."

The Best on the Market.

Insist on Getting our Registered Guarantee with Every "American."

Ten Thousand Miles and Repeat.

Easily read from the Saddle.

Price, **$2.00.**

Requires No Care.

The "American" Cyclometer, Model B, is not a dinkey toy, too small to be of any use; it does not get out of order if you run it backwards like others that are being put on the market. A cyclometer, though built like a watch, if too small cannot be depended on. The "American" tells you the small fractions of a mile; others do not. *The "American" leads; let those who can follow.* **Cuts now ready for 1896 Catalogues.**

AMERICAN CLOCK CO., 14 and 15 Tremont Row, Boston, Mass.

[1896]

BLOOD POISON

Primary, Secondary, or Tertiary BLOOD POISON permanently cured in 15 to 25 days. You can be treated at home for same price under same guarantee. If you prefer to come here we will contract to pay railroad fare and hotel bills, and no charge if we fail to cure. If you have taken mercury, iodide potash, and still have aches and pains, Mucous Patches in mouth, Sore Throat, Pimples, Copper Colored Spots, Ulcers on any part of the body, Hair or Eyebrows falling out, it is this Secondary BLOOD POISON we guarantee to cure. We solicit the most obstinate cases and challenge the world for a case we cannot cure. This disease has always baffled the skill of the most eminent physicians. $500,000 capital behind our unconditional guarantee. Absolute proofs sent sealed on application. Address COOK REMEDY CO., 1480 Masonic Temple, CHICAGO, ILL.

[1897]

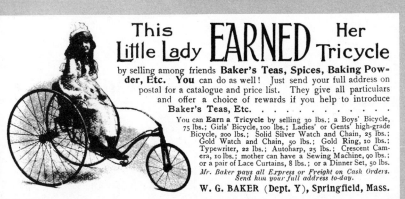

90

TROLLEY CAR OF THE
FUTURE.

A glimpse into the future reveals the Trolley Theatre, Restaurant, Cigar Store, Barber Shop and various other trades on wheels. The twentieth century man will receive his shave and breakfast while going to business in the morning—dine and be amused while returning at night.—*Electrical World.*

"LOOKING BACKWARD" or forward fifty years, you will always find

Williams' Shaving Soap

keeping step with every new invention or improvement for the welfare of man, and indispensable to his comfort and happiness.

WILLIAMS' SHAVING SOAP is used by the leading and most successful barbers everywhere. It was adopted as Standard by the U. S. Naval department, years ago. It is used at the various *Army* Posts—also on all the principal R. R. and Steamship Lines. You may be sure of finding it on the "Trolley Car of the future."

Williams' Shaving Stick, 25 cts.
Yankee Shaving Soap, 10 cts.
Luxury Shaving Tablet, 25 cts.

The J. B. WILLIAMS CO.,
Glastonbury, Conn., U. S. A.

LONDON : 64 Great Russell St.
SIDNEY : 161 Clarence St.

[1897]

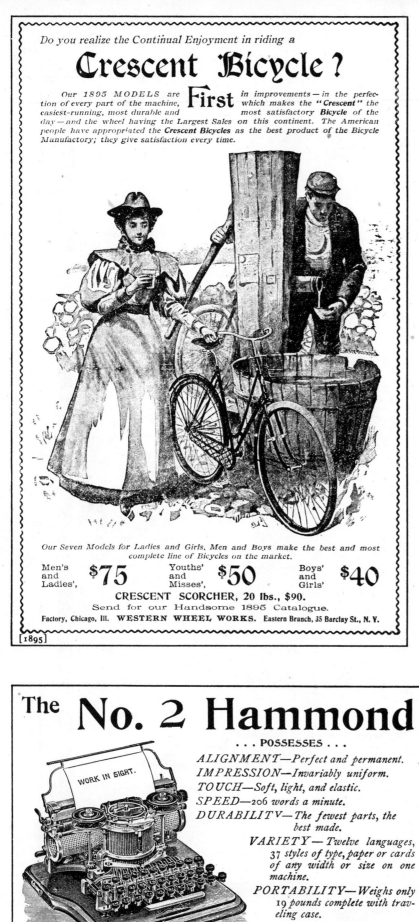
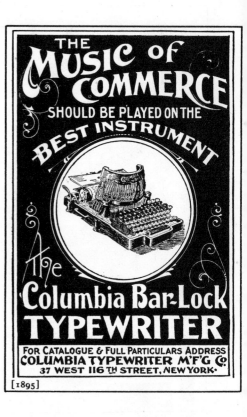
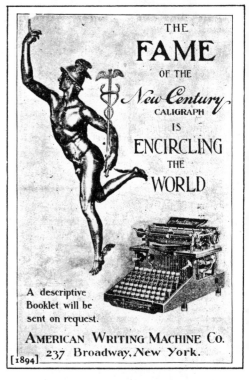

1900-1909

THE WORLD'S WORK

SEPTEMBER, 1904

AUTOMOBILES FOR COMMON USES

THE development of the automobile has been deflected somewhat from a natural course because its possibilities of swiftness have caused it to become a plaything of the idle rich. But gas- and steam-engines will soon propel loads wherever there are good and reasonably level roads; and, within a few years, pleasure vehicles will be made for persons of modest means and of quiet habits. For, of course, the making of cars chiefly for speed will cease to be the main work of the builders as soon as their novelty wears off. The sensation of running along country roads at the speed of locomotives will presently become commonplace; and then the many factories will turn their attention more to simpler cars and to freight-cars.

The durability and the trustworthiness of motor-cars have now been pretty well proved. The recent trip, for instance, made by Mr. L. L. Whitman, of San Francisco, from that city to New York in a single car in thirty-three days shows the endurance of the machine. The journey was about 4,500 miles, and he travelled an average of more than 135 miles a day. Such a performance shows that the mechanism of good cars has passed the experimental stage. Every year we may expect safer, more trustworthy, simpler, and cheaper machines, until one shall cost less than a horse and wagon, and may be run with safety by any man or woman of usual care. Such machines can be made to do all that light wagons now do, and they can be run for less cost for fuel and oil than the feeding of a horse, and with less care than a horse and wagon require. The sooner the fashion for speed subsides, the sooner will the manufacturers give their attention to the building of motor-cars for these humbler and more general uses.

The time may not be far off when the mechanism will be so simplified that light machines will be more common than horses and buggies, where there are good roads.

96

[1906]

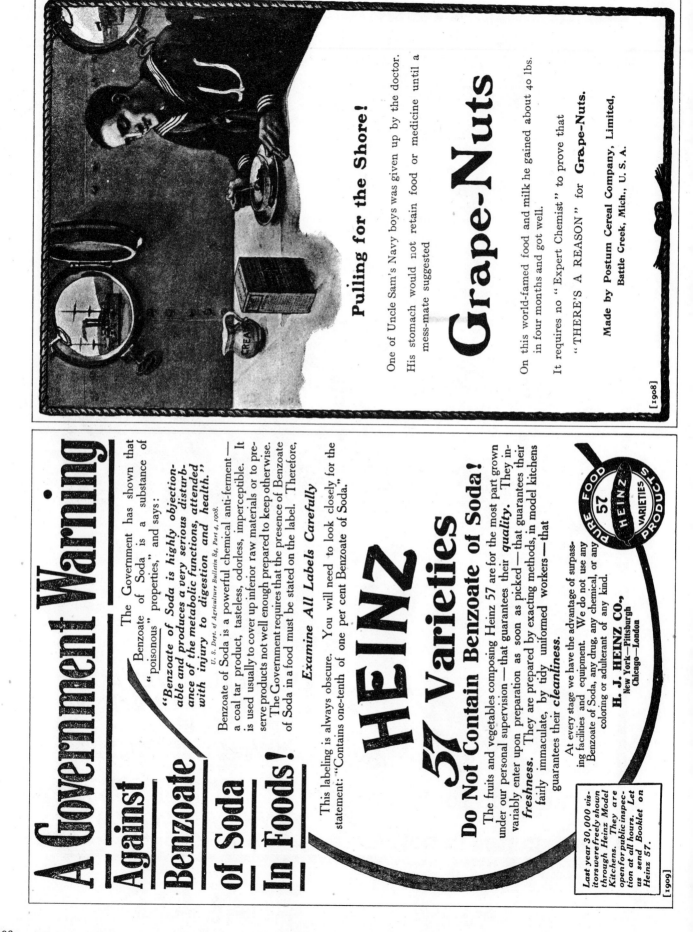

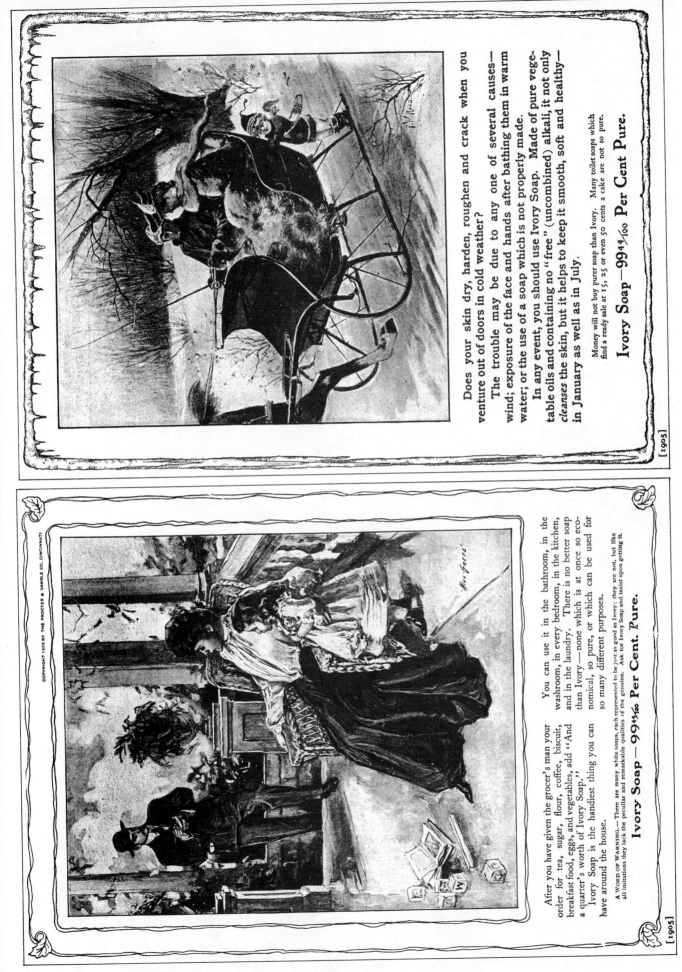

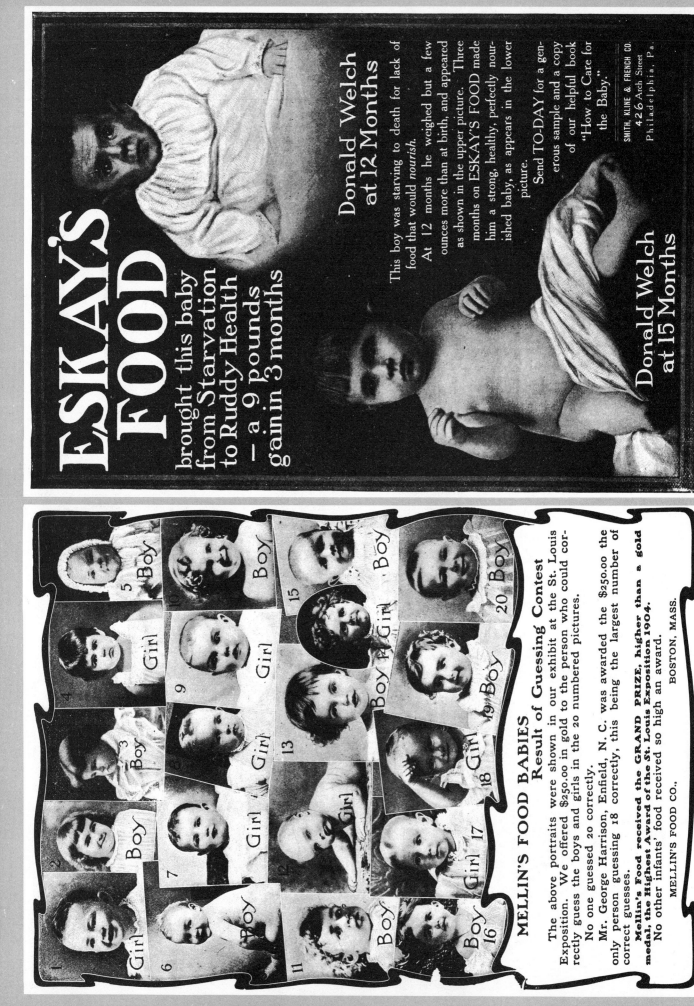

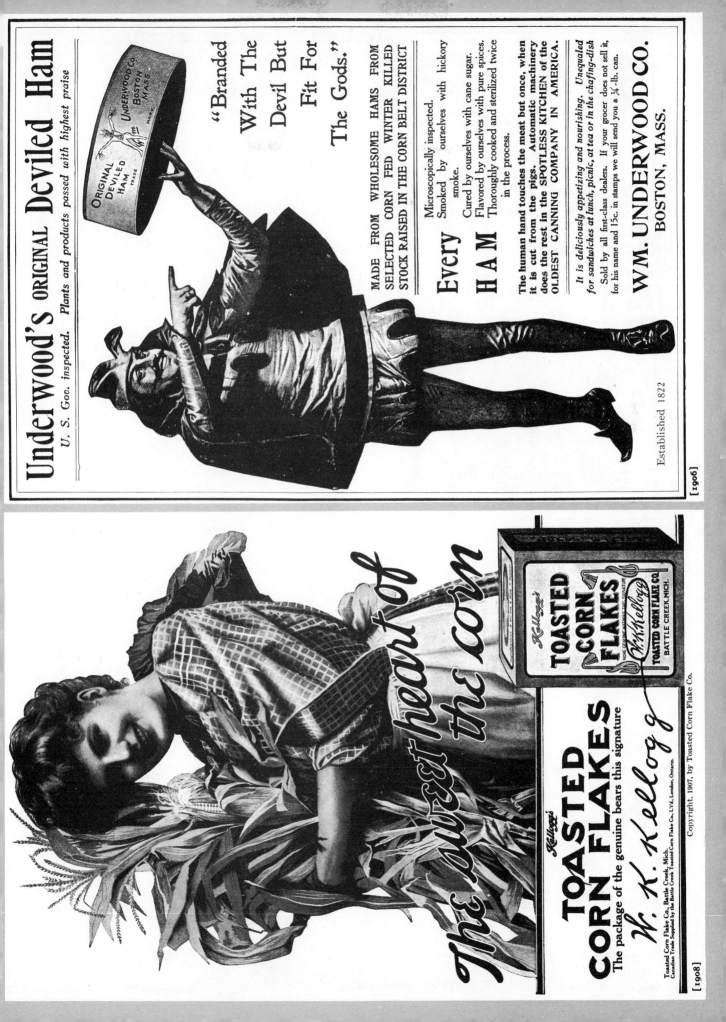

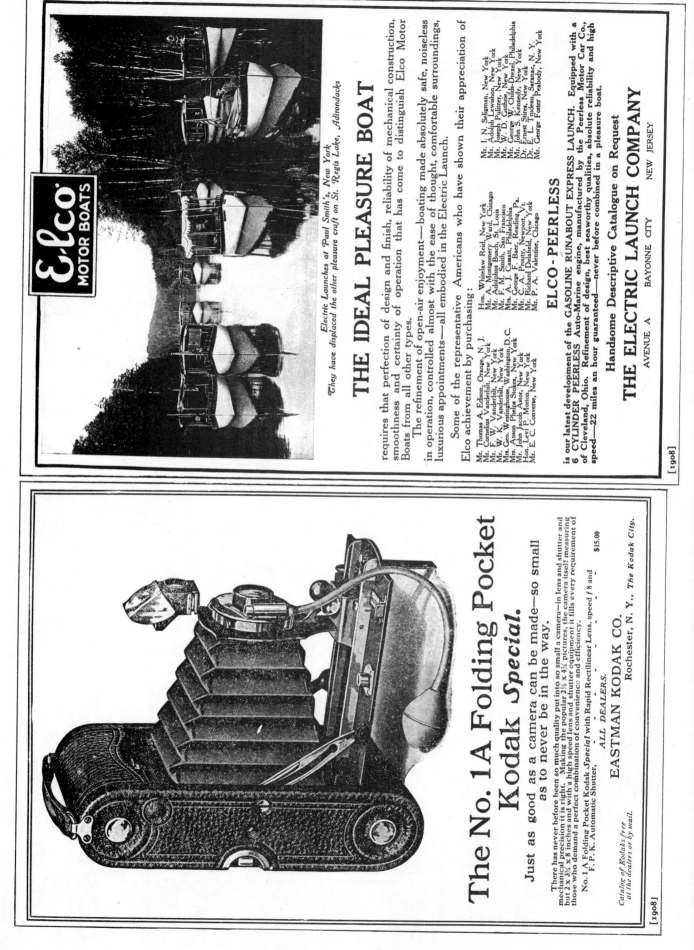

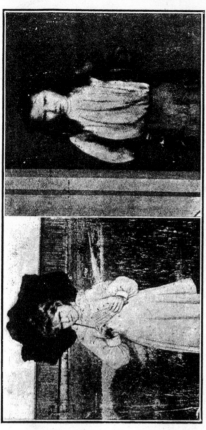

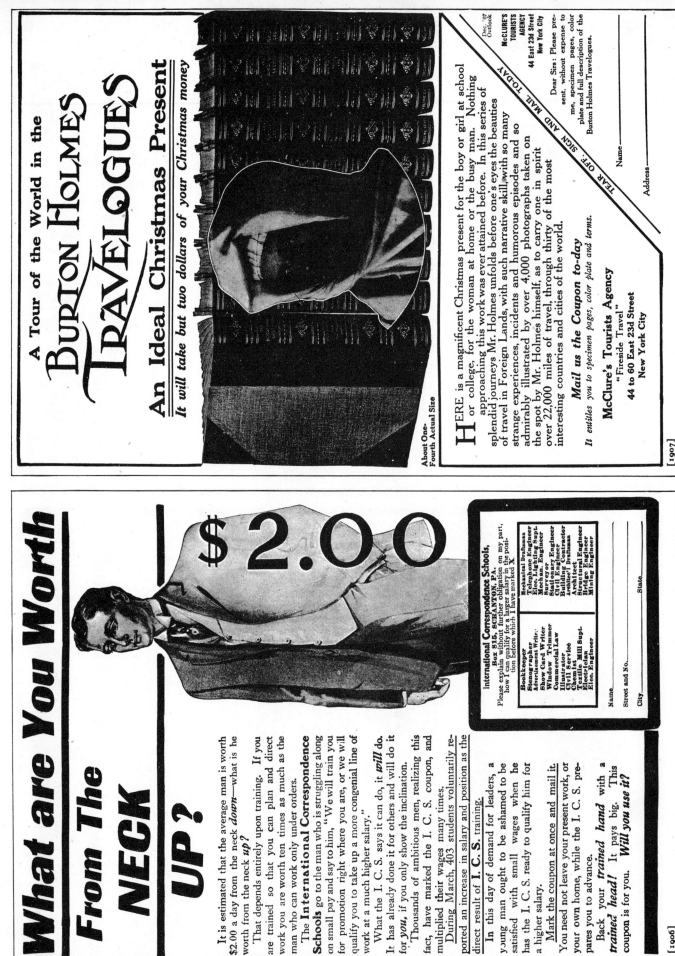
106

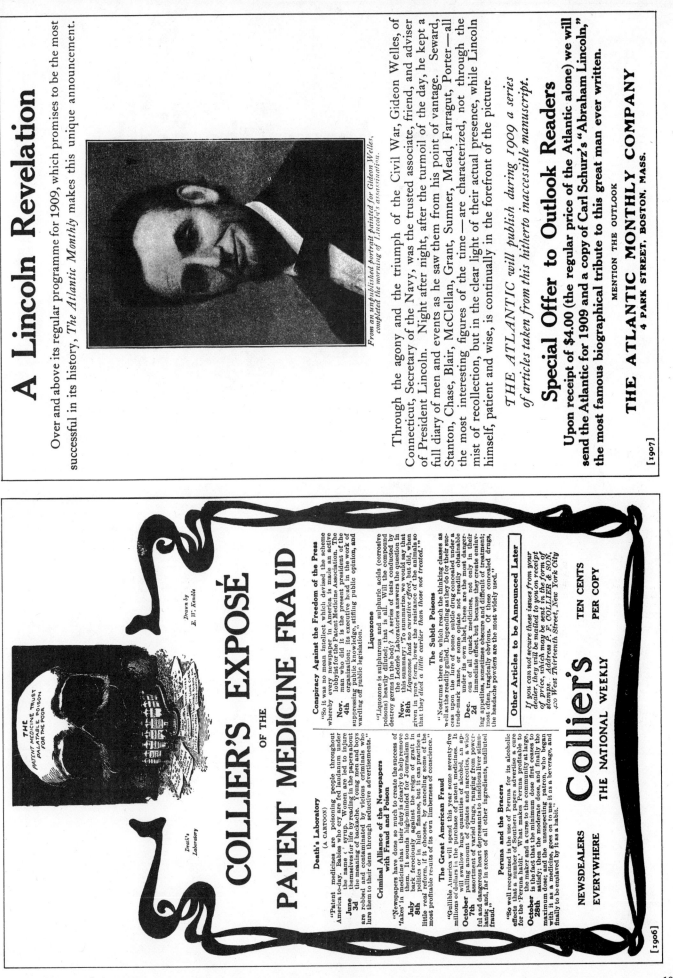

Four Times Around the Earth

Repair Expense $127.30

Most repair bills are unnecessary. We proved that fact when ten

cars ran 118,503 miles (more than four times around the earth) on repair expenses of $127.30.

These figures are sworn to by ten individual owners. One car, with limousine body, ran 17,003 miles. Repair expense—NOTHING. Another, 11,000 miles. Repair expense—30 cents. A third, 10,595 miles. Repair expense—NOTHING. Total, three cars, 38,598 miles, on repair expenses of *30 cents.*

All these cars were Winton Sixes. Pretty sturdy cars, eh?

One owner, after running from Cleveland to New England and back (2038 miles) said: "It was like a sealed bonnet run. Never touched the motor. And we didn't find a hill that was hard for us."

So it's a hill climber, too.

While you are buying a car, why not get *the one* that tops it over all the rest?

The prime secret of motor car supremacy is *Continuous Power.* No automobile on earth can have Continuous Power unless it has *Six Cylinders.*

The Winton Six has Six Cylinders. Therefore, it's right in principle.

And because it's right in practice, too, it's the quietest, prettiest running car of them all. None better on hills. None more flexible. None more reliable.

We are using the same, identical motor for 1910 as in 1909—couldn't improve it.

The 1910 buyer gets four forward speeds, a larger clutch, the best carburetor we have ever seen, dual ignition, a superb, roomy body, suspended low on semi-elliptical springs, 124-inch wheel base (4 inches increase), and an inswept frame, allowing short turning radius.

Starts from the seat without cranking—A feature not to be found on any other car of any type. A feature worth the price of one's self-respect.

At $3000 the 48 horse-power Winton Six represents the absolute limit of motor car value.

Let us send you the details. We want you to know about "Sixes vs. Fours;" you don't have to be a mechanical expert to understand the facts. And by all means get the full details about the ten Winton Sixes that ran more than four times around the earth on $127.30 repair expense.

Clip the coupon and send it today.

THE WINTON MOTOR CARRIAGE CO.
Member A. L. A. M.
CLEVELAND, U. S. A.

Winton Branch Houses (owned and operated by the company) in New York, Boston, Philadelphia, Baltimore, Pittsburg, Detroit, Chicago, Minneapolis, Seattle and San Francisco.

THE WINTON MOTOR CARRIAGE CO.
102 Berea Road, Cleveland, Ohio.
Please send Winton Six literature to

....

[1909]

The Remington Typewriter

With Wahl Adding and Subtracting Attachment

It Writes
It Adds
It Subtracts

You cannot do these three things mechanically on any other machine

represents the complete and perfect union of the writing machine and the adding machine. It completes the circle; finishes the labor saving; leaves nothing more for mechanical ingenuity to contrive in the field of billing, order and general accounting work.

The Wahl Adding and Subtracting Attachment bears our guarantee and is made for the Remington Typewriter exclusively.

Illustrated descriptive booklet sent on request.

Remington Typewriter Company (Incorporated)
New York and Everywhere

[1908]

A Course in Practical Salesmanship
Tuition FREE ~ All Expenses Paid

IN these times of keen business rivalry, the services of the Trained Salesman command a high premium.

The Oliver Sales Organization is the finest body of Trained Salesmen in the world. It is composed of picked men, and is under the guidance of Sales Experts.

In less than ten years it has placed the Oliver Typewriter where it belongs—in a position of absolute leadership.

Its aggregate earnings are enormous and the individual average is high.

The scope of its activities is as wide as civilization and the greatest prizes of the commercial world are open to its membership.

The organization is drilled like an army. It affords a liberal education in actual salesmanship, and increases individual earning power many per cent, by systematic development of natural talents.

Its ranks are recruited from every walk of life. Men who had missed their calling and made dismal failures in the over-crowded professions have been developed in the Oliver School of Practical Salesmanship into phenomenal successes.

Because every Business Executive is interested in the very things the Oliver stands for—economy of time and money—increase in efficiency of Correspondence and Accounting Departments.

The OLIVER Typewriter

The Standard Visible Writer

is simple in principle, compactly built, durable in construction, and its touch is beautifully elastic and most responsive.

In versatility, legibility, perfect alignment, visibility, etc., it is all that could be desired in a writing machine.

It's a constant source of inspiration to the salesman, as every day develops new evidence of its wide range of usefulness.

Just as the winning personality of a human being attracts and holds friends, so does the Oliver, by its responsiveness to all demands, gain and hold an ever-widening circle of enthusiastic admirers.

If you wish to learn actual salesmanship and become a member of the Oliver Organization, send in your application **immediately,** as the ranks are rapidly being filled.

You can take up this work in spare time, or give us your entire time, just as you prefer. Whether you earn $300 a year, or **twelve times $300** a year, depends entirely upon **yourself.**

We offer to properly qualified applicants the opportunity to earn handsome salaries and to gain a knowledge of salesmanship that will prove of inestimable value.

Can you afford to vegetate in a poorly-paid position, when the way is open to a successful business career?

Address at once.

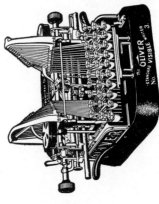

The Oliver Typewriter puts the salesman in touch with the men worth knowing—the human dynamos who furnish the brain power of the commercial world.

THE OLIVER TYPEWRITER CO., 161 Wabash Ave., Chicago
WE WANT LOCAL AGENTS IN THE UNITED STATES AND CANADA.
PRINCIPAL FOREIGN OFFICE—75 QUEEN VICTORIA ST., LONDON.

[1906]

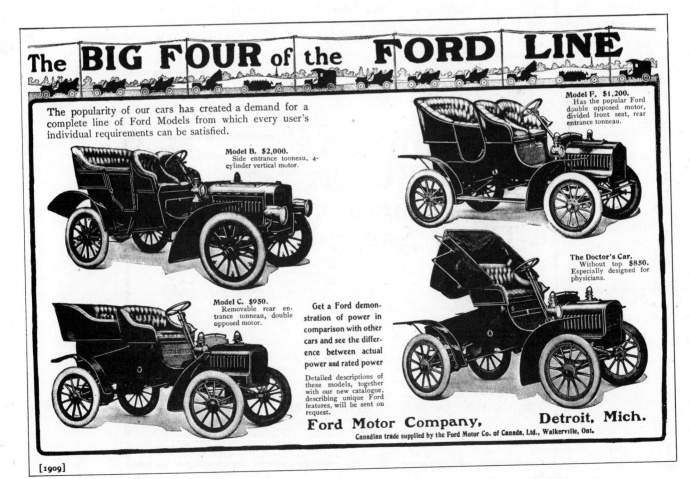
113

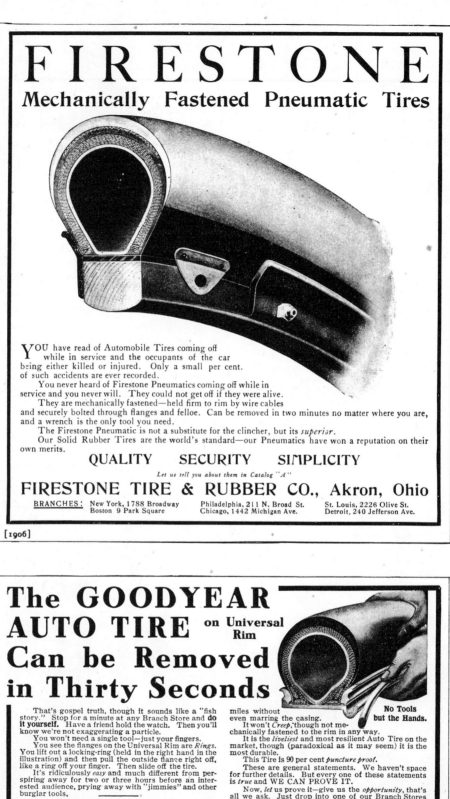

114

The Ultimate Car Is The Stearns

The Stearns is the dream of the real motor car lover, no matter what car he may own.

He may be content for a while with a lesser car. But his desire for the best, if he can afford it, will bring him in time to the Stearns.

For the Stearns is the autocraft of motordom. It leads so far, and has led so long, that none dispute its place.

Improvements are possible some time. We spend $40,000 per year to find them—in our experimental department.

But to build anything better, with man's present knowledge, is utterly out of the question.

30-60 H. P. Chassis with Limousine Body

Good for 60,000 Miles

The Stearns car, if properly cared for, grows better with use. It is better the second year than the first.

We win most of our races with cars which have run ten thousand miles or over.

The life of a Stearns, if not misused, is more than 60,000 miles. That is the result of perfection.

Cars that seem to be cheaper are not nearly so cheap, if you figure the cost by the year.

No New Yearly Models

Whenever our engineers work out and demonstrate an improvement, it is added at once to the car. So any buyer, at any time, gets a car of our latest construction.

Then keep it and care for it. Use it until it wears out. There will never be a car materially better, for invention in this line has about reached the limit.

Get the economy that comes from long service. Secure the full value of our costly construction. Then you will know why a car like the Stearns is worth more.

Where the Stearns Leads

The steel used in Stearns cars costs 25 cents per pound. It is made from imported ores.

Every important part of the car is made in our own factory—made without regard to cost.

The result, for one thing, is the safest car in the world. There is twice the strength needed where strength means additional safety.

The Stearns is a powerful car, conservatively rated. Its engine is famous for a seemingly exhaustless reserve power.

The car has a double carburetor. A change from low to high motor speed brings an automatic change of the carburetor. This is the secret of the car's flexibility.

This is the Envied Car

The Stearns is a stunning car, low and rakish. There is no other car so attractive.

It is a car to be proud of—a car that excites admiration. Every man envies the owner of a Stearns.

Yet the owner knows that, in the long run, inferior cars will cost more than he paid.

If you think you would like such a car as this, please send for our latest catalog.

The *Stearns*
The Ultimate Car

A Reminder
The F. B. STEARNS CO., Cleveland, O.

Please mail me the Catalog No. 16

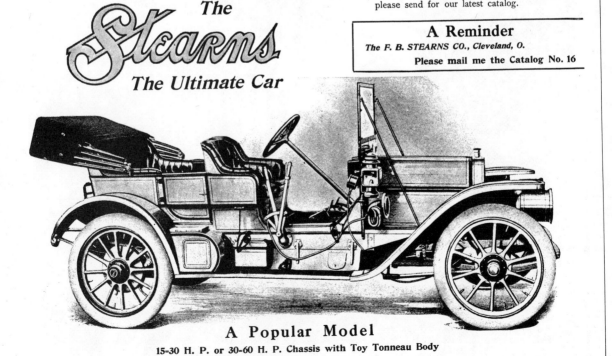

A Popular Model
15-30 H. P. or 30-60 H. P. Chassis with Toy Tonneau Body

[1907]

"The White Line Radiator Belongs to the Stearns"

116

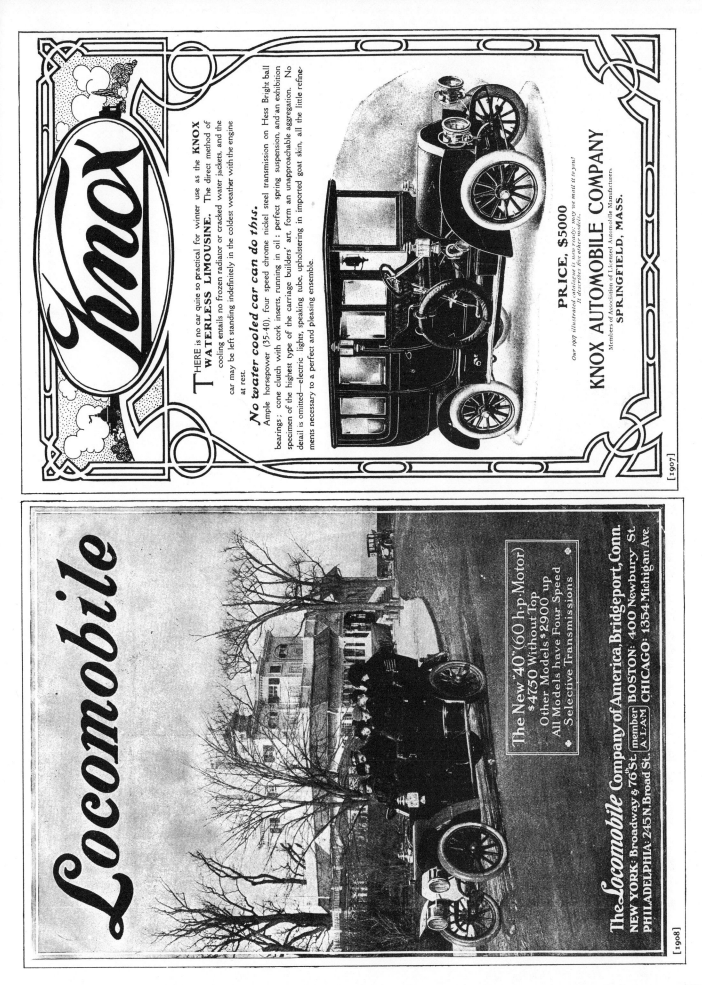
117

Avoid a Trip to the
Police Court

The fine amounts to little—it's the hours of delay, the inconvenience and possible humiliation for you and for those in your company that try the patience and spoil the pleasure of the whole trip,

All this can positively be avoided by equipping your car with

The Warner
Auto-Meter
(Registers Speed and Distance)

This little instrument always *tells the truth*. It registers with ABSOLUTE ACCURACY from ¼ mile to 60 miles per hour. It attaches to any Automobile made.

Without it you never know your *exact speed* — and the temptation to go a little faster and a little faster is almost irresistible—you know how it is. And you know, too, what happens to you and your party when you *think* you are going 8 miles an hour and the Policeman's stop watch says 15.

Don't guess yourself into trouble—KNOW and keep out of it. The Warner Auto-Meter is your salvation.

And it's your ONLY salvation.

Because the Warner Auto-Meter is the only speed indicator which is sensitive enough to be absolutely and unfailingly accurate at *speeds under 10 miles an hour.*

Because it's the only one which works perfectly in all positions and at all angles, on rough roads or smooth, up hill or down.

Because it's the only one which changes with the *speed alone* and in which the indicator does not dance back and forth from the jar of the car.

The Warner Auto-Meter is the only speed indicator which is actuated by the same fixed, unchangeable Magnetism which makes the Mariner's Compass reliable FOREVER under all conditions.

No one else can use Magnetism to determine the speed of an Automobile, though it's the only *positive* and *sure* way. Because there is just one way in which Magnetism can successfully be used for this purpose and *we have Patented that way.*

There is nothing about the Warner Auto-Meter which can give out, or wear out, or get out of adjustment. It is the only speed-indicator made without cams, plates or levers, and in which there is *no friction.* Friction wears away the cams and levers in other speed indicators, which are necessarily so small that *1-1000 of an inch* wear will throw out the reading from *one to five miles per hour.*

One Warner Auto-Meter will last a lifetime. It is as sensitive as a Compass and as *Solid as a Rock.* Otherwise it couldn't stand our severe service-test, which is equivalent to a trip of

160,000 Miles at 50 Miles per Hour on Granite Pavements Riding Solid Tires.

The practical Warner Testing Machine is shown in Fig. 1. The wheel connection of the Auto-Meter is attached to a shaft running

Figure 1

200 revolutions per minute. Across this shaft lies a plank which is hinged at one end and has the Auto-Meter attached to the other. Brazed to the shaft is a knob of steel, which at every revolution "bumps" the plank, giving to the Auto-Meter *200 shocks per minute* while it is showing a speed of *50 miles per hour.*

Each one of these shocks is more severe than would be suffered in an entire season's riding. After running 10 hours a day for THREE MONTHS, actual tests show the Auto-Meter to be recording the speed with the same accuracy as at first within 1-1000 of 1%, or less than *6 inches per mile.*

No other Speed Indicator on Earth could Stand this Test.

This is why we sell each Auto-Meter on a
10 YEARS GUARANTEE
and why we gladly renew any Auto-Meter (which has not been injured by accident) if the Magnet (the HEART of the instrument) is less accurate than 1-10 of 1% after 10 years use.

We will gladly tell you more about this wonderful instrument if you will write us,

If you write TODAY we will send you something every motorist will prize—our Free Book—"Auto Pointers."

The Warner Instrument Co.,   104 Roosevelt St., Beloit, Wis.
(The Auto-Meter is on sale by all first-class dealers and at most Garages.)

[1906]

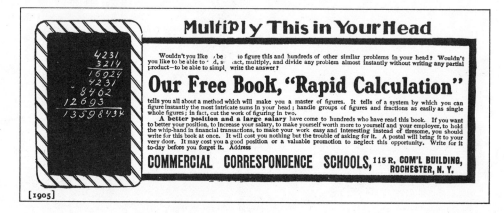

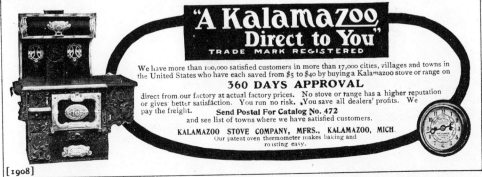
119

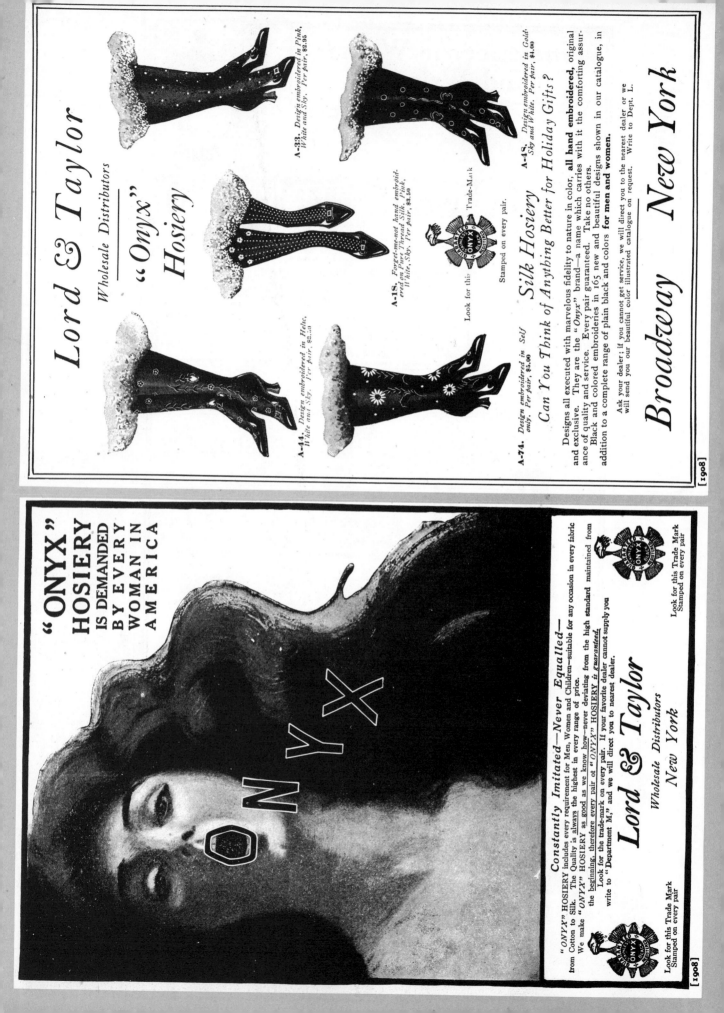

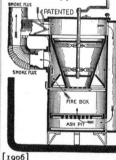
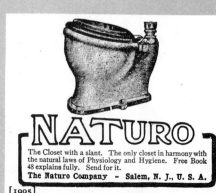

124

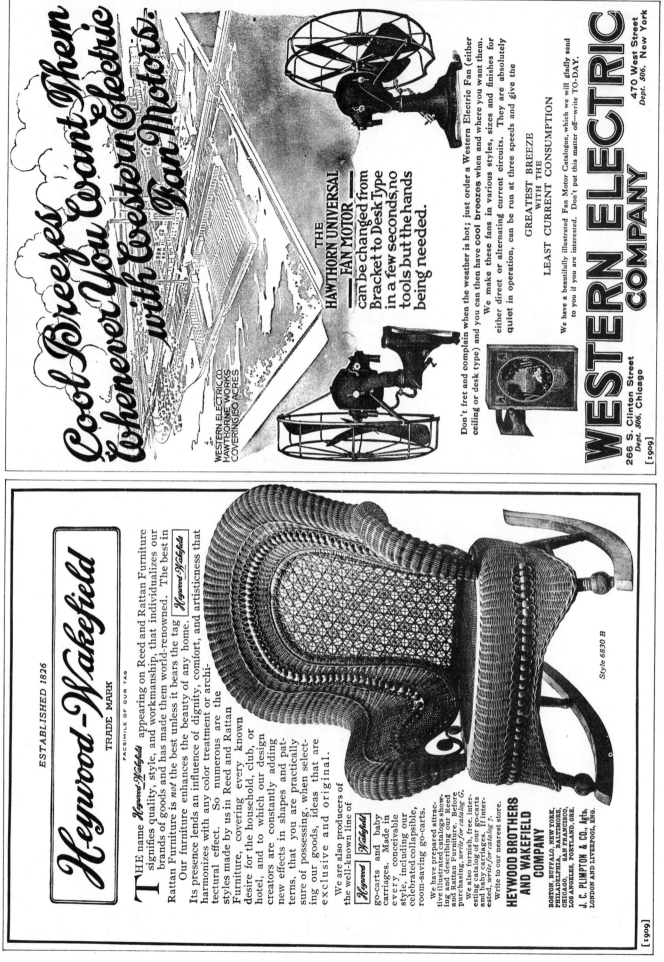

126

128

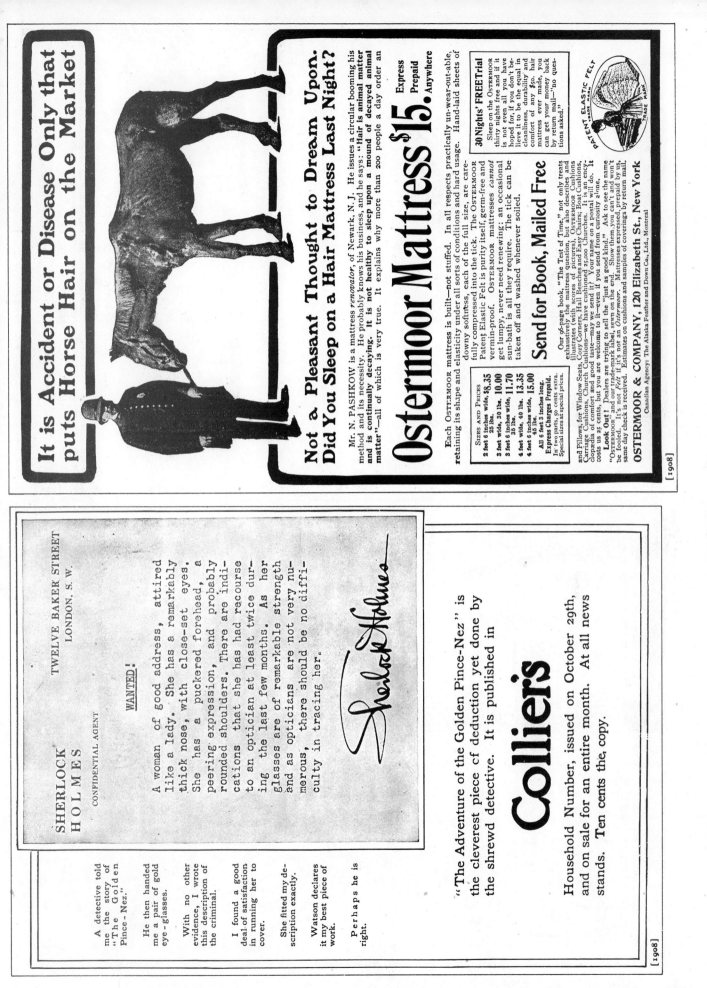

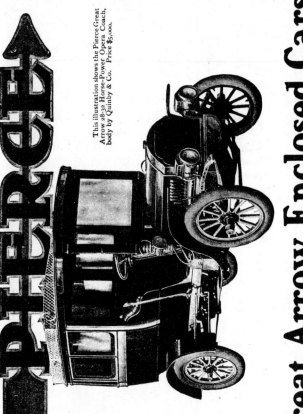

PIERCE

Great Arrow Enclosed Cars

This illustration shows the Pierce Great Arrow 28-32 Horse-Power Opera Coach, body by Quinby & Co. Price $5,000.

THESE three types of enclosed cars have been built with a special thought for the user who expects the same perfection in the appointments of his automobile that he does in those of his carriages.

These cars have the perfect mechanism of the Pierce cars together with the most attractive and tasteful bodies ever turned out by Quinby. To appreciate their perfection they should be seen. We have been working steadily toward a very high standard in car-building, and believe now that the Pierce cars are American cars built by Americans for American conditions, American roads and the American temperament. Full descriptive booklet together with technical description of mechanisms will be mailed on request, or can be had of numerous Pierce agents all over the United States.

This illustration shows the Pierce Great Arrow 28-32 Horse-Power Suburban Car. Price $5,000.

This illustration shows the Pierce Great Arrow 28-32 Horse-Power Landaulette Car. Price $5,000.

THE GEORGE N. PIERCE COMPANY, Buffalo, N. Y.

Manufacturers of Pierce Cycles   **Members of Association of Licensed Automobile Manufacturers.**

$1,000 IN PRIZES

EVERY artist and designer should write at once for full particulars of our offer of prizes as follows: First prize of $250 and a second prize of $100 for the best design of an open body for a motor car; first prize of $250 and a second prize of $100 for the best design of an enclosed or Limousine body for a motor car; first prize of $200 and a second prize of $100 for the best color scheme for motor car bodies. Full description and outline drawings of Pierce cars will be supplied to artists for coloring.

[1905]

Columbia Mark XLV 35-40 H.P. Gasolene Cars.

A SURPLUS of material for every strain but no excess of material where it is not needed. Every part and piece of chassis from selected stock subjected to the most thorough mechanical and laboratory tests, so that parts that most frequently break in cars of ordinary construction—axles, frame, springs, casings, transmission, etc.—are made unbreakable under any stress of normal use, however severe. Exclusive features of unequaled merit are: New carburetor which positively maintains a correct explosive mixture; new system of spark and throttle control with ball-joint connections from levers mounted on non-revolving head within the steering-wheel; new method of releasing compression in starting; new steering mechanism and other improvements adding to efficiency of the motor and ease of control and care-taking.

COLUMBIA supremacy in body designs and furnishings has never been questioned. We supply the Mark XLV Chassis with the following styles of bodies: Standard Double Side Entrance Tonneau, $4,000; Royal Victoria, $5,000; Double Victoria, $5,000; Landaulet, $5,500; Limousine, $5,500; Each pattern reaches the limit of elegance and sumptuous appointment.

Catalogue of Columbia 35-40 and 18 h.p. GasoleneCars will be sent on request. Also separate catalogues of Columbia Electric Carriages and Columbia Electric Commercial Vehicles.

35-40 H. P. Touring Car

ELECTRIC VEHICLE COMPANY

HARTFORD CONN.

134 WEST 39th ST   1413 MICHIGAN AV
NEW YORK   CHICAGO
74 STANHOPE ST
BOSTON

MEMBER OF ASS'N LICENSED AUTOMOBILE MANUFACTURERS

[1905]

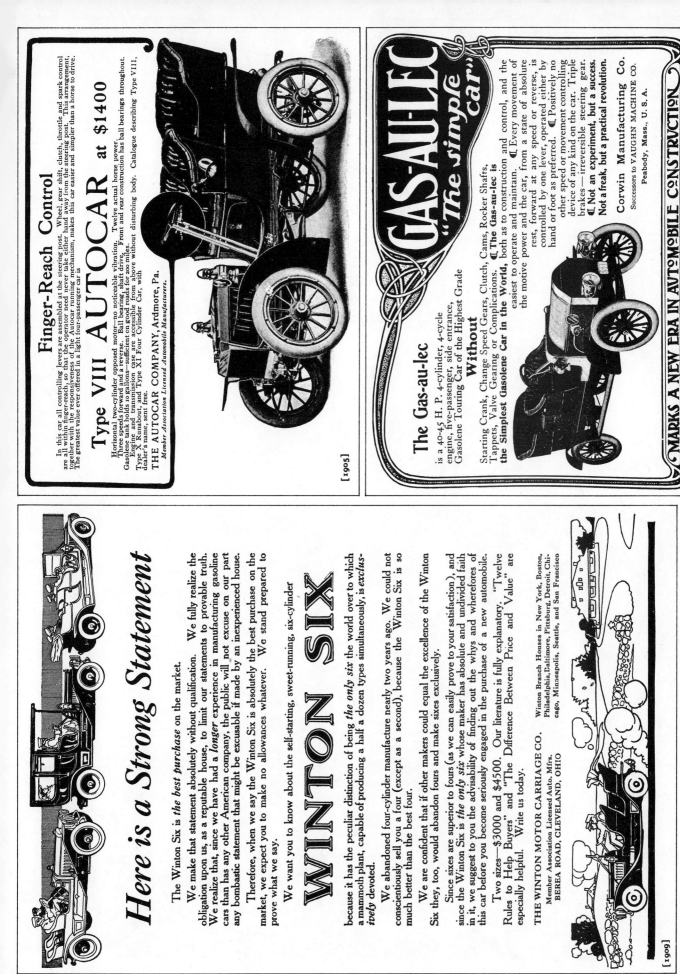

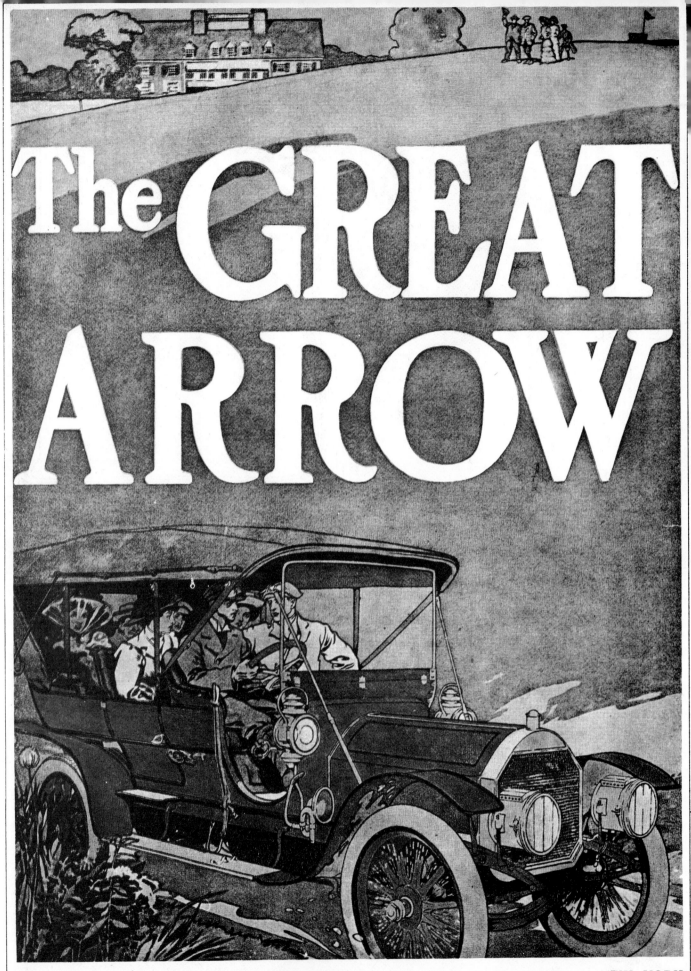

The GREAT ARROW

THE GEORGE N. PIERCE COMPANY, MEMBERS OF THE A. L. A. M., BUFFALO, NEW YORK

[1907]

The Outlook

MARCH 22, 1913

LYMAN ABBOTT, Editor-in-Chief   **HAMILTON W. MABIE,** Associate Editor
THEODORE ROOSEVELT
Contributing Editor

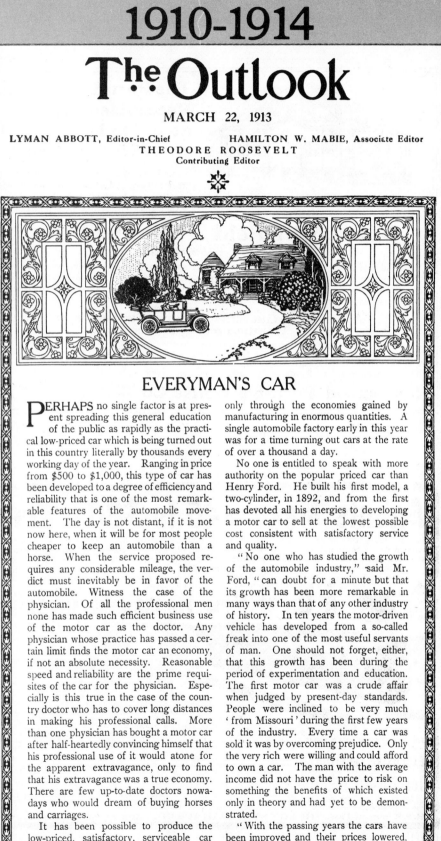

EVERYMAN'S CAR

PERHAPS no single factor is at present spreading this general education of the public as rapidly as the practical low-priced car which is being turned out in this country literally by thousands every working day of the year. Ranging in price from $500 to $1,000, this type of car has been developed to a degree of efficiency and reliability that is one of the most remarkable features of the automobile movement. The day is not distant, if it is not now here, when it will be for most people cheaper to keep an automobile than a horse. When the service proposed requires any considerable mileage, the verdict must inevitably be in favor of the automobile. Witness the case of the physician. Of all the professional men none has made such efficient business use of the motor car as the doctor. Any physician whose practice has passed a certain limit finds the motor car an economy, if not an absolute necessity. Reasonable speed and reliability are the prime requisites of the car for the physician. Especially is this true in the case of the country doctor who has to cover long distances in making his professional calls. More than one physician has bought a motor car after half-heartedly convincing himself that his professional use of it would atone for the apparent extravagance, only to find that his extravagance was a true economy. There are few up-to-date doctors nowadays who would dream of buying horses and carriages.

It has been possible to produce the low-priced, satisfactory, serviceable car only through the economies gained by manufacturing in enormous quantities. A single automobile factory early in this year was for a time turning out cars at the rate of over a thousand a day.

No one is entitled to speak with more authority on the popular priced car than Henry Ford. He built his first model, a two-cylinder, in 1892, and from the first has devoted all his energies to developing a motor car to sell at the lowest possible cost consistent with satisfactory service and quality.

"No one who has studied the growth of the automobile industry," said Mr. Ford, "can doubt for a minute but that its growth has been more remarkable in many ways than that of any other industry of history. In ten years the motor-driven vehicle has developed from a so-called freak into one of the most useful servants of man. One should not forget, either, that this growth has been during the period of experimentation and education. The first motor car was a crude affair when judged by present-day standards. People were inclined to be very much 'from Missouri' during the first few years of the industry. Every time a car was sold it was by overcoming prejudice. Only the very rich were willing and could afford to own a car. The man with the average income did not have the price to risk on something the benefits of which existed only in theory and had yet to be demonstrated.

"With the passing years the cars have been improved and their prices lowered,

Self AMERICAN Starting
AMERICAN UNDERSLUNG

"Nearly a Quarter-Century of Leadership"

For nearly a Quarter-Century the Stevens-Duryea has originated, and put into successful practice, the most important, vital and most imitated mechanical principles in the fine motor-car of today.

And now, having been the leader in establishing these principles, the Stevens-Duryea has brought out the new Model C-Six, an entirely new car with a still further advancement of these fundamentals. At the same time it assumes

A New Leadership

The result of which is to give the motorist the greatest possible enjoyment of his motoring, and pride in his car.

This means first, **the maximum of active power delivered to the rear wheels;** power-loss being reduced to the minimum by the Three-Point Support of the Unit Power Plant. Wheel-power is what you want — not wasted engine-power. It means going more miles a day, more easily than was ever possible before in any car of any power.

This means next, **the new quietness and smooth-running,** which have been obtained by an infinite number of improvements in design and manufacture. The Model C-Six is by far the quietest car we have ever seen.

The new motoring enjoyment is also due to the entire ease with which the motorist rests in the car. A new design of springs dampens the recoil. The Three-Point Support prevents the lurching of the engine from being communicated to the passengers, who rest in an easy position in

a wealth of depth of upholstery. The patented rear seat of the tonneau is entirely adjustable. There is plenty of room and the doors are wide. The rail of the car is upholstered for the entire length. The windshield thoroughly ventilates the driver's compartment, and the top, when up, attaches firmly to it—no rattle, or noise. Equipment is complete. Control is easy, and precision instruments are within easy reach, and are distinctly separated so as not to confuse the driver.

The new idea of beauty creates, for the first time, one true and artistic unit out of all the exterior elements of the car, with graceful lines flowing from the radiator to the rear of the car. This is a distinctive and beautiful style, and so correct and sound that it will compel admiration for a long time to come.

In the new Model C-Six the motorist is constantly in a position of rest and free from care or strain. He can go about his motoring feeling that he is in just the right car — the handsomest, most advanced, latest and best creation in the motor-car world.

$4500 to $5950 — Open and Enclosed Bodies, two to seven passengers.   Shall we send the new catalogue?

Stevens-Duryea Company Chicopee Falls Mass
"Pioneer Builders of American Sixes"

Model C-Six
Seven Passengers
$4750

[1912]

HUDSON "33"

See the Triangle on the Radiator

The 1912 Torpedo—$1600 Complete

Get this Car and be One Year Ahead of Others

All dealers are now showing the 1912 models of the HUDSON "33"

No other manufacturer has been able, as yet, to duplicate all the advanced ideas that are found in the Hudson "33."

The original "33" upset the calculations of many manufacturers. Nothing quite so simple, so handsome, so quiet or of so much worth had been brought out. No doubt was expressed by anyone in the trade as to the value of the car or the correctness of its design, for Howard E. Coffin, its builder, was admitted to be the most advanced creator of new, startling and successful ideas that the industry has produced.

He had built four famously successful cars before he turned his attention to the HUDSON "33." Each of those cars had served as a model for less clever makers. You will find duplicates of his earlier designs under many different names. The HUDSON "33," however, was so radically different from anything that had ever been done that it was impossible to so quickly change other designs to conform to it.

This season some manufacturers are using some of the ideas which Mr. Coffin introduced last year on the HUDSON "33." The indications are that by 1913 a great many other cars will be close duplicates in all essentials of the HUDSON "33."

If you choose a HUDSON "33" you get a type of car that will be in general use next year. You will, in addition, get a much better value than was the original HUDSON "33"—that of 1911.

The 1912 car is a distinct advancement over that model. It is little different mechanically; but in the way of refinement, in extra equipment and in other details which add to the life, appearance, power and comfort-giving qualities of an automobile, it is much better.

The Car Which Last Spring 2,000 Failed to Get

No car is talked about so much as the HUDSON "33." Everybody who knows anything at all about automobiles knows the wonderful value and advanced ideas of the "33."

The entire year's production of the factory was contracted for by the trade in less than a month. Orders from 687 individuals were placed the first day the car was offered for sale and at the close of the 1911 season we had more than 2,000 orders which we could not fill.

That is the story of the HUDSON "33."

No dealer was able to take care of his trade. We have orders on hand now that will take months to fill.

See the HUDSON "33." People buy it because of its recognized value. What others do in this respect should be your guide.

Go to your dealer's and see the 1912 HUDSON "33." If that is not convenient, write for literature.

The HUDSON "33" is furnished in four models, all on the same chassis. The price of each model is $1600. The Touring Car carries five passengers; the Torpedo, four; the Roadster and the Mile-a-Minute Roadster, two each. All models except the last are equipped with fore-doors, genuine mohair top and wind shield. Equipment includes 4-inch tires, Demountable Rims, extra rim, tire irons, highest grade black enameled lamps, Bosch magneto, Prest-O-Lite tank, tools, etc.

HUDSON MOTOR CAR COMPANY

7027 Jefferson Avenue, Detroit

75 *This plant, covering 6 acres—2 city blocks—was erected especially for the manufacture of the HUDSON "33."*

[1912]

THE NEW
Harley-Davidson
"THE SILENT GREY FELLOW"

The Motorcycle That Is Not Uncomfortable

The Free-Wheel Control permits the HARLEY-DAVIDSON to be started like an auto.

UNTIL the New HARLEY-DAVIDSON was produced motorcycles were more or less uncomfortable. With only the saddle springs and the resiliency of the tires to absorb the jolts, how could they be otherwise? When a motorcycle struck a 3 inch bump the tires and the saddle springs absorbed 1 inch of the shock—the rider got the rest.

Motorcycle manufacturers have long tried in vain to overcome this. They put longer saddle springs on and found that while this eliminated the hard jolts, when the machine struck bumps or crossings it added a "spring board like" action which threw the rider off the seat. This was even more objectionable than the jolts and jars and was actually dangerous. Other experiments were tried, but the problem remained unsolved, until William S. Harley, America's foremost motorcycle designer and engineer suspended or floated the seat between two springs held under heavy compression. Hence the name *Ful-Floteing* SEAT.

Jolts and jars were eliminated—it was like riding on air. The "spring board like" action was gone. The rider really floated over bumps and rough roads. The *Ful-Floteing* SEAT had solved the problem.

In addition to its comfort, the new Harley-Davidson is clean—all moving parts where oil is used are encased in oil tight cases, and the machine is so silent that it cannot be heard across the street.

Sectional View of Ful-Floteing Seat

HARLEY-DAVIDSON MOTOR CO.
225 B Street   MILWAUKEE

The new Garford "Six" was designed contrary to the usual custom. Instead of utilizing, re-designing or substituting any old parts, this car is new in its entire construction.

From the smallest steel bolt to the handsome, graceful and noiseless one-piece-all-steel body, it is a distinct 1913 creation.

In it are embodied more new and practical six-cylinder improvements and conveniences than in any other "Six" built.

As one illustration, your attention is directed to the single, parabolic electric headlight, sunk flush with the radiator. This new method of lighting eliminates the rattling cumbersome and unsightly headlights that were always in the way. It gives the car a much cleaner and much more finished appearance.

And this is but one of the many exclusive Garford features.

A Garford owner recently wrote: "It strikes me that in the new Garford 'Six' you started your improvements from where all the others left off."

So, if you are in the market for a "Six," we believe we can offer you even more for $2750 than most other manufacturers can for double that price.

Literature on request.

Electric Starter, which never fails to start instantly—winter or summer	Big, single electric parabolic headlight, sunk flush with the radiator	One piece, all steel body, steel Pullman car construction — no joints, no rivets, no wood	60 horsepower, long-stroke motor—3¾ in. by 6 in.	Center Control	Bosch Magneto
All lights are electric	Electric horn	Warner Auto-Meter driven from the transmission	Wheel Base, 128 inches	Left Hand Drive	Equipment—everything complete from tools
			Tires 36 x 4½	Three Speed Transmission	to top.
			Demountable Rims	Full Floating Rear Axle	

The Garford Company, Dept. 4, Elyria, Ohio

KEY TO DASH BOARD

1, Clock; 2, Speedometer; 3, Carburetor Adjustment; 4, Ammeter; 5, Ignition Switch; 6, Lighting Switch; 7, Dash Light; 8, Carburetor "Flooder"; 9, Self-Starter Button; 10, Clutch Pedal; 11, Brake Pedal; 12, Accelerator; 13, Muffler Cut-out; 14, Control Lever; 15, Brake Lever; 16, Steering Column; 17, Dash Ventilator; 18, Horn.

Electric Lighting
Electric Self-Starter
Standard Equipment

The Control System

No motor cars have more attractive and utilitarian dash boards than the new Abbott-Detroit models.

Every convenience necessary for the **complete control** of the car is at hand. There is even an electric light for illuminating the dash board at night.

THE ELECTRIC SELF-STARTER

The Abbott-Detroit electric self-starter consists of an electric motor built in the side of the crank case and connected with the crank shaft through an independent train of gears enclosed in timing gear compartment of crank case, this construction insuring perfect lubrication.

It is **controlled** by means of a **button** on the **toe board.**

In operation it is **simple, positive and reliable**—a lady or child can operate it.

As soon as the gasoline motor starts, an over running roller clutch releases these gears and they remain **idle** while the gasoline motor is running.

This self-starter is **not** an **experiment**, not an attempted **combination** of ignition, lighting and starting, but a **real, dependable self-starter**, built as a part of the engine and included in the regular equipment.

Call at one of our **salesrooms** and ask to have its operation explained.

Control and Emergency Brake Levers

ELECTRIC LIGHTING SYSTEM

The electric lighting system is equally complete. The current is generated by means of a dynamo, operated from the engine, and a large capacity lighting battery is provided which takes care of the lights when the motor is standing still.

Thus a **sufficient amount of current** is **always available** for lighting all the lamps **brilliantly.**

A switch on the dash board makes it possible to light all the lamps except the tail lamp from the driver's seat.

The tail light is electrically lighted and is controlled by independent switch integral with it.

" The demand of the day is that an organization shall be judged by its product and not by what it claims for itself."

Abbott-Detroit advertising for 1913 will be printed in serial form.

This is the fifth of the series. The sixth will appear in the Saturday Evening Post, Dec. 21st; Collier's, Dec. 14th; Life, Dec. 26; Literary Digest, Dec. 7.

Copies of previous advertisements sent on request.

An ammeter shows at all times the amount of electric current produced and used. An **automatic** switch prevents the discharge of the battery through the dynamo when the engine is idle.

Two large black enameled, nickel trimmed **electric head lights**, two electric **side and tail lamps**, fitted with Tungsten globes, an **extension auxiliary light** which can be used for examining the motor or interior of the car, a **dash light** for lighting the speedometer, clock, ammeter and other fittings on the dash and foot board, complete the electrical equipment.

CLOCK AND SPEEDOMETER SET

Mounted securely on the extreme left hand side of the dash is a clock and speedometer set which **accurately** indicates **time, speed** and **total mileage.**

To the right of this, on the other side of the ammeter, is a carburetor adjustment device.

In addition to the starting button, the foot board carries the muffler cut-out and accelerator throttle pedal. Two large pedals, one operating the clutch and the other the service brakes, are located on either side of the steering column.

EXTRA STRONG BRAKES

Internal expanding and external contracting brakes, with 16 in. x 2 in. drums on the 44-50 and 14 in. x 2 in. on the 34-40; lined with a friction-proof material, are mounted on the rear hubs.

The brake shoes are made of cast iron and substantially connected to the supports in such a way that they will **absorb** and **dissipate heat** at a **surprisingly rapid rate**, thus being able to withstand the exceedingly hard wear and tear incident to mountainous driving.

STEERING GEAR

The steering wheel, 18 inches in diameter and made of aluminum fitted with a **corrugated ebony rim**, is placed at just the right angle and height for comfortable driving.

Furthermore, the steering gear has been so accurately designed that the **34-40 models will turn around in a circle 39 feet in diameter** and the **44-50 in a 42-foot circle.**

Control and emergency brake levers are within easy reach of the right hand and are **inside the body.**

The spark and throttle levers are mounted on sectors on the steering column, and can be manipulated without taking the hands off the steering wheel.

End of rear axle, showing underslung springs and external and internal hub brake system.

Thus you will see that **every movement of the car, its speed, direction, motor operation, starting, stopping, signaling — everything can be controlled from the driver's seat** with ease and dispatch.

Let our dealers show you these cars, or write for advance catalog.

Front wheel and steering knuckle showing sharp turning ability.

Models and Prices

34-40	Fore-Door Roadster, 116-inch wheel base	$1700
34-40	5 - Passenger, Fore - Door Touring Car, 116-inch wheel base	$1700
44-50	5 - Passenger, Fore - Door Demi-Tonneau 121-inch wheel base	$1975
44-50	7 - Passenger, Fore - Door Touring Car, 121-inch wheel base	$2000
44-50	Battleship Roadster, 121-inch wheel base	$2150
44-50	7-Passenger, Fore-Door Limousine 121-inch wheel base	$3050

Abbott-Detroit

Built for Permanence and Guaranteed for Life

ABBOTT MOTOR COMPANY
637 Waterloo Street,   Detroit, Michigan

*The Haynes
in the
Royal Gorge*

The Haynes Goes Everywhere

AND the best part of it is that ever since 1893 the Haynes has been going everywhere that any automobile could go. Eighteen years of the history of automobiling are built into the 1912 Haynes. This means a whole lot to you who are considering the buying of your first automobile this year, or the buying of another car to take the place of the old one that is worn out or isn't good enough.

This eighteenth year of the Haynes car is a year of triumph for the pioneer American builder of automobiles. Last year automobile experts, and the public as a whole, declared the Haynes had reached the limit of quality production at a $2100 price. It was hard to figure how any more automobile worth could be put into a car at the price of the splendid 1911 Haynes, but there *is more* in the 1912 Haynes, and the price remains $2100.

The 1912 Haynes is not radically different from its recent predecessors. It is not radically better, but it does represent more all-'round value than *anybody* has ever before been able to put into a car selling at the Haynes price.

The 1912 Haynes is a bigger car—120-inch wheel base; it's a roomier car—wider rear seat and more depth both in the tonneau and in front; it's a more powerful car—the 4½x5½ motor gives forty to forty-five horse power; it's a safer car—larger brakes give one square inch of braking surface to every thirteen pounds of car, and it is a snappier, more stylish car—the whole car is finished in black with seventeen hand-rubbed coats of paint, and the trimmings are of black enamel and nickel.

The 1912 Haynes is now ready for delivery. You can see the new models at our branches and agencies, or we will send you a catalogue and name of dealer nearest you. The line is complete, meeting every demand—5-passenger Touring, 40 h. p., $2100; 4-passenger, 40 h. p., Close-Couple, $2100; Colonial Coupe, 40 h. p., $2450; 7-passenger Touring, 50-60 h. p., $3000; 4-passenger Close-Couple, 50-60 h. p., $3000; Model 21 Limousine, 40 h. p., $2750; Model Y Limousine, 50-60 h. p., $3800. Complete regular equipment for all models is of the very highest class. All models are so designed as to permit installation of electric lighting equipment at nominal cost. Address

Haynes Automobile Company, Dept. A.1. Kokomo, Indiana | **NEW YORK, 1715 Broadway
CHICAGO, 1702 Michigan Avenue**

What more is there to be said?

Every now and then, swift currents of discussion swirl around the Cadillac.

For long, long periods, it almost seems as though there were no effort to combat its dominating prestige.

And during these periods of peace, warm words of praise and appreciation are spoken, even by makers of and dealers in other cars.

But "business is business"—and human nature is human nature.

And sometimes the *overwhelming favor* in which the Cadillac is held, becomes almost unbearable to some of those interested in cars aspiring to compete.

And then there comes a little fighting flurry, and fretful things are said, and for a while, few there are who do not endeavor to establish equality with the Cadillac.

But the storm dies down,—the public never wavers nor changes,—and even those other dealers and other makers go back to their old attitude of admiration.

Was there ever another trade condition like this condition—in which the major part of a tremendous industry *almost revolves around one car?*

You know it to be true—you know that the Cadillac is a criterion wherever motor cars are discussed.

And you know that Cadillac owners remain unmoved, no matter what the flurry.

You know that argument adverse to the Cadillac is wasted argument with them.

You know that they are solidly entrenched in supreme content.

And in the face of that big fact—which has expressed itself in sales aggregating one hundred and thirty millions of dollars ($130,000,000.00)—how unnecessary for us to importune or to urge.

All the Cadillac arguments we could advance in a score of announcements would not be one-hundredth part as impressive as the positive knowledge you hold in your own mind at this moment.

You know that the Cadillac is *in very fact* the standard of the world.

What more is there to be said?

CADILLAC MOTOR CAR CO., DETROIT, MICH.

Appreciation of Cadillac luxury as exemplified in the enclosed types, reaches its height among those who can afford any car, no matter what its price.

THE CADILLAC LIMOUSINE

The Cadillac Limousine has rapidly advanced to the position of leadership of enclosed cars.

It finds its greatest sale among those who place luxury, comfort, ease, richness, taste, dignity, elegance and refinement above all

INTERIOR OF CADILLAC LIMOUSINE

price consideration and who are satisfied with nothing short of that which represents these qualifications in the highest degree.

The improved Delco automatic cranking device, the electric lights both inside and out, the powerful, quiet motor, the ample wheel base, the large wheels and tires, the flexible yielding springs, the deep, soft comfortable upholstering, the richness of trimmings and finish, all contribute to the luxuriousness of this splendid car.

The body is made of aluminum by the latest improved methods. The forward or driver's compartment, which is three-quarter enclosed, is upholstered in hand buffed, dull finished, deep grained black leather with French roll across front of cushions. The top deck above forward compartment is American black walnut.

The rear or passenger compartment with its two revolving seats, which may be folded up close to sides of body when not in use, affords accommodations for five passengers.

This compartment is upholstered in best quality blue broadcloth, trimmed with broad and narrow lace to match. The seat cushion has over-stuffed front of latest French construction.

The interior fittings include speaking tube; rosewood lever lock handles; robe rail covered with goat skin on doors; two slip pockets on center partition, edges bound with narrow lace; toilet case.

The electric lighting equipment consists of two head lights, two pillar lights, two interior lights, tail light and speedometer light.

Price F. O. B. Detroit $3,250

THE CADILLAC COUPE

The Cadillac Coupe is a worthy companion of the Cadillac Limousine. It is the leading car of its type.

The body is made of aluminum by the latest improved methods. There are accommodations for four passengers, two alongside the driver and one on drop seat in front. The driver's seat is hinged, permitting entrance at and exit from the right side of the car.

INTERIOR OF CADILLAC COUPE

The upholstering is in hand buffed black leather, trimmed with broad and narrow lace.

The equipment includes the improved Delco electric system, embodying automatic self-cranking device, electric lighting and ignition.

Price F. O. B. Detroit $2,500

CADILLAC MOTOR CAR CO., - - Detroit, Michigan

[1912]

144

Society's Town Car

The electric automobile has become a necessity to the woman with many social engagements. And the Detroit Electric has justly earned its title, "Society's Town Car." In the changeable spring weather—as at other times—this beautiful car carries you in elegant comfort and independent privacy to the reception, tea, theatre or dance. For shopping, also, it is the ideal of convenience

Remember, too, that the Detroit Electric is built and backed by the world's largest makers of electric pleasure vehicles. Your choice of many models.   Catalog on request

ANDERSON ELECTRIC CAR COMPANY
DETROIT, MICH.

Builders of the Detroit Electric

Largest manufacturers of electric pleasure vehicles in the world

[1914]

147

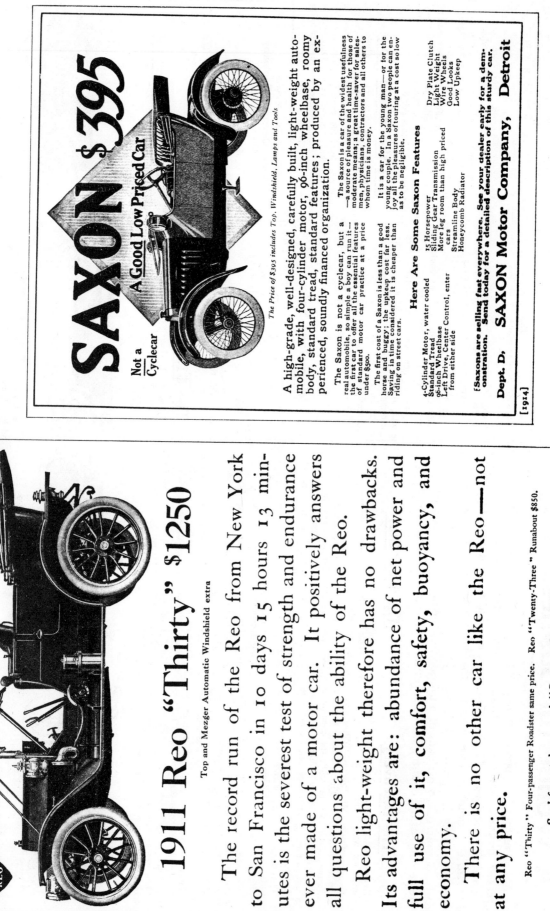

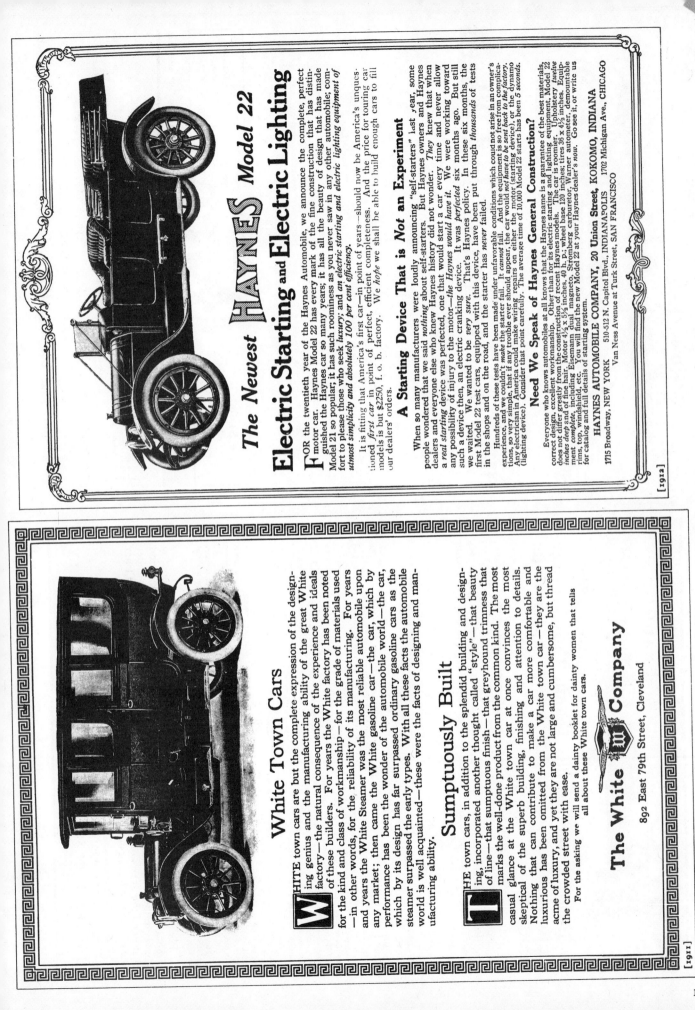
149

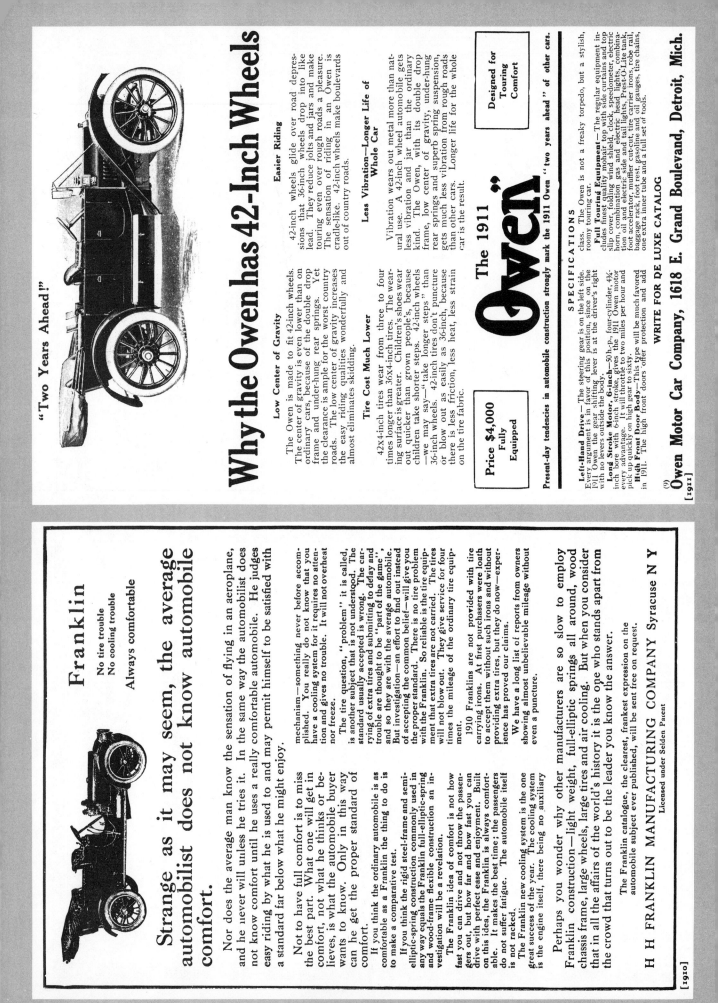

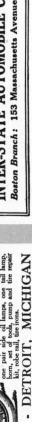
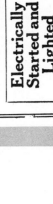

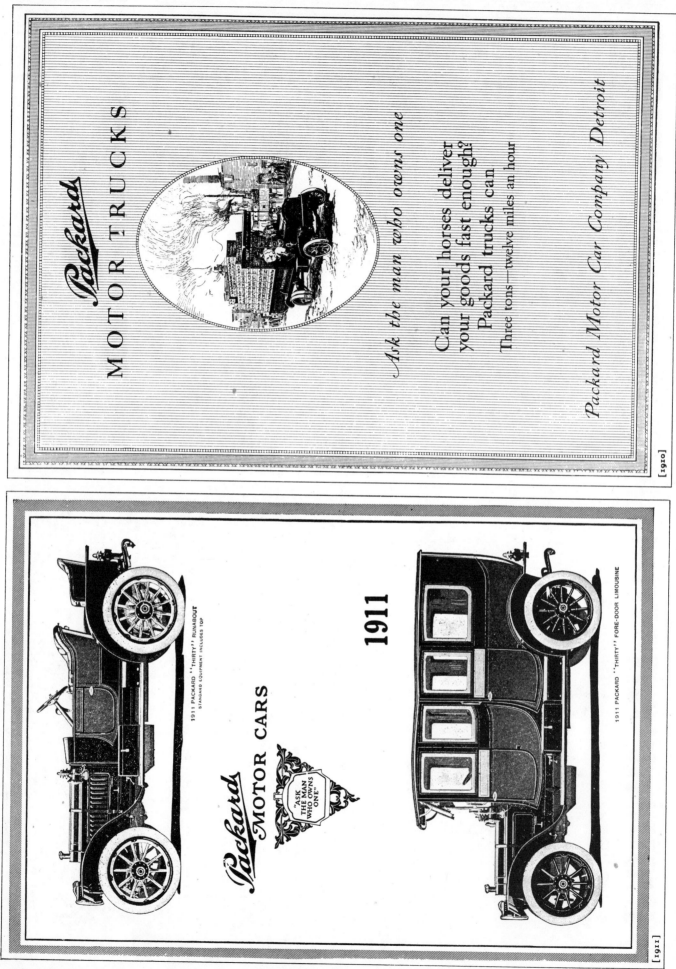

Packard MOTOR TRUCKS

Ask the man who owns one

Can your horses deliver your goods fast enough? Packard trucks can

Three tons—twelve miles an hour

Packard Motor Car Company Detroit

[1910]

1911 PACKARD "THIRTY" RUNABOUT
STANDARD EQUIPMENT INCLUDES TOP

Packard MOTOR CARS

"ASK THE MAN WHO OWNS ONE"

1911

1911 PACKARD "THIRTY" FORE-DOOR LIMOUSINE

[1911]

152

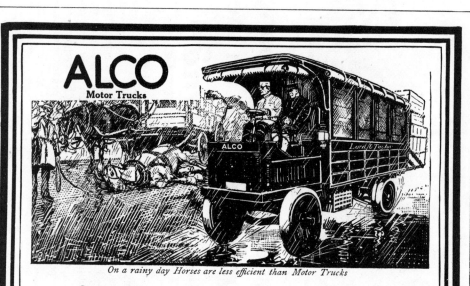

On a rainy day Horses are less efficient than Motor Trucks

Giant Locomotive Steels Go Into Alco Trucks

EVERYONE marvels at the locomotive. Its wonderful strength, its great power, its fleetness, excite enthusiasm in every red-blooded person.

Fifty thousand of its kind have been built by the American Locomotive Company. It has hauled you, your family, the things you eat and the things you wear.

Its success is due to a considerable degree to the stuff that is in it—the steels. They are rare steels. Millions of miles of service over railroads under the watchful eyes of men who know, in the tropics and in frigid zones, have tested these steels. Raging blizzards, driving storms, steep grades, sharp curves, rough road beds, have proven this metal's pre-eminence.

No one has cataloged these steels like the American Locomotive Company. No one knows what strains they will bear, what shocks they will stand, what vibrations they will endure as does the American Locomotive Company.

There is only one vehicle today that approaches this locomotive. *That vehicle is the Alco motor truck.* It is made by the American Locomotive Company.

That same good stuff that goes into these locomotives goes also into Alco trucks. The steels in the Alco are the same steels.

Three generations of engineers and 76 years of transportation experience have produced the Alco. It is an experience that no one else building motor trucks possesses. It is a rare experience—and the most logical one in the world upon which to produce motor trucks that endure. A motor truck today is a *road* locomotive.

With others only *claiming* the similarity, the American Locomotive Company *actually builds* both—the American Locomotive and the Alco Motor Truck.

And here is evidence that the truck profits by the relationship:

Sixty-two per cent of all Alco Trucks were purchased on re-orders.

A re-order is a dollars and cents expression of a satisfied owner.

Possibly the Alco is serving—*and saving*—in the very same line of business as yours. The new 64 page Alco catalog will inform you.

Write for it today.

AMERICAN LOCOMOTIVE COMPANY, 1916 Broadway, NEW YORK

Builders also of Alco 6-cylinder and 4-cylinder Motor Cars and Alco Taxicabs

Chicago Branch: 2501 Michigan Ave.
Boston Branch: 567 Boylston St.

Canadian Headquarters:
4280 St. Catherine St., W., Montreal

Movers of the World's Goods since 1835

Capital, $50,000,000

[1912]

To Skid Or Not To Skid

HEAVY CAR TYPE

TOWN CAR TREAD
NEW **FISK** TIRE

The Fisk Town Car Tread Tire
is a positive non-skid tire, furnishing on wet pavements and slippery
streets, the protection for which
every motorist is looking.

Substantial and effective in appearance, this tire combines the
strength, the quality and the exclusive features that are found
always in the famous *Heavy Car
Type Construction*—the construction that has earned for Fisk Tires
their reputation for exceptional
mileage and long service.

Write for Particulars of This New Tire

THE FISK RUBBER COMPANY
OF N. Y.

Department D   CHICOPEE FALLS, MASS.

[1912]

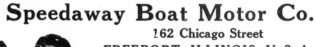

The Men We Love and The Men We Marry

Are there generally two men in a woman's life — the man she loves and the man she marries?

A woman, keenly observant, and who has seen much of girls and women, holds that it is more often true than many suppose. Then she explains how it comes about: what it can mean, in suffering, to a woman, and what is the duty of a woman to be the wife of the man she married, not that of the man she wishes she had married.

A thoroughly feminine article is this. Men will not understand it, but women will.

It is in the October LADIES' HOME JOURNAL.

15 Cents Everywhere

[1910]

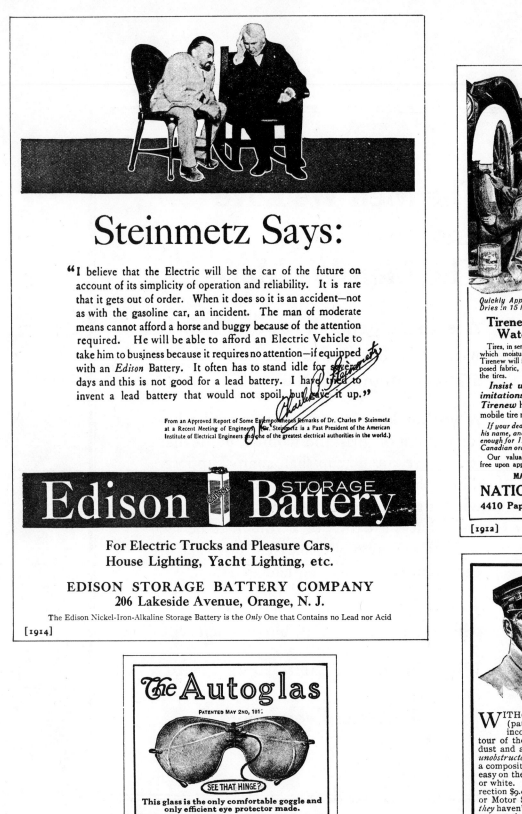

Steinmetz Says:

"I believe that the Electric will be the car of the future on account of its simplicity of operation and reliability. It is rare that it gets out of order. When it does so it is an accident—not as with the gasoline car, an incident. The man of moderate means cannot afford a horse and buggy because of the attention required. He will be able to afford an Electric Vehicle to take him to business because it requires no attention—if equipped with an *Edison* Battery. It often has to stand idle for several days and this is not good for a lead battery. I have tried to invent a lead battery that would not spoil, but I gave it up."

From an Approved Report of Some Extemporaneous Remarks of Dr. Charles P. Steinmetz at a Recent Meeting of Engineers. (Dr. Steinmetz is a Past President of the American Institute of Electrical Engineers and one of the greatest electrical authorities in the world.)

Edison STORAGE Battery

For Electric Trucks and Pleasure Cars,
House Lighting, Yacht Lighting, etc.

EDISON STORAGE BATTERY COMPANY
206 Lakeside Avenue, Orange, N. J.

The Edison Nickel-Iron-Alkaline Storage Battery is the *Only* One that Contains no Lead nor Acid

[1914]

TIRENEW TRADE MARK

Makes Tires Look New and Last Longer

Tirenew is a scientific preservative of automobile tires—a liquid, unvulcanized rubber coating, made of pure para gum. It will not flake or rub off—wears like rubber.

Made in two shades—white and tire gray.

Tirenew makes the tires look bright and new, and gives the entire car a well-groomed appearance.

Quickly Applied Dries in 15 Minutes

Tirenew Protects Tires from Water, Oil and Sunlight

Tires, in service, quickly become a mass of cuts through which moisture enters, causing the inner fabric to rot. Tirenew will flow into these cuts, *waterproof* the exposed fabric, *prevent decay,* and increase the life of the tires.

Insist upon getting Tirenew. Avoid imitations that contain injurious ingredients. *Tirenew* has received the endorsement of automobile tire manufacturers.

If your dealer cannot supply you, send $1.00 and his name, and we will send you a trial can of Tirenew, enough for 12 tires, prepaid or through your dealer. Canadian orders, $1.25.

Our valuable booklet entitled "Tire Care" sent free upon application.

MANUFACTURED ONLY BY THE
NATIONAL RUBBER CO.
4410 Papin St.,   ST. LOUIS, U. S. A.

[1912]

The Autoglas

PATENTED MAY 2ND, 1911

SEE THAT HINGE?

This glass is the only comfortable goggle and only efficient eye protector made.

WITHOUT rims, hinged at the center, it is neat and inconspicuous. Conforms to the contour of the face, and at the same time affords absolutely unobstructed vision.

Price, with plain amber lenses, $5.00
Or with wearers correction, $9.00

Any Optician, Sporting Goods or Motor Supply House can equip you. If your dealer hasn't them, write to us. We will see that you get them.
Over 12,000 now in use.

F. A. HARDY & CO.
Department D.   CHICAGO, ILL.

[1913]

The Autoglas

The **Best** Eye Protector for Motorists

WITHOUT rims, *hinged at the center* (patented feature), it is neat and inconspicuous. Conforms to the contour of the face; excludes wind as well as dust and at the same time affords *absolutely unobstructed* vision. Temples covered with a composition of silk and cotton makes them easy on the ears. Lenses either amber color or white. Price $5.00, or with wearer's correction $9.00. Any Optical, Sporting Goods, or Motor Supply House can equip you. If *they* haven't them, write to *us. We'll* see that you get them.

Over 12,000 now in use.

F. A. HARDY & CO.
OPTICIANS
900 Silversmith Building   Chicago, Ills.

[1912]

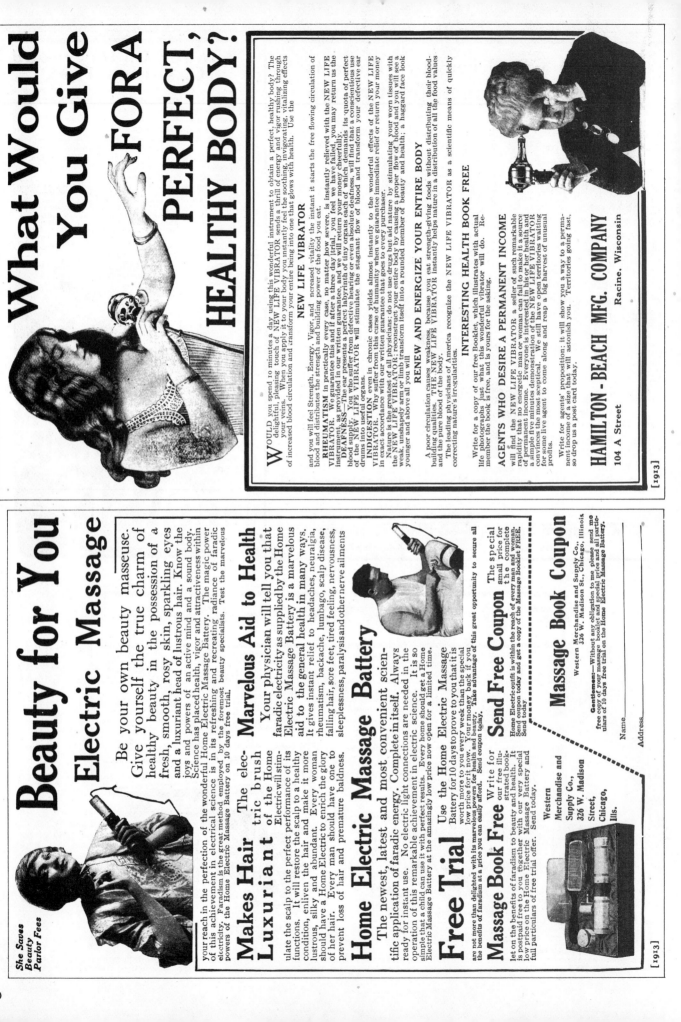

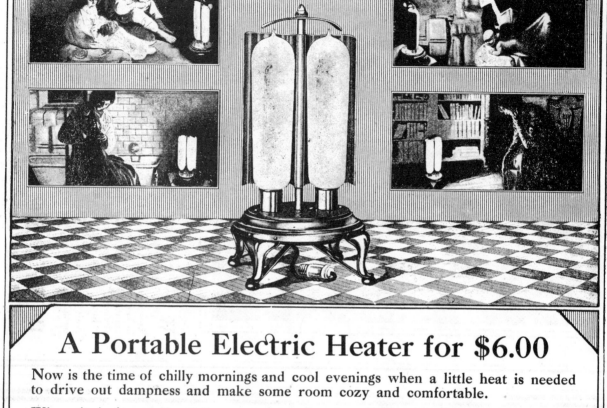

A Portable Electric Heater for $6.00

Now is the time of chilly mornings and cool evenings when a little heat is needed to drive out dampness and make some room cozy and comfortable.

When it isn't worth while to start a fire in range or furnace, then you will appreciate the warm Electric sunshine of this

G-E Twin Glower Radiator

A child can carry it from room to room and attach it to any lamp socket. At the turn of a switch, the heater bulbs glow ruddy with radiant heat that warms as sunshine warms.

Like electric light, it is absolutely safe, odorless and clean—and it cannot rob the air of its oxygen as do other types of portable heaters.

This Twin Glower Radiator takes no more electricity than an ordinary electric flatiron and, therefore, costs very little to operate.

It is finished in highly polished nickel that remains permanently clean and bright. Complete with cord and attaching plug—all ready for use—this G-E Radiator sells for only $6.00—costing less than any other luminous electric radiator. Electric shops, stores carrying electrical goods or any lighting company can supply you.

General Electric Company

Largest Electrical Manufacturer in the World
General Office: Schenectady, N. Y.
ADDRESS NEAREST OFFICE

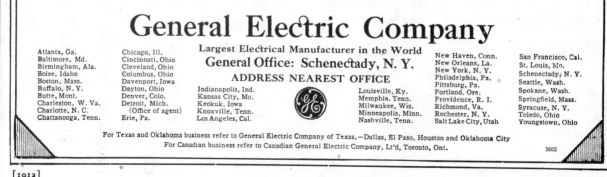

Atlanta, Ga.
Baltimore, Md.
Birmingham, Ala.
Boise, Idaho
Boston, Mass.
Buffalo, N. Y.
Butte, Mont.
Charleston, W. Va.
Charlotte, N. C.
Chattanooga, Tenn.

Chicago, Ill.
Cincinnati, Ohio
Cleveland, Ohio
Columbus, Ohio
Davenport, Iowa
Dayton, Ohio
Denver, Colo.
Detroit, Mich.
(Office of agent)
Erie, Pa.

Indianapolis, Ind.
Kansas City, Mo.
Keokuk, Iowa
Knoxville, Tenn.
Los Angeles, Cal.

Louisville, Ky.
Memphis, Tenn.
Milwaukee, Wis.
Minneapolis, Minn.
Nashville, Tenn.

New Haven, Conn.
New Orleans, La.
New York, N. Y.
Philadelphia, Pa.
Pittsburg, Pa.
Portland, Ore.
Providence, R. I.
Richmond, Va.
Rochester, N. Y.
Salt Lake City, Utah

San Francisco, Cal.
St. Louis, Mo.
Schenectady, N. Y.
Seattle, Wash.
Spokane, Wash.
Springfield, Mass.
Syracuse, N. Y.
Toledo, Ohio
Youngstown, Ohio

For Texas and Oklahoma business refer to General Electric Company of Texas,—Dallas, El Paso, Houston and Oklahoma City
For Canadian business refer to Canadian General Electric Company, Lt'd, Toronto, Ont.

3802

[1912]

162

Every Reader of The Literary Digest can have a Roll of ScotTissue Towels at Absolutely no Cost to Himself

We want you to know of the advantages of the ScotTissue Towels right in your home and we are willing to buy a roll for you. Just write us, giving the name of the nearest druggist, and we will send you by return mail, an order or coupon, which will be redeemed by your druggist for a roll of ScotTissue towels, and a booklet telling of many uses.

This offer is only for readers of The Literary Digest and will not be made again—there are no strings to it—we want to get the roll of ScotTissue Towels in your home, and we take this method of doing it. The coupon is redeemed by us from the druggist at the full retail price of the towels, 35 cents. (50c West of Mississippi River).

ScotTissue Towels not only have the advantage of being hygienic and sanitary, but they are the greatest *convenience* in the home. In the kitchen they have a number of uses and advantages in addition to replacing the ordinary roller towel. They can be used for polishing cut glass; for absorbing surplus grease from fried foods; for wiping windows. Then, too, after shaving they dry the skin without friction, and eliminate the necessity for using powder.

Physicians and Dentists will immediately recognize the value of ScotTissue Towels in their own offices and homes; absolutely clean and sanitary, used once and thrown away, they eliminate the laundering necessary for the fabric towel.

Sit right down and write us for this coupon—then use the towels—and learn of the many uses for ScotTissue Towels both in the home and in public places.

Scott Paper Company

608 Glenwood Avenue   *Philadelphia, Pa.*

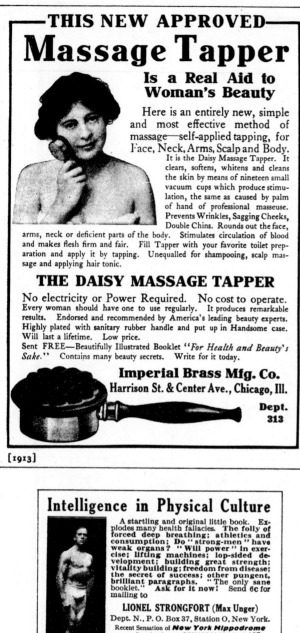

Victor Exclusive Talent

The best friends you can have—who cheer you with their music and song, who unfold to you all the beauties of the compositions of the great masters, who through their superb art touch your very heart strings and become to you a well-spring of inspiration.

Painting adapted from the
Chicago Tribune cartoon of John T. McCutcheon.

Copyright 1913 by
Victor Talking Machine Co., Camden, N. J.

Victor-Victrola

"HIS MASTER'S VOICE"

[1912]

169

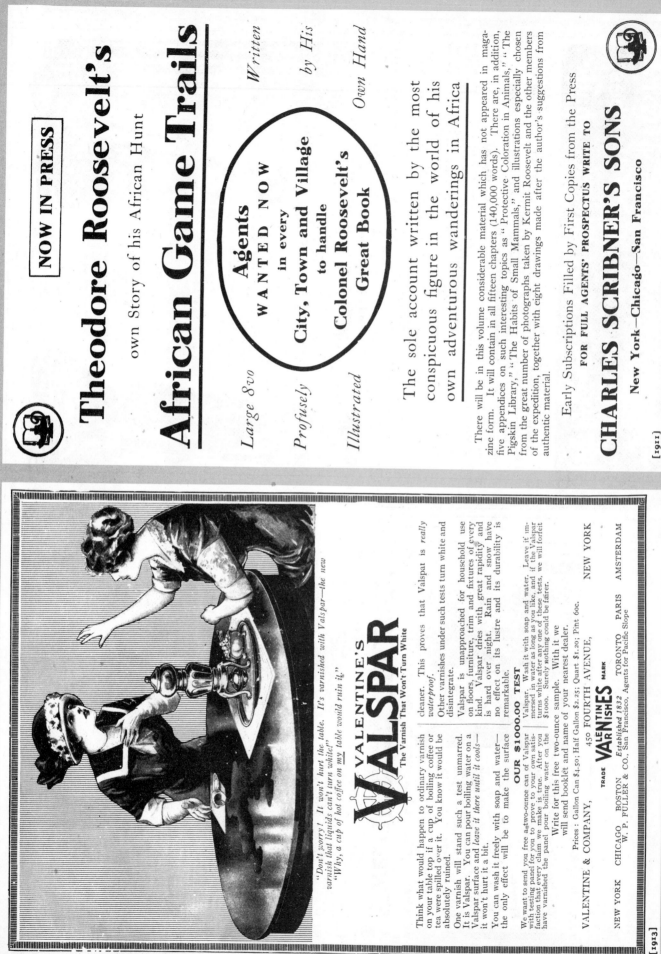

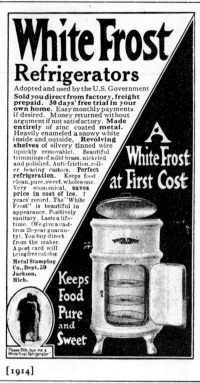

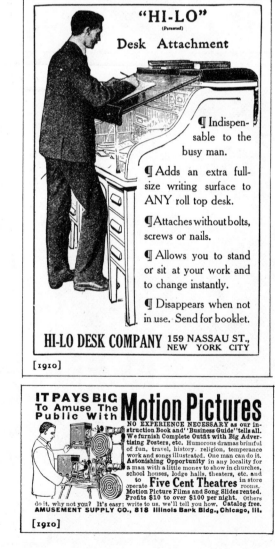

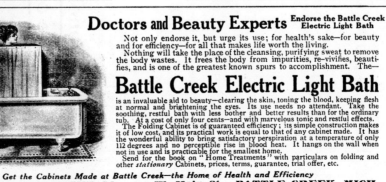

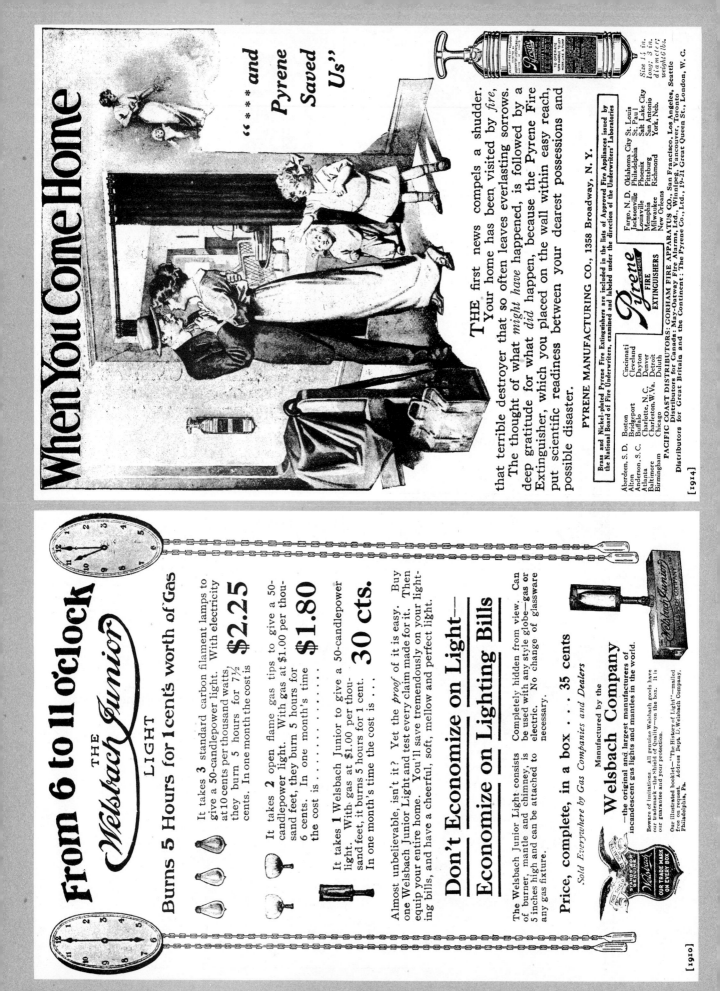

Synopsis of Course

1. Nine great laws that govern life.
2. What food is and its true purpose.
3. Digestion, assimilation and metabolism.
4. Chemistry of the body and the chemistry of food.
5. How wrong eating causes disease.
6. How foods establish health by removing causes of disease.
7. Scientific eating explained, sample menus.
8. Harmonious combinations of food tables.
9. How to select, combine and proportion your food according to age, sample menus.
10. How to select, combine and proportion your food according to occupation and season of year, sample menus.
11. Obesity, cause and cure, sample menus.
12. Emaciation, cause and cure, sample menus.
13. The business man—right and wrong ways of living, sample menus.
14. The new Vleno System of Food Measurement.
15. Food and morality.
16. Tea, coffee, liquor, tobacco, etc.
17. Superacidity, fermentation, gastric catarrh and ulcer, intestinal gas and auto-intoxication. Causes, sample menus.
18. Superacidity, fermentation, gastric catarrh and ulcer, intestinal gas and auto-intoxication. The remedy, sample menus.
19. What to eat and omit for all stomach and intestinal disorders. Ready reference lesson.
20. Intestinal congestion(constipation), cause and cure, sample menus for the four seasons of year.
21. Appendicitis—cause; sample menus.
22. Nervousness—cause and cure, sample menus.
23. Curative menus; for each season of year for manual laborer and sedentary worker.
24. Diagnosis simplified and made practical.

[1915]

Eat to Live 100 Years

Health, Efficiency and Length of Life Depend on the Foods You Eat

Many authorities agree that over 90% of all sickness originates in the stomach due to wrong eating. Yet not one person in a hundred has any knowledge of how to properly select, combine or proportion his food, which is the fuel of the human system, so as to get any power out of it.

If your stomach only had a window in it so that you could look in and see what happens down there after almost any meal, you would be amazed. Many foods, harmless in themselves, when eaten in combination with other harmless foods produce a chemical reaction and literally explode.

No wonder most people are below par physically most of the time—no wonder the average life of man is only 39 years when it should be three times as great.

Yet the improper combination of foods is only part of the great wrongs we do our systems. Few people know anything about selecting or proportioning their food. We try to run the human system on fuel as unfitted as mud, wet leaves, soggy wood and dynamite would be for a furnace.

Eugene Christian's Course in Scientific Eating

No Money in Advance—Examine It Free

Eugene Christian has long been recognized as a world authority on food and its relation to the human system. Over 23,000 people have come under his care and the results of his work have bordered on the miraculous. Without drugs or medicines of any kind—simply by teaching the proper selection, combination and proportion of foods under given conditions (and they vary according to age, climate, occupation, etc.), he has cured nearly every known non-organic ailment by removing the cause and has doubled the personal efficiency of his patients almost times without number.

24 BOILED DOWN LESSONS

Scientific Eating contains the boiled down essence of Eugene Christian's twenty years' experience in actual practice. Every step is logically explained. Reasons are given for each statement which anyone can easily understand and it is a simple matter to follow the simple directions. And the beauty of Eugene Christian's methods is that you get results with the very first meal. No special foods are required. You don't have to upset your table to follow his directions. Neither do you have to eat things you don't enjoy—nature never intended that you should.

AN AID TO SUCCESS

You can't do good work unless you feel full of "pep" and ginger. The best ideas, plans, and methods—the biggest business deals are put over when you are bubbling over with vitality. It is impossible to be really fit unless your food is scientifically chosen to supply the nutritive elements your mind and body demand. Man is made up of the sum total of what he eats. You can't add up to a very high state of efficiency if you don't know how to select your food, for the wrong foods counteract the good in right foods—and very often two right foods in combination make a wrong food. Eugene Christian has time and again turned sluggish, slow, unsuccessful men and women into very dynamos of success, achieving efficiency and greatly prolonged the lives of thousands by merely teaching them food values.

Send No Money

The price of Eugene Christian's course, complete in 24 lessons, is only $3 and it contains rules, methods and menus that are literally priceless. But we do not ask you to pay a single penny until you have examined this great work in your own home. Merely fill out and mail the coupon enclosing your business card or giving a reference, or write a letter and the entire course of 24 lessons will be sent, all charges paid, the day we hear from you. Keep it five days. Study it at your leisure. Then if you feel you can afford not to be master of the invaluable information it contains, send it back and you owe us nothing. Mail the coupon now, however, as this offer may never again be repeated.

Corrective Eating Society, Inc., 49 Richard Ave., Maywood, N. J.

Corrective Eating Society, Inc.
49 Richard Ave.,
Maywood, N. J.

Send me the "Christian Course in Scientific Eating." I will either remail it within five days, and owe you nothing, or send you $3.

Name ....
Address ....
City .... State ....

What People Say

"I am feeling fine again, thanks to you and your course on Scientific Eating. There ought to be 100,000 men practicing Scientific Eating in America."—F. A. Fulby, Niagara Falls, South Ont., Canada.

"I am delighted beyond expression with the lessons. They have proved invaluable to me and have revolutionized both my diet and my health."—Olive M. Sees, 725 East Tipton St., Huntington, Ind.

"Your work on Scientific Eating is wonderful. It is with much pleasure that I recommend your course to prospective students everywhere."—Chas. A. Ittel, 1212 Termont Avenue, North Side, Pittsburg, Pa.

"Your Course in Scientific Eating is wonderful because it has simplified both the chemistry of the body and the chemistry of the food and teaches one how to unite these two branches of science so as to make our food prevent and cure disease."—Eugene A. Ayers, Harrington Park, N.J.

"I think the Almighty sends men on the earth at different periods with independence and fearless minds to rectify the wrongs that have been taught and reveal the truth in all its simplicity."—Edward Brook, 10 No. 10th W. Sts., Salt Lake City, Utah.

"I have read of you for years and I have recently looked over some of your work. You are doing much for humanity. I congratulate you on your latest contribution to the health and happiness of man."—Dr. V. M. George, 2305 N. High St., Columbus, Ohio.

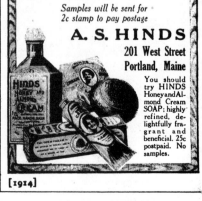

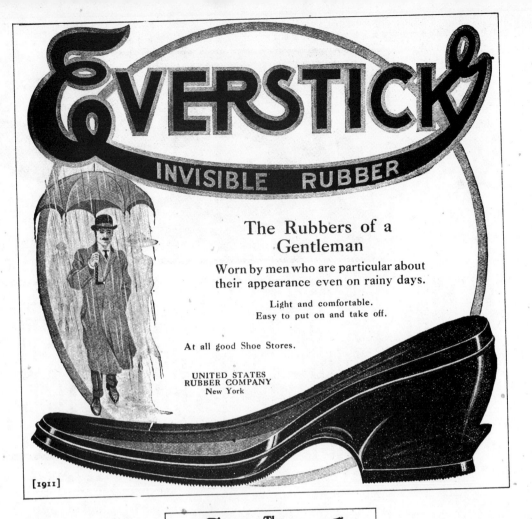
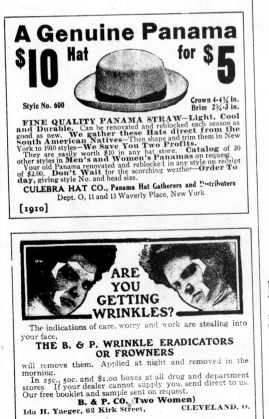

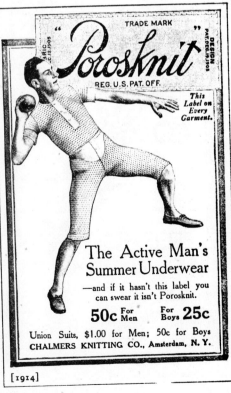
177

178

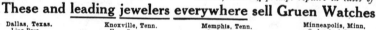

The chain chart images show:

WALDEMAR 15222
WALDEMAR 15498
WALDEMAR 19677
WALDEMAR 18882
WALDEMAR 18166
WALDEMAR 5180
DICKENS 1155
DICKENS 9327
DICKENS 11521
DICKENS 5428
DICKENS 7086
DICKENS 1768

ROBERT HILLIARD
The Famous Actor, now Appearing in New York in " The Argyle Case," Wears a Waldemar

These are the watch chains now worn by men who set the styles

When a man buys a watch chain he chooses a *pattern* to suit his individual taste—but he wants a *style* which will always be in good taste.

A watch chain is the only piece of jewelry worn universally by men. It is the most prominent piece a man can wear. Every man with any regard for his personal appearance wants his watch chain right.

SIMMONS CHAINS
TRADE MARK

are always "correct" in style. That is one reason why first-class jewelers have handled them for forty years. A man in the smaller cities and towns can be just as sure as a New Yorker that he is getting the "proper thing" if he buys a *Simmons Chain*.

Waldemar and Dickens are the most popular styles this year. Lapels, vests and fobs are also in good taste. For women there are chatelaines, neck, eyeglass and guard chains and bracelets.

The beauty of design and finish and the satisfactory service of the *Simmons Chains*, have made them a standard among well-dressed men and women.

The surface of a *Simmons Chain* is not a wash or plate. It is a rolled tube of 12 or 14 karat *solid gold*, of sufficient thickness to withstand the wear of years.

If your jeweler hasn't *Simmons Chains* write us for Style Book—make your selection and we'll see that you are supplied.

DOUGLAS FAIRBANKS
The Popular Actor who Made a Great New York Success in "Officer 666," Wearing a Dickens

R. F. Simmons Co. (Established 1873) 177 N. Main St., Attleboro, Mass.
Look for SIMMONS stamped on each piece—your protection and guarantee for wear.

[1912]

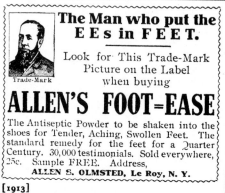
182

Why Oats Give Vim

"He feels his oats"—said of men or of horses—describes exuberant vitality.

Because the oat, as an energy-giver, is the greatest grain that grows.

Nature seems to have lavished on oats the sources of animal vim.

An extract of oats is employed as a tonic. A diet of oats, if continued a month, often multiplies vitality.

Active children crave oatmeal. Instinct seems to tell that it feeds activity.

Brain workers, from known necessity, depend largely on oatmeal. In one university, 48 out of 50 leading professors regularly eat oatmeal.

Inquiries made of 12,000 physicians show that four-fifths eat oatmeal

A canvass of homes where reside the successful shows that seven-eighths are oatmeal homes.

A canvass of homes where reside the incapable shows that not one in each twelve serves oats.

A canvass of 61 poorhouses shows that but one in thirteen of the inmates came from an oatmeal home.

———

Oats contain more of the brain-building elements than any other grain.

Oats contain more of the nerve-building elements than any other cereal food.

Oats have amazing energy value.

The person who wishes to live life at its full should make one meal a day on oatmeal.

Quaker Oats

The Richest Oats Made Delicious

The oats in Quaker Oats are selected by 62 siftings. We get from each bushel but ten pounds of these rich, plump grains.

When these selected grains are prepared by our process they form the finest oat food in existence. It has come to be the choice of the millions.

The cost, despite the quality, is but one-half cent per dish.

Regular size package, 10c

Family size package, for smaller cities and country trade, 25c.

The prices noted do not apply in the extreme West or South.

The Quaker Oats Company

CHICAGO

Look for the Quaker trade-mark on every package

(144)

[1911]

184

Sing, smile — and soothe your throat with WRIGLEY'S SPEARMINT

Enjoy it because of its *value.* It keeps your mouth pure and cool — and your throat refreshed. It brightens teeth, sharpens the appetite, and aids digestion.

It's clean, pure, healthful if it's WRIGLEY'S.

It's the hospitality confection. - It's ideal to have in the house for family or friends. It stays fresh until used. *Be SURE it's WRIGLEY'S. Look for the spear.*

BUY IT BY THE BOX
of twenty packages for 85c of most dealers.

Chew it after every meal

WRIGLEY'S SPEARMINT PEPSIN GUM

THE FLAVOR LASTS

Wm Wrigley Jr Co. CHICAGO

THE FLAVOR LASTS

[1914]

Have Your Own Private STEEL GARAGE

Protect Your Car From Fire and Theft **$92.50**

Have your own Garage. Make sure no one is using your car without your knowledge. Save $25 to $35 monthly garage charge. Save $50 to $100 cost of building by ordering

Edwards Fireproof Steel Garage

Shipped complete, F. O. B. Cincinnati, on receipt of $92.50. Blue prints and simple directions come with shipment. Sizes come 10 feet wide, 14, 16, 18 or 20 feet long, 10 feet high. Ample room for largest car and all equipment. Fireproof, weatherproof, indestructible. Locks most securely. An artistic structure any owner will be proud of. Booklet, with full description and illustration, sent on request.

THE EDWARDS MANUFACTURING CO.
742-782 Eggleston Ave.   Cincinnati, Ohio

[1912]

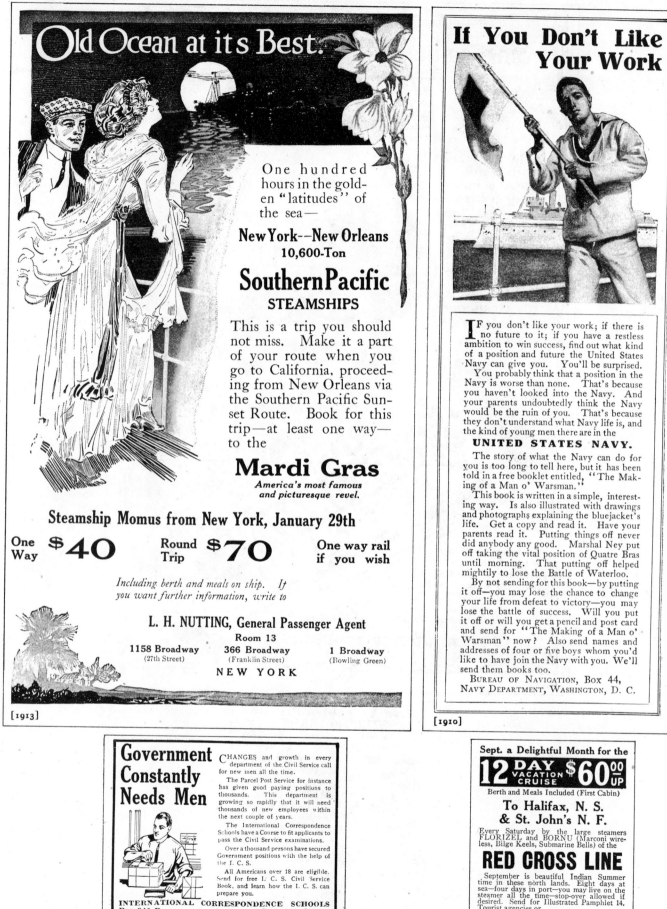

186

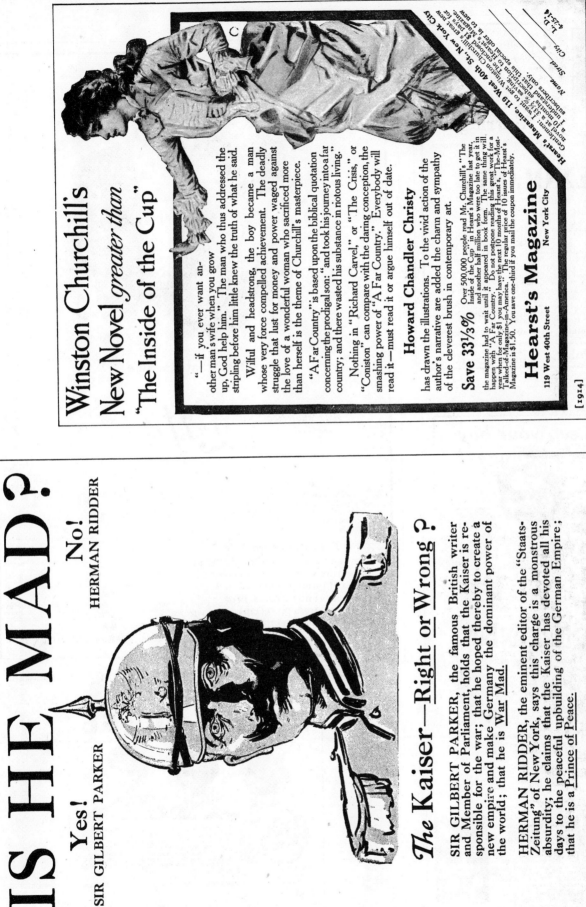

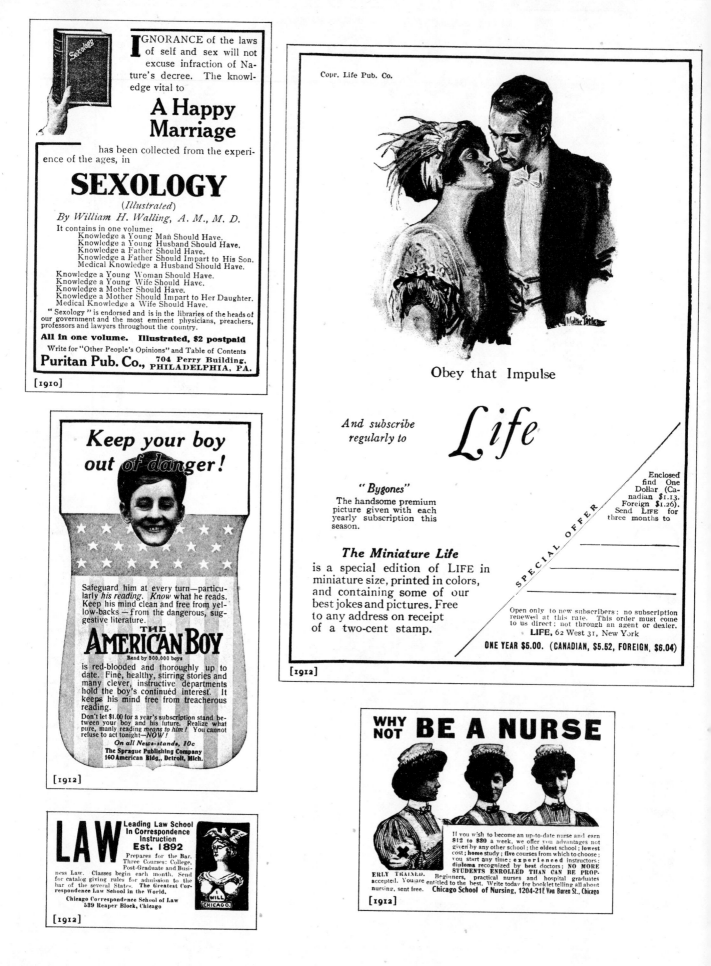

1915-1919

THE LITERARY DIGEST

PUBLIC OPINION (New York) combined with THE LITERARY DIGEST

Published by Funk & Wagnalls Company (Adam W. Wagnalls, Pres.; Wilfred J. Funk, Vice-Pres.; Robert J. Cuddihy, Treas.; William Neisel, Sec'y), 354-360 Fourth Ave., New York

Vol. LXII, No. 2   New York, July 12, 1919   Whole Number 1525

DOUGH-BOYS' FLY-SWATTING SHOCKS THE TEUTONS

NO doubt by way of retaliation for all the mean things said about the Huns during the period of the war, the German newspapers are now publishing stories of atrocious crimes committed by American soldiers in the occupied territory of Germany, says Richard Henry Little in the Chicago *Tribune*. Mr. Little met a German who had been traveling in the occupied zone, however, and was by him informed that there was no foundation for these stories. The German farmer folk, said this man, in the region where the Americans are located, regard the latter as kind, agreeable beings, albeit lunatics and also millionaires. They complained of no outrages perpetrated by the O. D. boys, but they did mention a few of their funny ways, which are utterly beyond the Teutonic understanding, and hence are viewed, if not with suspicion, at least with astonishment, not unmixed with pity that human beings should permit themselves to get that way. The edifying information furnished Mr. Little by the obliging traveler is set out, in part, as follows:

"The peasants told me," said he, "you might never know an American was mad unless a fly came into the room. When the American sees a fly a strange, hard glitter comes into his eyes. Then you see he is crazy. His mania makes him want to hit the fly. He folds up newspapers and tiptoes over behind the fly and strikes at it with great viciousness. If it does not die, he pursues it, calls in more soldiers, and strikes at the fly."

The traveler said some German farmers who had observed this strange action on the part of American soldiers were willing to make allowances. They said probably in America flies were large and that their bite caused instant death. Therefore, Americans had formed the habit of killing all flies they saw.

The traveler said another proof the farmer in the occupied zone had that Americans were stark, raving mad was because they made them open their windows at night and let in the deadly night air, which every German peasant knows is most poisonous.

The German farmer likes to close all windows at night and plug up every keyhole to keep out the deadly night air, but, if the Americans catch them with the windows closed, they haul them into court and fine them.

The peasants say the American soldiers told them it was one of President Wilson's fourteen points that all Germans should have their windows open at night, which is proof to some that Americans want to kill the Germans off with consumption, while others say it shows Wilson is as mad as the rest of the Americans.

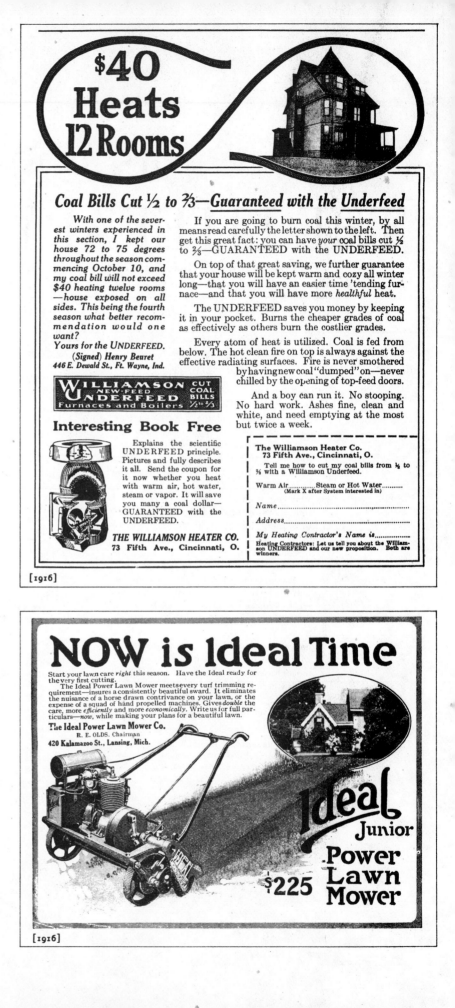

ALADDIN Homes

$989 for this 7-Room Aladdin

HERE is your opportunity to own a home and dodge high building prices. You can do it even though building prices are going up! THE ALADDIN READI-CUT SYSTEM OF BUILDING stands between you and present high prices. It offers you this ideal home or one hundred other attractive homes at substantial savings in price. Think of the home pictured above containing large living room and dining room, large kitchen, grade cellar entrance, three large bedrooms, bathroom, closets and porch for $989.00 for complete material, readi-cut. This is only one of a hundred homes with prices from $200 to $8000 shown in the handsome book. Let us send you a copy of this book entitled "Aladdin Homes." Send stamps today for your copy.

Avoid High Building Prices

Of course, the cost of living has been raised. And so has the cost of building. Yet, you can avoid these higher prices by eliminating waste. The Aladdin Readi-cut System of Construction eliminates the usual 18% waste of lumber, waste in measuring, cutting and fitting. This saving matched against wasteful methods *offsets the higher price* of building materials. Twenty feet of lumber from a sixteen-foot board—the Aladdin catalog tells how.

Dollar-a-Knot Guarantee

The famous guarantee of $1 per knot paid for every knot found in Aladdin Red Cedar Siding is continued for 1917, AND we have swept the last knot from Aladdin lumber inside and out. Every Aladdin House in 1917 will be furnished with knotless siding, knotless shingles, knotless outside finish, knotless porch work, knotless flooring, knotless inside finish, knotless door casings, stairwork—knotless inside and outside. Where else can you buy as good a home?

Styles for Every Taste

In the one hundred and twenty pages in the Aladdin catalog you will find the style of home you desire at a price that represents a big saving over general prices today. Small homes of three rooms to the largest sizes containing ten or more rooms are pictured and described with prices given for complete material. Single and double garages for all sizes of cars are shown in detail. Send for your copy today—better do it now before it is delayed.

Dwellings, Bungalows, Summer Cottages, Garages

Aladdin Houses are erected the same as other houses. Aladdin Houses are cut-to-fit—no waste of lumber or labor. The Aladdin price includes all materials cut-to-fit as follows: Lumber, millwork, flooring, outside and inside finish, doors, windows, shingles, lath and plaster, hardware, locks, nails, paint, varnishes. The complete material is shipped to you in a sealed box car, complete, ready to erect. Safe arrival of the complete material in perfect condition is guaranteed. Send stamps today for a copy of "Aladdin Homes," No. 190.

The Aladdin Co.

"Homebuilders to the Nation"

666 Aladdin Ave., Bay City, Mich.

Canadian Branch: Sovereign Construction Co.,
C. P. R. Bldg., Toronto, Ont.

[1917]

194

The Telephone of Tomorrow

Private business is always the pioneer, the trail-blazer and pathfinder—for government and public. And private business is making wide and clear the once hidden road to Tomorrow's Telephone—to the ultimate developement of wire communication—to the Automatic Telephone.

Business must avail itself of all things most efficient —of all things simple and sound to the core—of all things making for certainty, economy and high morale— in short of the best as soon as it appears.

Business cannot afford to do otherwise. That is why business in America—wherever that business is dealing with large problems and mighty forces—has blazed the way for Tomorrow's Telephone by investigating the Automatic, buying the Automatic, using the Automatic.

Governments abroad and at home are already traveling the clear road blazed by private enterprise.

England, France and Germany agree on this one point: That the Automatic Telephone must be used for government service because it is the type to which all telephones must eventually rise.

Our own War and Navy Departments, the United States Naval Torpedo Station, the fortifications at Sandy Hook, the Arsenal at Springfield, have used the Automatic Telephone for years and are each year adding to their equipment.

A few weeks ago the Federal Reserve Bank of New York bought the Automatic because the directors decided to transform their business telephones from a liability to an asset. They saw what many another great business has seen—that the Automatic Telephone is the only one giving 24-hour, 365-day secret service for a minimum labor and investment cost.

The Bethlehem Steel Company, the Alfred Du Pont Estate, the Tonopah Mining Company, Armour and Company, Mayo Hospital at Rochester, Minn., Sears, Roebuck and Company, The Great Northern Railway, the University of Chicago, the Baldwin Locomotive Works and hundreds of others have installed the Automatic Telephone and are constantly adding to the original installation.

Everywhere the signs read plain. Everywhere the trails and roads of telephony lead toward Tomorrow's Telephone, the Automatic. An unusually interesting and valuable booklet, "Your Telephone—Asset or Liability," has been prepared especially for the use of the executives of the larger business concerns and public institutions. A copy will be mailed on request.

Automatic Electric Co.

Makers of 600,000 Automatic Telephones in Use the World Over

Dept. 55, Morgan and Van Buren Streets, Chicago

OFFICES:

New York [1916]   Toledo   Buffalo   Pittsburgh   Detroit   Philadelphia   Boston   St. Louis

It's the Same Old "Juice"

—the Electricity that whizzes the Big Trolley Car along or pours from the Fiery Little Columbia to drive the Youngsters' Train

ELECTRICITY for hustling the big trolley car along the street comes from mammoth generators whose energy is reckoned in thousands of horsepower. . . . The youngsters' train gets its snap and go from the Fiery Little Columbia. . . . In both cases it is identically the same kind of electricity running the same type of motor. The only difference is in degree and size.

Toys themselves appear to enjoy the frolic when spun around by Columbias. No connection with the house-lighting fixtures is needed—the whole outfit may be toted up to the garret, out on the lawn, anywhere, everywhere, wherever the good time is—and with absolute safety.

What a marvelous thing this Columbia Dry Battery is—and what a lot of uses! Motionless, yet moving toys at a merry clip; cold, yet firing the fuel in autos, motorboats, trucks, tractors, and farm engines; silent, yet giving a vigorous tone to telephones, bells, and buzzers; lightless, yet illuminating lanterns, pocket lamps, and other portables. . . . Fahnestock Spring Clip Binding Posts may be had without extra charge

THE STORAGE BATTERY

WHEN you place a Columbia Storage Battery in your car you equip with *definite power guaranteed for a definite time.* The famous Columbia Pyramid Seal stamped on the connectors is the symbol of that guarantee.

Columbia Storage Battery Service is all around. Stop in and see how easily and gladly they make certain that each and every user gets the actual performance to which his orginal purchase entitles him.

Columbia Dry and Storage Batteries

[1919]

HUGHES Electric Ranges

Making a Nation of Better Cooks

No more cooking by guesswork. Electric cooking is replacing guesswork with an almost scientific exactness. It makes cooking successes the rule, failures rare. It gives food a richer, better flavor, a deliciousness before unknown. The Hughes Electric Range is setting this new standard of cooking excellence — making a nation of better cooks.

The absolutely even heat of a Hughes Electric Range gives a uniformity of results hitherto impossible. Constant watching is unnecessary; the results are assured in advance.

The Hughes Electric oven, with its heavily insulated, heat retaining walls, saves greatly in meat shrinkage and gives the meat a finer, better flavor. Cakes and bread rise evenly and brown uniformly, because of the wonderfully even heat throughout the oven. There are no air currents to carry off the rich juices, nor gaseous fumes to contaminate the food.

With such a range as this, every woman can become a better cook. When to her care in preparation is added perfection in cooking, is it any wonder that Hughes Electric Ranges are being bought by thousands, that every range installed in a neighborhood becomes the center of a growing group of users?

Learn more about this wonderful range in our book, "What Every Kitchen Needs." It tells what the greatest cooking experts, such women as Janet McKenzie Hill, Marion Harris Neil, Alice Bradley and Mrs. Lemcke-Barkhausen, think of the Hughes Electric Range, and includes their favorite recipes, with statements as to how electric cooking improved them. Send 6c in stamps for this book.

Ask your electric service company about Hughes Ranges — made in 20 models — sold and recommended by electric service companies throughout the country.

HUGHES ELECTRIC HEATING CO.

5641 West Taylor Street, Chicago

Canadian Factory: 364 Richmond St. W., Toronto, Ont.

Hughes Range — only electric range ever awarded gold medal — awarded Panama-Pacific Gold Medal.

[1917]

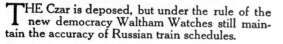

RUSSIA Comes to WALTHAM for TIME

THE Czar is deposed, but under the rule of the new democracy Waltham Watches still maintain the accuracy of Russian train schedules.

Russian officials recognized the need of a railroad watch of super-excellence. For Russia's trains travel vast distances and her time tables are extremely complicated. Russia required the most accurate and dependable watch that could be found.

So she sent her horological experts to search for a timepiece that would meet the standard she had set. London, Geneva and Paris exhibited their finest offerings. But these picked watches of European make failed to survive the exacting tests to which they were subjected.

Next those critical experts crossed the sea to inspect the Waltham Vanguard, which watch was finally chosen in competition with the best that Europe or America has produced.

The Vanguard has long been recognized as the "world's master railroad watch." And there are more Waltham watches in use on the railroads of the world than all other makes combined. Especially is this true in the United States and Canada.

With the dethronement of the Czar, autocracy passed away and a new Russia was born. And one of the few welcome heritages from the old regime was the Waltham Vanguard, which watch continues to guide the running time of trains in "All the Russias."

The Vanguard
The World's Finest Railroad Watch

Ask your jeweler to point out the advantages of the Waltham *jeweled main wheel* which makes a Waltham so easy to wind and set; also the *diamond end-stones* and the *Breguet hairspring* which make it impossible for the hairspring to catch in the regulator; the *recoiling click* which prevents injury to the time-keeping qualities if the watch is wound too tight; and the exclusive *winding indicator* on the dial which tells at a glance whether or not your Waltham needs winding.

23 and 19 jewels

WALTHAM WATCH COMPANY
WALTHAM, MASS.
CANADA: 189 St. James Street, Montreal
Manufacturers of the Waltham Speedometer and Automobile Clocks

WALTHAM
The World's Watch Over Time

[1917]

The Brunswick
ALL PHONOGRAPHS IN ONE

The Ultona

Now! The Final Achievement
Brunswick introduces a new Method of Reproduction, a real sensation

HERE, at last, is the supreme phonograph achievement of recent years . . . . The Brunswick Method of Reproduction.

It includes two distinctly new improvements, two inventions that absolutely revolutionize old standards.

Some maker was bound to build this ultimate phonograph, freed from ancient handicaps.

The honor has come to The House of Brunswick, a pioneer in developing the all-record idea. The first Brunswicks met with phenomenal success, showing that we might spend thousands of dollars in perfecting this idea.

Better Than Ever

Now, with the new Brunswick Method of Reproduction, distinctly new, we offer a super-phonograph.

It not only plays *all* records, but plays them at their *best*.

This is accomplished chiefly by The Ultona, our new all-record reproducer, and the new Brunswick Tone Amplifier.

Tone values are now given a naturalness hitherto unattained. Some of the gravest problems in acoustics are solved.

The Ultona is an amazingly simple contrivance. It plays all records according to their exact requirements. The proper diaphragm is presented to each record, whatever make, and the exact needle, the exact weight.

So you see that this is not a makeshift, not an attachment, but a distinctly new creation.

Simplicity Itself

At the turn of a hand you adapt The Ultona to any type of record. A child can do it. It is practically automatic.

Now your library of records can be bought according to your favorites. For instance, each record maker has a famous tenor. On a one-record instrument you are confined to one. Others are barred. And who likes to be restricted? Who wants to be confined to buying from only one catalog, when there are several from which to choose?

The Ultona, we think, is the greatest feature offered any music-lover. And it is obtainable *solely* on the new Brunswick.

Another vast improvement in tone projection comes in our all-wood Tone Amplifier, built like a violin. All metal construction is avoided, thus breaking away from the usual custom.

Wood, and *rare* wood at that, is the only material that gives sound waves their proper vibration.

With The Ultona and the new Brunswick Tone Amplifier, phonographic art is brought to higher standards.

See and Hear

You cannot afford now to make a choice until you've heard the latest Brunswick. Until you become acquainted with The Brunswick Method of Reproduction. Until you hear this marvelous instrument. You are invited particularly to examine The Ultona and note how simply it adapts itself to each type of record.

Once you hear the new Brunswick, you'll be delighted and convinced that this super-phonograph is in a class heretofore the ideal, but unattained. All you want in any phonograph is found in this composite type. Plus superiorities not found elsewhere.

A Brunswick dealer will be glad to play this super Brunswick for you and explain the new Brunswick Method of Reproduction.

Brunswick Models—Price $32.50 to $1,500

THE BRUNSWICK-BALKE-COLLENDER COMPANY

Canadian Distributors:
Musical Merchandise Sales Co.
Excelsior Life Bldg.
Toronto

General Offices: Chicago

Branch Houses in Principal Cities of the United States, Mexico and Canada

Dealers:
Write for our Profitable Plan
with all the details

(1164)

How Miller Cords Outran 21 Prominent Makes

A Heroic Tire Contest on 17 Packard 'Buses, Going 78,000 Miles a Month

NO more convincing proof of a tire's supremacy has ever been submitted to the court of public opinion. It comes from the private tests of the Eldorado Stage Company, Los Angeles, Cal. They're one of the largest users of tires in the world. To them it meant a huge sum of money to establish which tire carries a heavy load lightly, and runs the farthest.

Twenty-two leading makes of tires were tested on the Eldorado's seventeen 12-Passenger Packards. They travel an average of 153 miles daily—a combined distance of 936,000 miles a year. That's more than 37 times around the world.

Proof of Uniform Mileage

This is the "Service de Luxe" for which the Miller Tires competed and won. Their victory was based—not on exceptional mileage of a single casing—but on long distance uniformity, tire after tire.

Once the burro was the only transportation where today this grand fleet carries thousands of passengers between Los Angeles, Bakersfield and Taft. Here Nature has painted with lavish hand a wide panorama of peaks, canyons, rivers, verdant hills and valleys.

Parlor Car Comfort

Next time you visit California don't miss this enchanting trip—made in parlor car comfort in an Eldorado stage running on buoyant Miller Cord Tires.

All Millers are uniform because their workmanship is uniform. The Eldorado tests have reaffirmed it. You can get these championship tires—but only from the authorized Miller Dealer. If you don't know his name, write us.

THE MILLER RUBBER COMPANY
Dept. A-155, Akron, Ohio
Makers of Miller Red and Gray Inner Tubes —the Team-Mates of Uniform Tires
Also Miller Surgeons Grade Rubber Goods—for Homes as Well as Hospitals
TO DEALERS: Your Territory may be open—write us

miller
GEARED-TO-THE ROAD
UNIFORM MILEAGE
Tires

Grandfather
Father
Son

1902 Pierce Arrow

1910 Pierce Arrow

1918 Pierce Arrow

Genuine
Pantasote
Top Material

was used on the first Pierce-Arrow cars. It has been standard equipment on Pierce-Arrow cars ever since. Facts like this explain Pantasote prestige.

Throughout all these years Pantasote has rendered Pierce-Arrow owners dependable service and has fulfilled the rigid requirements demanded by the makers of this master car.

Pantasote was on the first Pierce-Arrow because it was the best Top Material. It is on the last Pierce-Arrow for the same reason.

What better proof of top material quality could be asked for?

Pantasote costs more than other top materials. The makers of cars listed here can truthfully say that they provide the most expensive of all top materials. They give the car owner the most costly and the best.

CARS
using
Pantasote
Standard Equipment

Pierce-Arrow	Chandler
Locomobile	Premier
Marmon	Cadillac
White	Reo-Six
Mercer	Columbia
Hudson	Cole
Chalmers	Westcott

TO USE THIS
LABEL ON
MATERIAL NOT
Pantasote
IS A PENAL
OFFENSE

Avoid misrepresentation, even though it be unintentional. Look for this label on tops represented as Pantasote.

THE PANTASOTE COMPANY
1700 Bowling Green Building   New York, N.Y.

Is this 1897 Haynes car the oldest Haynes in use?

Built in 1897
"Ready to run anywhere" says the owner, Walter E. Smith of Bound Brook, N.J.

Hundreds of Haynes cars have seen ten to nineteen years service. One Haynes of the vintage of 1900, owned by Chas. Menges, of Pittsburgh, Pa., has been in a repair shop only twice, during a service of 100,000 miles.

A four cylinder Haynes built in 1909 has run 300,000 miles. A large number of cars have made over 100,000 miles which include slow delivery work and trucking.

It means something to careful car buyers that Haynes cars built two decades ago are still in the harness—for Haynes cars of today are built even better than the old timers. They have the stamina!

HAYNES

"Better Than The Years"

America's Greatest "Light Six"

is more complete and desirable than ever, with the same high speed 55 H. P. engine—too good to change. Makes possible 1 to 60 miles per hour "on high" —develops more power than any other engine of equal bore and stroke. So economical of upkeep that it is economy to choose it in preference to cars of lower price but higher maintenance cost.

America's Greatest "Light Twelve"

is the only light weight twelve of high class. Every improvement in automobile engineering is embodied, supplemented by the latest in conveniences. Wire wheels and cord tires are standard equipment. The engine—with $2\frac{3}{4}$ in. x 5 in. bore and stroke—has overhead valves and aluminum pistons, and works with the same smooth efficiency as that of the Haynes "Light Six."

See your Haynes dealer for demonstration of "Light Six" and "Light Twelve." Compare the combination of beauty, power, flexibility—with cars of a much higher price rating and you'll be amazed at the value it offers.

THE HAYNES AUTOMOBILE CO., 32 South Main Street, Kokomo, Indiana

1916—Built better than ever—

Haynes "Light Six" Prices:
Model 36—5-passenger Touring Car - - $1485
Model 36—4-passenger Roadster - - 1585
Model 37—7-passenger Touring Car - - 1585

Haynes "Light Twelve" Prices:
Model 40—5-passenger Touring Car - - $1985
Model 40—4-passenger Roadster - - 2085
Model 41—7-passenger Touring Car - - 2085

All prices f. o. b. Kokomo

NEW CATALOG
giving full information of the latest Haynes models gladly mailed on request.

[1916]

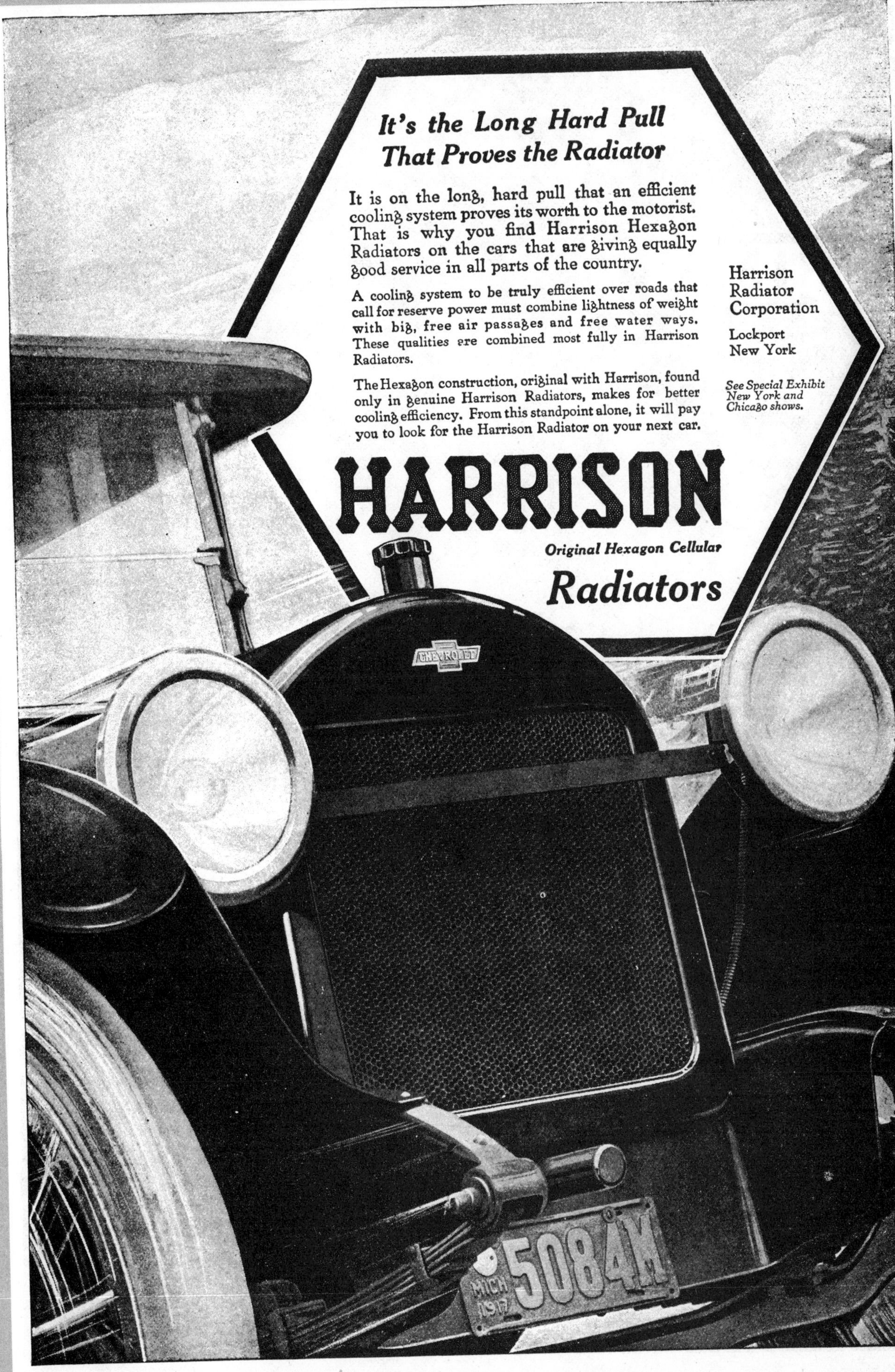
It's the Long Hard Pull
That Proves the Radiator
It is on the long, hard pull that an efficient cooling system proves its worth to the motorist. That is why you find Harrison Hexagon Radiators on the cars that are giving equally good service in all parts of the country.
A cooling system to be truly efficient over roads that call for reserve power must combine lightness of weight with big, free air passages and free water ways. These qualities are combined most fully in Harrison Radiators.
The Hexagon construction, original with Harrison, found only in genuine Harrison Radiators, makes for better cooling efficiency. From this standpoint alone, it will pay you to look for the Harrison Radiator on your next car.
Harrison Radiator Corporation
Lockport New York
See Special Exhibit New York and Chicago shows.
HARRISON
Original Hexagon Cellular
Radiators
CHEVROLET
MICH 1917
5084M

Automobiles
BIDDLE

In the training camps or at the front — through the cities' busy thorofares or along the broad boulevards of Florida's coast resorts, this car carries a message of speed, flexibility and service.

Various types of coach work

Biddle Motor Car Company
Philadelphia, U.S.A.

[1917]

Jordan Bodies Are All Aluminum

Rumbles, ripples and rust are the bane of the sheet metal body.

That is why the finest custom made bodies in the world are fashioned from aluminum.

All the new Jordan bodies are made from aluminum. It takes that smooth, velvety finish—it will not ripple nor rust—and the rumble of the sheet metal is gone.

The Jordan Suburban Seven is one hundred pounds lighter.

It is the first car of its type without the unsightly body bulge.

The sides run straight fore and aft. The edges are beveled sharply. The doors are wide and square.

The car is three inches lower, beautifully upholstered, equipped with Marshall cushion springs and a new type of cushion to conform to the natural position of the body.

The equipment includes curtains that open with the doors; beveled edge plate glass in rear panel; smaller wheels and tires; rim wind sport clock; tonneau light; Macbeth lenses; motometer—and a real tailored top.

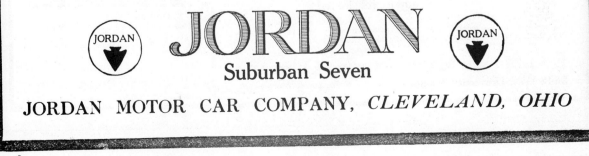

JORDAN
Suburban Seven

JORDAN MOTOR CAR COMPANY, *CLEVELAND, OHIO*

Now Is the Time to Buy

STAUDE Mak-a-Tractor

"America's Most Useful Farm Implement"

TAKE that Ford car of yours and turn it into a 4-horse team for the cost of one good horse. Make it do field work and heavy road hauling as well as pleasure driving. Make it do the work of four horses for the cost of feeding one horse, and turn 20 acres of your hay and oats land to growing crops that people can eat.

The STAUDE Mak-a-Tractor has made good in every state in the union. On more than five thousand farms it has been doing the work of a 4-horse team—in the field and on the road.

NOW is the time to buy your STAUDE Make-a-Tractor. There is no longer the slightest doubt of its being the most efficient and inexpensive light farm tractor that has ever been developed. Buy now and you won't have to carry your horses through the winter, with oats and hay way out-of-sight.

Immediate Delivery on 1918 Models!

The STAUDE you get will be the very latest and finest model. And you get it at once. Our attachment will add $1,000.00 to the value of any Ford car—new or second-hand. It will do all of your fall work—haul the crops to town twice as fast—and be ready for pleasure driving in 20 minutes.

This fifth wheel or bolster enables you to set the front end of any wagon over the tractor wheels for road hauling. All the load is carried by the tractor wheels and the rear wagon wheels. An ideal way to haul heavy loads to town.

Automatic force-feed oiling system has sight-feed on dash and forces supply of oil to all moving parts of motor. Same system as used on the many high-priced cars. Improves operation of the Ford on the road for pleasure driving.

Tractor drive wheels are steel—8 inches wide—with removable mud lugs for use in soft ground. Will not sink in any ground fit to work over. Extension rims furnished for very loose soil.

Tractor-hub and axle bear all the weight of rear end of car, pushing car ahead and pulling implement. Implement is hitched to tractor axle. Short arrow points to roller pinion gear which fits on end of regular Ford axle and intermeshes with bull gear. Ford axle merely turns the pinions. Tractor wheel hubs have roller bearings.

Tractor frame work clamps to Ford chassis without boring holes. Tractor frame connection is flexible and easily detached to roll back the tractor wheels and replace regular wheels for pleasure driving.

Our 1918 cooling system is the most efficient cooling device ever placed on tractor or pleasure car. Consists of special Perfex Radiator, Injector Water Circulator, Giant Suction Fan with broad belt and lagged pulley. Gives you greatly increased cooling capacity over the regular Ford. No change in appearance.

Bigger Value Than Ever At Our New Prices!

All orders now being filled with our new 1918 Model 2-speed outfit—2½ miles per hour for plowing and 5 miles per hour for hauling. New cooling apparatus cools twice as fast as our 1917 job. Overheating is now impossible if directions are followed.

Prices—Effective Aug. 25

STAUDE Mak-a-Tractor with 6-tooth pinions, force-feed oiling system and new 1918 cooling system...................... **$225**

STAUDE Mak-a-Tractor with both 6 and 8-tooth pinions, force-feed oiling system and 1918 cooling system..................... **$240**

STAUDE Mak-a-Tractor with both 6 and 8-tooth pinions, force-feed oiling system, 1918 cooling system, and fifth-wheel attachment for hauling........................ **$260**

STAUDE Mak-a-Tractor with both 6 and 8-tooth pinions, force-feed oiling system, 1918 cooling system, fifth-wheel attachment and belt-power pulley device.............. **$285**

A youth or a woman can easily drive it in plowing or other field work, as it starts and runs entirely on high gear and steers more easily than on the road. When through work you can remove the tractor and replace regular rear wheels for pleasure driving in twenty minutes.

Belt Power Pulley Attachment

Mail the Coupon for Facts!

Don't fail to immediately investigate the lowest-priced and most efficient farm tractor device on the market — proven satisfactory in every state in the Union. Mail the coupon for descriptive catalog and name of nearest dealer.

E. G. Staude Manufacturing Company

2648 West University Avenue   St. Paul, Minnesota

[1917]

210

No longer do Ford owners stand in dust, mud, slush, rain, snow, cold, heat, or at ANY TIME, and crank their engine by hand—all this annoying, disagreeable, dirty work has been done away with.

Ford owners now sit in the car and merely press the foot pedal of the Stewart Starter, and instantly their engine starts.

There is no hesitancy—no delay with a Stewart Starter on a Ford car. When the foot pedal is pressed, the smooth, quick, effective force of compressed air gets immediate action. It is the correct type of starter, located in the correct place, and it spins the motor exactly as when cranking by hand.

Stewart Starter weighs only 40 pounds which is evenly carried in center of car, giving perfect weight balance, not an unnatural strain on one side of car. Needs no attention. Nothing to replenish. Installation is simple—no cutting or changing any part of your Ford car, as you have to do in putting on other starters.

Stewart Starter also supplies air for your tires. No more back-straining job of hand-pumping. When your tires need more air, you simply attach the hose connection

Stewart Starter
for FORD Cars
Always Starts Your Engine—$40
and Pumps Your Tires

(furnished as part of the Stewart Starter equipment) and your tires are blown up while you stand and look on. Saves buying a tire pump. Saves tires from going bad because of not being fully blown up.

Get your Stewart Starter TODAY, and put a stop to hand-cranking forever. Its cost is only $40, one-half that of other starters.

30 days' Trial Offer

If not thoroughly satisfied with any Stewart Product after 30 days' use, the purchaser's money will be cheerfully refunded without question or argument.

Stewart-Warner Speedometer Corp'n
Chicago, U. S. A.
Branches and Service Stations in 60 Cities and Towns

Stewart Motor-driven **Tire Pump**
Don't pump tires by a back-straining hand-pump any longer; buy a Stewart Motor-Driven Tire Pump **$12**

Stewart **Hand-operated Warning Signal**
"Makes them pay attention" **$3.50**

Stewart **Vacuum Gasoline System**
Always insures a positive, automatic, even flow of gasoline to carburetor **$10**

Stewart **Motor-driven Warning Signal**
Contains a real motor **$6**

Stewart **Speedometer for FORD Cars**
Ford owners choose the Stewart: used by over 1,700,000 car owners on their cars every day **$10**

Stewart Products

[1916]

211

A new creation! A more beautiful Packard is here announced. Now—a remarkable accomplishment in *body designing* matches the achievement of the epoch-making Twin-six motor. And thereby is rounded out the smartest and *most efficient* motor carriage we have ever built. Branches and dealers today have ready for your inspection models in the new, *third* series—3-25 and 3-35. Open car prices are $3450 and $3850 at Detroit.

THE "BULL DOG"

Mack
TRUCKS

Through Service

Full-powered, like a giant locomotive, the MACK truck sweeps over the world's highways. It follows no prescribed track but moulds its routes according to the demands of transportation.

First manufactured twenty years ago, the MACK introduced the motor truck idea in the United States. Practical years of experience have followed with refinements in design that have produced the most endurable performance truck on record. In Los Angeles, a MACK truck has traveled 50,000 miles with an actual cost for repairs and parts of less than $20.00.

MACK capacities:—1, 1½, 2, 3½, 5½, 7½ tons.

Tractors, 5, 7, 11 and 15 tons.

Write for Traffic Catalog No. 5

INTERNATIONAL MOTOR COMPANY
New York

PERFORMANCE COUNTS

[1918]

DOBLE-DETROIT

STEAM CAR

Uses Only Kerosene for Fuel

The Car That Meets War Time Requirements of Economy and Fuel Conservation

The Doble-Detroit Steam Car uses only kerosene—or even lower grade and cheaper oil for fuel.

There are no gasoline jets—no preheating or vaporizing devices.

Cold kerosene is sprayed into the combustion chamber and ignited by an electric spark.

That is one of the big differentiating factors between the Doble-Detroit and former steam propelled vehicles.

It is one of the things that make the Doble-Detroit essentially a war time car.

It is one of the things that make the introduction of the Doble-Detroit at this time particularly important and timely.

The motor car has long since passed the luxury stage.

It has become so vital a part of the life and business of the nation that it is an economic necessity.

And the motor car, we believe, finds its highest expression in the Doble-Detroit Steam Car.

The Doble-Detroit is electrically controlled.

That is another of the big differentiating factors between it and other steam propelled vehicles.

Electricity ignites the fuel and starts the car on the pressure of a button.

It makes possible the use of kerosene or lower grade oil as the sole fuel.

It makes possible a combustion chamber and generating system of marvelous compactness and efficiency.

It makes possible the automatic control of the steam pressure under varying conditions.

In a word, in the Doble-Detroit car the use of steam is refined and simplified—its efficiency is greatly increased—its control is made amazingly simple and easy.

As we said last month, we firmly believe the Doble-Detroit to be the nearest approach to the ultimate car that has yet been achieved.

This belief is based upon years of actual performance.

Doble-Detroit Steam Motors Co.
Detroit

[1917]

214

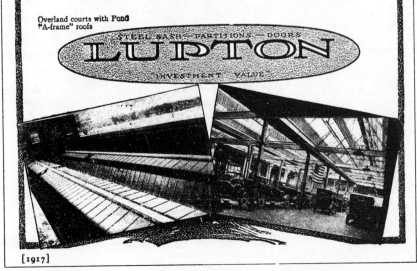

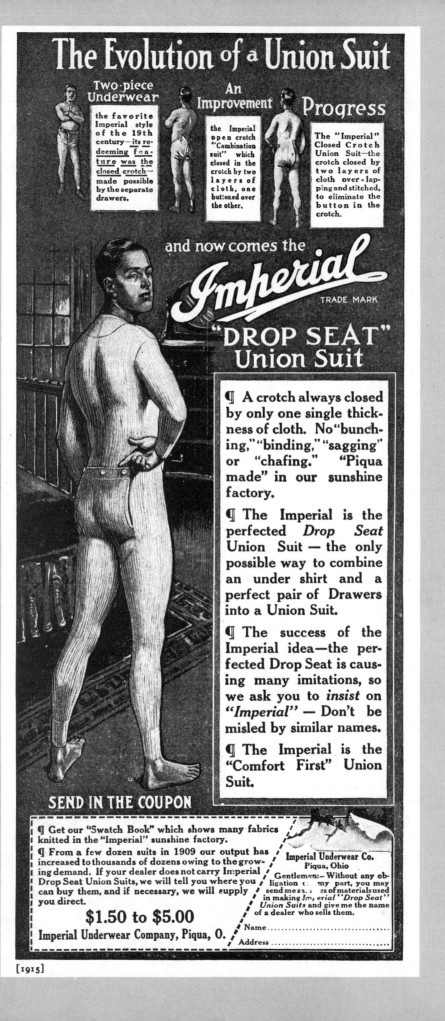

FASHION FIRST!

Wanamaker's FASHION *Mail Order* CATALOG

Yes, it is a "regular" Mail Order Catalog, but *specializing in fashions*, including women's, misses' and children's inner and outer wearing apparel.

Price range? *The happy medium!* Going as low as quality can be bought for. Fifty-eight years of successful store-keeping have established this absolutely trustworthy standard of merchandising.

Can you be sure of *correct and newest fashions?* You couldn't be *more* sure than at Wanamaker's! Our home is in the fashion center of New York and we are in constant touch with our Paris office. We go to press weeks after most of the other Mail Order Catalogs are completed, so for our catalog we are able to choose and design the very *latest* fashions.

If you want a copy of this catalog, please send for it right away because the edition is limited and a delay in writing may lose the chance to get YOUR copy.

P.S. *Letter postage is back to its old rate! A penny postal will bring this catalog today. Please ask for Catalog R. Address*

John Wanamaker
Mail Order, New York

A Giant Among Newspapers

While the population of the city of Boston is small compared with other leading American cities, yet it should be remembered that the Boston Shopping Zone (30-mile radius) contains a population of 2,219,064, and is one of the wealthiest and most densely populated sections of the United States. *That is the real "Home" of The Boston Post.*

The Boston Post

Average Net Paid Circulation, as Shown by October, 1917, Sworn Statement to United States Government.

Boston Sunday Post	Boston Daily Post
345,302	**521,499**
Largest Sunday Circulation in New England	Largest Morning Circulation in United States

HALF A MILLION BUY THE BOSTON POST EVERY WEEKDAY. This big family of American Men and Women makes it tower Head and Shoulders above all other Boston newspapers—and overtops, by a Wide Margin, any other morning newspaper in the United States.

The Boston Post has been truly called **"EVERYBODY'S NEWSPAPER."** It is the favorite in the homes of millionaires as well as in homes of moderate means.

EVERY WEEK FOR OVER SIX YEARS the Boston Post has carried the largest volume of Local and National Display Advertising among Boston newspapers, and leads the second paper by more than two million lines annually.

If you have anything to sell in this, one of the most concentrated markets in the United States, the Boston Post is your DOMINANT Advertising Medium.

[1917]

Why Live An Inferior Life?

I know that I can easily, quickly and positively prove to you that you are only half as alive as you must be to realize the joys and benefits of living in full; and that you are only half as well as you should be, half as vigorous as you can be, half as ambitious as you may be, and only half as well developed as you ought to be.

My Free Book Will Add to Your Self-Understanding

THE fact is that no matter who you are, whether you are young or old, weak or strong, rich or poor, I can prove to you readily by demonstration that you are leading an inferior life, and I want the opportunity to show you the way in which you may completely and easily, without inconvenience or loss of time, come in possession of new life, vigor, energy, development and a higher realization of life and success.

Become Superior to Other Men

The Swoboda System can make a better human being of you physically, mentally and in every way. The Swoboda System can do more for you than you can imagine. It can so vitalize every organ, tissue and cell of your body as to make the mere act of living a joy. It can give you an intense, thrilling and pulsating nature. It can increase your very life. I not only promise it, I guarantee it. My guarantee is unusual, startling, specific, positive and absolutely fraud proof.

Why Take Less Than Your Full Share of Life and Pleasure?

Are you living a full and successful life? Why not always be at your best—thoroughly well, virile, energetic? Why not invest in yourself and make the most of your every opportunity? It is easy when you know how. The Swoboda System points the way. It requires no drugs, no appliances, no dieting, no study, no loss of time, no special bathing; there is nothing to worry you. It gives ideal mental and physical conditions without inconvenience or trouble.

Your Earning Power

your success, depend entirely upon your energy, health, vitality, memory and will power. Without these, all knowledge becomes of small value, for it cannot be put into active use. The Swoboda System can make you tireless, improve your memory, intensify your will power, and make you physically just as you ought to be.

The Swoboda System is as effective for Women as for Men

[1917]

Send for My Book—FREE

It explains the SWOBODA SYSTEM OF CONSCIOUS EVOLUTION and the human body as it has never been explained before. It will startle, educate and enlighten you.

My book explains my new theory of the mind and body. It tells, in a highly interesting and simple manner, just what, no doubt, you, as an intelligent being, have always wanted to know about yourself.

You will cherish this book for having given you the first real understanding of your body and mind. It shows how you may be able to obtain a superior life; it explains how you may make use of natural laws to your own advantage.

My book will give you a better understanding of yourself than you could obtain from a college course. The information which it imparts cannot be obtained elsewhere at any price. It shows the unlimited possibilities for you through conscious evolution of your cells; it explains my discoveries and what they are doing for men and women. Thousands have advanced themselves in every way through a better realization and conscious use of the principles which I have discovered and which I disclose with my book. It also explains the dangers and after-effects of exercise and excessively deep breathing.

Tear Out Coupon Above and Mail Now

Write to-day for my Free Book and full particulars before it slips your mind.

You owe it to yourself at least to learn the full facts concerning the Swoboda System of Conscious Evolution for men and women. Mail the coupon above, or a post card now, before you forget.

Alois P. Swoboda, 2013 Aeolian Bldg., New York City

CREATOR OF CONSCIOUS EVOLUTION

Swoboda

What Others Have to Say

"Worth more than a thousand dollars to me in increased mental and physical capacity."

"I was very skeptical, now am pleased with results; have gained 17 pounds."

"The very first lesson began to work magic. In my gratitude, I am telling my croaking and complaining friends, 'Try Swoboda'."

"Words cannot explain the new life it imparts to both body and brain."

"It reduced my weight 29 pounds, increased my chest expansion 5 inches, reduced my waist 6 inches."

"My reserve force makes me feel that nothing is impossible, my capacity both physically and mentally is increasing daily."

"I think your system is wonderful. I thought I was in the best of physical health before I wrote for your course, but I can now note the greatest improvement even in this short time. I cannot recommend your system too highly. Do not hesitate to refer to me."

"You know more about the human body than any man with whom I have ever come in contact personally or otherwise."

A Few of Swoboda's Prominent Pupils

F. W. Vanderbilt	Howard Gould
W. G. Rockefeller, Jr.	W. R. Hearst
Woodrow Wilson	A. W. Armour
Alfred I. Du Pont	Charles F. Swift
Simon Guggenheim	Oscar Straus
Frank A. Vanderlip	Maxine Elliott
Charles Evans Hughes	Anna Held

Robbed of Health and Beauty

SLOWLY and stealthily, Pyorrhea has taken away the things that made her life worth while. That unaccountable depression, those nervous fears, that drawn and haggard look—these are the things Pyorrhea has brought her in place of health and beauty.

Pyorrhea begins with tender and bleeding gums; then, the gums recede and expose the unenameled tooth-base to decay. Perhaps the teeth loosen and fall out, or must be extracted to rid the system of the infecting Pyorrhea germs that often cause rheumatism, anaemia, indigestion, and other serious ills.

Four out of five people over forty have Pyorrhea; and many under that age have it also. The best way to end Pyorrhea dangers is to stop them before they begin. Start to use Forhan's today.

Forhan's for the Gums will prevent Pyorrhea—or check its progress if used in time and used consistently. Ordinary dentifrices cannot do this. Forhan's keeps the gums firm and healthy—the teeth white and clean.

How to Use Forhan's

Use it twice daily, year in and year out. Wet your brush in cold water, place a half inch of the refreshing, healing paste on it, then brush your teeth *up and down*. Use a rolling motion to clean the crevices. Brush the grinding and back surfaces of the teeth. Massage your gums with your Forhan-coated brush—gently at first until the gums harden, then more vigorously. If the gums are very tender, massage with the finger, instead of the brush. If gum-shrinkage has already set in, use Forhan's according to directions and consult a dentist immediately for special treatment.

35c and 60c tubes in the United States and Canada. At all druggists.

Forhan Company, New York, N. Y.
Forhan's, Ltd., Montreal

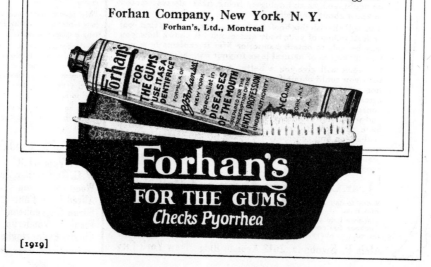

Forhan's
FOR THE GUMS
Checks Pyorrhea

[1919]

GROWING OLD GRACEFULLY

The key to health in old age is the *prevention* of bowel disorder. Constipation, which becomes more and more chronic with advancing years, frequently makes the burden of old age seem heavy indeed. Yet in most cases constipation can be entirely prevented by a little care in the matter of diet and by supplying in Nujol an efficient substitute for the mucus which exhausted nature no longer provides.

Nujol is not a bowel stimulant. It acts as an internal lubricant, softening the contents of the intestines and so promoting normal evacuations.

Your druggist has Nujol. Avoid substitutes. Nujol is sold only in pint bottles bearing the Nujol trademark.

STANDARD OIL COMPANY
(New Jersey)

Bayonne   New Jersey

Nujol
FOR CONSTIPATION

Send for booklet, "THE RATIONAL TREATMENT OF CONSTIPATION." Write your name and address plainly below. Dept. 62

.... Name.................................., Address........................... City........................... State...........................

[1917]

Y OUR vacation as well as your other summer activities will mean more to you if your hair looks its best every minute. With the very first use of a

Canthrox Shampoo

you discover that the soft massy fluffiness it develops has made your hair seem much heavier than it really is, and that the strands are so easy to manage that arranging them becomes a pleasure. Canthrox is not a cleanser for all purposes, but it is made expressly for shampooing the hair, stimulating its growth and removing dandruff.

Less Trouble than a Trip to the Hairdresser

To use: Just dissolve a teaspoonful in a cup of hot water and apply. The refreshing lather dissolves all dandruff, excess oil and dirt, so that they are entirely removed and the scalp is left sweet and clean.

15 Exhilarating Shampoos—50 Cents at Your Druggist's

This is about three cents for each shampoo. No good hair wash costs less.

FREE SAMPLE—Canthrox Shampoo proves its value without cost to you. We gladly mail one shampoo free.

H. S. PETERSON & CO., 212 West Kinzie Street, Dept. 51, CHICAGO, ILLINOIS

[1919]

FAUST INSTANT COFFEE & TEA

For the most delicious cup of coffee or tea, merely put soluble powder in cup, add hot water and serve. Made in a second—No Waste—No Grounds or Leaves — No Boiling or Cooking — No Pots to clean.

Send dealer's name and 35c. (foreign 45c.) for coffee or tea. Dealers supplied direct or by any jobber. Jobbers—Write Us.

Until recently all Faust Instant Coffee (known "over there" as U. S. Trench Coffee) was being shipped to our soldiers.

Victory now enables us to again supply the public.

FAUST CHILE POWDER

IS A "DIFFERENT" SEASONING.

You use it instead of pepper, spices, etc. It's a combination of all of them, except salt. For salad dressings, meats, gravies, stews, soups, there's nothing quite so good. Sold by most dealers in 15c., 25c. and 1-lb. cans. If your dealer hasn't it, send 20c. for 2-oz. can and Recipe Pamphlet prepared by Henry Dietz, famous chef of historic Faust Cafe and Bevo Mill.

Dealers—Ask Your Jobber. Jobbers—Write Us.

C. F. BLANKE TEA & COFFEE CO., Dept. 4, Saint Louis, Mo.

[1919]

Ashamed of Corns

As People Should Be—They Are So Unnecessary

The instinct is to hide a corn. And to cover the pain with a smile.

For people nowadays know that a corn is passé. And that naught but neglect can account for it.

It is like a torn gown which you fail to repair. Or a spot which you fail to remove. The fault lies in neglecting a few-minute duty—just as with a corn.

Any corn pain can be stopped in a moment, and stopped for good. Any corn can be ended quickly and completely.

All that is necessary is to apply a little Blue-jay plaster. It is done in a jiffy. It means no inconvenience.

Then a bit of scientific wax begins its gentle action. In two days, usually, the whole corn disappears. Some old, tough corns require a second application, but not often.

Can you think of a reason for paring corns and letting them continue? Or for using harsh or mussy applications? Or of clinging to any old-time method which is now taboo?

Or for suffering corns—for spoiling hours—when millions of others escape?

Can you think of a reason for not trying Blue-jay? It is a modern scientific treatment, invented by a famous chemist. It is made by a house of world-wide fame in the making of surgical dressings.

It has ended corns by the tens of millions—corns which are just like yours. It is easy and gentle and sure, as you can prove for yourself tonight.

Try Blue-jay on one corn. If it does as we say, keep it by you. On future corns apply it the moment they appear. That will mean perpetual freedom. A corn ache, after that, will be unknown to you.

BↃB Blue=jay For Corns

Stops Pain Instantly—Ends Corns Completely

Large Package 25c at Druggists

Small Package Discontinued (888)

How Blue=jay Acts

A is a thin, soft pad which stops the pain by relieving the pressure.

B is the B&B wax, which gently undermines the corn. Usually it takes only 48 hours to end the corn completely.

C is rubber adhesive which sticks without wetting. It wraps around the toe and makes the plaster snug and comfortable.

Blue-jay is applied in a jiffy. After that, one doesn't feel the corn. The action is gentle, and applied to the corn alone. So the corn disappears without soreness.

BAUER & BLACK, *Makers of Surgical Dressings, etc.,* **CHICAGO and NEW YORK**

[1918]

A Cough is a Social Blunder

People who know have no hesitation in avoiding the cougher. They know that he is a public menace. They know that his cough is a proof of his lack of consideration of others.

And they know that he knows it too, so they are not afraid of hurting his feelings.

For there is no excuse for coughing. It is just as unnecessary as any other bad habit. For it can be prevented or relieved by the simplest of precautions—the use of S. B. Cough Drops.

S. B. Cough Drops are not a cure for colds. They are a preventive of coughing. True, they often keep a cough from developing into a sore throat or cold. And they are a protection to the public because they keep people who already have influenza, colds and other throat troubles from spreading them through unnecessary coughing. Have a box with you always.

Pure. No Drugs. Just enough charcoal to sweeten the stomach.

One placed in the mouth at bedtime will keep the breathing passages clear.

Drop that Cough
SMITH BROTHERS *of Poughkeepsie*
FAMOUS SINCE 1847

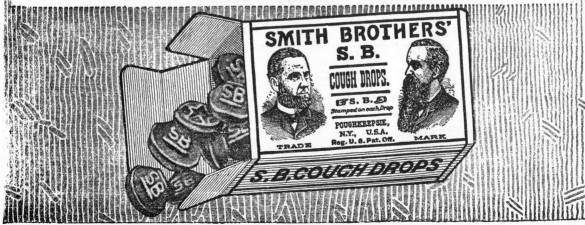

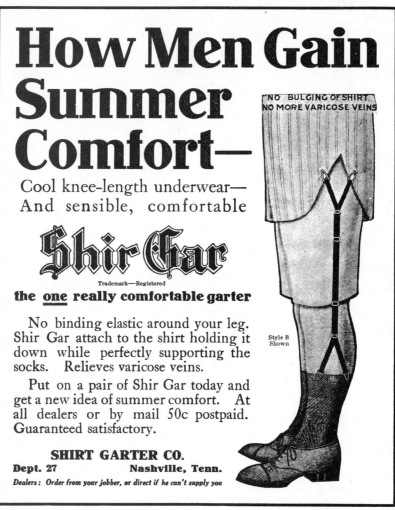

[1916]

[1917]

I Really _Must_ Use Something to Keep the Skin Soft

and free from the irritating effects of the sun and the wind. Then, too, the _dust_ is bad for one's complexion.—I don't know of _anything_ so _good_ as

Hinds HONEY AND ALMOND Cream

Copyright 1918
A. S. Hinds

for this purpose. _Everybody_ in our house uses it, and always has ever since I can remember.—I want _you_ to try it and see how quickly it cleanses and soothes and softens, no matter how rough or irritated the skin may be. I am _sure_ you will like it from the moment its refreshing fragrance greets you.—No grease, no danger of injury or growth of hair;—just delightful benefit and gratification.

Hinds Cold Cream: Semi-greaseless, highly refined. For complexion and massage.

Hinds Disappearing Cream: Vanishing, greaseless, fragrant, cleansing. Relieves catchy fingers. Ideal base for face powder.

Hinds Cream Soap: Adds to the skin-health and beauty of its users. Makes a rich, creamy lather in soft or alkaline water. Has unusual cleansing and softening qualities.

Hinds Cre-mis Face Powder: Wonderfully soft, delicate and clinging. White and all tints.

Hinds Cre-mis Talcum: Charms by its fragrance; purified, borated. Superfine quality. Makes velvety soft skin.

SAMPLES: Be sure to enclose stamps with your request. 3 kinds of Cream, 5c. Talcum, 2c. Trial cake Soap, 6c. Sample, Face Powder, 2c. Trial box, 12c. Attractive week-end Box, 35c postpaid.

Hinds Cream Toilet Necessities are selling everywhere, or will be mailed, postpaid in U. S. A., from Laboratory

A. S. HINDS
220 West Street, Portland, Maine

[1918]

228

ANSCO
CAMERAS & SPEEDEX FILM

Ansco Vest-Pocket No. 0.
Size of picture, 1⅝ x 2½ in. Equipped with Modico Anastigmat Lens, F 7.5, $15; Ansco Anastigmat Lens, F 6.3, $25. Fixed focus model with single achromatic lens, $7.

THE only self-opening camera, and the only camera in the world for 1⅝ x 2½-inch pictures which, in the anastigmat series, has a device for focusing, is the Ansco Vest-Pocket No. 0. Without the focusing device, an anastigmat lens would be of no greater value than a cheap lens.

Speed to get the picture where the picture is—not where the light is most favorable—is the great anastigmat advantage. In addition, the pictures are so clear and sharp that they may be enlarged to many times their size without sacrificing detail.

The Ansco Vest-Pocket No. 0 is small and light enough to carry in the ordinary waist pocket all the time and, by enlarging, produces large pictures of professional quality.

Catalog and specimen picture on Cyko Paper from your dealer or from us, free upon request.

The Sign of the Ansco Dealer

ANSCO COMPANY
BINGHAMTON, NEW YORK

[1916]

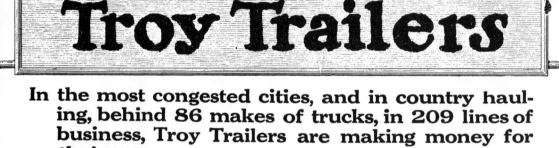

Troy Trailers

In the most congested cities, and in country hauling, behind 86 makes of trucks, in 209 lines of business, Troy Trailers are making money for their owners—

Robbins & Myers Co.—"We are hauling practically double tonnage with one motor truck."

Pillsbury Flour Mills—"Have just purchased a second one."

Oscar F. Mayer & Bro.—"Your Trailer is bringing us big dividends every day."

Crucible Steel Co. of America—"Of great value—proven satisfactory."

Continental Motors Corp.—"Helping us considerably in solving our transportation problem."

Hendee Mfg. Co.—"The fact that we ordered another Troy Trailer shows our confidence."

Studebaker Corp.—"Get excellent service from them."

Ford Motor Co.—"We now haul with 3 trucks and 2 Troy Trailers what formerly required 5 trucks."

H. G. Williams & Co.—"We are hauling 60% more slate ore daily with one truck and 3 Troy Trailers than 3 trucks alone formerly hauled."

Saxon Motor Co.—"A very cheap way to reduce our cost of freight handling."

Bethlehem Steel Co.—"Save us considerable expense."

Firestone Tire & Rubber Co.—"We find them very economical and a saving in labor."

Prest-O-Lite Co.—"Will do everything that the makers claim for it."

Procter & Gamble Co.—"Troy Trailers are the best buy on the market today."

Salt Lake Pressed Brick Co.—"We are satisfied that these Troy Trailers will give us a long satisfactory service."

Dayton Metal Products Co.—"Found our Troy Trailer to be satisfactory in every way."

Peoples Coal & Ice Co.—"We think the general makeup of a Troy Trailer makes it the best trailer on the market."

New York Shipbuilding Corp.—"We heartily recommend them."

Send for "Some Users" of Trailers—from one-truck owners to fleet operators

The Troy Wagon Works Co., Troy, O.

Oldest and largest makers of Trailers, making possible highest grade construction at lowest cost

1920-1924

THE AMERICAN MAGAZINE

November, 1923

More Than 2,000,000 Circulation

The Income I Would Be Satisfied With

FIRST PRIZE

$2,500 a Year Makes Four of Us Happy

FOR the present I am satisfied with our income. But I am neither a plutocrat nor a hypocrite, as one might suppose from such a statement.

In my twenty-eight years of life I have learned that one of the chief joys of existence is anticipation; that it is better to look forward to having a little more each year than suddenly to be presented with an income adequate to fulfill all desires.

Our income is twenty-five hundred dollars a year, and there are four of us—my husband, myself, and our two babies. We are buying our house through a building and loan association. My husband carries life insurance. We give regularly to the church through an envelope system. We have plenty of good, if not fancy, food, and substantial clothing, and we invest in all the electrical labor-saving devices for the household. Moreover, we can afford to entertain our friends simply, though we seldom go out. We do not need to, for we have plenty to amuse us at home.

When my husband was in the army, shortly after we were married, and when he spent a year in France, we learned that the greatest calamity we could face was separation; so now, even if we are obliged to stay at home because of our children, we are happy to be together. We subscribe to several good magazines, we own a phonograph, and a library of perhaps a thousand volumes. We usually spend our "recreation" money upon records and books; there is seldom a week that goes by without finding some addition to our store.

Both of us have money-making side lines that afford us no end of fun. It is with these extra, unexpected small sums that we buy luxuries, such as presents for each other and toys for the children. If our income were larger we could not possibly enjoy these little surprises so much.

Therefore, the income I would be (and am) satisfied with is the income I actually have.
MRS. E. L.

SECOND PRIZE

I Am Satisfied With What I Have

I WRITE in the present tense, for I have arrived at salary satisfaction. I am a Methodist preacher, and began my work nineteen years ago at $345 per year. When I married I was receiving $750 a year. My wife and I have always lived according to my salary. The increase has been steady. We now receive $3,250 cash, and the church furnishes our house, valuing the rent at $400. My perquisites average about $150. We have two children. We have no money discords, for our tastes are simple and alike. We are saving an amount which, with the minister's pension, will meet any normal needs of old age.

More money would not make us live differently under present conditions. It certainly would not extend our influence, but would, in fact, lessen it. For instance, I need a car in my work. The church recognizes that, so we purchased a small machine. A finer car would attract attention to itself and detract from my ministry, so I would not be happy using it.

My income will be adequate to educate my children. I shall give them a trained self-sufficiency, and that is all the inheritance they will need. The children are allowed all the perquisites. These for ten years have gone into an accumulating fund for their education. They are now actively interested in watching the fund grow. They are learning the worth of a dollar, and will demand its value when they spend it. They give a tenth of their funds to the church and benevolent work, just as we do.

We have sufficient funds for literature, music, and entertainment. Fortunately, we have always lived near fine free libraries. Our savings will take care of some traveling we will do later on, when the children are a bit older.

Financial satisfaction depends upon one's philosophy of life. We are busy realizing that the "Kingdom of Heaven is within," and right around us. We are learning to admire the rainbow's beauty rather than to seek the pleasure of its fabled gold.
O. E. A.

Maxwell

Maxwell

More miles per gallon
More miles on tires

BRAKES seem to be one of the overlooked features of a motor c
In a Maxwell they have had the extreme of attention.
For instance, a road engineer, in about 500,000 miles of experim
tal driving, has constantly tested and studied them.
That is why you can check the speed of a Maxwell in an instant and br:
it to a standstill either by foot brake or hand brake.

Special steels in a Maxwell are largely responsible. They give it ex
strength in wear and endurance, but they make the car light in weight.

Thus when you call on it to halt, the brakes are not required to "wrestl

...ith superfluous weight, and the momentum of the car is easily stopped. These ...re steels made to Maxwell's own formulae. They equal, pound for pound, ...he steels in any car built. But no car has steels just like them.

In a large measure they contribute to Maxwell's growing prestige, as ...xpressed in figures like these: nearly 400,000 now in use; and 100,000 more ...or the year 1920.

MAXWELL MOTOR CO., Inc.   DETROIT, MICHIGAN
MAXWELL MOTOR CO. OF CANADA, LTD., WINDSOR, ONTARIO
MAXWELL MOTOR SALES CORPORATION, EXPORT DIVISION, 1808 BROADWAY, NEW YORK

Stop! Look! Think!
—and you'll get your Philco now

Safety demands the strongest, toughest, most powerful battery you can get—a battery that will stand by you in emergencies—that won't expose you to the embarrassments, humiliations and DANGERS of battery failure.

Thousands upon thousands of car owners today—in record-breaking numbers—are replacing their ordinary batteries with dependable, long-life, *super*-powered Philco Batteries.

They know the Philco Battery—with its tremendous power and staunch, rugged, shock-resisting strength—will whirl the stiffest engine—give them quick, sure-fire ignition—*get them off at a touch of the starter*.

The Philco Battery is guaranteed for two years—the longest and strongest guarantee ever placed on a battery of national reputation. But with its famous Diamond-Grid Plates, Slotted-Rubber Retainers, Quarter-Sawed Hardwood Separators and other time-tested features, the Philco Battery *long outlasts its two-year guarantee*.

Why continue taking chances on ordinary batteries? Why wait for an emergency to show you the absolute need for a dependable, power-packed Philco? Install a Philco NOW and be safe. It will cost you no more than just an ordinary battery.

RADIO DEALERS—Philco Drynamic Radio Storage Batteries are shipped to you charged but absolutely DRY. No acid sloppage. No charging equipment. No batteries going bad in stock. Wire or write for details.

Philadelphia Storage Battery Company, Philadelphia

The famous Philco Slotted-Retainer Battery is the standard for electric passenger cars and trucks, mine locomotives and other high-powered, heavy-duty battery services.

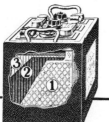

3-Point Superiority

1. The Famous Diamond-Grid—the diagonally braced frame of a Philco plate. Built like a bridge. Can't buckle—can't warp—can't short-circuit. Double latticed to lock active material (power-producing chemical) on the plates. Longer life. Higher efficiency.

2. The Philco Slotted Rubber Retainer—a slotted sheet of hard rubber. Retains the solids on the plates but gives free passage to the current and electrolyte. Prevents plate disintegration. Prolongs battery life 41 per cent.

3. The Quarter-Sawed Hard-Wood Separator—made only from giant trees 1000 years old; quarter-sawed to produce alternating hard and soft grains. Hard grains for perfect insulation of plates. Soft grains for perfect circulation of acid and current—quick delivery of power. Another big reason why Philco is *the* battery for your car.

LOOK FOR THIS SIGN

of Philco Service. Over 5500 stations—all over the United States. There is one near you. Write for address, if necessary.

PHILADELPHIA
DIAMOND
GRID
Battery

With the PHILCO Slotted Retainer

SLOTTED·RETAINER
BATTERIES

with the famous shock-resisting Diamond-Grid Plates

[1923]

THAT TREACHEROUS SKID

Endangers human life

IT TAKES little, so very little, to make driving dangerous and uncertain.

Bare rubber tires are treacherous. *When dry* they hang on like a bull dog—*when wet they* slip and slide — they cannot be trusted, no power on earth can control their movement.

Make driving safe — use WEED CHAINS when conditions make the "going" uncertain.

Safety lies in WEED CHAINS.

Put them on with the first drop of rain or flake of snow to safeguard your own life as well as the lives of others.

The few moments required to attach WEED CHAINS are not worth considering when one realizes that neglecting to put them on may mean unending sorrow and regret.

Your accessory dealer carries WEED CHAINS *in sizes to fit all tires— Balloon, Cord or Fabric.*

Insist on the genuine, time tested WEEDS.

AMERICAN CHAIN COMPANY, INC.

BRIDGEPORT, CONNECTICUT

In Canada:
Dominion Chain Co., Limited, Niagara Falls, Ont.

District Sales Offices:
Boston Philadelphia New York Chicago San Francisco Pittsburgh

World's Largest Manufacturers of Welded and Weldless Chains for All Purposes

WEED CHAINS

[1924]

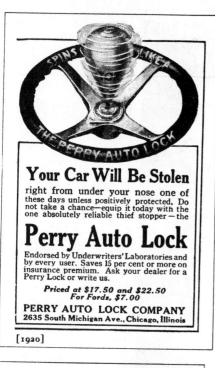

Let your next tire be

FISK

Trade Mark Reg U.S Pat Off.
Time to Re-tire?
(Buy Fisk)

*Y*OUR second Fisk tire will mean a repetition of the big and satisfying mileage of your first one.

Sold only by dealers

The Phaeton

Unheard-of Performance Results From Chrysler Engineering

If the Chrysler Six were merely another new car, its influence in the industry would be little felt.

But it is in reality the first step in the general revision of motor car design which is bound to follow its advent.

For it is an entirely new *type* of car, built on a new *kind* of engineering, which produces results radically *different* from any heretofore registered in the industry.

Where past development has halted, the Chrysler Six has advanced in seven-league boots.

In the motor car industry it is the turning point which inevitably arrives in every industry—when revolutionary improvements render the original invention almost obsolete.

No other interpretation can be placed upon a car which with a 3-inch motor delivers 68 horsepower and a speed of 70 miles per hour.

Such tremendous power and speed from a motor of such size are unprecedented.

The difference of Chrysler Six engineering is emphasized a hundredfold by the further fact that this motor yields better than 20 miles to the gallon of gasoline.

This is efficiency of the kind shown by the compound locomotives of today as compared with the first engines that ran on rails in America.

There has been no effort in Chrysler engineering to search out new principles.

On the contrary, the safe, sound fundamentals are its basis. Their application is the point of difference.

All previous experience has been taken into account. Good points have been separated from the bad. They have been improved upon and others added.

Nothing but engineering of the highest scientific character could produce such a vibrationless engine as the Chrysler Six.

There is no other explanation for the fact that you can comfortably drive the Chrysler Six at 60 miles an hour or more over a cobbled street; or safely take it around turns at 50 miles an hour.

That is balance in the *nth* degree—scientific balance, if you please.

Chrysler Six disposes for all time of the idea that weight and length are necessary to easy riding—that a great cumbersome engine is necessary for power.

For the first time, a car of Chrysler Six size has been engineered to afford not only comfortable seating space but comfortable riding.

Even the side-sway is gone, because the springs of thin chrome-vanadium leaves are placed close to the wheel-hubs and parallel to the wheels.

Details by the score could be quoted to

show that the Chrysler Six is as far in advance of ordinary practice as the harvester of today is ahead of the first clumsy reaping machine.

The Chrome-Molybdenum tubular front axle combines with Chrysler pivotal steering to steady and ease handling as never before. It is specially designed to take up the torsional strains of front wheel braking.

There is an oil-filter that cleanses all motor oil once in 25 miles; an air-cleaner for the carburetor; Chrysler-Lockheed hydraulic four-wheel brakes that make deceleration as swift and sure as the motor's acceleration.

Everything that Chrysler advanced design means in the operation and comfort of a motor car will be made clear to you in a half hour's riding and driving of the Chrysler Six.

Any Chrysler Six dealer will gladly afford you this demonstration, and supply you with all the structural details.

All Chrysler Six dealers are in position to extend the convenience of time-payments. Ask about Chrysler's attractive plan.

CHRYSLER MOTOR CORPORATION, DETROIT, MICHIGAN
Division of Maxwell Motor Corporation

The **Chrysler Six**

Pronounced as though spelled, Cry-sler

[1924]

238

The New ESSEX

A SIX

Built by Hudson under Hudson Patents

Essex closed car comforts now cost $170 less than ever before. Also with this lower price you get an even more attractive Coach body and a six cylinder motor built on the principle of the famous Hudson Super-Six.

It continues Essex qualities of economy and reliability, known to 135,000 owners. It adds a smoothness of performance which heretofore was exclusively Hudson's. Both cars are alike in all details that count for long satisfactory service at small operating cost.

Ideal Transportation

You will like the new Essex in the nimble ease of its operation. Gears shift quietly. Steering is like guiding a bicycle, and care of the car calls for little more than keeping it lubricated. That, for the most part, is done with an oil can.

The chassis design lowers the center of gravity, giving greater comfort and safety, at all speeds, on all roads. You will be interested in seeing how this is accomplished.

Greater fuel economy is obtained. The car is lighter, longer and roomier. You will agree that from the standpoint of appearance, delightful performance, cost and reliability, the new Essex provides ideal transportation.

A Thirty Minute Ride Will Win You

The Coach $975

Touring Model – $850

Freight and Tax Extra

ESSEX MOTORS
Detroit, Michigan

[1923]

What Cadillac brought to General Motors

SAID the Royal Automobile Club of London: "We will award the Dewar Trophy each year to the motor car demonstrating the greatest advance in the industry."

In 1909, three Cadillacs were taken from the dealer's storehouse in London to compete against the best that Europe could produce.

They were torn apart; the parts were tossed into a heap; it was impossible to tell from which of the cars any given part had come.

Then an amazing thing occurred. Mechanics, with only the most ordinary tools, stepped up to the pile, reassembled the three Cadillacs and sent them whirling around the track.

No other competing car could be rebuilt without filing and hand fitting. Cadillac had revealed to the world an unsuspected American achievement—perfect interchangeability of parts.

So the Dewar Trophy was won for American industry.

In 1912, Cadillac built the first car ever equipped with a complete electrical system of starting, lighting and ignition, and so won the Trophy a second time.

By a long succession of similar triumphs the leadership of Cadillac was gained. That leadership it kept and brought to General Motors.

* * * *

General Motors has built for Cadillac a wonderful new plant. It has contributed the united experience of its seventy-one divisions and subsidiaries to Cadillac craftsmanship; it has put its research laboratories at the service of Cadillac engineers.

Thus, giving and receiving, the two have reinforced each other. From the strength of the parent company Cadillac draws increased strength. From twenty years of Cadillac fidelity General Motors inherits a splendid tradition and an enduring ideal.

THE DEWAR TROPHY
which Cadillac
twice won.

CADILLAC
STANDARD OF THE WORLD

GENERAL MOTORS

Maker of PASSENGER CARS AND TRUCKS
BUICK · CADILLAC · CHEVROLET
OAKLAND · OLDSMOBILE · GMC TRUCKS

Its Divisions and Subsidiaries make these ACCESSORIES, PARTS AND EQUIPMENT
which contribute to the merit of many other trustworthy cars
Fisher Bodies · Remy Starting Systems · Delco Starting Systems · Harrison Radiators
Jaxon Rims · Klaxon Horns · Hyatt Roller Bearings · Frigidaire
New Departure Ball Bearings · AC Spark Plugs · Delco Light and Power Plants

[1923]

240

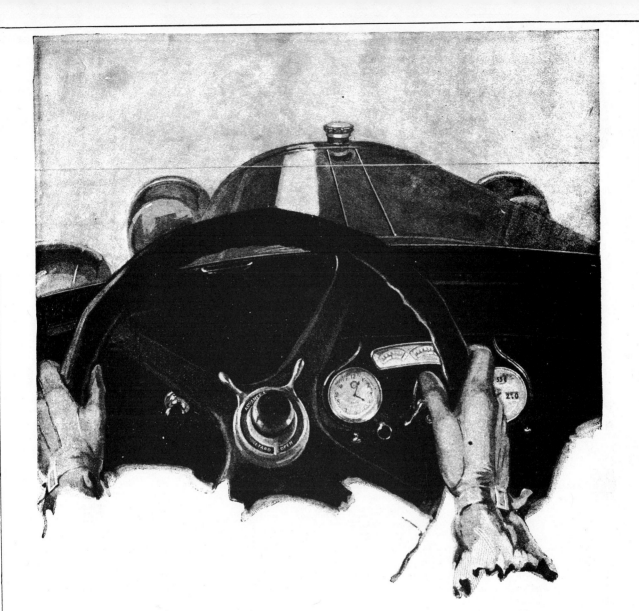

So quietly and smoothly does the
new V-63 operate that owners
say they are scarcely aware that
there is a motor beneath the hood.

CADILLAC
V-63

The Standard of Comparison

A Better Value For The 1923 Buick Open Cars

Buick open cars bring a comfort and convenience to winter driving, surpassed only by the more expensive closed models.

Close fitting curtains, that open with the doors, are provided with a weather strip of special design to seal their joints. The tight fitting windshield is adjustable from the inside, and with the curtains, insures a snug and cozy interior.

A more satisfying sense of safety is found in the wide visibility that the curtain design affords and in the signal pocket for the driver.

Combining this weather protection with the traditional Buick performance completes a value in a car that has no superior.

The Buick Line for 1923 Comprises Fourteen Models:

Fours—2 Pass. Roadster, $865; 5 Pass. Touring, $885; 3 Pass. Coupe, $1175; 5 Pass. Sedan, $1395; 5 Pass. Touring Sedan, $1325. Sixes—2 Pass. Roadster, $1175; 5 Pass. Touring, $1195; 5 Pass. Touring Sedan, $1935; 5 Pass. Sedan, $1985; 4 Pass. Coupe, $1895; 7 Pass. Touring, $1435; 7 Pass. Sedan, $2195; Sport Roadster, $1625; Sport Touring, $1675. Prices f. o. b. Buick Factories; government tax to be added.

WHEN BETTER AUTOMOBILES ARE BUILT. BUICK WILL BUILD THEM

BUICK MOTOR COMPANY, FLINT, MICHIGAN
Division of General Motors Corporation

Pioneer Builders of Valve-in-Head Motor Cars
Branches in All Principal Cities—Dealers Everywhere

[1923]

244

Columbia Grafonola

Music Wherever You Are

When the Grafonola takes a vacation with you, it gives you lots of fun and asks for mighty little care. Its strong, long-running motor requires a minimum of winding. The Non-Set Automatic Stop, an exclusive Columbia improvement, lets you listen in peace to the very end of every record.

There's nothing to move or set or measure. Just put on your record and the Grafonola plays and stops itself.

Full, pure, unmuffled tone. Exquisite beauty of design. The greatest convenience of mechanism. That's the unrivalled combination you always get in the Columbia Grafonola.

COLUMBIA GRAPHOPHONE CO., NEW YORK
Canadian Factory: Toronto

Columbia Grafonolas: Standard Models up to $300; Period Designs up to $2100

[1920]

ATWATER KENT
RADIO EQUIPMENT

"Look, Ben!"

"HERE's the equipment you want. This is part of my new radio set. Did you ever see anything more beautifully made?

"You should have heard the set over at Hayden's house last night. They have a stage of radio frequency amplification, a detector and two-stage audio amplifier with this tuner and a loud speaker.

"WE had Boston and Fort Worth and almost everything between. Why, it was just like having the entertainers right in the room!

"You know one reason I haven't been keen to have a radio set of my own was because of that stuttering and whistling. But there wasn't any of that in Hayden's set. It was so clear that I was sold right then and there.

"YES, I knew you'd ask about the price. Well, just shop around as I have and compare values.

"I feel confident you will never be satisfied until you have ATWATER KENT radio equipment."

A circular describing the entire line of Atwater Kent radio equipment is yours for the asking.

ATWATER KENT MANUFACTURING COMPANY
4965 STENTON AVENUE
Philadelphia

[1923]

Front Seats
in the theatre of the world

A FASCINATING place, the theatre of the world! Its program for one short week includes addresses by the President of the United States, four great concerts by the New York Philharmonic Orchestra, a Sunday morning full musical church service with a sermon by one of the nation's greatest preachers, the ringside report, blow by blow, of a heavyweight boxing championship, and a bewildering array of music, educational talks, and last-minute news reports from all over the country.

Something over ten million people go to this theatre by radio every week—but they don't all sit in the front seats!

Dr. Lee De Forest, discoverer of the 3-electrode vacuum tube, which makes all present-day radio possible. Below is the De Forest D-10 Reflex Radiophone.

Up in the gallery sit the newcomers in radio, getting enough with their simple sets to make them wish for more. Nearer yet to the great stage sit the owners of more powerful receivers—and in the front seats, getting every word of the great national performance, clearly, distinctly, without the blur of a word or a note—sit the satisfied owners of De Forest Radiophones.

The proved supremacy of De Forest Radiophones is a natural thing. Remember that Dr. De Forest discovered the vacuum tube, without which there would be no present-day radio receiving or broadcasting. Every tube set made, no matter by what maker, rests on De Forest's discovery. Remember that De Forest did the first broadcasting in the world. Twenty-three years ago De Forest was the pioneer in radio—and De Forest is the pioneer in radio today.

The three-tube D-7-A Reflex Radiophone at $125.00 has external batteries; the four-tube D-10 Reflex Radiophone at $150.00 has a drawer of its cabinet for dry cells. Both operate long distances on indoor loop, with wet or dry cells, with headphones or loud speaker. (Prices plus approximately 6% for territories west of the Rockies.)

After you get through experimenting you will come to De Forest, so you might as well get the facts now.

FREE RADIO CATALOGS

for the asking, with prices and full details of De Forest sets, tubes, and parts. Drop us a postcard:

De Forest Radio Tel. & Tel. Co.
DEPT. L3, JERSEY CITY, N. J.

If located west of Pennsylvania address

De Forest Radio Tel. & Tel. Co.
Western Sales Division
Dept. L3, 5680—12th St., Detroit, Mich.

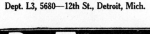

[1923]

One year married and all talked out

HERE are two young married people. For a year they have been spending their evenings together—and now, as the second year of their married life begins, they are *all talked out.*

He sits in moody silence under the lamp. The click of her needles is the only sound that breaks the veil of depression in the room.

Is there anything that would brighten their evenings?

How can they get more things to talk about; how can they turn their silent, lonely hours into real human companionship?

The answer to this question—and to the question of thousands of married couples like them—is contained in a free book that you may have for the asking. It is called "Fifteen Minutes a Day," and in a vivid, stimulating way tells how every man and woman can gain the knowledge of life and literature, the culture, the broad viewpoint that will turn lonely evenings into fine comradeship.

Think of it. You know in advance what most people are going to say. No new ideas, nothing that stimulates you, or makes you think: "My, I'd like to see those people again." But a few people get more interesting every year; they have always a new subject, new interests. Instead of growing mentally fat for lack of exercise, they keep their minds fit

Send for this free book that contains Dr. Eliot's plan of reading.

and healthy by exercising them —fifteen minutes a day!

Send for the free book. Read in it how Dr. Eliot, for forty years President of Harvard, tells just what great books he chose for the most useful library in the world; why he chose them, and how he has arranged them with notes and reading courses so that every man or woman can get from them, in even fifteen minutes a day, the things that make an interesting and responsive companion.

Every well informed man and woman should at least know something about this famous library—

Dr. Eliot's Five-Foot Shelf of Books

Every reader of this page is cordially invited to have a copy of this useful little book which tells all you want to know about this wonderful library. It will be sent free; merely clip this coupon and mail it today.

FIFTEEN MINUTES A DAY

[1923]

Of Course It's a CROSLEY
Better-Costs Less
Radio

THINK of the boundless delight of that dear old mother, confined to the house by the rigors of winter or the infirmities of age, when she listens in for the first time on a Crosley Radio. Imagine the joy of the kiddies, when they awaken you Christmas morning with the glad tidings that "Santa has brought us a Crosley Radio." Then decide to make this a Crosley Christmas.

There can be no gift with greater possibilities for continued happiness than a Crosley set. It carries Christmas along through the year, continually giving new thrills and happiness, and bringing pleasant thoughts of the giver.

It is a delight to operate a Crosley. The immediate response to the turn of the dials; the clearness of reception from far distant points; the real ease with which local stations may be tuned out; all help to make Crosley reception distinctive and exceptionally pleasurable. The very low cost at which this really remarkable radio performance can be obtained places Crosley sets within the reach of all—the ideal Christmas gift.

BEFORE YOU BUY—COMPARE   YOUR CHOICE WILL BE A CROSLEY

For Sale By Good Dealers Everywhere

Crosley Regenerative Receivers are licensed under Armstrong U. S. Patent 1,113,149. Prices West of the Rockies add 10%

Write For Complete Catalog

THE CROSLEY RADIO CORPORATION
Powel Crosley, Jr., President

122 Alfred Street   **Cincinnati, O.**

Crosley Owns and Operates Broadcasting Station W L W

[1924]

Crosley
Head Phones
Better — Cost Less
$3.75

Crosley One Tube
Model 50, $14.50
With tube and Crosley Phones $22.25

Crosley Two Tube Model 51, $18.50
With tubes and Crosley Phones $30.25

Crosley Three Tube Model 52, $30.00
With tubes and Crosley Phones $45.75

Crosley Trirdyn Regular, $65.00
With tubes and Crosley Phones $80.75

Crosley Trirdyn Special, $75.00
With tubes and Crosley Phones $90.75

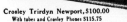

Crosley Trirdyn Newport, $100.00
With tubes and Crosley Phones $115.75

Mail This Coupon At Once

The Crosley
Radio Corp'n.
122 Alfred St.
Cincinnati O

Mail me, free of charge, your catalog of Crosley receivers and parts with booklet entitled "The Simplicity of Radio."

Name_____

Address_____

251

Church Seats
sani~white

Why not an ALL-WHITE *bathroom?*

CHURCH Sani-White Seats carry out the keynote of the "all-white bathroom." They are plated with an ivory-white sheathing without seams or joints. This sheathing cannot absorb moisture or hold dirt—it is cleaned as easily as porcelain and is equally sanitary. A white glossy surface that cannot be contaminated and is guaranteed never to change color, crack, craze, warp, or chip.

If you are about to build, make sure of the economy and sanitation that comes from the use of Church Seats by clipping out and handing to your architect the specification at the left.

Replace unsanitary seats

IF you want to replace unsightly toilet seats in your home, telephone your plumber and ask him to install Church Seats. He can attach them in a few minutes. They will last for years.

Upon request, we will mail you a small cross-section of a Church Seat showing the impervious ivory-white sheathing, with the interesting booklet, "Why White?"

Architects, Plumbing Jobbers, Contractors and Dealers—write for Catalogue and Style Poster.

C. F. CHURCH MANUFACTURING CO.,
Established 1898
Holyoke, Mass.

Clip—To remind the Architect

THE closet shall be ......Plate No....... complete as described *with exception of seat* which shall be Church Sani-White, Plate 142, as made by C. F. Church Mfg. Co., Holyoke, Mass. (Plumbers are glad to furnish Church Seats with any make of bowl).

Music that Charms

For an hour of relaxation at home in the evening there is nothing like the charm of sweet music to banish dull care. Nothing will give you greater enjoyment. And if you want to be popular, favored, the "life of the party" everywhere, learn to play a

BUESCHER
True Tone Saxophone

It's so easy anyone who can whistle a tune can learn to play the Buescher. Three free lessons give you a quick easy start. You can pick it up yourself and later get a teacher if you wish to join a band or orchestra. It's great fun practicing because you learn so rapidly.

We want you to try a Buescher Saxophone six days free in your own home. See what you can do in that time, then if you like it pay a little each month. But first, clip the coupon and get the beautiful free book. No obligation. Do this right now.

BUESCHER BAND INSTRUMENT CO.
Everything in Band and Orchestra Instruments
775 Buescher Block,   Elkhart, Indiana

Love's enchantment; melody divine; who can resist the charm of the soft sweet Saxophone song.

THE TRUMPET YOU HEAR ON THE PHONOGRAPH

The Buescher-Grand Trumpet, too, is easily learned and easy to play. With the mute in, it's so sweet and soft and mellow in tone that practice at home or in school will not bother anyone.

Free!

This beautiful book shows how easy it is to learn to play a Buescher. In it you will find the first lesson chart. It shows all the different models and tells what each is used for. Hundreds of pictures. 64 pages. You must have this fine book.

204

Mail

BUESCHER BAND INSTRUMENT CO.
775 Buescher Block
Elkhart,   Indiana
Gentlemen: Without obligation to me send your beautiful book "The Story of the Saxophone" described above.
Check here ☐
If you prefer other literature describing other band or orchestra instruments, check below.
Cornet ☐   Trumpet ☐   Trombone ☐
Tuba ☐
Mention any other........................

Easy to Play - Easy to Pay

Write plainly, Name, Address, Town and State in Margin Below

[1925]

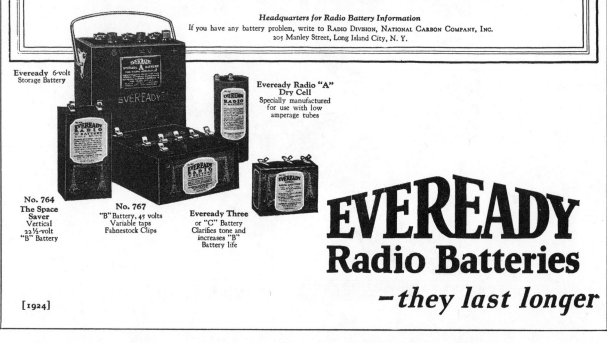

KOTEX

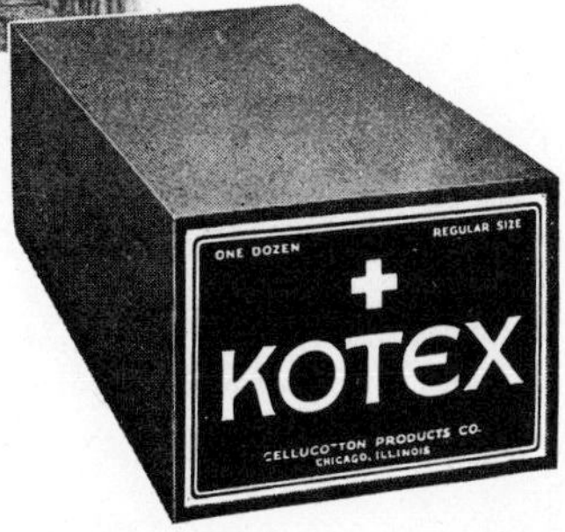

At stores and shops that cater to women

NEW but tried and proved, Kotex enters universal service from a romantic background. For, although a woman's article, it started as Cellucotton—a wonderful sanitary absorbent which science perfected for use of our men and allied soldiers wounded in France.

With peace came an idea suggested in letters from nurses in France, regarding a new use for this wonderful absorbent, and early in 1919 our laboratory made the first sanitary pads of Cellucotton enclosed in gauze and placed them on sale in various cities. Requests for more followed every sale, and we devoted two years to perfecting the new article—named KOTEX from "cotton-like texture"—and to the building of machinery which makes and seals it hygienically without contact of human hands. Kotex are now ready for every woman's use. Satisfactory beyond description—ask any trained nurse.

Cheap enough to throw away

The gauze envelope is 22 inches long, thus leaving generous tabs for pinning. The filler, forty layers of finest Cellucotton, is 3½ inches wide by 9 inches long. Kotex are cool, more absorbent, and of lasting softness. Kotex are cheap in price and easy to throw away.

CELLUCOTTON PRODUCTS CO.
208 South LaSalle Street, Chicago, Illinois

Copyright 1921, Cellucotton Products Co.

12 in box for 60c

If KOTEX are not yet for sale in your neighborhood, write us for the names of nearest stores and shops that have them. Or send us sixty-five cents and we will mail you one box of a dozen Kotex in plain wrapper, charges prepaid.

INEXPENSIVE, COMFORTABLE, HYGIENIC and SAFE ~ KOTEX

[1921]

255

The Transformer, wired ready to put up, with 17 beautiful colored lamps, comes packed in an attractive blue and orange box.

A new touch of beauty for the wired home

Tiny jewels of light that add a touch of fairy-land to any decoration—globules of radiant color, as unusual as they are charming—these are at the command of every wired home in the

G-E Christmas Arborlux

the quality tree lighting set manufactured by the General Electric Company.

Not only is this set a safe, reliable and beautiful outfit for Christmas tree illumination but it also offers a hostess, wonderful means to distinctive decoration for lawn parties, banquets and similar occasions.

Furthermore, the outfit includes a sturdy transformer, which, when not being used for the lights, will operate any electrical toy, thus being a year-'round utility for the home with children. It attaches to any alternating current lighting socket or convenience outlet.

The G-E Arborlux is superior to cheaper outfits for similar purpose because it is substantially constructed and so wired, that, if one light should fail or be broken, the rest of the lights continue to burn. This is not so with the cheaper "series wired" sets.

A novel effect can be secured by arranging Arborlux lights with ferns on the banquet table.

Insist on the G-E Arborlux for your tree this Christmas—and for use throughout the year. If the nearest electrical store cannot supply you, write us for leaflet B-3630 and the name of a nearby dealer.

General Electric Company

General Office Schenectady, N.Y.   Sales Offices in 33A-119X all large cities

[1922]

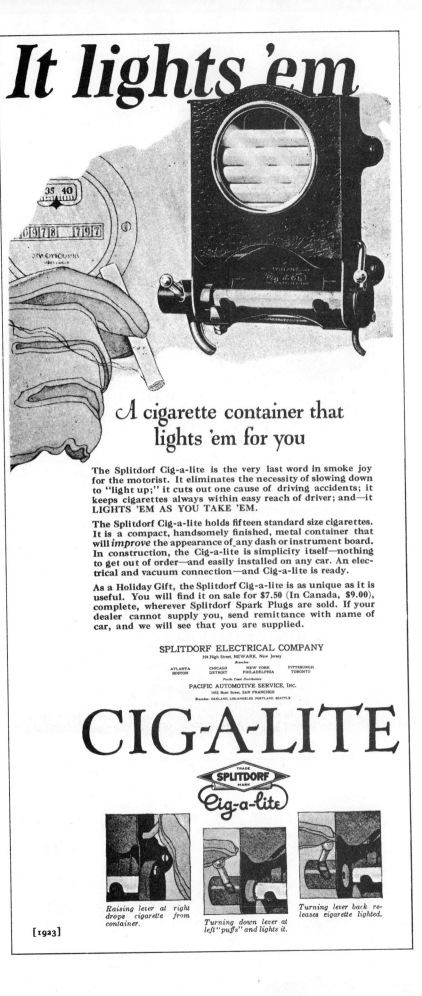

It lights 'em

A cigarette container that lights 'em for you

The Splitdorf Cig-a-lite is the very last word in smoke joy for the motorist. It eliminates the necessity of slowing down to "light up;" it cuts out one cause of driving accidents; it keeps cigarettes always within easy reach of driver; and—it LIGHTS 'EM AS YOU TAKE 'EM.

The Splitdorf Cig-a-lite holds fifteen standard size cigarettes. It is a compact, handsomely finished, metal container that will *improve* the appearance of any dash or instrument board. In construction, the Cig-a-lite is simplicity itself—nothing to get out of order—and easily installed on any car. An electrical and vacuum connection—and Cig-a-lite is ready.

As a Holiday Gift, the Splitdorf Cig-a-lite is as unique as it is useful. You will find it on sale for $7.50 (In Canada, $9.00), complete, wherever Splitdorf Spark Plugs are sold. If your dealer cannot supply you, send remittance with name of car, and we will see that you are supplied.

SPLITDORF ELECTRICAL COMPANY
394 High Street, NEWARK, New Jersey

Branches:

| ATLANTA | CHICAGO | NEW YORK | PITTSBURGH |
| BOSTON | DETROIT | PHILADELPHIA | TORONTO |

Pacific Coast Distributors:

PACIFIC AUTOMOTIVE SERVICE, INC.
1452 Bush Street, SAN FRANCISCO

Branches: OAKLAND, LOS ANGELES, PORTLAND, SEATTLE

CIG·A·LITE

TRADE **SPLITDORF** MARK
Cig-a-lite

Raising lever at right drops cigarette from container.

Turning down lever at left "puffs" and lights it.

Turning lever back releases cigarette lighted.

[1923]

How many of you who envy the perennial beauty of some favorite of the stage know the simple secret of her perpetual loveliness?

No life is more arduous than hers, no environment more trying to the complexion. Still she comes before the footlights year after year, young and radiant because she has not transgressed Nature's simplest law.

She who prizes beauty must obey Nature's law!

FAULTY ELIMINATION is the greatest enemy that beauty knows. It plays havoc with the complexion; brings sallow skin, dull and listless eyes.

When intestines fail to function normally, when they become clogged with digestive waste, poisons generate and spread throughout the system, destroying health and beauty, paving the way for sickness and disease. You can prevent faulty elimination and establish regular habits by eating the proper food.

Bran is a bulk food which your own physician has recommended highly. Perhaps you have tried to eat ordinary bran and found it dry and tasteless.

There is a bran that's good to eat

Post's Bran Flakes is bran in its most delicious form. You can eat it every day and enjoy it. Served with milk or cream it is a splendid breakfast cereal. It makes the lightest muffins and the most tempting bran bread.

Post's Bran Flakes provides the intestines with bulk they need to function normally and bring the body such vital food essentials as phosphorus and iron, proteins, carbohydrates and the essential Vitamin B.

Post's Bran Flakes is the best-liked bran. Millions eat it every day as an "Ounce of Prevention." Try it. Now you'll like bran.

Send for "An Ounce of Prevention"—

Let us send you a free trial package of Post's Bran Flakes and our booklet showing different ways of serving bran. Postum Cereal Company, Inc., Dept. 4-112, Battle Creek, Michigan. Makers of Post Health Products: Post Toasties (*Double-Thick Corn Flakes*), Post's Bran Flakes, Postum Cereal, Instant Postum, Grape-Nuts.

everybody
every day
eat

POST'S
BRAN FLAKES
as an ounce of prevention

[1923]

© P. C. Co., 1925

TIFFANY & CO.

JEWELERS AND SILVERSMITHS

TIME-HONORED QUALITY

MAIL INQUIRIES GIVEN PROMPT ATTENTION

FIFTH AVENUE & 37TH STREET
NEW YORK

[1924]

Brain fatigue
now known to come from two causes

Both causes are corrected through the rough-age and food-iron in Pillsbury's Health Bran.

IT is common knowledge today that intestinal putrefaction causes brain fatigue, often reducing efficiency 50 per cent and more.

Doctors know that to secure full brain efficiency, constipation must be permanently corrected *at the source*, which is our diet. The normal person each day requires nearly an ounce of cellulose, or roughage, in his food. Our modern diet is dangerously deficient in this laxative food essential. What is the result?

Instead of passing through the system in 24 hours, food is retained 50 to 60 hours. Putrefaction sets in. Auto-intoxication, headache, reduced energy and impaired efficiency quickly follow. All too often the health itself is undermined; 85% of all sickness follows constipation.

Doctors today widely recommend that Pillsbury's Health Bran, the natural *cellulose* food, be made a part of each day's diet. The large, coarse, crisp Pillsbury flakes supply exactly the needed bulk and roughage.

Pillsbury's Health Bran also supplies iron—organic iron which makes rich blood. It is second only to egg yolks in its iron content!

One-fifth of the blood supply of the body goes to the brain, where it carries away the poisons produced by brain activity. If the blood flow is insufficient, brain fatigue is intensified.

Pillsbury's Health Bran is rich in lime, which strengthens the bones and teeth. And it contains important vitamines. Enjoy this natural food-laxative with every meal—eat at least three large tablespoonfuls each day, and in stubborn constipation as much with each meal. Your grocer will supply you with the large 20 ounce package—fully 50% more for your money than any other package of flaked bran.

Special Pillsbury recipes on package

Pillsbury's
Health Bran
One of the family

Send for a copy of our new Pillsbury's Health Bran recipe book. Pillsbury Flour Mills Co., Minneapolis, U. S. A.

Eat More Wheat

FOOD-IRON

Note in the official chart below that natural bran holds second place among all these foods in its food-iron content.

EGG YOLK
WHEAT BRAN
MOLASSES
BEANS, DRIED
WHEAT, ENTIRE
WHEAT, SHREDDED
OYSTERS
ALMONDS
OATMEAL
SPINACH
BREAD, BOSTON BROWN
DATES
MAPLE SYRUP
PRUNES, DRIED
COCOA
DANDELION
PECAN NUTS
CURRANTS
BREAD, GRAHAM
WALNUTS
RAISINS
PEANUTS
BARLEY, PEARLED
BEANS, LIMA, FRESH
PEAS, FRESH

FAMILY OF FOODS
Pillsbury's Best Flour
Pancake Flour
Buckwheat Pancake Flour
Health Bran
Wheat Cereal
Rye Flour
Graham Flour
Farina

Pillsbury's Health Bran

Why men crack

An authority of international standing recently wrote:
"You have overeaten and plugged your organs with moderate stimulants, the worst of which are not only alcohol and tobacco, but caffein and sugar." . . . He was talking to men who crack physically, in the race for success.

YOU know them. Strong men, vigorous men, robust men—men who have never had a sick day in their lives. They drive. They drive themselves to the limit. They lash themselves *over* the limit with stimulants. They crack. Often, they crash.

You have seen them afterward. Pitiful shells. The zest gone, the fire gone. Burnt-out furnaces of energy.

"He was such a healthy-looking man—"

He was. His health was his undoing. His constitution absorbed punishment. Otherwise he might have been warned in time.

"*For every action there is an equal and contrary reaction.*" You learned the law in physics. It applies to bodies.

For every ounce of energy gained by stimulation, by whipping the nerves to action, an ounce of reserve strength is drained. If the reserve is great, its loss may not be felt immediately. But repeated withdrawals exhaust any reserve. Physical bankruptcy. Then the crash.

The last ten years have been overwrought. Men have disregarded much that they know about hygiene—about health. "Keeping up with the times." Inflated currency, stimulated production, feverish living, goaded nerves. It is time to check up.

It is time to get back to normal, to close the drafts, to bank some of the fires. It is time to remember some of the simple lessons of health you learned in school.

Avoid stimulants. What is good for the boy is good for the man. Life is worth living normally. The world looks good in the morning to the man whose head does not have to be "cleared."

Borrowed Energy Must Be Repaid!

Two million American families avoid caffein by drinking Postum. And two million American families are better off for it. They have deprived themselves of nothing.

The need they feel for a good, hot drink is amply satisfied by Postum. They like its taste. They like its wholesomeness. They prefer the energy—*real energy*—of body-building grain in place of artificial energy borrowed *from the body's own reserve* by drug stimulation.

Postum is made of whole wheat and bran roasted. A little sweetening. Nothing more.

It is not an imitation of coffee or anything else. It is an excellent drink in its own right. It has a full, rich flavor inherited directly from nourishing wheat and system-toning bran. Instead of retarding or upsetting digestion, it is an actual help, making the meal more appetizing and warming the stomach without counteracting these good effects by drugging.

There isn't a wakeful hour, a taut nerve, or a headache in it. You can drink it every meal of the day, relish it, crave it, knowing that it is a help, not a hindrance, to health and efficiency

A Sporting Proposition

You have a good many years yet to live, we hope. A good many years to do with as you please. We are going to ask you, in the interest of your health, usefulness and happiness during these remaining years, to try Postum for thirty days.

To make it a sporting proposition, we will give you the first week's supply of Postum. Enough for a cup with every meal for a week. But we want you to carry on from that point for thirty days. You can't expect to free yourself from the accumulated effects of a habit of years in two or three days, or even a week.

There is a woman in Battle Creek, Michigan, famous for her Postum. She has traveled all over the country, preparing it. She has personally served it to over half a million people, at expositions, food fairs, and at Postum headquarters in Battle Creek, where she has 25,000 visitors yearly. Her name is Carrie Blanchard. Men who have tasted Carrie Blanchard's Postum have the habit of remembering its goodness.

We have asked her to tell men about Postum made in the Carrie Blanchard way. She wants to start you on your thirty-day test with her own directions—in addition to the week's supply.

You men who have not cracked—it might be well to accept Carrie Blanchard's offer.

Carrie Blanchard's Offer

"Men have always been partial to my Postum. Anybody can make it as well as I can—but there are a few simple things to remember.

"I have written these things down, and will be mighty glad to send my directions to anyone who will write. I also want to send enough Instant Postum, or Postum Cereal (the kind you boil), to get you well started on your thirty-day test.

"If you will send in your name and address, I'll see that you get the kind you want, right away."

TEAR THIS OUT—MAIL IT NOW

YOUR GROCER SELLS POSTUM IN TWO FORMS. Instant Postum, made in the cup by adding boiling water, is the easiest drink in the world to prepare. Postum Cereal (the kind you boil) is also easy to make, but should be boiled 20 minutes. Either form costs less than most other hot drinks.

Holeproof Hosiery

NEVER forget that the exquisite *appearance* of Holeproof Hosiery—the lovely new colors, the lustrous fabric, the *style*—is but one part of its superiority. For in Holeproof, as in no other hosiery, there *is* quality to match beauty! Amazing ability to *wear,* to withstand laundering. Luxury that is *economy.*

Why? Because we use only highest quality materials. Because we have had more than a half century's experience in knitting fine hosiery.

The very newest shades and colors are being shown now at all good stores: Peach, Rose Beige, Airedale, Silver—and many others. Silk, silk-faced and lusterized lisle. Styles also for men and children. Holeproof is sold only through retail stores. If not available locally, write for booklet and prices.

HOLEPROOF HOSIERY COMPANY, Milwaukee, Wisconsin
Holeproof Hosiery Company of Canada, Limited, London, Ontario

© H. H. Co.

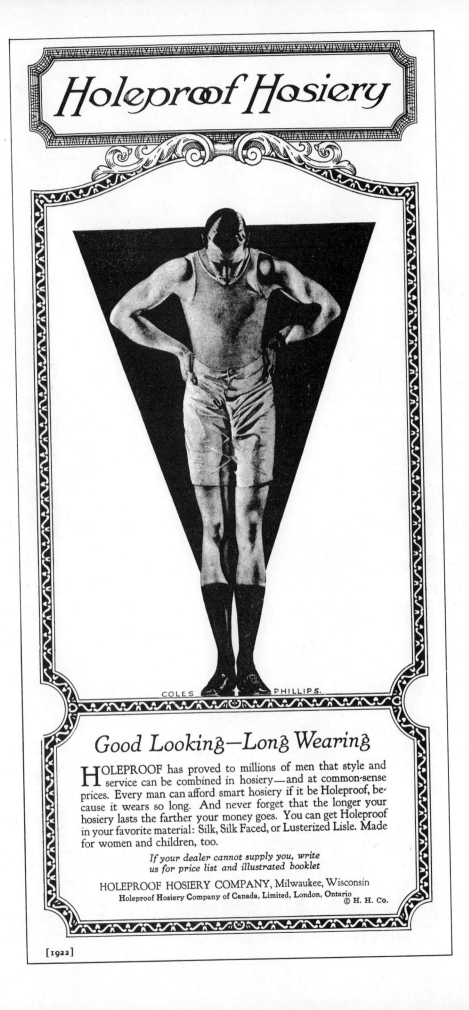

Holeproof Hosiery

COLES PHILLIPS.

Good Looking—Long Wearing

HOLEPROOF has proved to millions of men that style and service can be combined in hosiery—and at common-sense prices. Every man can afford smart hosiery if it be Holeproof, because it wears so long. And never forget that the longer your hosiery lasts the farther your money goes. You can get Holeproof in your favorite material: Silk, Silk Faced, or Lusterized Lisle. Made for women and children, too.

*If your dealer cannot supply you, write
us for price list and illustrated booklet*

HOLEPROOF HOSIERY COMPANY, Milwaukee, Wisconsin
Holeproof Hosiery Company of Canada, Limited, London, Ontario

© H. H. Co.

[1922]

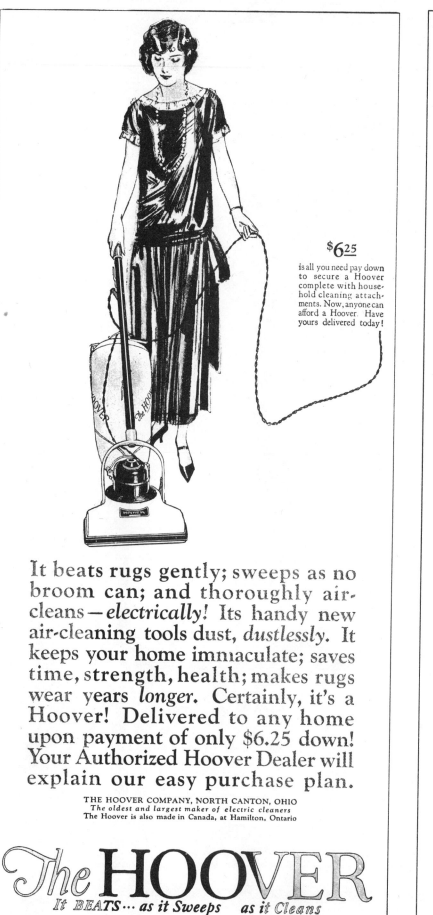

$\$6^{25}$ is all you need pay down to secure a Hoover complete with household cleaning attachments. Now, anyone can afford a Hoover. Have yours delivered today!

It beats **rugs gently**; sweeps as no broom can; and thoroughly air-cleans—*electrically!* Its handy new air-cleaning tools dust, *dustlessly.* It keeps your home immaculate; saves time, strength, health; makes rugs wear years *longer*. Certainly, it's a Hoover! Delivered to any home upon payment of only $6.25 down! Your Authorized Hoover Dealer will explain our easy purchase plan.

THE HOOVER COMPANY, NORTH CANTON, OHIO
The oldest and largest maker of electric cleaners
The Hoover is also made in Canada, at Hamilton, Ontario

The HOOVER
It BEATS ... as it Sweeps   as it Cleans

[1924]

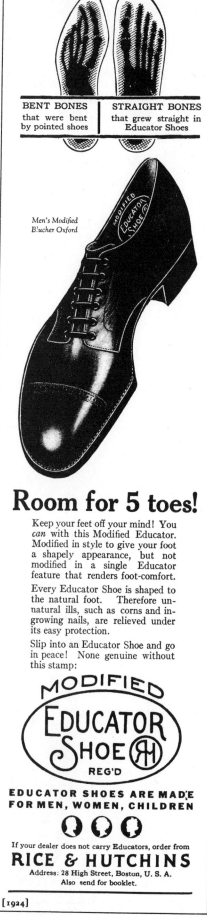

| BENT BONES that were bent by pointed shoes | STRAIGHT BONES that grew straight in Educator Shoes |

Men's Modified Blucher Oxford

Room for 5 toes!

Keep your feet off your mind! You *can* with this Modified Educator. Modified in style to give your foot a shapely appearance, but not modified in a single Educator feature that renders foot-comfort.

Every Educator Shoe is shaped to the natural foot. Therefore unnatural ills, such as corns and ingrowing nails, are relieved under its easy protection.

Slip into an Educator Shoe and go in peace! None genuine without this stamp:

MODIFIED
EDUCATOR
SHOE ℞
REG'D

EDUCATOR SHOES ARE MADE FOR MEN, WOMEN, CHILDREN

If your dealer does not carry Educators, order from

RICE & HUTCHINS
Address: 28 High Street, Boston, U. S. A.
Also send for booklet.

[1924]

264

That Will-o'-the-wisp—Smartness

Now you can capture it in clothes of your own making

YOU have seen it on the street in the swing of a skirt over a pert little pair of French heels. In the ball-room in the caressing petals of some slim flirt of a frock. It has teased you from the gay jauntiness of sport togs. Sometimes dashing, sometimes luring, sometimes happy-go-lucky —what is this will-o'-the-wisp, this shy, elusive spirit of smartness?

Have you thought that only the original creator himself could capture this indefinable air of chic? That mere "home made" clothes could never embody the real charm of Paris?

Then you will be overjoyed to realize that the clothes which you make from now on may embody not only the perfect workmanship which has always been the product of your needle, but this hitherto elusive charm. And they will actually cost less than any clothes ever cost you before!

Magic? No indeed—all because of the wonderful Deltor, a marvelous new picture-guide individually planned for the particular garment you have chosen. A picture-and-word

story of how Parisian professionals would put your very own frock together! Not a part of the pattern itself but a separate service enclosed in the envelope with your new pattern.

First—

It saves ¼ to 1⅜ yards of material — 50c to $10 — because of its professional, individual cutting guide.

Next—

It guides you in putting your garment together so that you can attain the elusive fit, drape and finish of an expert.

And last—

It gives you Paris' own touch in finish — those all-important things upon which the success of your gown depends.

Today, drop in at the Butterick pattern counter. Select the styles that you like best. None are too complicated, none possess too much *flair* for you now. For the Deltor will guide you to clothes that you will love to make and wear.

The Deltor is patented all over the world; it accompanies Butterick Patterns and *Butterick Patterns only.* Ask for it.

BUTTERICK · *Style Leaders of the World*

The DELTOR
Saves You
50¢ to $10 *on Materials Alone*

© 1923, H. J. H. Co.

56 is just a number—58 is just a number—but *57* means good things to eat

Here are Heinz *57* Varieties. *How many do you know?*

1 Heinz Baked Beans with Pork and Tomato Sauce
2 Heinz Baked Beans without Tomato Sauce, with Pork—*Boston Style*
3 Heinz Baked Beans in Tomato Sauce without Meat—*Vegetarian*
4 Heinz Baked Red Kidney Beans
5 Heinz Peanut Butter
6 Heinz Cream of Tomato Soup
7 Heinz Cream of Pea Soup
8 Heinz Cream of Celery Soup
9 Heinz Cooked Spaghetti
10 Heinz Cooked Macaroni
11 Heinz Mince Meat
12 Heinz Plum Pudding
13 Heinz Fig Pudding
14 Heinz Cherry Preserves
15 Heinz Red Raspberry Preserves
16 Heinz Peach Preserves
17 Heinz Damson Plum Preserves

18 Heinz Strawberry Preserves
19 Heinz Pineapple Preserves
20 Heinz Black Raspberry Preserves
21 Heinz Blackberry Preserves
22 Heinz Apple Butter
23 Heinz Crab-apple Jelly
24 Heinz Currant Jelly
25 Heinz Grape Jelly
26 Heinz Quince Jelly
27 Heinz Apple Jelly
28 Heinz Dill Pickles
29 Heinz Sweet Midget Gherkins
30 Heinz Preserved Sweet Gherkins
31 Heinz Preserved Sweet Mixed Pickles
32 Heinz Sour Spiced Gherkins
33 Heinz Sour Midget Gherkins
34 Heinz Sour Mixed Pickles
35 Heinz Chow Chow Pickle
36 Heinz Sweet Mustard Pickle
37 Heinz Queen Olives

38 Heinz Manzanilla Olives
39 Heinz Stuffed Olives
40 Heinz Ripe Olives
41 Heinz Pure Olive Oil
42 Heinz Sour Pickled Onions
43 Heinz Worcestershire Sauce
44 Heinz Chili Sauce
45 Heinz Beefsteak Sauce
46 Heinz Red Pepper Sauce
47 Heinz Green Pepper Sauce
48 Heinz Tomato Ketchup
49 Heinz Prepared Mustard
50 Heinz India Relish
51 Heinz Evaporated Horse-Radish
52 Heinz Salad Dressing
53 Heinz Mayonnaise
54 Heinz Pure Malt Vinegar
55 Heinz Pure Cider Vinegar
56 Heinz Distilled White Vinegar
57 Heinz Tarragon Vinegar

If you know only 4 or 5, you can be assured that the other 53 or 52 are just as good. If your grocer does not have the ones you want please write us

H. J. HEINZ COMPANY, *Pittsburgh, Pa.*

[1923]

266

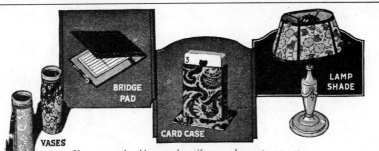

VASES   BRIDGE PAD   CARD CASE   LAMP SHADE

You can make things to beautify your home, to use as gifts, bridge prizes; to sell at church affairs; to amuse the children on rainy days.

Astonishing variety of things you can make by lepaging

THE astonishing variety of practical, useful and attractive things you can make by this wonderful new art of lepaging is simply remarkable.

". . . I have always used LePage's Glue for mending, but until I got Le-Page's Craft Book *I had no idea* how many lovely, useful things I could *make* with it . . ."

Easier and quicker than sewing

". . . You are really right about Le-Page's Craft being easier and quicker than sewing. I made a desk set complete in one afternoon and am very proud of it . . ."

The popularity of this book is such that in less than a year over 300,000 women have mailed us ten cents each for copies of it.

Things you can make for Easter

THE fascinating articles shown in the group above were every one made by lepaging. They give only a hint of the hundred and more things you can make.

Try lepaging. Send the coupon with 10 cents today for a copy of the new edition, lavishly prepared in colors, and try lepaging for yourself. LePage's Craft League, 54 Essex Avenue, Gloucester, Mass.

[1924]

See How Easily You Can Learn to Dance This New Way

Arthur Murray, Dancing Instructor to the Vanderbilts

Courtesy of Metro Pictures Corp.

No matter how skeptical you may be about being able to learn to dance by mail, Arthur Murray's new sixteen-lesson course will quickly prove to you that you can easily learn to become a perfect dancer without a teacher on the ground to direct your steps—without music or partner—right in your own home. If you will follow simple instructions shown on diagrams, practice the steps a few times to fix them in your memory, there is no reason why you should not be able to dance on any floor, to either band or phonograph music, and to lead, follow and balance correctly, no matter how expert your partner may be.

Whether you want to learn the Fox Trot, One Step, Waltz, or any of the newer steps, you won't have the slightest difficulty in doing so through this new method. Arthur Murray guarantees to teach you, or your lessons won't cost you one cent.

Send No Money—Not One Cent

FREE TANGO LESSON

Arthur Murray has diagrammed the principal steps in the famous Tango as danced by Rodolph Valentino in such a simplified way that you can quickly and easily master this fascinating Tango, after you have the Murray foundation to your dancing. Send for this Tango today and you will soon be able to amaze all your friends with your ability to dance it perfectly.

More than 90,000 people have learned to become perfect dancers by mail. In fact, about five thousand people a month are becoming wonderful dancers through Arthur Murray's amazing new method.

Send the coupon today, and Arthur Murray will send you the NEW 16-LESSON COURSE AND THE FREE FASCINATING TANGO.

Prove for yourself how quickly and easily you can learn all of the newest steps and dances. Don't send any money now—just the coupon. When the postman hands you the 16-lesson course just deposit $1.00 with him, plus a few cents postage, in full payment. And if within five days you are not delighted, return the complete course and your money will be promptly refunded. Otherwise the course becomes your personal property without any further payments. Send the coupon NOW. Don't delay. Return the coupon at once and the 16-lesson course will be promptly mailed to you.

ARTHUR MURRAY, Studio 719, 801 Madison Ave., New York

[1923]

"Slip into a Bradley and Out-of-Doors!"

Today!

SELECT your Bradley bathing suit today! It is none too early — if you want what you want. After all, Bradley can make only so many of these gorgeous Bradleys every year. The early shopper gets the pick of the patterns. All are beautiful, but there may be one that happens to capture your fancy to the exclusion of all the others.

The stores will be sold out later in the season. Now is the time to select *your* color, *your* weave, *your* size — your *ideal*.

Bradleys are made in all the authentic styles for men, women, and children.

One-piece, two-piece, skirted, and conforming — in various weights and color-harmonies at a wide range of prices.

Pick yours early — while the picking is good. Write us for the name of the store that features Bradleys.

BRADLEY KNITTING CO., DELAVAN, WIS.
The Home of Outdoor Style

Will Your Hair Stand Close Inspection?

Is it soft and silky, bright and fresh-looking full of life and lustre

YOUR hair, more than anything else, makes or spoils your whole appearance.

It tells the world what you are.

Wear your hair becomingly; always have it beautifully clean and well kept, and it will add more than anything else to your attractiveness and charm.

Beautiful hair is not a matter of luck. You, too, can have beautiful hair.

Beautiful hair depends almost entirely upon the way you shampoo it. Proper shampooing is what brings out all the real life and lustre, all the natural wave and color and makes it soft, fresh and luxuriant.

When your hair is dry, dull and heavy, lifeless, stiff and gummy, and the strands cling together, and it feels harsh and disagreeable to the touch, it is because your hair has not been shampooed properly.

When your hair has been shampooed properly, and is thoroughly clean, it will be glossy, smooth and bright, delightfully fresh-looking, soft and silky.

While your hair must have frequent and regular washing to keep it beautiful, it cannot stand the harsh effect of ordinary soaps. The free alkali in ordinary soaps soon dries the scalp, makes the hair brittle and ruins it.

That is why discriminating women, everywhere, now use Mulsified cocoanut oil shampoo. This clear, pure and entirely greaseless product brings out all the real beauty of the hair and cannot possibly injure. It does not dry the scalp or make the hair brittle, no matter how often you use it. If you want to see how really beautiful you can make your hair look, just follow this simple method.

A Simple, Easy Method

FIRST, wet the hair and scalp in clear warm water. Then apply a little Mulsified cocoanut oil shampoo, rubbing it in thoroughly all over the scalp, and throughout the entire length, down to the ends of the hair.

Two or three teaspoonfuls will make an abundance of rich, creamy lather. This should be rubbed in thoroughly and briskly with the finger tips, so as to loosen the dandruff and small particles of dust and dirt that stick to the scalp.

After rubbing in the rich, creamy Mulsified lather rinse the hair and scalp thoroughly—always using clear, fresh, warm water. Then use another application of Mulsified, again working up a lather and rubbing it in briskly as before.

You will notice the difference in your hair even before it is dry, for it will be soft and silky in the water.

Rinse the Hair Thoroughly

THIS is very important. After the final washing, the hair and scalp should be rinsed in at least two changes of good warm water. When you have rinsed the hair thoroughly, wring it as dry as you can, and finish by rubbing it with a towel, shaking it and fluffing it until it is dry. Then give it a good brushing.

After a Mulsified shampoo you will find your hair will dry quickly and evenly and have the appearance of being much thicker and heavier than it really is.

If you want to always be remembered for your beautiful, well-kept hair, make it a rule to set a certain day each week for a Mulsified cocoanut oil shampoo. This regular weekly shampooing will keep the scalp soft and the hair fine and silky, bright, fresh looking and fluffy, wavy and easy to manage—and it will be noticed and admired by everyone.

You can get Mulsified cocoanut oil shampoo at any drug store or toilet goods counter, anywhere in the world. A 4-ounce bottle should last for months.

Splendid for children —Fine for men.

Mulsified
Cocoanut Oil Shampoo

Spend your Vacation on Board a Cunarder!

Over to Europe and back for $170.

"The Proudest Moment of Our Lives Had Come!"

"It was our own home! There were two glistening tears in Mary's eyes, yet a smile was on her lips. I knew what she was thinking.

"Five years before we had started bravely out together! The first month had taught us the old, old lesson that two cannot live as cheaply as one. I had left school in the grades to go to work and my all too thin pay envelope was a weekly reminder of my lack of training. In a year Betty came—three mouths to feed now. Meanwhile living costs were soaring. Only my salary and I were standing still.

"Then one night Mary came to me. 'Jim', she said, 'why don't you go to school again—right here at home? You can put in an hour or two after supper each night while I sew. Learn to do some one thing. You'll make good—I *know* you will.'

"Well, we talked it over and that very night I wrote to Scranton. A few days later I had taken up a course in the work I was in. It was surprising how rapidly the mysteries of our business became clear to me—took on a new fascination. In a little while an opening came. I was ready for it and was promoted—with an increase. Then I was advanced again. There was money enough to even lay a little aside. So it went.

"And now the fondest dream of all has come true. We have a real home of our own with the little comforts and luxuries Mary had always longed for, a little place, as she says, that 'Betty can be proud to grow up in.'

"I look back now in pity at those first blind stumbling years. Each evening after supper the doors of opportunity had swung wide and I had passed them by. How grateful I am that Mary helped me to see that night the golden hours that lay within."

In city, town and country all over America there are men with happy families and prosperous homes because they let the International Correspondence Schools come to them in the hours after supper and prepare them for bigger work at better pay. More than two million men and women in the last 29 years have advanced themselves through spare time study with the I. C. S. Over one hundred thousand right now are turning their evenings to profit. Hundreds are starting every day.

You, too, can have the position you want in the work you like best. You can have a salary that will give your family the kind of a home, the comforts, the little luxuries that you would like them to have. Yes, you can! No matter what your age, your occupation, or your means—you can do it!

All we ask is the chance to prove it. That's fair, isn't it? Then mark and mail this coupon. There's no obligation and not a penny of cost. But it may be the most important step you ever took in your life. Cut out and mail the coupon *now*.

[1921]

271

How to Make a Hit with Influential People !

SOMETHING about Richard Bradley made him attract unusual attention wherever he went. You would instinctively pick him out of a crowd as worthy of note. In a gathering of any sort—at the club, at dinners or business meetings—the most important people present could always be found around Bradley, eager to make friends with him. And as for the ladies—well, to use a colloquial expression, they literally 'threw themselves at him."

It wasn't Bradley's physical appearance, or the way he dressed or acted, that caused him to attract such favorable attention. In these things he was not unlike other men. But here was a vividness and charm about him which you felt the moment you saw him; and in his eye was the glint of steel acquired only by men who are doing things in a big way.

Yet he had started life as an errand boy with a grammar-school education. And now at 29 years of age he was making $12,000 a year in a keenly-competitive business in which none but mature men of high education were supposed to be able to succeed.

BRADLEY and I saw each other often, and, naturally, I valued his friendship highly. One day he dropped in to see me with a "tip" on a big job he said I could get if I'd go after it. It *was* a big job—right in my line—but I felt it was altogether too big for me at that time. I doubted if I could get it; and even if I could, I didn't see how I could possibly be worth the large salary it paid. As I told this to Bradley a look of surprise, then of utter amazement, flashed across his face.

"*Too big for you!*" he exploded—"what nonsense! *Nothing is too big,* or too important, or too good for you—or for anyone else. Get that foolish nonsense out of your mind. The reason why you and lots of other fellows aren't getting more money is *because you let the world bluff you.* You've already got the ability—much more than many men holding high positions—but you haven't yet learned the knack of making people pay you big money for it."

Bradley then told me some *astonishing things* about men and women, life, business and the world in general. I was utterly astounded at what he said. It seemed as though a curtain had suddenly been lifted from my eyes and I could now see clearly for the first time. Then he drew his chair close to mine and told me a mental knack to use in dealing with people so as to *immediately destroy any advantage they have over you, and to gain the advantage yourself.*

"And now," continued Bradley, in a tone of friendly command, "telephone to the man I told you about and ask for an appointment."

I SAW my man the following day, and *did exactly what Bradley told me to do both before and during the interview. And I got that job!* Yes, actually landed a job I was afraid to tackle until Bradley told me such astonishing things. You can well imagine my delight! It pays me *three times more than I ever thought myself capable of earning!* All my friends are wondering how I did it! I've the satisfaction of knowing I'm making good in a big way—got it straight from the president at luncheon. If it hadn't been for Bradley I'd still be asleep in a rut letting the world bluff me out of money which is rightfully mine. *But now I know the knack of getting big money!*

WHAT Bradley told me was this: "You know that until recent generations our ancestors, as a race, were oppressed, exploited and *held down* by the governing classes. They were bluffed into believing that kings and the ruling classes were infinitely *better* and altogether *superior* to them. The ruling classes forced this *bluff* on the people by means of artificial standards of society and a lot of flub-dub magnificence.

"Today you and the rest of us laugh at this. We know it to be *bunk.* But just as we inherit our type of body, so do we *inherit* our *state of mind.* Our ancestors had a high respect for—*even fear of*—people in authority. Recent researches in psycho-analysis prove that even today most of us have an *undue respect for,* or *actual fear of,* people in positions of authority. We may not realize it. *Consciously* we may not have this fear; but, nevertheless, we have it—planted deep in our subconscious mind—*inherited from our ancestors.*

"That is why so few people get the rich rewards they are entitled to. They know they are worth more money, but they dislike to face the boss. They know they have the ability to hold a bigger job, but lack the know-how and the nerve to get it. *Tens of thousands of natural-born money-makers and leaders of men are today held down to underpaid jobs simply because they are bluffed by other men.* And many splendid men and women find themselves unable to enter high social circles, simply because of an *inherited state of mind.*

"But there's a simple way to *quickly overcome* this inherited handicap," continued Bradley. "It will not only wipe out your fears, but give you *invincible courage, dash and intrepidity* which sweeps everything before it, and makes people view you with amazed admiration. It will enable *you to dominate* other people instead of being dominated by *them.*" And then he told me the *actual methods* to use—the methods which enabled me to win and hold my big job which pays me *three times more than I ever thought myself capable of earning.*

Startling Revelations !

THE whole of these astonishing facts, with *all the powerful methods,* are clearly and fully told in "NERVE," a remarkable 6-volume pocket-size Course by William G. Clifford. That is where Bradley got his information which enabled him and his friend to accomplish such remarkable things. Within one hour after you start to read this astonishing Course your eyes will be opened as they never were opened before! There is nothing to laboriously study or learn. You can apply *at once* the powerful methods it gives you—methods which will *immediately* thrill you with invincible courage and give you *great power* over men and women and the world at large.

SEND NO MONEY. Merely fill in and mail the coupon. The complete Course "NERVE," in six attractive volumes, goes to you immediately. Simply pay the postman $1.25 plus postage and the complete Course is yours. If you are not delighted, return the Course within five days and your money will instantly be refunded.

You have always wanted to know how to *forcefully assert yourself* to command respect from other men; how to meet the biggest business and social leaders with the *impressive manner* that wins their admiration; how to *feel at ease* under all conditions; how to know if the other man is *bluffing* you and how to quickly *turn the tables on* him. All these things and more—including *the secret of making big money* —are clearly and specifically told in "NERVE," as you will quickly see to your great profit and delight.

We may be compelled to withdraw this remarkable offer at any moment, so it is suggested that you get "NERVE" *now—before it is too late!*

Big Cut In Price!

"NERVE" has created a **tremendous** impression. Letters and telegrams are snowing us under. Personal calls by the score. All from purchasers — telling how **greatly** they have been astonished — delighted — thrilled — pushed to success — by "NERVE."

Orders are **flooding** us for the big, new revised edition of "NERVE"—the $3 Course. Now we can cut costs by printing large editions. We'll share our saving with you.

If you **order immediately** we'll send you this $3 Course for only $1.25. A clear saving to you of $1.75. Value $3—now $1.25. But you must ACT QUICKLY!

$1.25

Special Quick-Action Offer!

Fairfield Publishers, Inc.
110 West 40th Street (Dept. 884), New York City

How to—

—gain the self-assurance that strongly impresses people;

—overcome nervousness in meeting people;

—meet and deal with "big" people as easily as you do your closest friends;

—develop an impressive, winning personality;

—dominate and control business and personal conditions;

—prevent people from dominating you;

—quickly make yourself more valuable and important to people you deal with;

—make people look upon you as a "winner";

—intensify your knowledge and skill, without further study, to make it bring you substantial and quick rewards;

—win your way into select social circles.

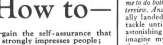

How Little Social Errors Ruined Their Biggest Chance

VIOLET CREIGHTON was proud of her husband. And she had reason to be. Six years ago he was at the very bottom of the ladder. Now he was almost near the top. One more decisive step—and they would be ready to step across the boundary, into the world of wealth, power and influence.

No wonder Ted was elated when he brought the good news home. "Well, Vi, it has come at last!" he beamed. "Crothers has left and I'm to have his place. I'm actually going to be one of the vice-presidents of the company."

Violet was duly surprised—and delighted. "The wife of an officer of the company," she laughed. "Sounds good, doesn't it?" and together they planned for the wonderful days to come, of the big things he would accomplish and the charming functions of which she would be hostess. Yet beneath their happy planning was a subtle, unexpressed fear which both realized—yet which both ignored.

An Invitation Is Received

The next evening, Ted brought even bigger news. They were to dine at the Brandon home—actually be the guests of William Brandon! Violet knew how happy Ted must be, how he had dreamed of and longed for this very opportunity. Yet, when he told her of the dinner invitation, there was a sudden tug of pain at her heart.

Oh, she was happy enough, and proud that Ted had reached his goal. But were they ready for it—would they enter their new social sphere gracefully and with a cultured charm, or would they make a blundering mess of it? She was afraid. She knew that failure now would hurt more than ever. And, with a woman's instinct, she knew that there was something Ted and she lacked.

"But do you think you should have accepted, Ted?" she queried. "You know how elaborately the Brandons entertain, and how—well, formal they are. Why, I don't even know whether it is correct for me to wear an evening gown!"

Ted was silent for a moment. "I couldn't possibly refuse," he said slowly. "We'll simply have to see it through. Mr. Brandon wants to have a long chat with me before the final arrangements are made. But I'll admit I'm kind of worried myself. Now, do you suppose I may wear a dinner jacket or must I wear full dress?"

For the first time, the Creightons realized that there was something more than business status if they were ever to be real successes—they realized that personality, culture, and social charm played an important part. And they felt keenly their lack of social knowledge, their ignorance as to what was correct and what was incorrect.

"I hope we don't make any bad breaks," Ted whispered, as they drew up before the Brandon mansion. And way down deep inside, Violet made a secret vow that she would try to be at her best tonight, to be polished and well-poised and impressive—for Ted's sake.

Bad Mistakes Are Made

They reached the Brandon home immediately before the arrival of Mr. Roberts and his wife. There was a certain tacit understanding that if anything prevented Ted from stepping into the vacancy Mr. Roberts would take his place. He was a severely dignified gentleman, and his wife had a certain distinction that immediately commanded respect and admiration. Violet was embarrassed when introductions were made and mumbled a mechanical "Pleased to meet you" several times. She wished she had prepared something brilliant to say.

Violet sat between Mr. Brandon and Mr. Roberts at the table. From the very first she felt uncomfortably ill at ease. Ted, sitting

He knew that the others were watching them, reading in their embarrassment their lack of social knowledge.

opposite her, was uncomfortable and embarrassed, too. He felt out of place, confused. Mr. Brandon immediately launched into a long discourse on the influence of women in politics, and under cover of his conversation the first two courses of the dinner passed rather pleasantly.

But then, something happened. Violet noticed that Mrs. Roberts had glanced at her husband and frowned ever so slightly. She wondered what was wrong. Perhaps it was incorrect to cut lettuce with a knife. Perhaps Ted should not have used his fork that way. In her embarrassment she dropped her knife and bent down to pick it up at the same time that the butler did. Oh, it was humiliating, unbearable! They should never have come. They didn't know what to do, how to act.

Mr. Brandon was speaking again. Ted was apparently listening with rapt attention, but inwardly he was burning with fierce resentment. It was unfair to expect him to be a polished gentleman when he had had no training! It wasn't right to judge a man by his table manners! But—why did Violet seem so clumsy with her knife and fork? Why couldn't she be as graceful and charming as Mrs. Roberts? He was embarrassed, horribly uncomfortable. If he could only concentrate on what Mr. Brandon was saying, instead of trying to avoid mistakes!

The Creightons Suffer Keen Humiliation

Violet, sitting opposite, listened quietly to the conversation. She wished that Mrs. Roberts would not watch her, that she would not make any more mistakes, that the ordeal would soon be over. The butler stopped at her side with a dish of olives. . . .

"I say, Creighton, are you listening to me or not?" With a start, Ted turned toward his host. He had *not* been listening. He had *not* been paying attention. How could he, when directly opposite him, before all the guests, his wife was taking olives with a fork! Violet glanced up and saw the look of horror in his eyes. She crimsoned, became embarrassed. But though Mr. Brandon seemed mildly surprised and Mrs. Roberts seemed very near the verge of smiling, the incident was smoothed over and conversation began once again.

For Ted, the evening was irretrievably spoiled. He knew that the others were watching Violet and him, reading in their embarrassment their lack of social knowledge, condemning them as ill-bred and uncultured. But when the ladies rose from the table to retire to the drawing-room, and he rose to follow, he knew by the amused glances of the others that they had hopelessly failed, that they had socially disgraced themselves.

He wasn't surprised, then, when Mr. Brandon remarked, after the other guests had left and Violet had stepped into the next room for her wraps, "I'm sorry, Creighton, but I've decided to consider Roberts for the vacancy. I need a man whose social position is assured, who can meet men of any position on their own footing. The executives in our company must be able to make a good impression wherever they go, and they must be the type of men one instinctively trusts and respects."

An Opportunity Is Lost, But a New One Is Found

At home that night, Violet refused to be comforted. "It was all my fault—I have spoiled your best chance," she cried. But

Ted knew that he was as much to blame as she.

"Another chance is bound to come," he said, "and we'll be ready for it. I'm going to buy a reliable, authoritative book of etiquette at once."

It was only when the famous Book of Etiquette was in her hands, and she saw how easy it was to acquire the social knowledge, the social poise and dignity they needed, that Violet was happy again. They would never make embarrassing blunders again. They would never be humiliated again. Here was the very information they needed—clear, definite, interesting information that told them just what to do, say, write and wear on all occasions under all conditions!

Ted and Violet read parts of the Book of Etiquette together every evening. It revealed to them all the mistakes they had made at the Brandon home and told them exactly what they should have done. It was positively a revelation! By the time they had finished that splendid book they knew that they would ever after be well poised and at ease even in the company of the most brilliant celebrities!

* * *

The Importance of the Book of Etiquette to YOU

The Book of Etiquette is recognized as one of the most dependable and up-to-date authorities on the conduct of good society. It has shown thousands of men and women how to meet embarrassing moments with calm dignity, how to be always at ease, how to do, say, write and wear always what is absolutely correct. It has made it possible for people everywhere to master quickly the secrets of social charm, enabling them to mingle with the most highly cultured people and feel entirely at ease.

In the Book of Etiquette, now published in two large library volumes, you will find valuable and interesting information on every question of social import. The entire subject of etiquette is covered completely, exhaustively. Nothing is omitted, nothing forgotten. You learn everything—from the correct amount to tip the porter in a foreign country to the proper way to eat corn on the cob. Wherever old traditions are attached to present conventions, they are revealed—why the bride wears a veil, why calling cards are used, why ostrich plumes are worn at Court. Every phase of etiquette has been brought up to date, and no detail, no matter how slight, has been omitted.

Five-Day FREE Examination

We would like to send you the famous Book of Etiquette free for 5 days, so that you can examine it at leisure in your own home. There is no obligation, no cost to you. Simply fill in the coupon and mail it to us at once. The complete, two-volume set of the Book of Etiquette will be promptly sent to you, and you have the privilege of examining and reading it at our expense for 5 days.

The Book of Etiquette is published in two handsome library volumes, bound in cloth and richly decorated in gold. Each volume contains interesting and valuable information that will be of permanent use to you—whenever you come into contact with men and women. Don't overlook this opportunity to examine this remarkable set without cost—mail the coupon NOW.

Within the 5-day examination period, decide whether or not you want to keep the Book of Etiquette. You have the privilege of returning the set to us within the 5 days, or keeping it and sending us only $3.50 in full payment. But remember, that this places you under no obligation—you may return the Book of Etiquette to us without hesitancy if for any reason you are not delighted with it. Clip the coupon and send it off *today*. Address Nelson Doubleday, Inc., Dept. 582, Oyster Bay, N.Y.

Did he have a right to suspect her?

DUNBAR was in a terrible state of mind. He was worried sick about his wife. He was madly in love with her and she had been acting very strangely during the past several months.

The thing that troubled him most was that she now responded very reluctantly to his affectionate advances. She wouldn't even let him kiss her. The whole state of affairs was driving him mad. He suspected everything. And, yet, he alone was to blame.

* * *

That's the insidious thing about halitosis (unpleasant breath). You, yourself, rarely know when you have it. And not only closest friends but wives and husbands dodge this one subject.

Sometimes, of course, halitosis comes from some deep-seated organic disorder that requires professional advice. But usually—and fortunately—halitosis is only a local condition that yields to the regular use of Listerine as a mouth wash and gargle. It is an interesting thing that this well-known antiseptic that has been in use for years for surgical dressings, possesses these unusual properties as a breath deodorant.

It halts food fermentation in the mouth and leaves the breath sweet, fresh and clean. *Not* by substituting some other odor but by really removing the old one. The Listerine odor itself quickly disappears. So the systematic use of Listerine puts you on the safe and polite side.

Your druggist will supply you with Listerine. He sells lots of it. It has dozens of different uses as a safe antiseptic and has been trusted as such for a half a century. Read the interesting little booklet that comes with every bottle.— *Lambert Pharmacal Company, Saint Louis, U. S. A.*

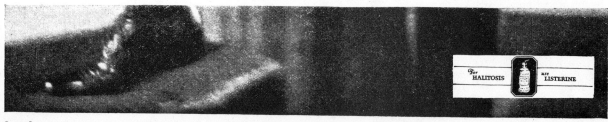

For HALITOSIS use LISTERINE

Malnutrition

More and more the main <u>source</u> of human ills is being traced to this one thing—*malnutrition*

Yet you can do much to protect yourself from its evils if you will

Malnutrition is not limited to the poor. It takes its toll from those whose tables are loaded with food as well as from starving people.

In the mouths of the American people are more than one billion bad teeth. At least one-third of our adult population suffer from indigestion or dyspepsia. Hardly a man or a woman today who is not from time to time troubled with constipation.

And all of these—dyspepsia, bad teeth, constipation—lead slowly but surely into far worse ills.

Doctors, dentists, and biological chemists—men spending their lives to find out just what your needs are—more and more are tracking down the main source of these conditions to this: *malnutrition*.

Malnutrition means that your body is not *taking up* sufficient nourishment for its daily needs. Food and nourishment, these authorities will tell you, are two very different things. Food is *what you eat*. Nourishment is *what your body gets out of it,* what it can digest.

In this food is nourishment you need, in the form your body can digest

AT LEAST one-third of all your nourishment *should* come from the *carbohydrates* (starches and sugars). For the *carbohydrates* are your greatest source of strength and vitality—your power to do work.

But if they are not rightly prepared—if they are not broken down as your body wants them, they may become a heavy burden and *still* leave you undernourished. They must be in a form your body can utilize.

* * *

Grape-Nuts gives you the *carbohydrates* in the most easily digested and most nourishing form.

Served with cream or rich milk Grape-Nuts gives you in most delicious form the essentials of a well-balanced ration.

More than three-fourths of the contents of Grape-Nuts are the precious *carbohydrates*.

They have been *dextrinized*, that is, scientifically broken down into the form *your body most readily digests and transforms into strength and vitality*.

No matter how much you have abused your body with difficult foods, you can digest Grape-Nuts quickly and easily. It is good for your digestion and it gives you nourishment you should daily have.

And Grape-Nuts *starts* digestion right. It comes in crisp golden kernels you must chew. This chewing keeps your whole mouth healthy, and starts the proper flow of the salivary and gastric juices—the first step towards sound digestion.

Eat Grape-Nuts for a week and see how much better you feel.

There is no other food like Grape-Nuts in form or taste. You will like it and it will do you good.

All grocers have Grape-Nuts. All restaurants serve it in individual packages of a single portion. The Postum Cereal Company, Inc., Battle Creek, Mich.

4 Sample Packages Free

Send today for four of the individual packages free. Enough Grape-Nuts for four nourishing breakfasts. Free offer also includes book of 101 delicious recipes selected from 80,000 prepared by housewives who regularly serve Grape-Nuts.

Postum Cereal Company, Inc.
Dept. M-10, Battle Creek, Mich.

Please send me free trial packages and booklet.

Name ....

Address.......................................

If you live in Canada, address **Postum Cereal Co.,** Ltd., 45 Front St., East, Toronto, Ont.

[1924]

Is there a greater war story than this?

What is the great story of the War? Is it the story of Joffre at the first Marne or of Foch at the second? Or the story of "They shall not pass" at Verdun? Is it the story of the first gas attack at Ypres? Or of Belleau Wood? Or of the Lost Battalion? These are all great stories of super-achievements on the field of battle.

But a different sort of story stands comparison with these. It concerns a side of the war the public knows little about. It is the story of a fight by the soldiers that the science of medicine called to the colors against a countless and implacable foe. The winning of that fight saved hundreds of thousands of wounded from torture and death during the period of the war alone. Since the end of the war it has saved uncounted thousands in addition. Its total saving of lives in homes, factories, hospitals throughout the civilized world will, as the years go on, amount to millions more.

TO tell the story properly it is necessary to go back more than half a century to that wizard of the microscope and test tube, Louis Pasteur. In 1852 Pasteur discovered germs and subsequently proved that contagious diseases and the infection of wounds are caused by malignant bacteria.

From then on medical science did its utmost to guard mankind from germ attack. During the next sixty years the new school of preventive medicine was born. Sanitation was developed. All known microbes were studied and classified. By 1914 the medical profession felt that modern surgical methods could cope with and prevent infection of wounds.

A Grim Disillusionment

Then war engulfed the world, and oh, what a grim disillusionment followed! Early in that war it became appallingly clear that the goal pointed out by Pasteur had not yet been reached; that man was still helpless before the savage, invisible, all-conquering germ.

The wounded poured into the Allied hospitals in overwhelming streams. The hospitals were thoroughly aseptic, no microbes could get in but the soldiers were covered with the indescribable dirt of the trenches. A bullet, a shell fragment, a bayonet thrust would gather bacteria as it passed through the clothing and deposit them deep within the vital parts of the body, there to breed galloping putrefaction while the wounded man lay on the field or in a shell hole waiting to be picked up. A simple scratch from a barbed wire barricade in the morning developed into a pus pocket by evening and amputation or death frequently followed within the week.

The Surgeons' Problem

The surgeons turned to antiseptics. In the years since Pasteur's discovery, only two types of antiseptics had been developed. One was the mild non-poisonous type. All it did was to make the surface of a wound an unpleasant resting place for the microbe. If the microbe had already started raising his family, it could do no more to prevent it than so much rainwater. The other type was the poisonous burning disinfectant. Though it would kill germs, it would also destroy flesh and tissue; if introduced into gaping wounds at sufficient strength to destroy germs it would eat through cells and membranes and create conditions as bad as the infection itself. In mild dilutions

these poisons were not powerful enough to check infection.

A Fearful Crisis

In this crisis the Allied surgeons appealed to the scientific world. Back from the war hospitals through all branches of the medical profession came the cry: "Find, oh find us something that will check this fearful horror! We are helpless before such infection; we must have something to check it!"

Among those who heard the call was the Franco-American surgeon, Dr. Alexis Carrel, who in 1912 had received the Nobel Prize for medicine. Dr. Carrel, who was then serving with the French armies, secured the assistance of the famous English chemist, H. K. Dakin. Backed with money and equipment provided by a great American philanthropic institution, the two scientists went to work in an effort to find a new antiseptic. They experimented day and night, for every hour was precious, at first at Beaujon Hospital, Paris, and later at Military Hospital 21, Compeigne. In an incredibly short time, when the magnitude of their task is considered, the two scientists made an announcement: "We think we have what you want," they said, "Try it and see."

The Turning Point

The surgeons of the Allied armies tried it and saw. They saw the fulfillment of the teachings of Pasteur. Here was the ideal antiseptic. It was non-poisonous and non-irritating. It could be used constantly in the deepest wounds without harm, yet it would destroy bacteria with an effectiveness undreamed of heretofore. Man had beaten the germ at last!

They named the new antiseptic the Carrel-Dakin Solution, in honor of its co-discoverers, and put it to work in all the Allied hospitals. Its triumph was complete. It drove the horror and agony of suppurating wounds from those hospitals as sunlight dispels shadows. Where seventy per cent of the wounded had been dying from infection, now less than one per cent died from that cause. Hundreds of thousands of men alive and whole today would be hopeless cripples or under the soil of France if the Carrel-Dakin Solution had not been found.

Is there a greater war story than this?

SEQUEL

After the extraordinary success of the Carrel-Dakin Solution in the war zone, it was quickly adapted for hospital use throughout the civilized world. It has performed the same miracles for surgical and civil wounds that it accomplished in the wounds of war. But it is limited to hospital and professional use for the following reason: The Carrel-Dakin Solution is unstable, it will not "keep." It has to be freshly made by experts every day and the mass of humanity has been denied its protection.

Ever since its discovery, however, chemists in all parts of the world have been trying to stabilize the Carrel-Dakin Solution, and American chemists finally succeeded in doing so. This meant that Zonite, as the improved Carrel-Dakin Solution is called, would keep indefinitely and could be put up in containers ready for household use.

Zonite has been distributed to druggists throughout the United States as rapidly as possible.

Placed on the market little more than a year ago, it is now guarding close to ten million people from infection and disease.

Facts About Zonite

Zonite is a non-poisonous, non-irritating, colorless liquid.

By scientific laboratory tests it has far greater germ-killing power than *pure carbolic acid* yet it may be used in a scratch or cut absolutely pure.

Physicians and health authorities are urging the use of Zonite as a mouth wash, throat and nasal spray, to prevent colds and more serious contagious diseases.

Dental authorities say that the use of Zonite as a mouth wash is the most effective home preventive of pyorrhea, trench mouth and infected gums known to dental science.

"The Zonite Handbook on the Use of Antiseptics in the Home" describes the many uses for this new form of antiseptic. A copy will be mailed free of charge upon request. Address Division "F" Zonite Products Company, 342 Madison Ave., New York.

Often a bridesmaid but never a bride

EDNA'S case was really a pathetic one. Like every woman, her primary ambition was to marry. Most of the girls of her set were married—or about to be. Yet not one possessed more grace or charm or loveliness than she.

And as her birthdays crept gradually toward that tragic thirty-mark, marriage seemed farther from her life than ever.

She was often a bridesmaid but never a bride.

* * *

That's the insidious thing about halitosis (unpleasant breath). You, yourself, rarely know when you have it. And even your closest friends won't tell you.

Sometimes, of course, halitosis comes from some deep-seated organic disorder that requires professional advice. But usually—and fortunately—halitosis is only a local condition that yields to the regular use of Listerine as a mouth wash and gargle. It is an interesting thing that this well-known antiseptic that has been in use for years for surgical dressings, possesses these unusual properties as a breath deodorant.

It halts food fermentation in the mouth and leaves the breath sweet, fresh and clean. Not by substituting some other odor but by really removing the old one. The Listerine odor itself quickly disappears. So the systematic use of Listerine puts you on the safe and polite side.

Your druggist will supply you with Listerine. He sells lots of it. It has dozens of different uses as a safe antiseptic and has been trusted as such for a half a century. Read the interesting little booklet that comes with every bottle.
—*Lambert Pharmacal Company, Saint Louis, U. S. A.*

For HALITOSIS use LISTERINE

Give the Railroads a Needed Rest Cure!

ABOUT TIME TO CALL A COP.

From "The Philadelphia Record," Jan. 7, 1923

The average person does not know that 99 different agencies seek to "regulate" the Railroads of the United States. There are 48 State Legislatures, the same number of State Utility Commissions, Congress, the U. S. Railroad Labor Board, and the Interstate Commerce Commission.

Think of 99 different doctors trying to "regulate" your physical system—and the resultant havoc to you. A railroad System suffers just as much.

During 1922 there were 134 measures in Congress affecting Railroads, and 228 measures in the State Legislatures. Politics, not the public good, played a large part in these bills. Few of them were constructive—many were meddlesome and hindering.

Under Government Control during the war, the Railroads suffered—and so did their stockholders—worse than any period in their long history.

What the Railroads need today is a rest from petty politics—a period free from doctoring—a hands-off policy—a long, delightful railroad legislative holiday. Then transportation problems would be solved by railroad heads—by the men whose long service in railroad management presupposes ripe judgment.

Today the Philadelphia and Reading Railway is efficiently handling the biggest volume of business in its history—and with 3,000 less employees than was thought necessary under Government control.

Let the Railroads have a rest cure for a while!

Philadelphia & Reading Railway

Agnew T. Dice

President

"Travel on the Reading"

[1923]

278

At thirty every woman reaches a crossroads Will she develop~or merely age?

LET your imagination play with those two sentences, the title of an article by Ethel Barrymore which recently appeared in McCall's Magazine. Sit down in front of your mirror and honestly analyze *your* appearance. Fine lines about the eyes and lips— a skin losing its freshness and vitality—these are the every-day tragedies that make maturity regarded with fear and hostility.

Modern Women Stay Young By Using Clay

You can prevent age from settling on *your* face. Even if its devastating work has begun you can overcome it. The means is so simple, so logical. *Clay* is the answer. Not ordinary clay, however, but *clasmic* clay—

Boncilla
BEAUTIFIER
The *Clasmic* Clay

—imported clay of most remarkable smoothness, compounded with the finest known East India balsams—the purest, blandest clay you have ever seen.

Do This For Your Complexion Tonight

Wash your face in warm water and then gently spread Boncilla Beautifier over face and neck. The very first sensation is delightful—refreshing, invigorating, soothing.

While this fragrant clasmic clay is drying, the rejuvenating balsams penetrate the pores, flushing them, cleansing them, stimulating them, removing every impurity; while its gently "pulling" action builds up drooping facial muscles and restores a firm, rounded facial outline.

When Boncilla Beautifier is dry, just remove it with a wet towel.

Your Face Is Alive!

Now you can look in your mirror unafraid. Note your smooth, firm, satin-soft skin, delicately radiant, free from the slightest suggestion of blackheads or pimples, or aging lines. Your face is young!

Remarkable Free Offer!

So that you may know for yourself that Boncilla Beautifier *Clasmic* Clay is just what you want, we want to send you a trial tube of Boncilla Beautifier absolutely free. Just mail the coupon below, with your name and address, and we will send you by return mail, our generous trial tube of Boncilla Beautifier, containing enough *clasmic* clay for two facial packs. Mail the coupon now.

Department Stores and Drug Stores Carry a Complete Line of Boncilla Preparations. Barber Shops and Beauty Shops give Boncilla Beautifier Clasmic Facial Packs.

If you live in Canada, mail the coupon to Canadian Boncilla Laboratories, 590 King Street, W., Toronto. If in England, mail to H. C. Quelch & Co., 4 Ludgate Square, London, E. C. 4.

Mail the FREE *coupon*

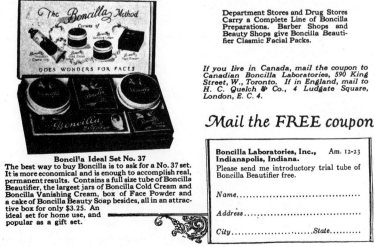

Boncilla Ideal Set No. 37
The best way to buy Boncilla is to ask for a No. 37 set. It is more economical and is enough to accomplish real, permanent results. Contains a full size tube of Boncilla Beautifier, the largest jars of Boncilla Cold Cream and Boncilla Vanishing Cream, box of Face Powder and a cake of Boncilla Beauty Soap besides, all in an attractive box for only $3.25. An ideal set for home use, and popular as a gift set.

Boncilla Laboratories, Inc.,   Am. 12-23
Indianapolis, Indiana.
Please send me introductory trial tube of Boncilla Beautifier free.

Name......................................

Address...................................

City......................State..........

[1923]

280

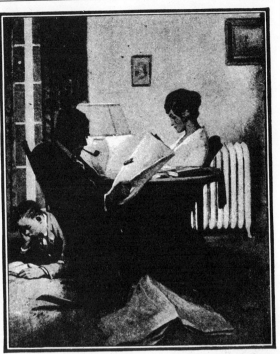

© ARCO, 1923

From a painting by VICTOR C. ANDERSON

"Put on your overcoat—
we're going into the parlor"

IN MANY HOMES a trip from one room to the next room is like passing from the Torrid to the Arctic zone.

The wind determines which side of the house is hot and which cold. And the family spends the winter huddling over a register or around a stove.

It's all so unnecessary.

For ARCOLA, connected with an American Radiator in each room, can warm your home as evenly and perfectly as our larger heating plants warm mansions and larger buildings all over the world. And radiator warmth

> **You need no overcoat in Mr. Butler's home!**
>
> "I AM using my ARCOLA now for the second winter. Our home is nice and warm all over, in all the rooms. When we had stoves we had to close off a part of our home. But now it's like summer time all year 'round."
>
> Leo Butler,
> Noblesville, Ind.

with ARCOLA is not only best but *cheapest.* Thousands of owners testify that ARCOLA is rapidly paying back its cost in the fuel it saves.

Life is short; don't shiver through it. Send today for the finely illustrated book about ARCOLA. It gives you all the facts and tells how simply and easily ARCOLA can be installed without disturbance to the family. It's *worth* sending for.

Simply send your name on a postcard to either address below; find out with what a small investment you can be warm in every room.

AMERICAN RADIATOR COMPANY
IDEAL Boilers and AMERICAN Radiators for every heating need

104 West 42nd Street, New York   *Dept. 125*   816 So. Michigan Ave., Chicago

[1923]

281

Is "ACID-MOUTH" at work on the teeth of your loved ones?

Here is the way to find out whether any member of your family is afflicted with "Acid-Mouth," the estimated chief cause of tooth decay.

Send coupon below for Free Litmus Test Papers
and 10-Day Trial Tube of Pebeco Tooth Paste

Place one of the blue Litmus Papers on the tongue, and let it stay there until thoroughly moistened. If it remains blue, there are no unfavorable acids present in the mouth. If it turns pink, then "Acid-Mouth" is working destruction on the teeth.

If the paper does turn pink, try this second test: First brush the teeth and gums thoroughly with Pebeco from the trial tube. Then place another Litmus Paper on the tongue. This time it will remain blue, thus establishing the fact that Pebeco Tooth Paste tends to counteract any undue acidity in the mouth.

Send each member of your family to a dentist twice a year, and have him or her use Pebeco regularly twice a day.

Pebeco is sold by druggists everywhere

Made by LEHN & FINK, Inc., Greenwich and Morton Streets, New York

PEBECO TOOTH PASTE

Lehn & Fink
New York

LEHN & FINK, Inc.
Greenwich and Morton Sts., New York

Please send me Litmus Test Papers and 10-day Trial Tube of Pebeco without cost or obligation to me.

Name

Street and No.

City

State

[1920]

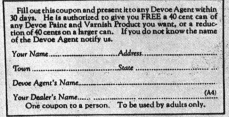

"Jones Must Be Broke"

SURFACE appearances . . . snap judgments . . . hasty conclusions. No matter how beautiful your home may be within, an outside surface of dilapidated paint is sure to give an unfavorable impression of your circumstances.

Confidence, consideration and respect surround the family whose home, inside and out, bears the beaming look of prosperity that only the proper use of Paint and Varnish can impart.

But remember... you can't get more out of the painting job than the manufacturer has put into the paint. For five generations Devoe has meant supreme quality in Paint and Varnish products.

When you paint with Devoe you get all the beauty and durability you can get out of any other product . . . plus a guarantee, backed by the Oldest Paint House in America, that Devoe will cost less money per job and give better results than any other paint you can buy.

This Coupon is WORTH 40 CENTS
Use It To-day

Fill out this coupon and present it to any Devoe Agent within 30 days. He is authorized to give you FREE a 40 cent can of any Devoe Paint and Varnish Product you want, or a reduction of 40 cents on a larger can. If you do not know the name of the Devoe Agent notify us.

Your Name.................................Address.................

Town.................................State.................

Devoe Agent's Name.................................

Your Dealer's Name...... .... (A4)

One coupon to a person. To be used by adults only.

New York   DEVOE & RAYNOLDS CO., Inc.   Chicago
Founded 1754

DEVOE
Paint and Varnish Products
THE OLDEST, MOST COMPLETE AND HIGHEST QUALITY LINE IN AMERICA

"**Standard**" PLUMBING FIXTURES

In a Bathroom Five Feet Square.
Standard Sanitary Mfg. Co.
Pittsburgh

[1923]

1925-1930

The American Magazine

June, 1926

We Save More Than Half of Our Income

I AM a teacher and receive a salary of $2,500 for nine months of teaching. Starting with $1,500 savings at the time of our marriage three years ago, my wife and I have increased our reserve fund to almost $6,000. For the ten months of the year during which we live in the town where I teach, our monthly budget is approximately as follows:

Income

Salary	$250
Interest from investments	30
TOTAL	**$280**

Expenditures

Rent	$35
Food	25
Clothing	20
Entertainment and Advancement	10
Insurance	8
Fuel	5
Light, Water and Telephone	4.50
Medical	3
Charity	2.50
Laundry	2
TOTAL	**115**
SAVINGS	**$165**

We are fortunate in securing a neatly furnished, comfortable four-room house, modern except that it is unheated, for $35 per month. Although not located in the most exclusive section of the city, it is in a substantial neighborhood and has a splendid yard with trees and a small garden. The owner returns during the two summer months when we are out of town, so we pay only ten months' rent. Some of our friends advise us to build a home; but for the present we believe it wiser to rent. We are just turning twenty-five, and have plans for more schooling and hopes for a better position before we shall have the pleasure of owning our own home. A few of our friends, who have undertaken to finance a home on limited means, remind one of the old saying about the farm owning the farmer, not the farmer the farm.

MY WIFE is an excellent cook and our simple foods are well-cooked and attractively served. We buy potatoes and apples by the bushel and canned foods by the case, thereby making a material saving. Rarely do we buy out of season foods like strawberries or tomatoes, because invariably we find that the flavor is not as good as the price. For vitamins during the winter we use lettuce now and then and drink milk at least once a day. When butter reaches peak prices we do not hesitate to use substitutes.

Contrary to the usual custom, my own clothes cost more than my wife's. This does not mean that I am better dressed than she, because she is an expert seamstress. She has her own electric sewing machine and makes all of her own dresses, and very lovely ones at that. Since taking a few lessons in hat designing, she makes most becoming hats at a cost less than half that of the ready-made kind.

Perhaps it is just as well that our town does not offer the great diversity of entertainment afforded by the large city. Occasionally we grasp an opportunity to attend a good play or an artists' recital, and perhaps twice a month go out to a movie, a dance, or card party. Our best entertainment, however, comes from reading, hiking, and listening to the radio. We use both the school and the city libraries, and a constant stream of books and magazines passes through our hands.

Almost every week-end sees us rambling in the woods. There we meet with a glorious array of adventures and pleasures. How good the food tastes when cooked over an open fire under the pines! Then to come home and lounge in an easy chair with the head-phones of a two-tube radio set against one's ears and a book live Stevenson's "Travels with a Donkey" in one's hand. Surely that is to taste real contentment!

Recently we have cashed in on these trips to the woods in an unusual way. We found a supply of insects and plants that are used in botany and biology courses in many schools over the country. A few letters to colleges and universities brought a number of orders. Already we have sold about one hundred dollars' worth, and are planning to extend operations next year. The money we have set aside for a "piano fund."

OUR medical fees go mainly for examinations and for dental work. At present we are in splendid health, and we have the worry-saving satisfaction of knowing that we can pay for the services of competent doctors if they should be needed.

We keep a few hundred dollars in a savings bank in case of need, but as soon as $750 is accumulated we invest $500 in a security bearing a higher rate of interest. Naturally, our investments are very conservative. They include $1,000 in United States postal savings certificates, $2,500 in gilt-edge first mortgage real estate bonds, and $2,000 in municipal bonds.

By acting as tutor in a boys' camp during the past two summers, I have more than paid all of our expenses for the summer months. This work has taken us outdoors to such an extent that it is almost as good as a vacation. But we are looking forward to this summer, when we expect to buy a small car and take a real vacation in the national parks of the West.

Frequently our friends ask us how we manage to save so large a slice of our modest income. The answer is simple: Our wants are few. We find that most of our real pleasures cannot be measured in terms of money. Consequently, with us, saving involves little sacrifice and becomes almost automatic, as it were. We try to practice the virtue of being content and happy in the present, but we are always looking toward the future, and trying to plan for it too.   C. M.

WHICH *two would you hire?*

experienced and intelligent   experienced and intelligent   experienced intelligent *and* CLEAN   experienced   experienced intelligent *and* CLEAN   experienced and intelligent

WHEN jobs seem scarce and the turn-downs many . . . that's a good time to check up on one's self.

More and more, employers are looking for *extra* qualifications in the people they hire.

What are these requirements that make the difference between getting a job and not getting it? . . . between being "unwanted" or *belonging* somewhere?

Self-Confidence...and how to get it

Commanding the respect of others, begins of course with improving one's *own* opinion of one's self.

But what many of us forget is that there's a way of building up our *self* respect that's as simple as it's certain: starting each day clean . . . *100%* clean.

Where personality comes from

Everyone has personality . . . if it isn't smothered by "complexes." All one needs to do is be one's natural self.

Here again, no better cure for self-consciousness has ever been invented than keeping clean, from the skin out, every day.

Character...what shows you have it

Suppose *you* were the employer. Fifty applicants to choose from, and not one you've ever seen before! How would you decide between the last half-dozen?

Necks, collars, shirts, stockings, hands, handkerchiefs, faces, complexions, hair . . . these are the things you'd notice, probably, to get a line on *character*.

Alertness, "pep," good looks

For waking people up, and putting them on their toes, nothing naturally is quite so good as the every-morning tub or shower.

For well-groomed hands, there's nothing like the regular use of a good hand brush.

For a healthy clear complexion, nothing is more necessary than a daily, *pore-freeing* wash with soap and water.

Since dust and dirt keep nice hair from looking nice, nothing takes the place of the frequent shampoo.

And, finally, nothing adds the sheer attractiveness to our clothes that fresh cleanliness does.

How wives and mothers can help

Attention wives and mothers! It concerns you, too, that cleanliness today has so much to do with the size of pay-checks.

For you are the ones who decide which is to be considered the most important in your household: clean clothes for everyone, or "keeping down the size of the wash".

You also can help by providing: an orderly, inviting bath room; a home that sparkles generally; and last but not least, the benefit of your own good example with respect to clean hands, face, hair, body, clothes.

Published by the Association of American Soap and Glycerine Producers, Inc., to aid the work of CLEANLINESS INSTITUTE. 45 East 17th Street. New York.

[1929]

IN choosing the particular system that is to bring the recognized advantages of electric refrigeration to your home, this is to be remembered: Kelvinator is the oldest system. Its performance, since 1914, in thousands of homes, is a guarantee of its performance in your home.

There is a Kelvinator to fit your present refrigeration

KELVINATOR CORPORATION
Division of Electric Refrigeration Corporation
2053 WEST FORT STREET, DETROIT, MICHIGAN
KELVINATOR OF CANADA, LIMITED, LONDON, ONTARIO   223

"My experience covers seven or eight years with one Kelvinator. It is difficult to believe that anything could give more unalloyed comfort and satisfaction than the Kelvinator I have."
(Name on request)

Kelvinator
The Oldest Domestic Electric Refrigeration

"Better-Always-Better"

The
PRESCOTT
Dining Room Suite

Do they know YOUR *son at* MALUCIO'S ?

HERE'S a hole in the door at Malucio's. Ring the bell and a pair of eyes will look coldly out at you. If you are known you will get in. Malucio has to be careful.

There have been riotous nights at Malucio's. Tragic nights, too. But somehow the fat little man has managed to avoid the law.

Almost every town has its Malucio's. Some, brightly disguised as cabarets—others, mere back street filling stations for pocket flasks.

But every Malucio will tell you the same thing. His best customers are not the ne'er-do-wells of other years. They are the young people—frequently the best young people of the town.

Malucio has put one over on the American home. Ultimately he will be driven out. Until then THE HOME MUST BID MORE INTELLIGENTLY FOR MALUCIO'S BUSINESS.

There are many reasons why it is

profitable and wise to furnish the home attractively, but one of these, and not the least, is—Malucio's!

The younger generation is sensitive to beauty, princely proud, and will not entertain in homes of which it is secretly ashamed.

But make your rooms attractive, appeal to the vaulting *pride* of youth, and you may worry that much less about Malucio's—and the other modern frivolities that his name symbolizes.

A guest room smartly and tastefully furnished—a refined and attractive dining room—will more than hold their own against the tinsel cheapness of Malucio's.

Nor is good furniture any longer a luxury for the favored few. The PRESCOTT suite shown above, for instance, is a moderately priced pattern, conforming in every detail to the finest Berkey & Gay standards.

In style, in the selection of rare and beautiful woods, and in the rich texture of the finish and hand decorating, it reveals the skill of craftsmen long expert in the art of quality furniture making.

The PRESCOTT is typical of values now on display at the store of your local Berkey & Gay dealer. Depend upon his showing you furniture in which you may take deep pride—beautiful, well built, luxuriously finished, and moderately priced.

There is a Berkey & Gay pattern suited for every home—an infinite variety of styles at prices ranging all the way from $350 to $6000.

* * * * * *

Write to the Berkey & Gay Furniture Company, Grand Rapids, Michigan, for an interesting booklet, "Some of the Things That Make Furniture Values," which points out sixteen important features of construction that you should consider in selecting furniture for your home.

THIS SHOP MARK IS INSET IN EVERY BERKEY & GAY PRODUCTION

IT IS THE CUSTOMERS PROTECTION WHEN BUYING AND HIS PRIDE EVER AFTER

BERKEY & GAY FURNITURE CO.

Wholesale Showroom: 115 W. 40th St., New York City

Associated Companies

WALLACE FURNITURE CO. ~ GRAND RAPIDS UPHOLSTERING CO
GRAND RAPIDS MICHIGAN

[1925]

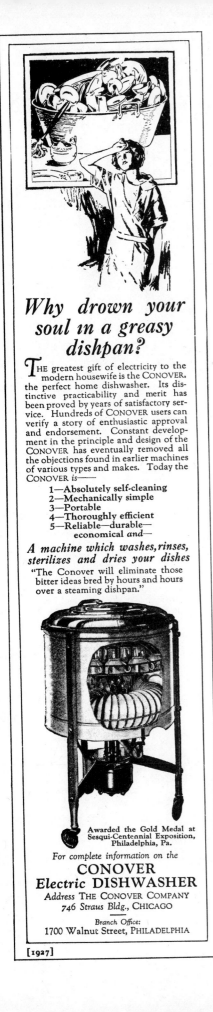

Make your Ice Box a Frigidaire

How Your Ice Box Is Quickly Converted Into a Frigidaire

1 *The frost coil is placed in the ice compartment of your refrigerator as shown above.*

2 *The compressor (shown below) is placed in the basement or other convenient location.*

3 *The frost coil and the compressor are connected by two small copper tubes, and a connection made to your electric wires.*

That's all. Your refrigerator becomes cold and stays cold.

You have Frigidaire electric refrigeration.

IT'S EASY. Frigidaire simply replaces the ice you now use. Your present ice box immediately gives you *electric* refrigeration. You enjoy the convenience, dependability and economy of Frigidaire.

Frigidaire maintains a constant, *dry* cold—keeps food fresh and wholesome in any weather—makes dainty ice cubes and delicious desserts—saves the possible annoyance of outside ice supply—adds greatly to the convenience of housekeeping. And Frigidaire is *not* expensive. In most localities its operation costs less than ice.

There are thirty household models of Frigidaire —eleven complete with cabinet, and nineteen designed for converting present refrigerators into Frigidaire. There are also Frigidaire models for stores, factories, hospitals, schools and apartments.

Frigidaire—pioneer electric refrigeration—is backed by the General Motors Corporation, and by a nation-wide organization of over 2,500 trained sales and service representatives.

Write for the Frigidaire book, "Colder than Ice." It gives complete information.

Prices:
(f.o.b Dayton O)
Frigidaire
complete with cabinet
$245 *up*

for converting present refrigerators into
Frigidaire
$190 *up*

To Salesmen—
There are a few openings in the Frigidaire Sales Organization for salesmen of experience and ability. The opportunity offered is one of a permanent and profitable business.

DELCO-LIGHT COMPANY
Subsidiary of General Motors Corporation
Dept. C-11, Dayton, Ohio

Makers of Delco-Light Farm Electric Plants, Electric Pumps, Electric Washing Machines, and Frigidaire Electric Refrigeration

PRODUCT OF GENERAL MOTORS

Frigidaire
ELECTRIC REFRIGERATION

[1925]

WHY
YOU SEE THIS
in Most New Homes

Majestic
Coal Window
The Mark of a Modern Home

You see the Majestic Coal Window in most new homes because it is the recognized leader of all coal windows. Builders know it protects the foundation and sidewalls when coal is delivered—saves grief and repair bills later. And they know that it is guaranteed breakproof—made of Certified Malleable Iron and Keystone Copper Steel —rust-proofed. No wonder more Majestics are in use than all other coal windows combined. When you buy or build you, too, will want the Majestic.

ANOTHER MAJESTIC PRODUCT
You'll Want in Your Home

A new convenience that costs but little— the Majestic Milk and Package Receiver. It receives deliveries from the outside—you remove them from within at your convenience. Saves steps—protects from annoyance, intrusion and theft. Outside door locks automatically when closed. Easily installed in old or new homes.

Write for catalog describing all styles of Majestic Coal Windows, Milk and Package Receivers, and many other Majestic Quality Products you will want in your home.

THE MAJESTIC COMPANY
1200 Erie Street, Huntington, Ind.

[1927]

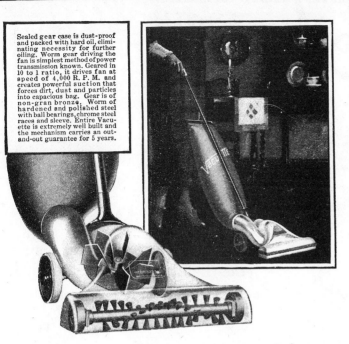

Sealed gear case is dust-proof and packed with hard oil, eliminating necessity for further oiling. Worm gear driving the fan is simplest method of power transmission known. Geared in 10 to 1 ratio, it drives fan at speed of 4,000 R. P. M. and creates powerful suction that forces dirt, dust and particles into capacious bag. Gear is of non-gran bronze. Worm of hardened and polished steel with ball bearings, chrome steel races and sleeve. Entire Vacuette is extremely well built and the mechanism carries an out-and-out guarantee for 5 years.

It's Easy to Vacuum Clean Without Electricity

JUST let a woman try the Vacuette on her own rugs and carpets and she wants it— right away. It's so light and easy to handle. It simplifies housekeeping so much. It's so thorough in its work.

It requires but little effort to glide the Vacuette over your floors. And that's all there's to it. For this remarkable vacuum cleaner operates without electricity. There are no connections to make and unmake. No heavy motor to push around. No trailing cord. No cost for current. No upkeep cost at all.

The Vacuette creates its own powerful suction that digs deep for hidden dirt. And the bristle brush revolving both forward and backward, takes up the surface litter—all of it. The ingeniously arranged bristles

weave in and out of the surface, loosening all embedded dirt, dust and litter and throws it directly into the path of the suction, to be drawn into the bag.

Over half a million American women have welcomed the Vacuette with open arms.

The Vacuette is remarkably inexpensive to buy. And it can be purchased on convenient time payments. A phone call to the Vacuette branch in your town will bring a Vacuette to your home for you to try without the slightest obligation. Or, write for our free booklet which describes the Vacuette in detail.

★ *Approved by Good Housekeeping* ✠
and Modern Priscilla

THE SCOTT & FETZER CO.
1922 W. 114th St.   Cleveland, Ohio
Vacuettes, Ltd., 48 York St., Toronto, Can.
*Vacuette Dist. Co. of Australia,
160 Castlereagh Street, Sydney.*

> *There's a remarkable opportunity for men of ambition and initiative to act as our county representatives, in charge of Vacuette sales. Hundreds of men are now earning far above the average income at this interesting, worthwhile occupation. Write for our booklet "Over the Hill to Better Things."*

Vacuette
non electric
VACUUM CLEANER

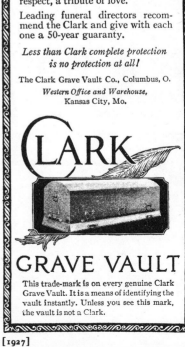

A GIFT OF THE CENTURIES

DOWN through countless centuries there has been slowly developing one of the great comforts for the human heart of today.

Scientists have searched out the secrets of Nature. Inventors have perfected metals. Mechanical experts have developed processes.

A quarter of a century ago these resulting factors were combined to provide at a reasonable cost the most positive and permanent burial protection ever known.

The immutable law of Nature which governed the designing of the Clark Grave Vault makes it absolutely positive in its protection. Not a particle of moisture can get inside.

And the use of perfected metals, Keystone copper steel, or Armco Ingot Iron, in heavy 12 gauge weight, gives permanence. In the quarter of a century this vault has been in use it has never failed.

Further, on the higher priced vaults there is added a plating of pure cadmium, by the Udylite process, which is exclusive on this vault. This results in the greatest rust-resistance known to science.

Representative families everywhere are demanding the Clark Grave Vault as a logical part of the burial equipment. It is a definite source of comfort in time of sorrow, a mark of respect, a tribute of love.

Leading funeral directors recommend the Clark and give with each one a 50-year guaranty.

*Less than Clark complete protection
is no protection at all!*

The Clark Grave Vault Co., Columbus, O.
Western Office and Warehouse,
Kansas City, Mo.

CLARK
GRAVE VAULT

This trade-mark is on every genuine Clark Grave Vault. It is a means of identifying the vault instantly. Unless you see this mark, the vault is not a Clark.

292

Now Comes – Simplified Electric Refrigeration

THE CREATION OF GENERAL ELECTRIC—
THE LEADING RESEARCH ORGANIZATION OF THE WORLD

THE GENERAL ELECTRIC ICING UNIT
is the revolutionary feature of new-day refrigeration.

* * *

THERE is now a new development in electric refrigeration for the home. An amazingly *simplified* icing unit by General Electric Company. A factor everyone, from now on, must take into account when considering an electric refrigerator. Electric refrigeration—above all things an *electrical* problem—has been solved *electrically* by the world's outstanding group of technical experts.

The General Electric icing unit is so supremely engineered and so precisely constructed that its operation is practically *noiseless* three feet from the refrigerator. It uses very little current and no special wiring is needed to hook it up—the regular house circuit is adequate.

The entire mechanism is housed in an hermetically sealed casing mounted on top of the cabinet. You *never* need oil it—*never* need touch it. It operates automatically, maintaining a *practically constant* temperature in the refrigerator.

Only an institution like General Electric Company—with its world-wide electrical resources—could have produced so outstanding an electrical achievement.

It marks 15 years of intensive research. Some 64 leading engineers cooperated in its development. Their goal was to

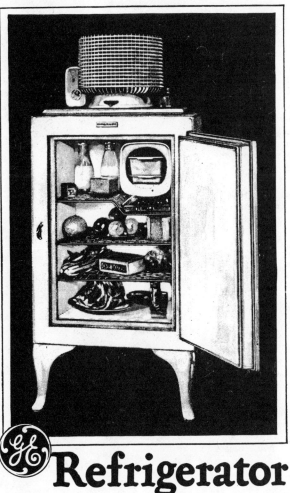

GE Refrigerator

Outstanding Advantages

Simplified—no pipes, no drains, no attachments. Portable—install anywhere. Just plug into nearest electric outlet and it starts.

Quiet—three feet away you can hardly hear it.

No Servicing—never needs oiling or attention. All moving parts are enclosed in an hermetically sealed housing.

Economical—uses very little current and maintains uniform temperature.

Clean—the circulation of air through the coils drives dust away from the top of the refrigerator.

Guaranteed by General Electric

* * *

produce the *simplest,* most *practical* electric refrigerator Electrical Science could achieve. Several thousand refrigerators —of 19 different designs—were built, field-tested and improved before production of the models now announced, was authorized. They embody the best thought of the leading electrical research organization of the world.

* * *

Now thousands who have debated the purchase of electric refrigeration will want to see this new creation, will wish to find out what General Electric has done in the field. Buying any other way is a mistake.

Remember that the efficiency of any electric refrigerator you may purchase rests basically on its efficiency as an *electrical* device.

The General Electric Refrigerator is obtainable in various sizes suitable for every home. Different models are now on display at lighting companies and dealers everywhere.

Write for Booklet No. 6-A. It tells all about this new-day refrigerator.

Electric Refrigeration Department
of General Electric Company
Hanna Building, Cleveland, Ohio

GENERAL ELECTRIC

[1927]

The song that STOPPED !

A CHILD of five skipped down the garden path and laughed because the sky was blue. "Jane," called her mother from the kitchen window, "come here and help me bake your birthday cake." Little feet sped. "Don't fall," her mother warned.

Jane stood in the kitchen door and wrinkled her nose in joy. Her gingham dress was luminous against the sun. What a child! Dr. and Mrs. Wentworth cherished Jane.

"Go down cellar and get mother some preserves . . . the kind you like."

"The preserves are in the cellar," she chanted, making a progress twice around the kitchen. "Heigh-ho a-derry-o, the preserves are . . ." her voice grew fainter as she danced off. ". . . in the . . ."

The thread of song snapped. A soft thud-thud. Fear fluttered Mrs. Wentworth's heart. She rushed to the cellar door.

"Mother!" . . . a child screaming in pain. Mrs. Wentworth saw a little morsel of girlhood lying in a heap of gingham and yellow hair at the bottom of the dark stairs.

The sky is still blue. But there will be no birthday party tomorrow. An ambulance clanged up to Dr. Wentworth's house today. Jane's leg is broken.

If a flashlight had been hanging on a hook at the head of the cellar stairs, this little tragedy would have been averted. If Jane had been taught to use a flashlight as carefully as her father, Dr. Wentworth, had taught her to use a tooth-brush, a life need not have been endangered.

An Eveready Flashlight is always a convenience and often a life-saver. Keep one about the house, in the car; and take one with you wherever you go. Keep it supplied with fresh Eveready Batteries — the longest-lasting flashlight batteries made. Eveready Flashlights, $1.00 up.

NATIONAL CARBON CO., INC.
New York   UCC   San Francisco
Unit of Union Carbide and Carbon Corporation

[1927]

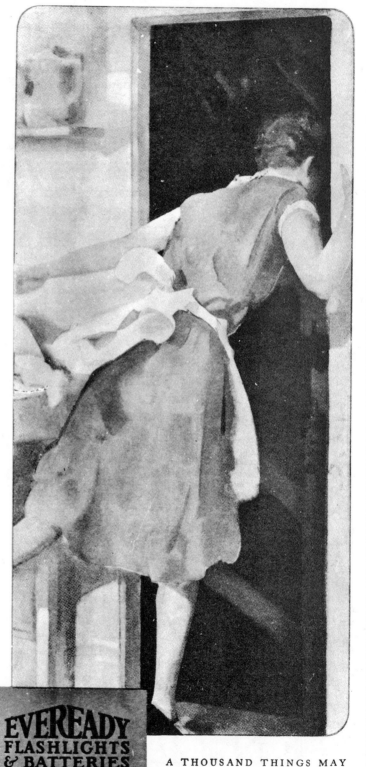

EVEREADY
FLASHLIGHTS
& BATTERIES
—they last longer

A THOUSAND THINGS MAY
HAPPEN IN THE DARK

The Improved QUIET SI-WEL-CLO

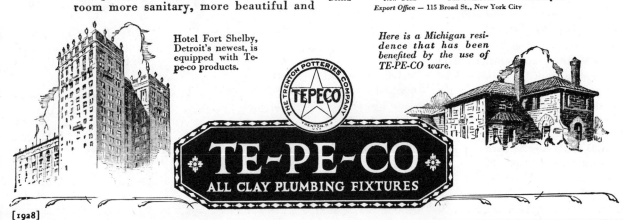

Shaped—
to conform to Natures Laws.....

MEDICAL science influenced the unique shape of the Improved Quiet Si-wel-clo. Authorities have agreed that a seat should encourage a natural sitting position. It stands to reason that the organs and muscles of elimination are not easily stimulated to action if forced into a position never intended by nature.

The exceeding comfort of the Si-wel-clo saddle seat minimizes the unhygienic tendency, especially noticeable in children, to grudge sufficient time for proper elimination. The decided dip in the rim elevates the front and rear of the bowl opening, reducing the possibility of soiling.

The Quiet Si-wel-clo water-closet makes a bathroom more sanitary, more beautiful and quieter. Dripping and gurgling sounds which emanate from ordinary water-closets are almost absent.

The Si-wel-clo is one of many charming and durable plumbing fixtures belonging to the TE-PE-CO family. They all carry the star in the circle trade mark as a guarantee of superb quality. Look for it whenever you equip a bathroom or kitchen. For your guidance we shall send you our booklet "Bathrooms of Character" upon receipt of 10¢ in stamps.

THE TRENTON POTTERIES COMPANY
Trenton, New Jersey, U. S. A.

Boston   New York   San Francisco   Philadelphia

Export Office — 115 Broad St., New York City

Hotel Fort Shelby, Detroit's newest, is equipped with Te-pe-co products.

Here is a Michigan residence that has been benefited by the use of TE-PE-CO ware.

TE-PE-CO
THE TRENTON POTTERIES COMPANY
TEPECO
TRENTON. N.J. U.S.A.

ALL CLAY PLUMBING FIXTURES

[1928]

TEENIE WEENIE

© 1925, R., M. & Co.

The TEENIE WEENIES go in the Pickle Business!

There was a mystery in the Teenie Weenie village. The little folks, no taller than a half used lead pencil, puckered up their tiny brows and did a great deal of thinking.

The General, who was the head of the Teenie Weenie clan, had been mighty busy for some days. Several times he had mounted his riding mouse, and galloped away on some mysterious errand.

"I'll bet you a grape seed the General's got something up his sleeve besides his arm," remarked the Dunce as he stretched himself out under a shady dandelion, beside the Sailor.

"Of course he has," said the Sailor, who was carving a set of wee fingerbowls out of cherry stones. "He'll tell us when he's ready, and I'll bet it'll be something worth listening to."

"Well, I'm ready to listen right now," said the Dunce with a yawn. And resting his head on one of the cherry stones he fell asleep.

That evening, word was passed about the village that the General wanted all the Teenie Weenies to meet in the old Derby hat, which served the little folks as a school house.

An hour before the appointed time the old hat was filled nearly to the crown with curious Teenie Weenies.

"Friends," said the General, as at last he stepped out onto the platform, "I have news for you—we are going into the pickle business!"

"*Pickle business!*" shouted the surprised Teenie Weenies.

"Yes, the pickle business," answered the General. "We are going to put Teenie Weenie Sweet Pickles on the market. I have a contract here that I am going to read to you."

"Yes, do—go on!" cried the excited little people.

"Well, then," began the General, "here it is." He unfolded a bit of paper no bigger than a postage stamp. It was filled with writing so small that a big person could not possibly have read it without the use of powerful magnifying glasses.

The General held up his hand again for silence, as the eager little people were buzzing like a hive of bees.

"We, the Teenie Weenies," read the General, "agree to furnish small sweet pickles of the highest quality, to be known as Monarch Teenie Weenie Sweets. These pickles we agree to select with care, and prepare in the cleanest possible way. We also agree to build Teenie Weenie barrels, in which the Teenie Weenie pickles are to be packed. We further agree that the barrels shall be made of selected hard-wood and bound with silvered hoops. These barrels we agree to make so strong that big boys and girls can play with them for years after they have eaten the pickles."

When the General had finished reading the contract, he beckoned to the Cook, who came staggering onto the platform with a Teenie Weenie pickle on his back. He dropped it onto the table, and began to cut it into pieces with a huge knife nearly an inch long.

The Turk quickly passed the pieces to the Teenie Weenies who ate them greedily, and all the little folks decided that they were the best they had ever tasted.

"That's the kind of pickle we are going to put up in quantities," said the General, after everyone had eaten a piece. "Now," he continued. "All those who wish to work in this new business, please stand up."

All the Teenie Weenies jumped to their feet, even the Dunce, who was fast asleep, managing to rise.

"Well, well, it looks as if you all wanted to go into the growing and packing of pickles," smiled the General, "so I will sign the contract."

Taking his tiny fountain pen from his pocket, the General signed the contract. "There," he said, as he carefully blotted his signature, "we are in the pickle business now, sure enough!"

And the little people gave three rousing cheers.

The Teenie Weenies set to work first at making the barrels. That was quite a task, for the barrels were to be seven and three-quarter inches high, which is fifteen and a half feet, Teenie Weenie measurement, a Teenie Weenie foot being half an inch according to our scale.

Some of the little men set up a sawmill and cut the wood into staves and barrel heads, while others made the beautifully silvered hoops. The Cook kept a huge kettle of wax heated with which the inside of the barrel was coated to make it airtight.

Every one of the little folks worked—even the Lady of Fashion helped, for she is extremely neat, and she watched to see that everything was done in the cleanest way possible.

"It certainly takes an awful lot of work to build these barrels," said the old Soldier, as he and the General stood watching the Teenie men put a barrel together.

"Yes, it does," answered the General, thoughtfully. "But it is worth while to do it well, for there are many boys and girls in this great world who are going to get a lot of pleasure out of these Teenie Weenie barrels, both while they have pickles in them, and after they're empty."

OUR HIGHEST QUALITY
TRADE MARK REG.

"SAFE AT HOME" *yet*

the door-knobs threaten them with the danger of disease

BRIGHT eyes and happy greeting! Mothers have a satisfied feeling when they know their children are "safe at home," out of the danger of traffic and questionable companions. And yet we now know that even the most innocent-appearing objects may be fraught with the dangers of unnecessary illness to children who are "safe" within their own homes.

Health authorities tell us that disease germs are everywhere. Door-knobs, chair-arms, banisters—a hundred places around the home that big and little hands must touch daily—carry the germs of illness. 3,000,000 people in the United States are sick every day. And yet much of this illness is *preventable*.

A campaign to protect health

THROUGHOUT the country mothers, teachers, doctors, Health Officers, are uniting in a health-campaign to prevent unnecessary contagion, and safeguard health. The Health Officers of 365 cities, in a recent report, advocate as an important measure in this campaign *the regular use of a reliable disinfectant in all your weekly cleaning water.*

"Do you disinfect these important places?" ask the Health Officers

EVERYBODY, the Health Officers say, disinfects the garbage pail, drain pipes, toilet bowl. But do you also disinfect these other important danger-spots, door-jambs, chair-arms, tables, banisters, and telephone mouth-pieces? Soap and water are not enough to destroy the germs on these surfaces. You must have a trustworthy disinfectant to drive germs out of your home.

"Lysol" Disinfectant is the standard disinfectant for this important weekly cleaning, the disinfectant used by physicians everywhere. Three times stronger than powerful carbolic acid, yet so carefully is it blended that in proper proportion it is not harsh for the most sensitive hands.

Use one tablespoonful to a quart of water. Its deodorant qualities and soapy nature help to clean as it disinfects.

Get "Lysol" at your druggists. The 16 ounce size is most economical. Be sure you get the genuine "Lysol."

MADE by LYSOL, INCORPORATED, a division of Lehn & Fink Products Company. Sole Distributors, Lehn & Fink, Inc., Bloomfield, N. J. Canadian Offices: 9 Davies Avenue, Toronto.

SEND FOR THIS *FREE* "Lysol" HEALTH LIBRARY

Three helpful, interesting volumes on keeping well: "Health Safeguards in the Home," "The Scientific Side of Youth and Beauty" and "When Baby Comes." You will enjoy reading and owning them. Send coupon for free set.

Lysol
Reg. U.S. Pat. Off.
and in Canada
Disinfectant

LEHN & FINK, Inc., *Sole Distributors*, Dept. AB-4, Bloomfield, N. J.

Name_____

Street_____

City_____ State_____
(Please print name and address plainly)

[1926]

in FLORIDA

Hollywood summer excursions by boat and rail offer wonderful vacation opportunities

YOUR SUMMER VACATION

Mail This Coupon Today
HOLLYWOOD RESORT AND INDUSTRIAL BOARD
Hollywood, in Florida
Please mail me full information about low cost summer excursions to Florida, with free illustrated folders.

Name _____

Street _____

City_____ State_____

[1926]

300

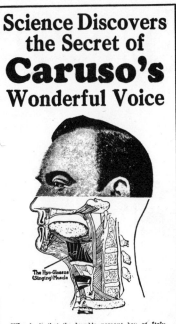

ATWATER KENT RADIO

In the summer home of BOOTH TARKINGTON is the *Atwater Kent Model 20 Compact* This Receiving Set is priced at eighty dollars.

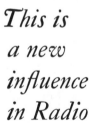

MODEL 10 (without tubes)—$80

RADIO SPEAKERS priced from $12 to $28

MODEL 20 — $80

Prices slightly higher from the Rockies west, and in Canada

This is a new influence in Radio

In many ways the Atwater Kent Model 20 Compact is a new influence in the progress of radio.

It is unobtrusive. It takes its place gracefully on a small table, a book rack or any other small piece of furniture, for it is a fine, simple electrical instrument only 6½ inches high and 19¾ inches long—no larger than a row of a dozen books.

So now Radio needn't disturb any room. You can fit it agreeably into your present arrangement of furniture and decorations, without buying anything new.

Already the Model 20 Compact has won its place in the fine homes of many famous people. It is the radio of today—and of tomorrow.

Write for illustrated booklet telling the complete story of Atwater Kent Radio.

ATWATER KENT MANUFACTURING CO.
A. Atwater Kent, President
4702 WISSAHICKON AVENUE · PHILADELPHIA, PA.

Hear the Atwater Kent Radio Artists every Sunday evening at 9.15 o'clock (eastern standard time) through stations—

WEAF	New York
WJAR	Providence
WEEI	Boston
WFI	Philadelphia
WCCO	Minneapolis-St. Paul
WCAE	Pittsburgh
WGR	Buffalo
WWJ	Detroit
WSAI	Cincinnati
WOC	Davenport
WCAP	Washington

Take it wherever you go!

UNDER a tree, on a mountain top—tune in. Out on the sea, lazing coolly on the deck—tune in! And off for a motor trip, put into the car one more suitcase—a Radiola Super-Heterodyne *complete*. Its loudspeaker is built-in, its loop in the cover, its batteries inside!

The Radiola Super-Heterodyne is made, now, in two portable models. It is the same far-famed "Super-Het"—with the same fine quality of tone—the same complete simplicity —the same distance performance. But it is portable now —and you can take your entertainment with you every- where!

Radio Corporation of America

Chicago　　　　　　　New York　　　　　　San Francisco

Radiola

REG. U.S. PAT. OFF.

PRODUCED ONLY BY RCA　　RCA

Radiola 24
Built in a suitcase of black cowhide, cobra grain. Open ready for use. And closed for carrying. With 6 Radiotrons UV-199 - - - $195

Radiola 26
Finished in Walnut. Complete for carrying. And with an extra bat- tery cabinet for home use. With 6 Radiotrons UV-199 - - - $225

[1925]

LOOK!

Run Any Radio from your Electric Current

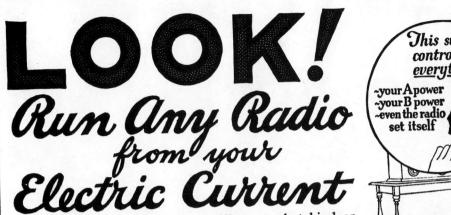

This switch controls everything

~your A power
~your B power
~even the radio set itself

All in ONE Cabinet

And remember, it makes no difference what kind or what make radio set you have, PHILCO Socket Powers will give you both A and B radio power from your electric light current—*dependably and constantly.* Here is your opportunity to do away with the ordinary "A" storage battery, dry cell batteries, and "B" batteries.

One switch controls everything. Snap it "ON" and from your house current you get a strong, steady flow of A and B power. Snap it "OFF" and your radio is silent.

No Hum No Distortion

Philco Socket Powers will give you radio reception without the least hum; without the least distortion. Your electric lighting current will now operate your radio set smoothly and perfectly—*any kind or any make of set.*

No more recharging to do; no more dry batteries to replace; no more fuss; no more bother, and better still, improved reception. *Everything contained in ONE Cabinet.*

Yours On Very Easy Payments

You can buy a PHILCO AB Socket Power on *Easy Payment Terms* from any Philco dealer in your town. You merely make a small first payment—balance monthly.

Go to your Electrical Dealer, Department Store, Electric Light Company, Music Dealer or Battery Service Station; tell them you read this advertisement and you want the PHILCO RADIO SOCKET POWER.

Installation FREE

No matter where you live there is almost sure to be an authorized PHILCO dealer near you who will deliver a brand-new Philco Socket Power to your home on the day and hour you desire. He will connect it to your radio set *at no additional cost to you.*

The Philco dealer in your community guarantees you complete satisfaction.

Trade In Your Old Storage Battery

Yes, any one of the many thousands of Philco dealers will make you a very liberal trade-in allowance for your old "A" storage battery on the purchase of a brand-new Philco Radio AB Socket Power.

It makes no difference what make of "A" storage battery you now have or how old or worn out it may be, the Philco dealer will give you a surprisingly liberal allowance.

Mail This Coupon Now

Visit the Philco dealer, or if you prefer, mail this coupon to us and we will give you the full details direct from the factory. We will send you complete information on our Easy Payment Plan and Trade-In Allowance offer for your old storage battery.

Sign your name and address to this coupon, and mail it to us today. The coupon is not an order. It does not place you under the slightest obligation. It is merely a request for the full details and free illustrated literature describing these famous Philco Socket Powers.

Philadelphia Storage Battery Co.
Philadelphia, Pa.
Dept. 1093

PHILCO Radio "AB" Socket Power

© H.B.B.

[1927]

305

Powered by Lycoming

The Cord car creates a place for itself
no other car has ever occupied.

CORD FRONT DRIVE

SEDAN $3095 · *BROUGHAM* $3095 · *CABRIOLET* $3295 · *PHAETON* $3295

Prices: F. O. B. Auburn, Indiana. *Equipment other than standard extra*

AUBURN AUTOMOBILE COMPANY · AUBURN, INDIANA

How Often Do You Buy a War Tax?

EACH time you buy a motor car you pay for five things in which you never can take a ride:

These are: war tax—freight charge—factory's profit—dealer's profit — salesman's commission.

Once every five years or more is often enough to afford yourself the luxury of such purchases.

Those who buy the Packard Six expect, on the average, to keep their cars more than five years, spending the minimum in war tax and other outside charges.

Packard encourages its owners in keeping their cars, through retaining the beauty of Packard lines and in announcing no yearly models. It is now more than ten years since Packard offered yearly models.

The most recent evidence of Packard's interest in its owners is the chassis lubricator and motor oil rectifier, found only in Packard cars. Together they double the life of the car.

The Packard Six Five-passenger Sedan is illustrated—$2585 at Detroit. Packard Six and Packard Eight both are furnished in nine body types, four open and five enclosed. Packard distributers and dealers welcome the buyer who prefers to purchase his Packard out of income instead of capital.

PACKARD

The PACKARD SIX

ASK THE MAN WHO OWNS ONE

[1925]

The World's Most

Luxurious
Low-Priced Automobile

Never before has a low-priced automobile exhibited such marvelous beauty, such interior smartness and completeness of appointment, as the Bigger and Better Chevrolet.

Built on a 107-inch wheelbase—4 inches longer than before—equipped with non-locking 4-wheel brakes and incorporating scores of vital contributions to every phase of motoring enjoyment, this great new car completely revolutionizes every existing standard of luxury in the low-price field.

You will be delighted with a ride in this beautiful car. Your Chevrolet dealer will be glad to arrange a demonstration.

The Roadster, $495; The Touring, $495; The Coach, $585; The Coupe, $595; The 4-Door Sedan, $675; The Sport Cabriolet, $665; The Imperial Landau, $715; Utility Truck (Chassis only) $495; Light Delivery (Chassis only) $375. All prices f. o. b. Flint, Mich.

CHEVROLET MOTOR COMPANY, DETROIT, MICHIGAN
Division of General Motors Corporation

Chevrolet
Enclosed Cars
with
Bodies by
FISHER

Bigger
and
Better

The $585
COACH
f. o. b. Flint, Mich.

QUALITY AT LOW COST

[1928]

Fresh and relaxed at the journey's end

ONE of the fine things about driving the new Ford is the way it takes you over the miles without fuss or fatigue.

Mentally you are at ease because you are sure of the mechanical performance of the car. No matter how long the trip, or rough or devious the roadway, you know it will bring you safely, quickly, to the journey's end.

Through thickest traffic, up steepest hills, along the open road, you will drive with security and confidence because the new Ford is so alert and capable and so easy to operate and control.

The steering wheel responds readily to a light touch. Gears shift smoothly and silently. The brakes take hold quickly and firmly even on rain-swept pavements.

Unusual acceleration, speed and power are especially appreciated in emergencies. A space little longer than the car itself is all you need for parking.

These features simplify the mechanics of driving and, together with reliability, add a great deal to the mental comfort of motoring.

Physically, too, you will feel fresh and relaxed in the new Ford because it is such a roomy, easy-riding car. The restfully tilted seats are generously wide and deeply cushioned, with coil

springs of both straight and hour-glass type. The backs are carefully designed to conform to the curves of the body.

Perhaps the most outstanding feature of the new Ford is found in its riding comfort. Somehow it seems to just glide along, as if every road were a good road. The rough spots are there, just as they have always been, but you do not feel them. It is almost as if a giant hand had smoothed the way before you. Even bad stretches may be taken at a reasonably fast pace without hard jolts or bumps or the exaggerated bouncing rebound which is the cause of most motoring fatigue.

One reason, of course, is the use of four Houdaille

Attractive colors give added charm to the trim graceful lines of the new Ford. Shown above is the new Ford Roadster in andalusite blue. On the left, the Fordor Sedan in rose beige.

hydraulic double-acting shock absorbers—two in the front and two in the rear. Of even greater importance, however, are the low center of gravity, the carefully planned balance of the car, and the many advantages of the transverse or crosswise springs.

These springs rest on their flexible ends with the heavy center part uppermost. Thus the very weight of the springs receives the benefit of spring action instead of hanging below as dead weight and increasing the hammer-like blows of road impacts.

Another element in decreasing unsprung weight (weight below the flexible ends of the springs) is the design and construction of the front axle and rear axle housing. Through the use of fine steel and electric welding, they are made of exceptional strength, yet kept comparatively light in weight. All of these factors, by reducing the force of every unevenness in the road, combine to give greater riding comfort, and contribute to better performance and longer life for every mechanical part.

FORD MOTOR COMPANY
Detroit, Michigan

BUICK

THE records of two million Buicks
—and the fact that motorists buy more than twice
as many Buicks as any other car priced above $1200
—reflect the policy of progress and permanence which
has enabled Buick to lead year after year

Dedicated from the dawn of the industry to a policy of progress—yet steadfastly adhering to those sound manufacturing practices which spell true goodness and reliability—Buick has enjoyed worldwide recognition as a builder of quality automobiles throughout a quarter of a century.

More than two million Buicks have been produced ... the first million in twenty years, the second million in four years. More than 1,500,000 of this twenty-five year total are still serving their owners. More than 80% of Buick owners buy Buicks again. And, as a final proof of leadership, more than twice as many people purchase Buicks year after year as any other automobile listing above $1200. Buick ideals, Buick policies and principles have won steadily increasing confidence and good will, until today Buick is recognized as the standard of comparison by the millions of motor car buyers in the Buick market.

The builders of Buick will continue to hold true to their trust. They will tread their chosen path of progress and of sound manufacture in the future as they have in the past. The public may rely to the fullest degree upon the integrity of Buick ideals as well as upon the permanence of the Buick pledge, "When better automobiles are built, Buick will build them."

GENERAL
MOTORS

SPRING
SHOWING

PONTIAC

$\mathcal{T}$HE New Pontiac Big Six, built by Oakland, exemplifies the value offered in General Motors Products—providing a car of exceptional beauty, performance, comfort and size at prices ranging from $745 to $895

The New Pontiac Big Six is built to appeal to those progressive people who want to step up the quality of their automobiles without stepping out of the low-price field.

Its big car performance is achieved through the use of numerous engineering advancements typified by a larger L-head engine with the G-M-R cylinder head, counterweighted crankshaft, Harmonic Balancer and adjustable full-pressure oiling system; the cross-flow radiator; a balanced line of drive and noiseless, dirt-and-weatherproof internal four-wheel brakes. Additional features include gasoline pump, larger carburetor, rattleproof spring shackles—and Lovejoy hydraulic shock absorbers at slight extra cost. Combined with this mechanical excellence is the big car beauty resulting from an overall length of 167 inches and new bodies by Fisher introducing the distinctive concave belt moulding. Fisher contributions to Pontiac's comfort, luxury and value include adjustable drivers' seats, Ternstedt period appointments and upholsteries of special weave.

The New Pontiac Big Six is clearly something new and different—a car offering every element of luxury, style and performance desired by that great group of progressive people who have been seeking a finer, low-priced automobile.

2-Door Sedan . .	$745
Coupe	745
Roadster	775
Phaeton . , . .	825
Convertible Cabriolet . , . .	845
4-Door Sedan . .	845

(Shown above—wire wheels extra)

Landaulet Sedan .	895

All prices f. o. b. Pontiac, Mich. plus delivery charges.

Spring covers, bumper, and rear fender guards regular equipment at slight extra cost.

Purchases may be arranged on the convenient G. M. A. C. Purchase Plan

GENERAL MOTORS 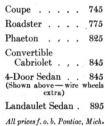 SPRING SHOWING

[1929]

PIERCE-ARROW

announces

lowest prices

in its history

Never were Pierce-Arrow motor cars so *distinctive* and *aristocratic* as they are today. ℂ Never before has it cost so little to own and operate a Pierce-Arrow. ℂ Yet on account of the price reduction just made, the *Series 80* five-passenger Brougham is now selling at $2495 at Buffalo—tax extra. ℂ Other popular models of the *Series 80* line are also priced below any previous figure.

5-Passenger Brougham

Now $2495

—*a reduction of* $500!

The Runabout, *now* $2495—*a reduction of* $400!

Also new low prices on the 5-passenger Standard Sedan and the 4-passenger Coupe

All prices at Buffalo, N. Y., tax extra

Pierce-Arrow *Series 80* cars have hand-hammered aluminum bodies covered with 14 coats of nitro-cellulose lacquer. Luxurious appointments . . . silver finish hardware . . . handsome vanity cases. Wide range of color and upholstery choices. 70-horsepower engine . . . Houdaille double-acting shock absorbers . . . special Pierce-Arrow four-wheel safety brakes. 14 to 17 miles per gallon of gasoline, 15,000 to 18,000 miles per set of tires. Nation-wide Pierce-Arrow flat-rate service effects great operating economy.

Pierce-Arrow *terms* are also notably liberal. One can purchase his car largely out of income if he chooses. Only a reasonable first payment is required. Select your favorite model now—from the Pierce-Arrow dealer in your community. A courteous demonstrator is at your command.

THE PIERCE-ARROW MOTOR CAR COMPANY, *Buffalo, N. Y.*

The AIRPLANE FEEL of the Franklin opens the road to new motoring thrills

You are driving the Franklin for the first time. "Incomparable," you say, as you start ahead in second speed, mounting to fifty-five miles an hour—as quietly as in high. There's a short, easy shift to high and you are even more thrilled! Actually you feel as though you were piloting an airplane. Such a surge of power. The acceleration is amazingly fast. How smooth —like a gliding gull. Relax—you can be more relaxed in the Franklin than in any other car. The riding comfort is truly restful. *Effortlessly and confidently* you control the car.

Air-cooling has made all this possible. Franklin is first to introduce such a revolutionary and different motor car. Will you drive it? We promise you will not only enjoy it—but you will instantly become a life member of the large and rapidly increasing group of Franklin enthusiasts.

FRANKLIN AUTOMOBILE COMPANY, SYRACUSE

The One-Thirty, $2180 ▾ ▾ ▾ The One-Thirty-Five, $2485 ▾ ▾ ▾ The One-Thirty-Seven, $2775 ▾ ▾ ▾ Sedan prices f. o. b. factory

FRANKLIN

[1929]

"*They said father didn't keep his Life Insurance paid up!*"

THE PRUDENTIAL INSURANCE COMPANY *of* AMERICA

EDWARD D. DUFFIELD, *President*   HOME OFFICE, *Newark. N.J.*

THE PRUDENTIAL HAS THE STRENGTH OF GIBRALTAR

[1926]

"I'd Like to Know *that* Man!"

Of course they would. Everyone would like to know a man so brilliant, so entertaining. They see how interesting and well-informed he is. But they don't know the story behind the man.

"I WONDER who he is? Let's ask!" They turned to his friend, Rollins.

"His name is Davis," he said.

"Isn't he interesting! How well he talks. I could listen to a man like that all evening!"

"Oh, come!" Rollins laughed, "You two would probably find him a bore after the first hour."

"A bore? Just listen to him! He seems to know about everything. See how he's holding those people fascinated."

"He must be highly educated. Isn't he, Mr. Rollins?"

As a matter of fact, *Davis never even finished elementary school!* His friend, Rollins, listening to him, was astonished. How had Davis suddenly become so well-informed? How had he suddenly developed this brilliant personality?

He spoke to him about it later—as one friend to another. "I say, Davis, how did you get this way? You must certainly read a lot."

Davis laughed. "You know how busy I am, Rolly. I don't get much time to read."

"But in this one evening you quoted from Dante, Browning, Kipling, Poe! How do you do it?"

"I try to make the most of what little time I have. I read the newspapers and magazines to keep up-to-date on current events. And once in a great while I browse through some of my favorite old classics. But for most of my reading I depend upon one volume alone—the Elbert Hubbard Scrap Book."

Elbert Hubbard's Scrap Book? What's That?

"Hubbard was a many-sided genius—writer, orator, craftsman. He began to keep a scrap book when he was quite young. He put into it all the bits of writing that inspired and helped him most. He kept this scrap book all through life, adding whatever he thought great and inspiring. As it grew, it became Hubbard's greatest source of ideas. He turned to it constantly; it helped him win fame as a writer and orator. At the time of his death on the sinking of the Lusitania, it had become a priceless collection of great thoughts—the fruit of a whole lifetime of discriminating reading."

"But what can this private scrap book mean to you? How can you—*use* it—as you say?"

"It was published after his death. Now anyone can buy it for the price of an ordinary best seller. I have a copy."

"So that's your secret! That's why you can talk so well on so many different subjects! That Elbert Hubbard Scrap Book has made you a popular man, Davis. The women just hung on your words tonight. You've become mighty interesting."

Examine It Free

The Elbert Hubbard Scrap Book contains ideas, thoughts, passages, excerpts, poems, epigrams—selected from the master thinkers of all ages. It represents the best of a lifetime of discriminating reading, contains choice selections from 500 great writers.

This Scrap Book is a fine example of Roycroft bookmaking. The type is set Venetian style—a page within a page—printed in two colors on fine tinted book paper. Bound scrap-book style and tied with linen tape.

The coupon entitles you to the special five-day examination. Send it off today, and the famous Elbert Hubbard Scrap Book will go forward to you promptly. When it arrives glance through it. If you aren't inspired, enchanted—simply return the Scrap Book within the five-day period and the examination will have cost you nothing. Otherwise send only $2.90 plus few cents postage in *full payment.*

You are the judge. Clip and mail this coupon NOW. Wm. H. Wise & Co., Roycroft Distributors, Dept. 810, 50 West 47th Street, New York City.

[1926]

A Corn cost him his job

He was called the best natured man on the pay-roll. Nothing ever seemed to faze his good humor. In a touchy situation, his tact and cool headedness were never known to fail.

Then came the amazing blow-up.

A testy old customer said some riley things—and Jenkins lost his temper.

Not even the most genial disposition can withstand the constant strain of an aching corn. It isn't only the local pain. It's the reaction to the whole nervous system. It makes a man feel mean all over, and act that way. But for business' sake, as well as comfort's sake, end that corn with Blue=jay. It stops the pain in ten seconds —and ends the corn itself in 48 hours.

Blue=jay

Business men appreciate Blue=jay particularly because it is so scientifically efficient. It leaves nothing to the user's guess-work. You do not have to decide how much or how little to put on. Each plaster is a complete standardized treatment—and it does the work.

THE QUICK AND GENTLE WAY TO END A CORN

© 1925 [1925]

One purpose ROOMS *make houses too* BIG

There is only one In-a-Dor Bed — *the* MURPHY

MANY houses built today are too big. They have too many one-purpose rooms and too much space to heat. The owners have too much furniture to buy, too much tax to pay, too much house to keep for the living accommodations provided.

One room, equipped with a Murphy In-a-Dor Bed, gives the service of two in an old type house. The sleeping porch is an upstairs sun room by day. The den or living room becomes a guest room in reserve. One room serves as a playroom and children's bedroom, leaving the living room free from the toys and noise of romping children.

Behind any standard three-foot door there may be a wonderfully comfortable full size Murphy In-a-Dor Bed, that does not interfere with the constant use of its concealing closet as wardrobe or dressing room.

Surprising, to those not informed, is the harmony between a Murphy In-a-Dor Bed and the other furniture. Authentic styles and beautiful finishes

may be selected for any scheme of furnishing, from simple to lavish. Surprising, too, is the ease with which a Murphy In-a-Dor Bed is swung on its pivot and lowered, balanced by special springs, to solid rest upon the floor. Installation, also, is easy. No special con-

struction is needed. Nothing gets out of order.

Murphy In-a-Dor Beds exemplify modern efficiency. They cut the cost of homes — in single or in multiple dwellings—without affecting the living capacity. Follow the trend of home building. Build as though you expect to live in your home forever. Build as though you intend to sell your home tomorrow.

MURPHY DOOR BED COMPANY

Valuable Book Free

Write for "More Home in Less Space." Full color illustrations show all styles and finishes of Murphy In-a-Dor Beds and pictures them fitted into various rooms of differing decorative schemes.

If you are planning to build or to invest in any type of residential building you should get and read this book. Write for it, today.

THE MURPHY IN-A-DOR BED

[1928]

NORTHWEST AT 125 MILES AN HOUR!

Features of Ford Plane

All-metal (corrugated aluminum alloys)—for strength, uniformity of material, durability, economy of maintenance, and structural safety . . .

Tri-motored (Wright or Pratt & Whitney air-cooled engines, totaling from 900 to 1275 horse-power)—reserve power for safety.

Speed range—55 to 135 m. p. h. Cruising radius, 580-650 miles.

Disposable load—3670 to 5600 pounds.

High wing monoplane (single, stream-lined, cantilever wing) — for strength, speed, inherent stability, visibility, clean design . . .

17 capacity (including pilot's dual-control cabin) —Buffet, toilet, running-water, electric lights, etc.

Durability—No Ford plane has yet worn out in service.

Price, $42,000 to $55,000 (standard equipped at Dearborn)—Exceptionally low because of multiple-unit on-line production methods.

Air passengers entering Northwest Airways Ford plane at Cicero Field, Chicago. Time, 3 P. M. They will be in Twin Cities, after a smooth, safe, glorious flight, at 6.40 P. M.! Modern air fields line the entire route.

Above the Twin Cities after gliding high in the air across some of the most beautiful and romantic country in America.

SPEED is an important consideration . . . but it is only one of many reasons that have made the Northwest Airways one of the most successful transportation companies in America, whether by land or sea or air.

This service, flying the skyways between Chicago and Twin Cities, was inaugurated in 1926, and has been in operation ever since, carrying mail, fast express and passengers. 95% of scheduled flights were completed!

Latest model Ford all-metal, tri-motored planes are now in regular service on the Northwest Airways. These big machines, with great reserve power, have three motors, developing 1275 horse-power! With twelve passengers and pilots, they can maintain a comfortable speed of over 100 miles an hour, and reach a maximum speed of 135 miles an hour. *With only one engine turning, each of these planes may extend its gliding range for many miles. Landing fields are always within gliding distance.*

All planes are delightfully furnished and decorated. Travelers are provided with every comfort, including a lavatory with running-water; so that this swift passage across the sky may be enjoyed in mental and physical relaxation.

The Northwest Airways pioneered in the establishment of co-ordinated air-rail service in this country. Connection is made with six railroads, three of which operate from the West and Northwest and three from the East.

Ford all-metal, tri-motored planes have been put into service over this great skyway not only because the air-minded American public recognizes them as safe and dependable commercial air transports, but also because they have proved so highly efficient in all sorts of service.

Visitors are always welcome at the Ford Airport at Detroit.

[1929]

FORD MOTOR COMPANY

HE THOUGHT:
*"How absolutely
lovely she is
tonight!"*

SHE THOUGHT:
*"How glad I am
I washed my hair
and changed to
this fresh dress!"*

Real cleanliness is the greatest beauty secret!

What is it that puts high-lights in your hair...glints of gold or copper? What is it gives your skin the vivid pinkness that even great painters find difficult to get on canvas? What is it that transforms the simplest summer frock ...makes it *charming?*

The answer, of course, is *real cleanliness.*

It isn't that we do not know these things. The question is, do we make *use* of this great aid to beauty as much as we might and should?

What doctors say about shampooing

The dryest hair is oily enough to catch the dirt that flies everywhere. As this grime kills hair luster, why let it accumulate?

Authorities advise a thorough shampoo every two weeks ... and *oftener* when a hair dressing is used, when you perspire freely, when your hair is naturally oily, when in work or play your head is exposed to more dust and dirt than is usual. And remember, any good toilet soap is a good shampoo soap.

[1929]

Don't fail, either, to wash your comb and brush thoroughly every few days.

Wash your face the only "best" way

The skin, also, is invisibly oily and dirt-catching ... and water alone will not remove this film. Soap, the real cleanser, is needed.

Skin specialists say that creams and powders, when used as a *substitute* for soap and water, increase rather than lessen the possibility of blackheads and "shiny nose". They call soap and water "the most valuable agent we have for keeping the skin of the face normal and healthy".

Elbows, underwear and finger nails

Are your elbows dark and roughened? Then *brush* them every night with warm soapy water and see this unloveliness gradually disappear.

If you aren't able to manage as many professional manicures as you would like, soap-scrub your nails once a day with a stiff brush, and push the cuticle back with the towel while drying. You'll find that except for occasional shaping and polishing, little else is needed.

From stockings and underwear to dresses, scarfs, gloves, etc., there's only one safe rule about your clothing: anything that is *doubtful* is definitely *too soiled to wear.*

The kind of beauty called "elusive"

Other people know when we do and do not take baths. Other people notice when the attention we give to cleanliness is the 100% and constant kind.

Isn't "daintiness" just another name for being *clean?* . . . and "elusive" beauty, probably mostly *extra* cleanliness? . . . of body, face, hands, hair, clothing, and all the many little details?

Published by the Association of American Soap and Glycerine Producers, Inc., to aid the work of CLEANLINESS INSTITUTE, *45 East 17th Street, New York.*

Portrait of a gentleman breaking a bad habit

Until the very moment of our picture the subject thereof was a confirmed user of old-fashioned sinking soaps.

He quaintly ignored the dangers lurking in the cake on the slippery tub-bottom. There was no one present to cry, "Watch your step!"

You see the painfully upsetting results.

WHILE the necessary curative measures were working their healing effects, the gentleman saw a new light.

They bathed him with Ivory, as is the almost universal medical practice.

For the first time he learned the joy of lavish lather.

He noticed the lily-white cake jauntily *afloat* and constantly, gloriously visible in the bed-side basin.

And he went forth preaching the gospel of Ivory—permanently cured of the catch-as-catch-can soap habit.

Fortunately for you it is not necessary to step on a sinker cake in order to learn that Ivory is the grandest soap a man can use, not only because it floats, but because it has every other attribute a fine soap ought to have.

IVORY SOAP

99 44/100 % Pure · It Floats

Guest IVORY *is a favorite in homes and hospitals because it is made to fit the hands, the face and the traveling soap-box. Only 5 cents for a' that.*

[1925]

Would you have told him the truth?

AGAIN—for the third time that year, Dobbs was told that he would probably find a greater opportunity elsewhere—that he was not needed—that he didn't quite fit with the organization.

And yet, strangely, in no case when he was handed his check was he ever told *specifically* why he was no longer wanted.

He was becoming discouraged—embittered. What *was* the thing that caused all this?

As he wandered from one job to another he came to be more and more behind in his accounts. He never seemed to get ahead—always broke, poor fellow.

You, yourself, rarely know when you have halitosis (unpleasant breath). That's the insidious thing about it. And even your closest friends won't tell you.

Sometimes, of course, halitosis comes from some deep-seated organic disorder that requires professional advice. But usually—and fortunately—halitosis is only a local condition that yields to the regular use of Listerine as a mouth wash and gargle. It is an interesting thing that this well-known antiseptic that has been in use for years for surgical dressings, possesses these unusual properties as a breath deodorant. It puts you on the safe and polite side.

Listerine halts food fermentation in the mouth and leaves the breath sweet, fresh and clean. *Not* by substituting some other odor but by really removing the old one. The Listerine odor itself quickly disappears.

This safe and long-trusted antiseptic has dozens of different uses: note the little circular that comes with every bottle. Your druggist sells Listerine in the original brown package only—*never in bulk.* There are four sizes: 14 ounce, 7 ounce, 3 ounce and 1¼ ounce. Buy the large size for economy. — *Lambert Pharmacal Company, Saint Louis, U. S. A.*

Turned down again
—perhaps it's *comedones**

Not a single dance with her. How he envied the other men as they gaily whirled her round the floor! Somehow *he* was always "just too late." He suspected she was purposely declining his invitations. But never for a moment did he guess that the reason was . . . comedones.

A great many young men suffer from comedones—commonly called blackheads. Skin can't be clean-looking, fresh, wholesome, if these disfiguring formations are present.

What's more, you may not even be conscious of *comedones*. But your friends notice them. You may wonder why invitations become fewer—why friends—girls in particular—seem to avoid you. You may never guess. Perhaps it's *comedones*.

Pompeian Massage Cream helps you overcome comedones. It gives you a clean, clear, ruddy complexion. It gets into the pores where comedones form, rolls out all dirt and oily secretions, and stimulates a healthy circulation, keeping skin clean, pores open.

Try this treatment

After you shave, spread Pompeian Massage Cream generously over your face—and *rub*. Continue to rub until the cream rolls out. Note how dark the cream looks. That's the dirt that was in your pores.

No need to have a dirty skin. Don't let comedones form. Use Pompeian Massage Cream every day. It means a healthy, wholesome skin. It means more joy in living.

Use at Home after Shaving

To get full pleasure and benefit, use Pompeian Massage Cream regularly at home after shaving. Your face will feel and look like a million dollars. For sale at all drug stores.

---

*WHAT ARE COMEDONES? (pronounced Cŏm'ē-dōnes)

Dictionary definition: A small plug or mass occluding the excretory duct of a sebaceous gland, occurring frequently upon the face, especially the nose, and consisting of retained semi-liquid glandular secretion or sebum. The outer end is often dark or black, due to accumulation of dust and dirt; hence it is often called blackhead.

SEND FOR
10-DAY TRIAL TUBE

For Men!

For 10c we will send a special trial tube containing sufficient cream for many delightful massages. Positively only one trial tube to a family on this exceptional offer.

Use this coupon now.

Tear off, sign and send

The Pompeian Laboratories,
Dept. A-37, Cleveland, Ohio,

Gentlemen, I enclose a dime (10c) for a special trial tube of Massage Cream.

Name...... ....

Street
Address...

City...................... State............

If you were free to *live*..

WERE you today to throw off the restraints of social conformity . . . would you, too, first satisfy that inborn craving for Ultraviolet? Would you discard the trappings of civilization to spend strenuous health-brimmed days in the beneficent sunlight?

For most convention-ridden people such action is denied. But the vital Ultraviolet portion of the sunlight can be brought right into the home by means of the justly-famous *Alpine Sun Lamp*. For years this apparatus has been used by physicians for the application of Ultraviolet as a powerful remedial agent. Now, with the growth of the preventive ideal, physicians are making it available to their patients for regular irradiation as a means to complete physical fitness.

To those who accept the obligation of a healthy body for themselves and their family...who glory in a robust tan throughout the year...the *Alpine Sun Lamp* has a vitally interesting message.

Ask your physician about it...and write for the treatise "*Ultraviolet for Health.*"

Modern bathroom fixtures by courtesy of the Crane Co.

The Original ALPINE SUN LAMP *Luxor Model*

Teeth may shine like tinted pearls
STILL

Pyorrhea attacks 4 out of 5..

Too often, all seems so safe because teeth gleam in their natural whiteness. Then suddenly Pyorrhea swoops down on the unwary.

Clean teeth still gleam. But gums break down and Pyorrhea poison sweeps through the system leaving in its wake a trail of havoc, often causing many serious ills which destroy happiness. And beauty vanishes with lost health.

As the penalty for neglect, 4 out of 5 after forty and thousands younger pay Pyorrhea's high price.

These Odds Can Be Bettered—Easily

For safety's sake, protect your gums as well as your teeth. Visit your dentist regularly. Have him examine your teeth and gums thoroughly. And start using Forhan's for the Gums, today.

Without the use of harsh abrasives Forhan's easily and safely restores teeth to their natural whiteness and protects them against acids which cause decay.

In addition, if used regularly and in time, it helps to keep gums sound and healthy and so safeguards precious health against the attack of dread Pyorrhea.

This dentifrice is the formula of R. J. Forhan, D. D. S., for many years a Pyorrhea specialist. It is compounded with the correct percentage of Forhan's Pyorrhea Liquid, used by dentists in the treatment of Pyorrhetic conditions.

Don't wait for danger signs, for gums to bleed and recede from teeth, or for teeth to loosen in their sockets. Be on the safe side and start using Forhan's for the Gums regularly, morning and night. At all druggists—in tubes, 35c and 60c. Forhan Company, New York.

Formula of R. J. Forhan, D. D. S.

Never Feel Down-in-the-Mouth

More and more people are using Forhan's Antiseptic Refreshant, morning and night, as an indispensable part of the correct practice of oral hygiene. This scientific triumph *cuts and neutralizes the after-taste effect of tobacco or too rich foods.* It leaves the mouth tingling with delightful freshness for hours after using. It is pleasant, refreshing, harmless and safe. For keeping breath and taste sweet and fresh use Forhan's Antiseptic Refreshant. There's nothing better! 35c and 60c in bottles.

Make This 10 Day Test

Here's something worth knowing. Gums need the same stimulating massaging that keeps a woman's face youthful and free from the wrinkles of age. Lazy, lethargic gums invite disease. Forhan's for the Gums is designed to keep gums firm, sound and alive. So make this test: Before brushing teeth with Forhan's exercise your gums, following closely the directions in the booklet that comes with each tube. Do this for 10 days . . . . See how much better your gums look and feel!

Forhan's *for the gums*

MORE THAN A TOOTH PASTE . . . IT CHECKS PYORRHEA

[1928]

We Stars

Must have fine teeth

By Edna Wallace Hopper

We on the stage must have beautiful teeth. I have consulted counter authorities on them.

For many years I did this: I used several kinds of tooth pastes to get their various effects. Then I used an antiseptic mouth wash to combat germ attacks. I used magnesia to neutralize the acids which cause tooth decay. Then I used breath deodorants. I spent a half-hour daily on my teeth. An authority told me the other day that my teeth were the marvels of all his experience.

But he also told me a new way—a way which eliminates the bother. Many great experts have combined to create a new-type tooth paste—a dentifrice which does everything at once. It contains olive-oil cleansers of the highest order. Polishers to beautify the teeth. Antiseptics to combat the germs. Iodine for the gums. Magnesia and other antacids to guard against acid attacks. Deodorants for the breath.

An army of experts combined their talents to create this new-type dentifrice. Now one application does all that I did with many.

The name of this tooth paste is Quindent, meaning five-in-one. It is made by Quindent Laboratories. They have furnished me sample tubes. Now dentists everywhere advise it, and druggists supply it.

It means so much to women that I urge them to try it. It combines all helps in one. Send the coupon for a sample tube. My Beauty Book will come with it. I will send enough for 20 uses to show you what Quindent means. Clip coupon now.

Trial Tube Free

Edna Wallace Hopper,   Q33-AM
536 Lake Shore Drive, Chicago
Ma me a test of Quindent

....

....

[1925]

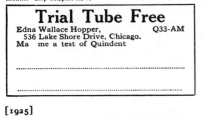

EUROPE $406
All Expense Tours and up

SELECT your trip abroad from 232 itineraries covering all countries of Europe during summer of 1929. Prices from $295 to $1074. England, Belgium, Holland, Germany and France —all expenses, $406. Tour prices include all necessary expenses from time of sailing until return. Congenial parties personally conducted by expert couriers. Delightful Tourist Third Cabin accommodations on Canadian Pacific steamships via the scenic St. Lawrence "water boulevard" to Europe. College orchestras on shipboard—just like a big house party! Large amount of motor travel in Europe. Thousands of satisfied clients recommend Guild tours. Ask for beautiful 40-page illustrated "Booklet E29."

Art Crafts GUILD TRAVEL BUREAU
Dept. 613, 180 N. Michigan Blvd., Chicago

[1929]

"Why Was I Fired?"

"I've worked my head off for them people!" exclaimed Jones to his wife. "Yet the very minute business gets slack, out I go!"

"AND THIS IS THE SECOND JOB YOU'VE LOST, DEAR," answered his wife sorrowfully. "We're surely up against hard luck."

A few hours before this conversation, Jones was himself the subject of a conversation between the business manager and his assistant.

"I don't like to let Jones go," the manager said. "Married man with a wife to support. But I simply must. He's willing enough and faithful, too. *But his English! You know how he talks, Bill.* Maybe he didn't go to school long enough—but if that's the case why doesn't he try to improve himself. After hearing him talk to customers and hearing him dictate letters I can understand why his sales record stands still. He's not a very big asset to the house and it would never do to advance him."

Don't Be a Job Hunter And so, Jones, because he was careless in his use of English, like many another man and woman before him, not only fails to advance, but is ACTUALLY REDUCED TO A JOB-HUNTING STATE— a condition he would never have reached if he had spent a few minutes of his spare time every day in improving his speech by a little study.

Be a Master of Words To-day you have your destiny in your own hands, because—whoever you are, and whatever your walk in life, the little book which we are offering you will OPEN YOUR EYES TO A NEW WORLD OF UNTOLD POWER AND ACHIEVEMENT—to use good English and to build a personality that charms.

Stepping Stone to Success Here is the stepping-stone by which thousands have climbed to success. *Salesmen—doctors— lawyers— merchants —clergymen — teachers — clerks— business men and women* everywhere attribute their success to the advantage they derived from the study and application of Grenville Kleiser's unique course in English, endorsed by such distinguished people as Booth Tarkington, Mary Roberts Rinehart, Irvin S. Cobb, and thousands of others.

Use Your Spare Moments This line of easy study places in your hands the systematized knowledge that others go to college for years to get—and sometimes leave without.

Grenville Kleiser can teach you by mail, in your home, at your own convenience, the power and use of words. This is no ordinary, lengthy course to be studied laboriously. On the contrary, you will find it marvelously simple, clear and concise. A few minutes a day spent in studying this course will soon make your speech, your conversation, your writing, vastly more interesting and profitable.

Get the Free Booklet It is possible for people in all stations of life to enjoy the great benefits of Grenville Kleiser's wonderful course in English. For not only are we offering this course for an astonishingly small investment, but you may pay for it on easy monthly terms. So that you may know what Grenville Kleiser's English course contains, we will send you by mail the book

"HOW TO BECOME A MASTER OF ENGLISH"

This instructive little book which we will give you FREE will show you how the Kleiser Personal Mail Course in Practical English and Mental Efficiency will enable you to win promotion and higher pay—use correct and forceful words—write convincing letters, sermons, advertisements, stories, articles—become an interesting talker, win power, success, and popularity.

Remember—it costs you nothing to investigate. Your signature on the coupon puts you under no obligation whatever. But a single day's delay may mean that you will forget, or the coupon be lost, and so deprive you of your opportunity. MAIL THE COUPON TO-DAY!—

The Coupon to Bigger Success

- -

FUNK & WAGNALLS COMPANY
354 Fourth Avenue, New York

Gentlemen: Send me by mail, free of charge or obligation, the booklet, "How to Become a Master of English," together with full particulars of the Grenville Kleiser Course in Practical English and Mental Efficiency.   Dept. 966

Name...

Local Address..................................

Post Office....................................

Date.................State......................

[1926]

"Use no soap except Palmolive"

says NIRAUS, of Madrid

Known throughout Spain as one of the foremost specialists on care of the skin

"All my clients are asked to use no soap except Palmolive. The pure palm and olive oils of which it is made give the skin deep, thorough cleansing. Daily cleansings with Palmolive have a tonic and rejuvenating effect on the skin."

Niraus
MADRID

Niraus' reputation extends throughout Spain. His salon is one of the handsomest in the South of Europe and his smart clientele includes many royal personages.

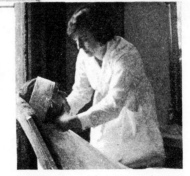

An assistant giving a facial treatment in the salon of Madame Elin Dahlstrand of Stockholm, who finds that "Palmolive Soap lather revives and strengthens the tissues."

THE basis of all complexion care is, or should be, to cleanse the skin thoroughly twice a day, using soap and water." That is the opinion of Niraus, well known beauty specialist of Madrid, Spain.

But Niraus warns against the use of ordinary soaps. He realizes that some soaps have a tendency to irritate the skin—bringing coarse pores, causing the texture to lose it smooth loveliness. For that reason he specifies one soap and one only—Palmolive. Like most modern beauty experts, Niraus believes in the use of vegetable oils in facial soap. These cosmetic oils are so bland, so gentle on the skin, that 18,012 beauty specialists, all over the world, advise the daily use of Palmolive.

"No soap but Palmolive"

"All my clients are asked to use no soap except Palmolive," says Niraus. "The pure palm and olive oils of which it is made give the skin the deep, thorough cleansing that is required in order to rid the pores of all accumulations."

Niraus is a skin specialist of wide experience and enviable reputation. He advocates this simple daily treatment, to be used morning and night: massage a fine creamy lather of Palmolive Soap gently into the skin, allowing it to penetrate the pores. Rinse, with warm water, then with cold. And you're ready for rouge and powder!

Use Palmolive every day. Consult your beauty specialist regularly. And remember—a clean skin is absolutely necessary in order to get best results from special beauty care. Palmolive is made entirely of palm and olive oils. These oils—and nothing else—give it nature's fresh green color. And these oils make it the perfect skin cleanser and beautifier.

One week's use will show you why millions use it for bath as well as face.

5075

Retail Price 10c

[1930]

326

"Yeast builds resistance,"

says PROF. DOCTOR PAUL REYHER

famous lecturer at the University of Berlin

"THE MEDICINAL USES of yeast are many-sided. There is a high percentage of Vitamin B in yeast ... Vitamin B bears a very close relation to the proper functioning of the nervous system. It also improves the appetite, regulates metabolism, promotes growth and raises the body's power of resistance to every kind of infection ... One can see, therefore, that yeast contains a remarkable healing factor."

Prof. Dr. Reyher [signature]

PROF. DR. PAUL REYHER

Lecturer, University of Berlin, on Vitamins, X-Ray and Pediatrics; Director, Children's Hospital, Berlin, which he built and equipped. The Germans refer to this hospital as "the jewel box" because of its perfect appointments and beauty of structure.

ANOTHER of the great medical leaders of Europe to add his voice to the movement of health preparedness is Prof. Dr. Paul Reyher, of the University of Berlin.

Dr. Reyher has made an exhaustive study of yeast. His findings extend new hope to all who suffer from indigestion, headaches, nervousness, depression, too frequent colds and sore throat—sure signs of constipation and lowered vitality.

In a recent survey throughout the United States, half the doctors reporting said they prescribed fresh yeast for constipation and its attendant ills.

Fleischmann's Yeast is fresh. Unlike dried or killed yeast it contains millions of living, active yeast plants. As these live yeast plants pass daily through your system, they rouse the muscles that control elimination, combat harmful poisons. Your digestion improves. Your skin clears.

Eat three cakes of Fleischmann's Yeast every day, one cake before each meal or between meals, plain or in water (hot or cold). To get full benefit from yeast you must eat it regularly and over a sufficient period of time. At all grocers and many leading cafeterias, lunch counters and soda fountains. Buy two or three days' supply at a time, as it will keep in a cool, dry place. Start now!

Write for latest booklet on Yeast in the diet—free. Health Research Dept. C-125, The Fleischmann Company, 701 Washington St., New York, N. Y.

FROM THROAT TO COLON is one continuous tube. 90% of ills start here. Poisons from clogged intestines easily spread through the system, lowering resistance to disease. But here is where yeast works. "Yeast builds resistance," says Dr. Reyher. It keeps the entire intestinal tract *clean, active* and *healthy.* Eat Fleischmann's Yeast regularly.

[1929]

UNIVERSITY OF BERLIN, *where Dr. Reyher is a noted lecturer.*

FLEISCHMANN'S YEAST
for HEALTH

Copyright, 1929, The Fleischmann Company

327

1930-1934

TIME

Vol. XXIV, No. 3   *The Weekly Newsmagazine*   July 16, 1934

AERONAUTICS

Sleepers

World's first aerial sleeper service was launched by Eastern Air Transport last autumn (TIME, Oct. 16) when an 18-passenger Curtiss *Condor* with two berths (upper & lower) was assigned to the night run between Newark and Atlanta. When airmail contracts were cancelled in February, Eastern Air discontinued the night run to Atlanta and, with it, air sleeper service. When the company began flying mail again three months later, the sleeper service was not resumed.

Meanwhile on the West Coast berth-plane service was inaugurated three months ago by American Airlines between Los Angeles and Dallas, Tex. Always more progressive in accepting what seems new, the West furnished American Airlines' sleepers with many a capacity load. Encouraged by its success, American Airlines last week inaugurated sleeper service on its six-hour New York-Chicago night run, using 160 m.p.h. Curtiss *Condors* with twelve berths, upper & lower. The same length as Pullman berths but nine inches narrower, the aerial berths are convertible by day into roomy club chairs.

FORWARD!

BETWEEN October 19th and November 25th America will feel the thrill of a great spiritual experience. In those few weeks millions of dollars will be raised in cities and towns throughout the land, and the fear of cold and hunger will be banished from the hearts of thousands.

Be sure that you do your part. Give to the funds that will be raised in your community. Give liberally.

And know that your gift will bless yourself. It will lift your own spirit. More than anything else you can do, it will help to end the depression and lay the firm foundation for better times.

The President's Organization on Unemployment Relief

Walter S. Gifford Director
WALTER S. GIFFORD

Committee on Mobilization of Relief Resources

Chairman
OWEN D. YOUNG

What is the
RECONSTRUCTION
Finance Corporation
Doing?

It is acting as a great
discount bank, and is loaning over $7,000,000 a day

★

THESE loans are made to every part of the United States through commercial banks, savings banks, trust companies, joint stock land banks, Federal intermediate credit banks, agricultural credit corporations, live stock credit corporations, and to the railroads, building and loan associations, mortgage loan companies, and insurance companies.

The applications come in through the 33 branches and are carefully inspected locally as well as in Washington. But action is rapid, and one day's operations will take in many of the above avenues of distribution in most sections of the country.

The amounts loaned vary from a few thousand dollars to several millions, and due consideration is given the necessity of each case.

WHAT ARE THE CHANGES IN THE ECONOMIC PICTURE?

THROUGH the Reconstruction Finance Corporation, the enlarged powers of the Federal Reserve System, the campaign against hoarding, and the United Action for Employment, great fundamental changes have developed.

Beginning in the summer of 1931 with the financial crisis in Germany, followed by the suspension of gold payments in England, a tremor of fear went through the entire world. The shock manifested itself in America by enormous gold withdrawals on the part of foreign central banks which had been leaving their money on deposit with us for years. Bank failures increased rapidly in this country as a result of the financial excitement, which encouraged the hoarding of currency and the sale of securities.

This picture is now changed. Money is being returned to circulation. The resources of banks that failed in March are about equalled by the resources of the banks that reopened. People are becoming impatient with anything which is obstructing the return to normal trade and normal living. The dollar is able to buy more in merchandise, services and securities than it has for many years. The *active dollar* is the only dollar that is valuable, and it is now putting its more slothful neighbor to shame.

THE NATIONAL PUBLISHERS' ASSOCIATION

*"As the most nearly self-contained nation, we have within
our own boundaries the elemental factors for recovery."*

(From the Recommendation of the Committee on Unemployment Plans and Suggestions of the President's Organization on Unemployment Relief)

MOBILIZATION FOR HUMAN NEEDS

If people are hungry this winter, they will have food. If they are cold, they will have clothing and shelter. Federal and State funds are being appropriated to supplement your local efforts toward relieving actual hunger and physical distress.

Eating is not living; it is existing. If we are to justify our claim to civilization, we must think beyond primary needs of food and shelter. We must face our responsibility for human service, broader in conception, deeper in sympathy and understanding.

Care of the aged, service to demoralized families, hospitalization of the needy sick, home nursing, settlements, guidance of youth, care of the children without a chance—these and hundreds of other services are in the hands of your local welfare organizations. Some of these programs were overshadowed during the past year by the desperate fight to supply food and warmth to every one in need. But they must not be forgotten. Huge public appropriations only to maintain life necessitate your and my partnership in making that life worth while.

This year there are social needs created by the misery of the lean years we have gone through. These critical needs must be met by the local welfare agencies which you have maintained in the past and which must look to you for support again at this time.

I join Newton D. Baker, Chairman of the National Citizens' Committee, and Mrs. Roosevelt, Chairman of the National Women's Committee, in asking you to support your Community Chest or your local welfare appeals to the limit of your ability. It is a cause well designated by the title given it, "Mobilization for Human Needs."

Franklin D Roosevelt

THERE'S ONE THING THAT THE BLUE EAGLE CAN NOT DO

THE BLUE EAGLE is restoring purchasing power. It is providing greater leisure through shorter working hours. It is eliminating destructive trade practices... But there's one thing the Blue Eagle can NOT do. *It can't sell your goods.* The business your company enjoys in the new deal depends entirely on your own policies—your own practices—and most of all, *your own products*... Today's buyers know the value of the dollar. They insist upon greater durability—more attractiveness—better service from the products they buy... That is why manufacturers of hundreds of articles have turned to Enduro—Republic's *perfected stainless steel.* It is a sales builder... And you will find Republic representatives ready to help *you* in the improvement of your present products—or in the development of new ones.

REPUBLIC STEEL CORPORATION

GENERAL OFFICES:　　　　Ⓡ　　　　YOUNGSTOWN, OHIO

334

THE BUSINESS LEADERS
OF TODAY
are the I.C.S. students of yesterday

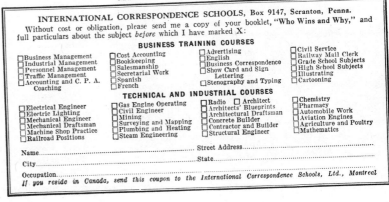

COL. EDWARD V. RICKENBACKER, *and a giant Fokker 30-passenger air-liner*

EVERY ONE has heard of "Eddie" Rickenbacker. Most of us think of him as a daredevil driver, a cool, skilful pilot, and a famous air-fighter. But how many realize that he is also an engineer of genius, and an executive of rare ability?

Today Colonel Rickenbacker is Vice-president Director of Sales for Fokker Aircraft Corporation in America; President of the Indianapolis Motor Speedway Corporation, and Chairman of the Contest Board of the American Automobile Association.

Eddie Rickenbacker was born in Columbus, Ohio, in 1890. He grew up in the street and on the lots. He led his own gang. He was all boy. But when he was 12 his father died and suddenly he had to be a man. He got himself a job in a glass-works, at $4.80 a week.

At 16 Eddie Rickenbacker had worked in many places, including a brewery, a shoe factory and a railway machine shop. Then came the turn of fate that shaped his life. He got a job with a man who repaired cars and bicycles.

The "fleet" of cars on which young Eddie got his first experience comprised a one-cylinder Oldsmobile, a Waverly electric and a Locomobile "steamer." He ran them and tinkered with them. But he wanted to know more about their inside workings than any one in the shop could tell him. That was when he enrolled for the Automobile Course with the International Correspondence Schools.

For two years he did a double shift — all day on the repair work and half the night at his lessons. When he felt he had mastered enough theory, he moved to a new job in a car factory. His dogged persistence and his real knowledge of automobiles won him promotion to the engineering department. At 18 he bore the title of "experimental engineer."

When he was 21 the lure of the racing game caught him, and for the next five years he made his reputation as a driver.

When the United States entered the World War, he was in the first contingent of the A. E. F. to cross. In seven months of flying he made history, bringing down a total of 26 hostile planes.

Captain Eddie Rickenbacker came home a national hero, but it did not spoil him. Following the war he was chosen to head a motor company that bore his name. Later he became Vice-president in charge of sales for the Cadillac-LaSalle division of General Motors. And when that organization bought a dominating interest in Fokker Aircraft Corporation, and needed an executive to "take the controls" in developing America's already quickened air-sense, Colonel Rickenbacker was selected.

Because of natural gifts, reinforced by the habit of study developed in his I. C. S. days, this boy whose start was so beset with difficulty has become a man outstanding in any field he enters.

Such a career is a ringing challenge to every ambitious young man in America. No matter what a man's previous education may be, no matter what his aims or his financial standing, the International Correspondence Schools can give him the training he needs to achieve success. Tonight, in thousands of homes, young men will be at work on their I. C. S. lessons under the study lamp. *They are the business leaders of the future.*

INTERNATIONAL CORRESPONDENCE SCHOOLS
Mail this Coupon for Free Booklet

[1930]

337

SINCLAIR LEWIS

etches another world "Type" for you

THIS TIME it is the modern loather of things as they are — the restless reacher for imaginary advantages beyond the horizon.

With his usual zest, with his deft and frank character sketching, Mr. Lewis gives us the first short story he has written since he was awarded the Nobel prize.

But this time it is not limited to Americans. The background is international. Starting thirty stories above Manhattan in the duplex living room of a Park Avenue penthouse apartment, the action shifts to England, to an Italian villa on Lake Maggiore, to a suburban German home, and back to New York.

Read *"Ring Around a Rosy"* In next Week's Issue **OUT JUNE 4!**

You will call it one of the outstanding short stories of the year, and Mr. Lewis is now writing another for THE SATURDAY EVENING POST.

THE SATURDAY EVENING POST

"AN AMERICAN 〔◉〕 INSTITUTION"

Starting in the June 27th Issue "Two Black Sheep"

— a rollicking serial By HARRY LEON WILSON

In it we find a French count disguised as an automobile mechanic in a Los Angeles garage and somewhat baffled by American idioms and idiosyncrasies, an American girl whose heart is in the pictures though her job is in Ye Olde Cheshire Tea Denne, who is disguised as a Balkan princess and is baffled by nothing under the sun, and many other delightful people who play minor parts of major importance in this Franco-American comedy. A worthy successor to Bunker Bean, Ruggles of Red Gap, Merton of the Movies and Lone Tree.

In the June 13th Issue "She Was Right Once"

By BOOTH TARKINGTON

A well-meaning bachelor tries to relieve the plight of a man hemmed in by his wife's relatives and dominated by a sister-in-law with a "female-infallibility-complex." The setting is one of those quiet little cities of the Middle West which Mr. Tarkington knows so well, where Hon. Chanley (Worm) Orde visits an old classmate, Bertram (Bum) Hastie. What happens provides a story with delightful Tarkington humor.

Many more articles, short stories, serials **5¢** *enough each week to make a bound bookful*

[1931]

COOL..REFRESHING
like the decks of an original
YANKEE CLIPPER

Close your eyes. You're at sea—judging by the freshness of the air! You can almost feel the deck of an old-time clipper ship under your feet . . . as you speed silently over the "boulevard of steel". Not only the blue-ribbon Yankee Clipper (12 noon E. S. T. from Grand Central), but *every* day train between New York, Providence and Boston on the Shore Line route is now air-conditioned! Notice how *clean* everything is—no dust or grime on anything you touch. And how cool and comfortable you are, no matter what the thermometer says outside. Almost hourly one of these fine trains leaves New York—with the most modern and efficient type of air-conditioning operating in each car.

For tickets and Pullman accommodations apply Grand Central Terminal, Pennsylvania Station or Consolidated Ticket Offices: 17 John Street and 155 Pierrepont Street, Brooklyn.

THE NEW HAVEN R.R.

[1934]

341

**N**O land gypsy ever enjoyed the freedom of that nomad of the water, the Chris-Crafter. To him the waterways of the whole world lie open There are no white lines, no straight pavements. Every bay and river invites the Chris-Crafter to rest or to explore, to hunt or to fish. The shorelines offer wide diversity of play and recreation. Thrilling races, regattas, boat parties, picnics, social affairs—all are within range of the fast, roomy Chris-Craft ✦ ✦ ✦ Every waterside family needs a Chris-Craft, and every member of the family will enjoy and use it. It handles even more easily than a motor car and has the same steering, starting and lighting equipment. There are fast, racy runabouts, luxurious sedans, commuters, cruisers and yachts in the 1930 Chris-Craft fleet. Let the Chris-Craft merchant help you select the one that fits your desire. Illustrated catalog may be had by writing Chris Smith & Sons Boat Company, 285 Detroit Road, Algonac, Michigan.

[1930]

24-foot Chris-Craft Runabout, 125 H. P., speed up to 35 M.P.H. $2850

NEW!

A 17-foot Runabout, 25 M. P. H., priced at $1295.

✦ ✦ ✦

A few desirable sales territories open. Wire for details.

Chris-Craft
World's Largest Builders of All-Mahogany Motor Boats

Runabouts—Sedans—Commuters—Cruisers—Yachts
25 Models—17 to 48 feet—$1295 to $35,000

Into the new... the unknown
AROUND THE WORLD
IN THE
FRANCONIA
WITH HENDRIK WILLEM VAN LOON

"Ghost ships of Magellan's fleet..."

The Franconia takes you where few have ventured ... to the South Sea Isles and the whole momentous and entrancing world of the Southern Pacific and the Indian Oceans. She alone among world-cruising liners sails to Tahiti and Rarotonga, Samoa, Viti Levu in the Fiji Islands ... to the very antipodes of the earth: New Zealand and Australia ... to Papua in New Guinea and Kalabahai on almost unknown Alor Island. She includes such favorite world-cruise features as Bali and Java, Singapore, Penang, Ceylon, South India ... turns southward again into sea-lanes where few great liners sail ... to the paradise of Mahe in the Seychelles ... to Madagascar and the populous, poly-colored East Coast of Africa... to South Africa... South America!

It is fitting that Hendrik Willem van Loon accompany such a cruise ... his informal, witty and learned talks on board will emphasize its deep significance,

"Islands arise, grow old and disappear ..."

widen its scope. It is fitting, too, that the ship which takes this eventful route around the world is the Franconia. Already a leader among world-cruising liners, the

Franconia will be completely reconditioned this Fall, so that she may sail on her great adventure resplendent and even more luxurious than heretofore.

"The rice fields of Java ..."

At this year's rates this unique opportunity demands your consideration. The whole cruise from New York to New York ... nearly five months ... costs but $1,200 up without shore excursions, $1,700 up including shore excursions. (Passengers joining the cruise on the Pacific Coast receive a rebate of $100—$125). Compare that with what you spend in just an ordinary winter-and-spring at home!

Franconia sails from New York Jan. 9th from Los Angeles Jan. 24th.

"A Voyage of Re-Discovery" is the title of an extraordinary 80-page booklet that should have a permanent place in your library. Besides all the facts of the Franconia's unique voyage, it includes a fascinating and very personal conception of this world cruise, written and illustrated by Mr. van Loon. Your copy may be had by addressing your local agent or

CUNARD LINE
25 Broadway, New York
THOS. COOK & SON
587 Fifth Ave., New York

"One of the few things I have discovered during the thirty years I have devoted (more or less) to a study of the past as revealed in the present and of the present as explained by the past is this: that in order to get the right point of view one needs the right perspective. And one does not get the right perspective by sitting with one's nose glued to the object under observation. You may well argue that the contemplation of self-government as practiced among the natives of New Guinea will hardly teach us how to do things in Washington and that a few days spent in the strange democratic commonwealth of Australia will not show us how to handle our own labor problems. Of course not. But we will gain a tremendously superior understanding about ourselves and our own problems if we contemplate our own achievements against a background of other habits and other customs.

That this trip happens to lead through one of the loveliest parts of the world is a most agreeable detail, but if it merely made the circuit of the Poles, I would still be on board the ship."

Hendrik Willem van Loon

ITINERARY
Jamaica* Panama Los Angeles
Hawaiian Islands
South Sea Islands
(Tahiti*,Rarotonga*,Apia*,Suva*)
New Zealand* Australia*
New Guinea*
Dutch East Indies
(Kalabahai*, Bali, Java)
Straits Settlements and Malaya
(Singapore, Penang)
India   Ceylon   Seychelles*
East Africa
(Mombasa*, Zanzibar*)
Madagascar*
South Africa (Cape Town*,
Durban*, Port Elizabeth*)
South America
(Montevideo*, Buenos Aires,
Santos*, Rio de Janeiro*)
Barbados*
*Franconia is the only world cruise to call here.

Franconia ONLY WORLD
CRUISE TO THE SOUTH SEAS AND SOUTHERN HEMISPHERE

[1933]

343

"Do you mean to say that's a movie camera?"

"It sure is ... and a good one, too. Eastman makes it."

[1934]

Ciné-Kodak *Eight*

Makes movies for 10¢ a "shot"*

"Imagine getting movies like these the first time you tried!"

"Pretty simple, wasn't it? All I did was press the button."

WHAT fun it is to make movies . . . movies that capture, and *save,* the joy of living. Gay, fleeting childhood, happy vacations, life's big events —now everyone can keep them in movies.

Ciné-Kodak Eight is a full-fledged movie camera—capable in every respect, beautifully built ;.. so easy to use ... so easy to own. Price, $34.50.

See the Ciné-Kodak Eight at your dealer's today—see the movies it makes ... then join the ranks of the Ciné-Kodak Eight fans. Eastman Kodak Co., Rochester, N. Y.

"Does your dad know you've got his camera?"

"Sure, he says I make swell movies and there's nothing about it for me to break."

* A "SHOT," in Hollywood movie parlance, is one continuous scene of a picture story. The Eight makes 20 to 30 such scenes—each as long as those in the average news reel—on a roll of film costing $2.25, finished, ready to show. *If it isn't an Eastman, it isn't a Kodak.*

344

Fly in Bed
VIA AMERICAN ✈ AIRLINES

DAY AND NIGHT
SERVICE
COAST-TO-COAST

SLEEPER PLANE SERVICE BETWEEN

New York and Chicago

Travel the modern way—by Sleeper Plane! Enjoy the most restful sleep as your plane carries you high above dust and dirt, over the smoothest air route between these two cities. Each section converts into exceptionally commodious upper and lower berth. Complete wash room facilities and every convenience for your comfort. Fly this scenic route day or night via the Delaware Water Gap, Buffalo and Detroit. Going by Sleeper Plane you have ample time for late appointments and theater at night. You can go to sleep as soon as you board the plane, and wake up in the morning at your destination clean and refreshed. Call American Airlines, any Western Union or Postal Telegraph Office, leading hotel or travel bureau.

AMERICAN AIRLINES, INC., CHICAGO
Day and night flying service, coast-to-coast, directly connecting 57 cities

SLEEPER PLANE SERVICE BETWEEN
Los Angeles—Fort Worth—Dallas
on the Southern Transcontinental, Fair Weather Route
You may sit up as late as you like. The roomy club chairs are oversize, lounge type, considerably wider than the standard airplane seat. Each passenger is provided with individual window, reading light, service call button, warm and cool air vent, ash tray and magazine pocket.

SHIP BY GENERAL AIR EXPRESS • CUT SHIPPING DAYS TO HOURS

[1934]

Why not let the Children see a WOGGLE FISH

WELL . . . maybe not a woggle fish, but if there is such a thing the Shedd Aquarium in Chicago has it . . . for here is the most complete aquarium in the world. Many of the fish swim in genuine sea water, brought from the ocean to Chicago in tank cars.

The Planetarium is another of the City's Wonders . . . wherein is depicted the behavior of the stars and planets, from sundown to dawn. This is one of two planetariums in the world.

The Field Museum . . . one of the finest natural history museums anywhere. The Merchandise Mart . . . largest floor area of any building. Soldier Field . . . scene of the historic Dempsey-Tunney fight, famous football games and the rodeo. The Board of Trade, Stock Exchange, Navy Pier (stretching a mile into Lake Michigan), Lincoln Zoo, the Art Institute, skyscrapers, lake boats, toy fairylands in State Street stores!

Why not let the children see these things—and partake of the joys which you and they can share right now?

It is such an easy undertaking . . . on your next weekend, or if you pass through Chicago east or west bound. Especially with the Palmer House to help you.

Here is the hotel that engineers and architects call "the safest hotel in the world." It provides playrooms for the children . . . enclosed or open-air, in charge of educational supervisors. It has a hospital with nurses and doctors always on duty. Trained children's attendants are available when parents wish to stay out beyond a youngster's bedtime. One floor is devoted exclusively to accommodation for women guests.

Right in the heart of the famous Loop, the Palmer House puts you in the center of everything worth seeing in Chicago. All forms of transportation pass nearby.

The rooms are moderately priced at $4, $5, $6 or more. . . . . . . WALTER L. GREGORY, *Manager*

PALMER HOUSE

CHICAGO

RATES: $4 *and more;* $6 *and more with twin beds (for two guests). Every room with private bath.*

"NEXT DOOR TO EVERYTHING" — STATE STREET, MONROE STREET AND WABASH AVENUE

[1931]

Turn the cold eye
of the
MIRROR
on
HART SCHAFFNER
& MARX CLOTHES

The mirror will prove that you get better style and fit. Pictured here is a 4 Star Worsted. It had to earn its name by surviving every hard test that science could invent—for all-wool, long wear, for skilled needlework. Now give it the severest test of all—The Mirror Test.

•

Insist on the Trumpeter label; it's a small thing to look for—a big thing to find

HART SCHAFFNER & MARX CLOTHES

WATCH OUT! Wolves are masquerading in sheep's clothing these days! Men's clothes represented as "all-wool" but containing sometimes as much as 80% cheap substitutes, are being sold widely. They *look* all right at first, but fade, shrink and pucker. To be *sure* of pure all-wool, look for the famous Trumpeter label

[1934]

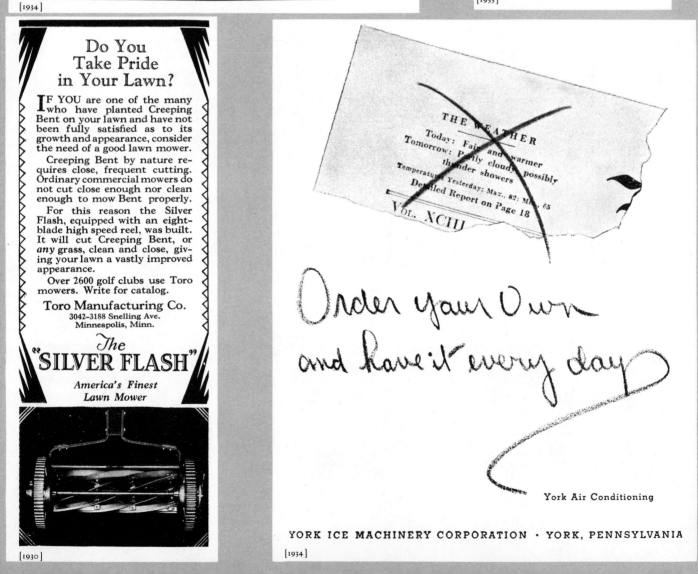

HONEYMOON HAPPINESS
Sky high

Just Married

"See that rangy bronzed fellow with the slim brunette," said the boss of the flying field. "They used to come over here late every afternoon to watch the planes. Anyone could tell they were engaged· they weren't out of each other's sight for a second. Finally, they decided to go up. It was a short flight, just over the ridge and back, and I saw them as they stepped from the cabin. Both wore a blissful expression. She spoke first: 'Wasn't it simply marvelous!'

"After that they flew pretty regularly. Then, first thing I knew, he was on the field in flying togs and going over the training ship with McAuliffe.

"A few weeks later he was asking me what I thought of the Curtiss Robin. Well, I said, she holds the world's endurance record but I wouldn't let records alone influence me. I'd consider the construction and the outfit that made it. Now, the Robin is a cabin plane. That gives you comfort. Its fuselage is of tubular alloy steel construction, providing strength far beyond any actual requirement. That gives you safety and reduces upkeep and depreciation. As for stability, the Robin is so easy to handle, it practically flys itself. You see, it's built by Curtiss-Wright and they have the greatest engineering staff in the country. As for price, Curtiss-Wright puts out a Robin, powered with an OX5 engine, at $2,495. Unlimited production facilities, I guess, is the reason they can give so much plane at the figure. Even with the bigger engines, the Challenger and Whirlwind, Robin prices are low.

"'I'm sold on it myself,' agreed the young fellow, and then, grinning, 'What's your opinion of it for a honeymoon?'

"Yes, he got his Robin. But I don't see how it left the ground with all the ribbons and shoes that were tied to it. A few days after the wedding when I went South to go over a near-by field, I spotted their ship. A mechanician satisfied my curiosity. 'Oh, them,' he said, 'those love birds are stayin' at the Inn. They'll go up about sunset so's to get closer to the moon.'

"They're back now, as you see. He has a local electric refrigerator agency and he flys twice a week to his home office in Cleveland to see about shipments and special orders. Doing quite a business, I hear."

The Robin Cabin Monoplane is now available in types and at prices to fit every need. A 4-passenger model powered with 185 h. p. Curtiss Challenger engine is $7,995; a 3-passenger model with 165 h. p. Wright Whirlwind is $5,995; and with the OX5 engine, $2,495.

Wheel landing gear is interchangeable with Edo Floats and the Robin may be converted to a seaplane in two hours. Curtiss Robin owners enjoy full day and night service at forty bases throughout the country.

Detailed and illustrated literature about the Robin—the family plane of America—will be gladly sent you. Write Dept. R7, Curtiss-Robertson Airplane Mfg. Co., division of CURTISS-WRIGHT, 27 West 57th St., New York.

CURTISS ROBIN
For Business · Pleasure · Instruction

They secretly pitied her husband
when they should have pitied their own

THEY had the old-fashioned idea that a woman isn't fair to her husband if she serves him canned vegetables.

But they didn't realize that canning does not change a vegetable. It merely seals in nature's original freshness and food value.

When perishable vegetables, such as peas, corn, string beans, tomatoes, asparagus or spinach, are put into a can, they are garden-fresh—only hours away from the soil. They are hermetically sealed before exposure to the air does any harm. They are cooked in the sealed can, without preservatives and with oxygen excluded. For these reasons, virtually none of the vitamin value is lost.

Furthermore, a canned vege-table represents a choice portion of the crop, grown from selected seed in an ideal climate and season, and picked when fully and naturally ripe.

So next time you buy a canned vegetable, remember that "canned" simply means: "garden freshness and goodness sealed in."

"Canned foods are the safest foods that come to our tables because of the sterilization to which they are subjected." The cans are specially made for food.

CONTINENTAL
NEW YORK, CHICAGO
CAN COMPANY
SAN FRANCISCO

[1934]

HOW TO MAKE YOUR SON THE HAPPIEST OF BOYS

IT is not the amount of money you spend on your boy's Christmas that counts—it is the amount of thought you put into the proper selection of your gift. The secret of giving your boy *lasting happiness* can be summed up in one word—*helpfulness.*

Help your boy. Give him a gift that will not only bring him fascinating fun, but, above all, help him to become keen-witted, quick-thinking, resourceful. You can do both these things if you give him a Lionel Electric Train. For Lionel Trains are more than toys. They teach boys how to develop skill with their hands and skill with their brains—and, above all, they help boys form the habit of thinking problems out for themselves because they make these problems a game.

For instance, your boy will not only have the fun of building his railroad and operating it; he will have the opportunity to tackle actual problems of railroad operation that give him training in both electricity and mechanics.

GIVE HIM THIS HELP. You can now buy your boy these sturdy trains for as little as $5.95—and they last for years and years. Clip the coupon below. Take it to a Lionel dealer. He will give you, **FREE,** the new 52-page Lionel Model Railroad Planning Book that shows (1) how to plan and build a model railroad system and (2) what to get to make it true-to-life to the last detail. *Note:* If it is not easy for you to go to a Lionel dealer's store—mail the coupon below to us and we will send you this expensive book if you send **10c** to cover handling and mailing costs.

LIONEL *Electric* **TRAINS**

[1932]

NOTICE TO ALL AUTHORIZED LIONEL DEALERS. *The bearer of this coupon is entitled to receive,* **FREE,** *one copy only of the new 1932 Lionel Model Railroad Planning Book.*

NOTICE TO THE PUBLIC. *If your dealer cannot supply you with a Lionel Railroad Planning Book, or if it is not easy to go to his store, mail this coupon to the LIONEL CORPORATION, Dept. 33, 15 E. 26th St., New York City. We will send you this expensive book if you enclose* **10c** *to cover handling and mailing costs.*

NAME_____

STREET_____

CITY_____STATE_____

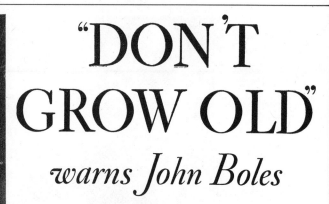

"DON'T GROW OLD"
warns John Boles

YOU CAN ESCAPE THE MASK OF AGE

JOHN BOLES, Universal, whose excellent singing voice and fine acting ability have made him one of the screen's most popular stars, tells you what he considers woman's most priceless possession.

Learn the complexion secret 98% of the famous screen stars know

"NOWADAYS no woman need be afraid of birthdays," John Boles says. "Charm isn't by any means measured by years!

"One of the most alluring women I know is . . . But it wouldn't be fair to tell! No one would ever guess—and she's admired wherever she goes.

"These days not only stage and screen stars but hundreds of other women, too, have learned a very important secret of allure. YOUTH is recognized for the priceless thing it is . . . complexions are kept glowing."

★

"To keep youth, guard complexion beauty," the fascinating actresses will tell you. "Keep your skin temptingly smooth, alluringly aglow!"

The actresses famous for their charm the world over use Lux Toilet Soap, and have for years. So well-known is their preference for this fragrant, beautifully white soap that it is found in theater dressing rooms everywhere.

In Hollywood, where 605 of the 613 important actresses use it, Lux Toilet Soap is official in *all* the great film studios.

Of the countless Hollywood, Broadway, European stars who use this white soap, some have the fine-grained skin that is inclined to dryness; some the skin that tends to be oily; some the in-between skin.

Whatever *your* individual type may be, you, too, will find Lux Toilet Soap the perfect soap—so neutral, so bland is its effect on the skin.

EVELYN LAYE, co-starring with John Boles in a recent picture, says: "Lux Toilet Soap is wonderful."

LUPE VELEZ, Universal's effervescent star, says of this white soap: "It keeps my skin like velvet."

Youth Lux Toilet Soap..10¢
The caress of dollar-a-cake French soap

LOST—
10 *years of*
H*appiness*

Theirs was such a happy little family. But what a change the last few months have wrought. Before her very eyes he has seemingly grown ten years older.. in looks.. in habits.. in desires. Once so eager.. so interested.. so full of life.. he has become jaded, unresponsive, morose.

Ask him what's wrong with him and he couldn't tell you to save his life. Yet it's pathetically simple.

Without knowing it he has fallen victim of that insidious modern malady which doctors call ASTHENIA*.

Without knowing it.. that's the disarming thing about this health-destroying blight. It drags you down.. slows your mind.. saps your vitality.. robs you of your joys and pleasures. Yet all the while you hardly realize that you are slipping.

Millions are in just that plight today. They toss and turn at night.. wake up with a headache.. drag through the day feeling weary and depressed—rarely, if ever, guessing the true cause.

Don't think.. just because you seem to be "regular".. that your system is free from those poisons which, in the majority of cases, are directly respon-

sible for that dull, achy, pepless condition known as ASTHENIA.

If you're not feeling up to par.. if you're tired, listless, irritable!.. if your work weighs you down.. it's time to *act* and act quickly!

Would you like to brush the cobwebs from your eyes.. know how it feels to be "walking on air".. ready and eager for any task.. able to do *everything* with new vim and pleasure?

Take Pluto Water.. *and see a new world in 10 days!* Take it as directed (one-fifth glass in four-fifths glass of hot water) every morning for 10 mornings. Don't miss a single day for 10 days straight! You'll be amazed how this gentle treatment will change your entire viewpoint.. make you as keen and alert as you have ever been.

After that take Pluto Water every Sunday morning regularly and you'll keep your body free of those accumulated poisons that produce ASTHENIA.

Then you'll understand why for nearly 90 years.. from all over the world.. people have traveled to French Lick Springs to partake of the famous 10-day Pluto Water treatment.. why physicians everywhere recommend it.

**GENTLE
EFFECTIVE
AGREEABLE**

Taken as directed.. one-fifth glass Pluto to four-fifths glass hot water.. Pluto Water is virtually tasteless. It is non-irritating and non-habit-forming.

THE FAMOUS
PLUTO SPRING

FRENCH LICK SPRINGS.. the home of Pluto Water.. is renowned the world over. It ranks with the celebrated European spas as a resort for health, rest and recreation. The magnificent French Lick Springs Hotel is noted for its lavish comfort.. its consummate service.. its perfect cuisine.. and the almost unlimited diversions it affords. Two excellent golf courses.. splendid riding facilities .. as well as all other out-door amusements are provided.

Pluto Water ends *ASTHENIA—the want or loss of strength.. diminution of the vital forces .. often due to poisons bred by intestinal microorganisms. Pluto Water—America's Laxative Mineral Water—is bottled and sealed at French Lick Springs Hotel, French Lick, Indiana—America's Greatest Health Resort. By actual comparison, Pluto Water is the least expensive laxative you can take. In two sizes—20c and 45c. At all drug counters; on trains, steamships; at clubs and hotels.

it's ASTHENIA*

Take PLUTO WATER and see a NEW WORLD in 10 Days!

[1932]

Should she have been frank?

She called this the "last straw" and left him.

• • •

THIS is a case where a woman paid a high price for silence. Like so many other commendable people she kept small irritations to herself. It was hard for her to speak out—even though a frank discussion might have smoothed trouble away.

Little things continually cropped up to mar her happiness. Possibly she should have overlooked them entirely. Certainly it was a grave mistake to harbor bitter thoughts. She allowed petty annoyances to pile up until her patience was almost exhausted. Then her husband grew a bit careless in his appearance—even failed to shave as often or as carefully as he should.

Is a woman correct in assuming a man is losing respect for her or himself when he becomes careless about shaving? We think not—discomfort is a more likely reason—although stubble is a handicap in almost every business or social contact. May we suggest today's Gillette blade is the answer in cases like this.

This blade is far keener and smoother—invites frequent, close shaving. Once or twice daily use will not irritate the tenderest skin. We urge you to try this remarkable blade on our positive money-back guarantee. If you don't agree every shave is by far the cleanest and smoothest you have ever enjoyed—return the package to your dealer and he'll refund the purchase price.

Gillette

RAZORS — Gillette — BLADES

[1932]

Thrilling!
Yes!…but tiring

Just as soon as you *do* tire, eat a few pieces of Schrafft's candy. Notice how quickly your energy comes back. Schrafft's candy is one of nature's shortest cuts to stimulation through food. For your health's sake keep a box handy when you work or play. Sold everywhere . . . . 60c to $2.00 the pound.

SCHRAFFT'S
*Selected Candies and Chocolates
belong in the picture
of Health ★*

SCHRAFFT'S gives you quick energy
for a QUICK COMEBACK

★Every day thousands of healthy people buy Schrafft's Candy in the famous Schrafft's Stores and Restaurants and they eat this delicious energy-food to fight fatigue and guard health.

SCHRAFFT'S   *New York and Boston* ⚓ OWNED AND OPERATED BY FRANK G. SHATTUCK COMPANY

[1931]

Foot-Joy
REG. U.S. PAT. OFF.
"The Shoe that's Different"

Ask for the best shoe store in any of the principal cities of America and you will nearly always be given the address of a Foot-Joy dealer. For these dealers endeavor to render you a service beyond the selling of shoes. When they fit you to a pair of Foot-Joy shoes they insure you against fatigue, leg and muscle strain, and the many ills that start with arch trouble. Ask us to send you illustrations of the latest smart styles.

FIELD & FLINT CO., Brockton, Mass.
Established 1857

Dealers in most of the larger cities.

In New York at 4 E. 44th Street

The above statement is also true of Foot-Joy shoes for women. Write for information.

Name..

Address....................................(TOD)

[1930]

The **MOST EXPENSIVE** gown in the world—not merely because of its beauty—but also because of the exquisite artistry of its designer, Vionnet. Though apparently simple, its classic loveliness is founded on the most intricate cutting and molding to the body lines.

*By courtesy of
Bergdorf-Goodman, N. Y.*

Obviously not for the masses

Like an expensive gown, the effectiveness of Pebeco is not due to obvious things. It hasn't the frills and furbelows of sweet taste and foamy lather. Its tremendous effectiveness lies in the character of its ingredients—and in the cool, lasting tang which is Pebeco's distinctive signature. 40% of Pebeco is an expensive ingredient not found in other tooth pastes—an ingredient that science has proved vital in the care of the teeth.

It is the *thinkers* who like Pebeco—the people who realize that irrelevant, candy-like tastes or extravagant claims in advertising cannot benefit the teeth—*that it is what is in a tooth paste that counts.*

Do your own thinking about what dentifrice to use...ask your retailer for PEBECO

LEHN & FINK, Inc., Bloomfield, N. J.

Pebeco is the **MOST EXPENSIVE** tooth paste in the world to make. But its cost to you is no higher than that of the average dentifrice.

*The tooth paste
for thinking people*

[1931]

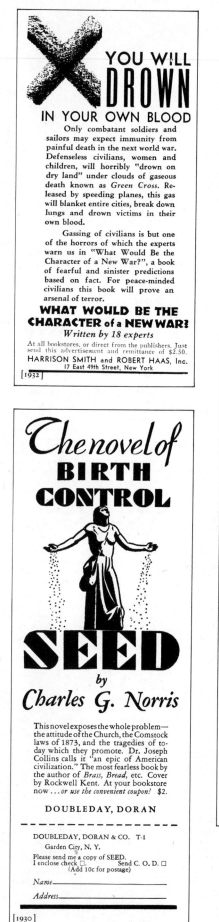

"Why did the Clark and Jones Company move to the office building across the street?"

THE REAL REASON why office tenants so frequently seek new quarters is that the washrooms and toilets in the buildings they leave have become worn out and shabby. Business men appreciate that it is lack of courtesy to customers and employees to have toilets of this kind. Fortunately, these unpleasant conditions can be remedied easily and at little cost, simply by installing new Church Sani-Black Toilet Seats.

It is the ease with which they may be installed—and their inexpensiveness—which makes Church Sani-Black Seats a profitable investment in any building and puts the appearance of the toilet above reproach. All that is necessary is to throw out the old seats and replace them with the new, everdurable Church Sani-Black Seats which fit any make of bowl. They are sanitary, clean, guaranteed to last for the life of the building.

Neat, clean and modern toilets do not only help induce old tenants to stay—they give the building a higher rental value and make it easier to find new tenants. The owners of hundreds of office buildings have profited in dollars and cents by installing Church Toilet Seats.

Are you sure that your tenants are entirely satisfied with their quarters? If not it may pay you to send for the illustrated booklet which we have prepared. It describes our full line of Sani-Black Seats for office and public buildings. C. F. Church Manufacturing Company, Holyoke, Massachusetts.

C. F. CHURCH MANUFACTURING CO., Dept. W-2, Holyoke, Mass.
   Gentlemen: Please send me the illustrated catalog describing Church Sani-Black Seats for (state kind of building)_____

Name_____

Address_____

City_____ State_____

CHURCH *sani*-SEATS

"TOILET SEATS FOR BETTER BUILDINGS"

[1930]

To Play Better
Play Safe

To get distance, direction, control on the green . . . to improve your form and your score . . . try giving support and protection against fatigue and strains to the vital but least rugged zone of your body.

More and more, thinking men agree with trained athletes in accepting Bauer & Black athletic supporters as essential sport equipment. Not only to guard delicate cords and structures, but to enjoy the snug comfort, security, freedom which make for brilliant performance.

The *de luxe* supporter is *Pal*. Strong, rubber-cored ribs knit into its light, porous pouch . . . an exclusive patented feature . . . provide supersupport and matchless comfort, never binding or chafing. Slow to absorb perspiration, soft as new after washing. Supreme quality and economy at a dollar and up.

Bike is a simpler, all elastic supporter, the choice of coaches, trainers and athletes for 55 years. Easy to wash . . . easy to wear . . . easy to buy at 50 cents upward. At all druggists and sporting goods dealers.

Pal
and BIKE

BAUER & BLACK

DIVISION OF THE KENDALL COMPANY
Chicago · · New York · · Toronto

What every man should know *about the need and functions of a supporter is concisely presented in our new treatise "Guard the Vital Zone."* Address Bauer & Black, 2542 S. Dearborn St., Chicago, for free copy.

[1930]

This Time he's setting the pace for All Three

Walter P. Chrysler's new Plymouth Six now on display

"LOOK AT ALL THREE!" said Walter P. Chrysler last April. "Look at all three!" he repeats today.

"For a lot of things have happened since the last time you looked!"

Today, he announces a brand new Plymouth! It's a Six with Floating Power. A BIG, *full-sized* Six!

Not just a new model . . . but a *complete new car that changes the whole picture of the low-priced field.*

This time it's Plymouth that's "out in front!" Setting the pace. Showing the nation what style can mean . . . what values can be these days.

The new Plymouth Six is Walter P. Chrysler's bid for first place in the low-priced field. He has declared war in a battle of engineering brains . . . and he adds with confidence: "May the best car win!"

Walter P. Chrysler stands where he does today because of his remarkable sense of knowing what the public wants. His new Plymouth Six was built to *earn* "Number One" place . . . by honestly winning the good-will of American motorists!

That's why it is not just a Six—but a Six with patented Floating Power. Completely vibrationless.

That's why it has hydraulic four-wheel brakes— so Free Wheeling can be enjoyed in security. And safety steel bodies—so you ride with peace-of-mind.

It has big-car roominess . . . big-car performance, and yet, because of brilliant engineering, it has amazing economy of gas . . . oil . . . tires . . . upkeep!

It's a solid car—solid-looking, and solidly built. Honest in every part and detail. It was created by hard, earnest effort . . . keen, straight thinking!

We ask you to look at the new Plymouth Six . . . to "Look at All Three." And decide for yourself . . . "Is Plymouth America's next 'Number One' Car?"

SOLD BY 7,232 DESOTO, DODGE & CHRYSLER

It's a **Six**—
with <u>Floating</u>
<u>Power</u>

DEALERS THROUGHOUT THE UNITED STATES

[1932]

IT'S WISE TO CHOOSE A SIX

... and the Chevrolet Six is priced as low as $495

More and more motor car buyers in the low-price field are learning that it's wise to choose a Chevrolet Six—for modern ideas of power, speed and smoothness can best be met with six cylinders.

The flow of power is smoother in a Chevrolet Six. Hills and bad roads are traveled easily and surely. High speeds are maintained without strain. And its six-cylinder smoothness saves the whole car from destructive vibration.

Yet, with all these advantages of six-cylinder performance—the Chevrolet Six is priced as low as $495, at the Flint factory. And it costs no more for gas, oil, tires, or upkeep.

In addition, the Chevrolet Six gives you the style, comfort and safety of beautiful Fisher bodies—built of selected hardwood-and-steel.

It gives you the travel-comfort and road-balance of four long semi-elliptic springs, controlled by four Lovejoy hydraulic shock absorbers.

It gives you safety and driving confidence by providing internal-expanding four-wheel brakes, completely enclosed against mud and water.

Near at hand is a Chevrolet dealer. See him today—and learn on what easy terms you can buy a Chevrolet Six.

CHEVROLET MOTOR COMPANY, DETROIT, MICHIGAN
Division of General Motors Corporation

CHEVROLET SIX

The Sport Roadster..$555	Roadster or Phaeton	*The* Sedan Delivery..$595
The Coach........$565		Light Delivery Chassis.........$365
The Coupe........$565		1½ Ton Chassis....$520
The Sport Coupe....$655		1½ Ton Chassis with Cab............$625
The Club Sedan....$625		Roadster Delivery..$440
The Sedan.........$675		(Pick-up box extra)
The Special Sedan..$725	*(Special Equipment extra)*	*All prices f. o. b. factory*
(6 wire wheels standard)		*Flint, Michigan*

[1930]

$495

ANNOUNCING THE

SUPERCHARGED AIR-COOLED

Twelve Cylinder

FRANKLIN

For four years Franklin engineers have studied, experimented, tested, proved — and now present the Supercharged, Air-cooled, Twelve Cylinder Franklin. For the first time in a motor car, this new Air-cooled Twelve incorporates the one thing that has given aviation its greatest impetus — the high-powered, multi-cylinder, air-cooled engine.

To see the car is to feel instantly the freshness and brilliance that Le Baron has styled into the Franklin Twelve — the year's pattern of beauty and luxury. And when you drive this responsive, amply proportioned car of 144-inch wheelbase, that feeling is immediately transformed into thrilling admiration for the sensational performance which carries you to new luxury in travel.

The Supercharged 150 horsepower air-cooled engine is extremely simple in operation, requiring 100 less parts than comparable water-cooled engines.

So accessible is the engine and so free of complication that low maintenance becomes an important feature. The Supercharger achieves flowing, turbine-like power, smoothness and acceleration by *forcing* a full charge of perfect mixture into *every cylinder equally*. Actual tests show gas consumption is appreciably lower. And engine life is much greater, for even at high touring speeds the engine is purring effortlessly. Pressure air-cooling adds greatly to the economical efficiency of the engine and allows you to *drive all day at high speed* without overheating or loss of power. In Franklin there is no water to boil, freeze or leak.

You are invited to examine and drive the new Supercharged Twelve as an example of the really modern motor car.

Franklin also offers the new Supercharged Airman, with 132-inch wheelbase, 100 horsepower engine. Franklin Automobile Company, Syracuse, New York.

Air-cooled **V** *Twelve*

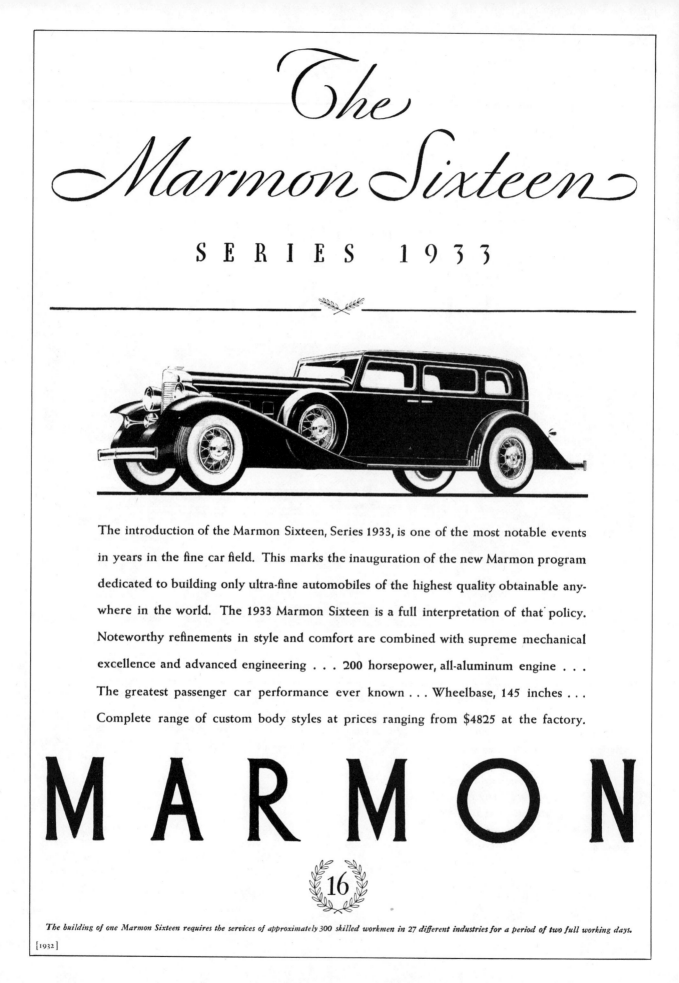

The Marmon Sixteen

SERIES 1933

The introduction of the Marmon Sixteen, Series 1933, is one of the most notable events in years in the fine car field. This marks the inauguration of the new Marmon program dedicated to building only ultra-fine automobiles of the highest quality obtainable anywhere in the world. The 1933 Marmon Sixteen is a full interpretation of that policy. Noteworthy refinements in style and comfort are combined with supreme mechanical excellence and advanced engineering . . . 200 horsepower, all-aluminum engine . . . The greatest passenger car performance ever known . . . Wheelbase, 145 inches . . . Complete range of custom body styles at prices ranging from $4825 at the factory.

MARMON

The building of one Marmon Sixteen requires the services of approximately 300 skilled workmen in 27 different industries for a period of two full working days.

[1932]

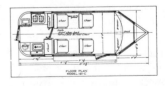
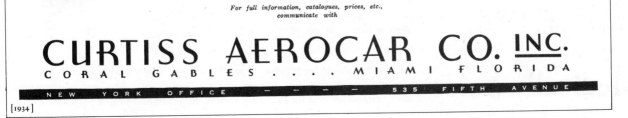

Acids.. Mercury.. even Arsenic..

found in many brands
of toilet tissue

YOU would never forgive yourself if your child . . . or any member of your family became ill from using carelessly purchased toilet tissue.

Yet how can you tell whether or not the toilet tissue you buy is safe . . . free from impurities? You can't—unless you insist on the brand of a responsible manufacturer. For two-thirds of the so-called "brands" of toilet tissue sold in stores today are unfit to use.

Tests of 660 brands made in a nationally known hospital laboratory prove that 455 toilet tissues are decidedly inferior and contain chemical impurities which are an actual menace to health.

Strong acids, mercury, sand, chlorine —and even arsenic were found.

In every test, the two health tissues,

ScotTissue and Waldorf, conformed to medical standards of safety. No harsh irritants were found. No harmful acids or chemicals. Both ScotTissue and Waldorf were extremely soft, absolutely pure, with a high degree of absorbency.

· · ·

Don't take chances. Rectal trouble is an extremely painful illness—often requiring an operation. Be safe! Buy only the tissues you know meet the standards which physicians approve. Scott Paper Company, Chester, Penna.

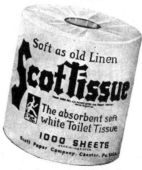

SCOTTISSUE, *an extremely soft, pure white absorbent roll. Now selling at the lowest price in 14 years.*

WALDORF, *a soft and absorbent roll, yet very inexpensive. Now selling at the lowest price in 14 years.*

Medically Safe

The hospital tests described above showed ScotTissue and Waldorf *entirely free from harsh irritants . . . and chemically pure.* These extremely soft, absorbent health tissues have always been approved for safety by doctors, hospitals and health authorities.

[1932]

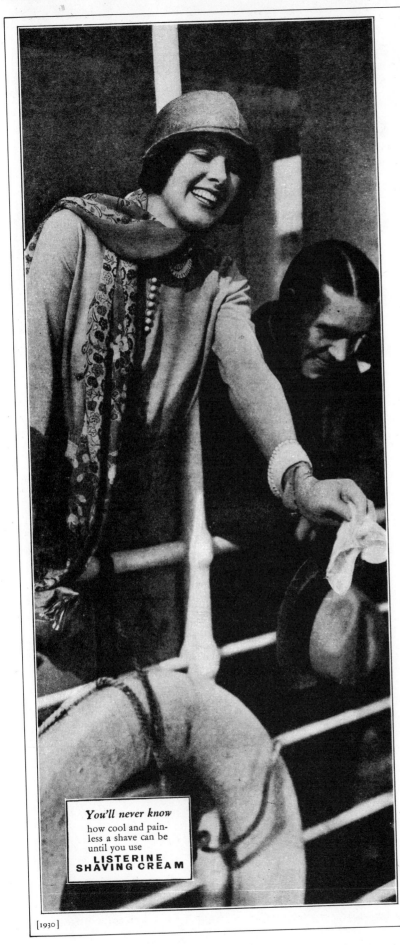

You'll never know
how cool and pain-
less a shave can be
until you use
**LISTERINE
SHAVING CREAM**

Look out, Europe, here she comes!

This is Mildred on her way to Europe—attractive, capable, the secretary of a well-known business man in Albany.

She has forgotten the sacrifices necessary to make this trip possible; the lunches she didn't eat; the little things she went without. They are all behind now. Europe and romance lie ahead.

There will be nice men on the boat who will dance with her again and again—so she thinks. *But she is mistaken. They will only dance once.*

There will be gay little bridge parties bright with badinage and the exchange of wit. *Sure there will—but she won't be included.*

Perhaps some attractive man will walk the moonlit decks with her and, recognizing the qualities that make her one woman out of a hundred, will ask her to marry him. Perhaps he will—*but the chances are against it.*

If you have ever come face to face with a real case of halitosis (unpleasant breath) you can understand how it might well be an obstacle to pleasant business, professional, and social relations. It is the unforgivable social fault.

The insidious thing about halitosis is that you never know when you have it. It does not announce itself to the victim. Important to remember, also, is the fact that few people escape it entirely. That is because every day in any normal mouth, conditions capable of causing halitosis are likely to arise.

Common causes are: stomach derangements due to excesses of eating or drinking, fermenting food particles in the mouth, defective or decaying teeth, pyorrhea, catarrh, and infections of the nose, mouth or throat.

The pleasant way to put your breath beyond suspicion, is to rinse the mouth with full strength Listerine, the safe antiseptic. Every morning. Every night. And between times before meeting others.

Since it is antiseptic, full strength Listerine checks food fermentation. It is also a remarkable germicide* which attacks infection from which odors spring. Finally, being a deodorant, it destroys the odors themselves, leaving both mouth and breath fresh, sweet, and clean.

Keep Listerine handy in home and office, and drop a bottle in your bag when travelling. It puts you on the safe side; makes you acceptable to others. Lambert Pharmacal Company, St. Louis, Mo., U. S. A.

•   •

*Though safe to use in any body cavity, full strength Listerine kills even the resistant Staphylococcus Aureus (pus) and Bacillus Typhosus (typhoid) germs in counts ranging to 200,000,000 in 15 seconds. (Fastest time science has accurately recorded.)

Rockwell Kent, with the Eskimos in Greenland,

...hears the tango played in distant Argentina

FOR the next eighteen months, Rockwell Kent, noted artist and author, will live in Greenland among the primitive Eskimos.

He has put civilization far behind him—telephones, motor cars, steam-heated apartments—and yet he will be in daily touch with the modern world and all that it is doing.

He will hear, over a new General Electric All-wave Radio Receiver that went with him, the news of busy America and Europe.

During the long Arctic nights, he will entertain his Eskimo friends with Spanish music from Madrid and Buenos Aires, symphony concerts played in Berlin, opera winged from Milan and Rome.

And every other week, he will listen to the voice of Mrs. Kent, speaking from the General Electric short-wave station at Schenectady . . . telling him the gossip of New York, of friends, of home.

After you've "gone places" with a new G-E set, you'll never be content with any other radio.

Any one of these new General Electric All-wave sets . . . founded on 28 years of short-wave pioneering achievement . . . will take you roaming all over the world for radio entertainment.

At the turn of a dial, you leave the U. S. A. behind and in a few seconds, oceans are bridged . . . and you're getting programs from European capitals, South America, distant Australia.

Switch to another broadcast band . . . and there are police calls, aviation signals, the conversation of amateur operators to thrill you.

And when you return to America once more, your favorite local and network programs hold a new delight for you . . . for only the new G-E bring them in with such brilliancy of tone.

Convince yourself with a thrilling "tone test"

Ask your nearest G-E dealer to demonstrate one of the new G-E All-wave models—highly improved descendants of the famous G-E sets that "won the tone tests". . . "Believe your own ears" as you compare this new G-E with your present radio . . . And bear in mind that this distance-defying G-E is less expensive than the standard-range set of three years ago.

A full line of superb instruments—table models, consoles, radio-phonograph combinations, including battery sets. Priced from $18.75 to $375. Prices slightly higher in the West, Mid-West and South. Subject to change without notice.

MODEL M-86—Typical of the many new G-E All-wave models is this smartly styled console. Priced at $119.50. Other long- and short-wave sets as low as $39.95.

Write the General Electric Co., Section R-4910 Merchandise Dept., Bridgeport, Conn.

GENERAL ⓖⓔ ELECTRIC RADIO

BORN OF THE PIONEERING ACHIEVEMENTS OF THE FAMOUS "HOUSE OF MAGIC"

[1934]

NOW..... from "RADIO HEADQUARTERS"
amazing Radio-Phonograph that plays the
New 30-Minute Records

New 9-tube De Luxe radio, combined with automatic record-changing phonograph, provides complete home entertainment in one moderately priced instrument.

LISTEN—with this new instrument—to Victor's new 12-inch records that play for 30 minutes—and 10-inch records that play proportionately as long!

Listen—through its automatic record changer that takes ten 10-inch records—to almost two hours of music, without repetition and without touching the instrument.

Listen—through its new De Luxe 9-tube Super-Heterodyne—to radio music with no distortion, no mechanical effect, none of the common set faults—thanks to a revolutionary new Synchronized Tone System!

Listen—and *marvel*—for this new instrument with all its new features—its automatic record changer, its long-play-

ing record clutch, its exclusive 10-Point Synchronized Tone System—costs no more than a high grade radio alone would have cost last year!

By all means, hear it! Hear the new Victor Program Transcriptions—with 15 minutes of music on each side!

And at the same time, see all the amazing values RCA Victor dealers have to show. Radios from $37.50 to $178, complete; radio-phonograph combinations from $129.50 to $995 ... all hallmarked by *two* famous trademarks—RCA and Victor.

RCA Victor Co., Inc.,   Camden, N. J.
"RADIO HEADQUARTERS"
A Radio Corporation of America Subsidiary

RCA Victor Radio-Phonograph Model RAE-26 —Nine-tube Super-Heterodyne radio with electrically reproducing phonograph and automatic record changer. Automatic volume leveler, Micro tone control, Pentode and Super-Control Radiotrons. Plays both old type records and new Victor Program Transcriptions, which give nearly four times as much music as present types. Complete with Radiotrons, $247.50.

RCA Victor
Radios
Phonograph Combinations
Victor Records

[1931]

PHILCO JR.

Genuine Balanced Superheterodyne

$18 75

Complete with Tubes
TAX PAID

Price slightly higher in Denver and West

THINK of it! A real PHILCO — a musical instrument of quality — for only $18.75. Designed in the great PHILCO Laboratories to meet present-day broadcasting conditions.

A real superheterodyne radio of superb tone — able to receive broadcasts from a surprising distance — a radio superior to many sets selling at twice its price.

A TRUE PHILCO THROUGH AND THROUGH

PHILCO Jr. is the latest development of the PHILCO research laboratories — built to precision standards in the great PHILCO factories. And it is designed to meet the safety requirements of the National Board of Fire Underwriters.

PHILCO Jr. is in a most attractive cabinet of pleasing design, a Balanced Superheterodyne with genuine Electro-Dynamic Speaker and Illuminated Station Dial — most unusual features in a radio so low in price. The new PHILCO High Efficiency Tubes are used throughout. PHILCO Jr. is a true PHILCO in every sense of the word — worthy of its honored name in appearance as well as in performance.

A GENUINE PHILCO AT AN UNHEARD-OF PRICE

See this wonderful new PHILCO Jr. Thrill to its superb tone and surprising distance range. Buy it. Take it home. Enjoy its splendid performance at a price that revolutionizes the whole world of radio entertainment! $18.75 — complete with the new PHILCO High Efficiency Tubes — *tax paid!*

PHILCO · PHILADELPHIA · TORONTO · LONDON

The complete PHILCO line offers supreme value in all price ranges . . .

$18 75 to $295
TAX PAID

PHILCO REPLACEMENT TUBES IMPROVE THE PERFORMANCE OF ANY SET

Philco-Transitone Radio (superheterodyne) for motor cars and boats, average price complete, installed and tax paid on cars equipped with aerial, $69.50. ALL ELECTRIC (no dry batteries) $79.50.

PHILCO
A musical instrument of quality

UNBALANCED RADIO   BALANCED PHILCO

BOTH
are Stokowski

ABOVE IS MODEL 112X Balanced Superheterodyne, eleven tube, Automatic Volume Control, $150. Other Philcos from $36.50 to $295, complete with Philco Balanced Tubes, including new Pentode Power Tube, illuminated station recording dial, hand rubbed cabinets, and many other exclusive Philco features . . . Philco replacement tubes, Philco Short Wave Converter, Philco Transitone for motor cars and boats, Philco Electric Clock and Radio Regulator.

WHEN you hear the Philadelphia Orchestra, conducted by Leopold Stokowski, on your own PHILCO Radio, you are hearing them as eloquently as if they were playing in your own home. You are hearing a real, living, personal rendition of the world's finest music interpreted by genius · · · Close your eyes, turn your back and listen. PHILCO is ONE instrument—but when you listen on your PHILCO to the Philadelphia Orchestra you are listening to MORE THAN ONE HUNDRED instruments · · · Just so you may, at any time, hear the instruments and voices of all the audible arts, in full, real and personally-present tone. PHILCO, a fine musical instrument and the most accepted radio, brings them to you in person · · · You may enjoy these voices of the air "in person" every day and night in the year, by the simple turn of a single dial on your PHILCO. Leading dealers everywhere will show it to you. See it. Hear it. Buy it. Enjoy it.

PHILCO · PHILADELPHIA · TORONTO · LONDON

Hear the greatest musical broadcasts of all time, by Leopold Stokowski and the Philadelphia Orchestra, over the entire Columbia Network, March 12, April 2 at 8:15 P. M. (E. S. T.)

·PHILCO
A musical instrument of quality

UNBALANCED RADIO   BALANCED PHILCO

[1932]

$\mathscr{B}$uilt for those who want THE BEST

THE NO. 40

THAT discerning class of people who seek to enrich their lives with the *better* things remain loyally Stromberg-Carlson in their radio tastes. And—Stromberg-Carlson remains faithful to this very considerable class, without which no standards of quality can be maintained.

Because every community has a group which always continues to want the best, Stromberg-Carlson tone quality, now for years the world's standard, remains unimpaired. For that same reason Stromberg-Carlson telephone standards* of radio design remain uncompromised; its insistence upon the truly artistic in fine cabinets remains unchanged.

True, Stromberg-Carlson prices do reflect lower present day costs, but, at any price, "there is nothing finer than a Stromberg-Carlson."

STROMBERG-CARLSON TELEPHONE MFG. CO., Rochester, N. Y.

*Since 1894 Stromberg-Carlson has manufactured instruments for telephone companies who must maintain this equipment at their own expense.

METER TUNING

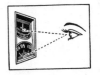

Essential if you are to have the benefits of Automatic Volume Control and yet get finest tone quality. Tuning Meter also shows relative signal strength of each station. "Cluster" arrangement of meter and dial on the Stromberg-Carlson allows both to be viewed simultaneously.

Stromberg-Carlson

MAKERS OF VOICE TRANSMISSION AND VOICE RECEPTION APPARATUS SINCE 1894

[1932]

375

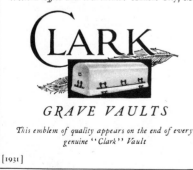

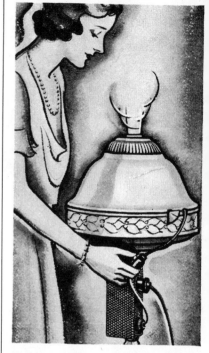

This cabinet is standard, but the cooling mechanism can be built into a piece of furniture or into any type of cabinet.

NOW YOU CAN

Turn on the Cold

AS EASILY AS YOU TURN ON THE HEAT!

This brings you news that will be as welcome as the first hint of autumn on a blistering August day. For it tells you how you can work in comfort even when the mercury climbs for a record and heat waves shimmer in a broiling sun outside your windows!

The Frigidaire Room Cooler is now ready—ready to transform hot, stuffy offices into places with an atmosphere so fresh and invigorating that "nerve-fag" never has a chance.

You can actually "turn on the cold" whenever you feel like it! For the minute you start it going the Frigidaire Room Cooler begins to draw the warm air in and throw the cold air out—all without creating annoying drafts or breezes. And as it takes out the heat, this marvelous device also takes out the humidity —just as a sponge picks up water.

Yet, despite the magic it performs, the Frigidaire Room Cooler is surprisingly simple—as simple as Frigidaire Refrigeration.

The Frigidaire dealer will be glad to tell you and show you how this appliance works and explain about the different models for offices, homes, stores, restaurants and other places where real warm-weather comfort is wanted.

We suggest that you get in touch with the Frigidaire dealer today. Frigidaire Corporation, Subsidiary of General Motors Corporation, Dayton, Ohio.

FRIGIDAIRE
Room Coolers

Also Electric Refrigerators for Homes ... Heavy-duty Refrigerating Equipment for Stores and Public Institutions ... Electric Water Coolers ... Ice Cream Cabinets ... Milk Cooling Equipment.

[1931]

73% _find relief from age-hastening ills_

"Change is remarkable", reports Dr. Langstroth

He credits diet, rich in vital protective factors

WHY some people age more quickly than others, why they develop degenerative diseases, was the subject for an interesting study recently made by Dr. Lovell Langstroth, a well-known California physician.

Dr. Langstroth asked 501 of his patients what they had been eating. They were all people in middle life, suffering from some ill characteristic of their age.

A careful study of their diets showed that most of them had not been getting enough of certain factors, now known to be essential for well-being.

These important factors are the vitamins!

When Dr. Langstroth put one hundred seventy-four of these patients on a diet rich in vitamins, he found that _seventy-three per cent_ were "much improved or completely relieved" of their ills.

The physician particularly noted how much better these people looked. Their skin was fresh, clean, and vital. Eyes had become bright and clear again. They carried themselves with a new alertness!

Why should adding vitamins to their diet have brought about this remarkable change?

First, because vitamins help people to stay active and well. To those who are under par, they offer a chance for renewed vitality.

Second, because vitamins _protect_ against many ills. They help to build up resistance against colds—nose and throat troubles. They aid digestion and help to keep appetite normal.

This is why people look and feel so much better when they get enough every day!

But how can they be sure of obtaining these factors? As Dr. Langstroth's study clearly shows, the average diet is too often lacking in vitamins.

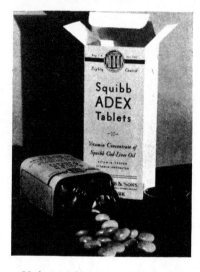

Under par? Here's a source of vitality

Squibb Adex Tablets provide Vitamins A and D, the "building up" elements of cod-liver oil, in a new palatable form. Taken every day, they help to renew vitality, to build resistance against colds, nose and throat troubles. People who can't take regular cod-liver oil will like Adex Tablets. Small, sugar-coated, and easy to swallow, they are agreeable to the most sensitive taste. And each Adex Tablet has the vitamin content of one-half teaspoonful of Squibb Cod-Liver Oil! Don't forget the name—_Adex_. At your druggist's.

Now a way has been found to make up this shortage. With _Squibb Vitamin Products!_

Squibb Vitamin Products, taken every day, enrich the diet in these important factors. They are palatable and easy to use. Begin now to build up vitality and resistance with them! Just ask today for Squibb Vitamin Products at any reliable drug store.

• • •

A sensible way to keep active and well— with these Squibb Vitamin Products

Squibb Chocolate Vitavose—If you feel sluggish, try this delicious new food drink. Chocolate Vitavose acts as an internal stimulant. Rich in Vitamin B*, it helps you to digest, to eliminate your food. Thus it tones the whole system! Drink Chocolate Vitavose regularly. It is delicious hot or cold! Children love Chocolate Vitavose, too. It adds such a rich, full flavor to their milk.

Squibb Mint-Flavored Cod-Liver Oil—A wonderful health-builder with the pleasant taste of mint. Rich in Vitamins A* and D*, it will increase vitality and build up resistance. The agreeable flavor makes it a favorite with the whole family!

Squibb Plain Cod-Liver Oil—"Bottled Sunshine" for babies. It helps them to build sound bones and teeth. _Guaranteed_ for its richness in Vitamin D*. It also supplies a protective amount of Vitamin A. Always get the Squibb Plain for babies.

Squibb Cod-Liver Oil with Viosterol-10 D—This is a special oil for children and babies who are growing rapidly or show a tendency toward tooth decay. It supplies _ten times_ as much Vitamin D as standard cod-liver oil. Also very rich in Vitamin A. Like the regular oil, it comes plain and mint-flavored.

Vitamin A*—Too little Vitamin A brings greater susceptibility to colds and to skin, sinus, and other troubles. Vitamin A helps build up resistance against them. It also has an important effect on growth.

Vitamin B*—A shortage of Vitamin B leads to poor appetite, loss of weight, low vitality, faulty assimilation, and sluggishness. Vitamin B gives tone to the digestive system, aids growth, and helps to keep the nervous system healthy.

Vitamin D*—Lack of Vitamin D results in soft, porous bones, rickets, and tooth decay. Vitamin D helps babies and children develop and maintain a strong, well-proportioned framework. It also helps them build strong, even teeth.

FREE: "Why You Need Vitamins," a booklet with a real message. Write for it! Address E. R. Squibb & Sons, 745 Fifth Ave., New York City.

SQUIBB VITAMIN PRODUCTS

PLUG IN FOR CORRECT TIME!

Electricity keeps the Telechron Clock in your home as accurate as the Telechron Master Clock in the power house

MUST YOU guess each morning which one of your clocks is right, if any? Do you ever forget the daily or weekly winding? It's disconcerting to miss a train by two minutes — unnerving to burn a batch of biscuits. Life moves so much more serenely, when it moves on schedule. . . . And Telechron was created just to keep life like that. ● Telechron does. You can connect it with the nearest electric outlet, set it and forget it. It will serve you faithfully for weeks and months and years. Its complete accuracy is assured by even impulses of alternating current, regulated at the power house by a Telechron Master Clock. You can *trust* Telechron! ● The very same precision is built into all the Telechron models. There are banjo clocks for the wall, graceful tambours for the mantel, compact little clocks for desk or radio, bedside clocks with alarm and illuminated dial, clocks in color for the kitchen — Telechron clocks — for every purpose and every price, from $9.95 to $55.★ Warren Telechron Company, Ashland, Massachusetts. In Canada, Canadian General Electric Co., Toronto.

★ The Revere Clock Company, of Cincinnati, Ohio, produces grandfather's clocks and other distinguished examples of fine cabinetwork equipped with Telechron motors, priced from $40 to $1200.

BELOW: *Vernon, particularly popular for bedside or dressing-table. Mahogany case. Three-inch gold-finish dial, illuminated by tiny Mazda lamp. Height 6⅛". Price* **$21.**

BELOW: *Madison, an attractive banjo clock in early-American design. Mahogany case with colored glass panels. Six-inch silvered dial. Height 32½". Price* **$50.**

This is the Telechron Master Clock in your power house. Checked by radio with naval observatory time, it governs the speed of the giant generators that supply impulses of alternating current to regulate the Telechron in your home.

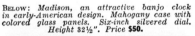

Telechron
electric time-keepers

...... !

the **MARCH**
of **TIME**

COMES BACK *on the* AIR!

In response to an ever-increasing demand for the return to the air of the MARCH of TIME, TIME, Inc., and the Columbia Broadcasting System have each arranged for a series of broadcasts of the program which made radio history last year with its stirring re-enactments of memorable scenes from the world's news.

SEPTEMBER

9

The Columbia Broadcasting System will present the MARCH of TIME as a sustaining feature, commencing

Friday night September 9, at 8:30 P. M. EDST — on the entire Columbia network — and every Friday throughout September and October. TIME's editors will assist with the selection of events and preparation of the script.

Starting November 4, TIME, Inc., will itself sponsor the program, every week following the Columbia series, and throughout the winter — at the same weekly hour.

TIME MARCHES ON!

1935-1939

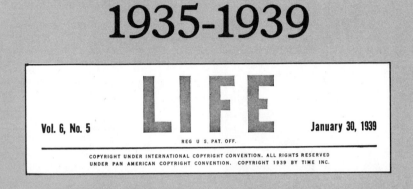

LIFE

REG U S. PAT. OFF.

Vol. 6, No. 5

January 30, 1939

●

Unpopularity Contest. Of profoundest importance in its bearing on America's chances of getting into a war is the sentiment of the American people toward other nations. This week FORTUNE releases the results of a poll which shows how Americans are losing their neutrality. Asked which foreign government and people they felt "least friendly" toward, only one in ten of those polled was indifferent, as compared with over half of those questioned in a similar poll in 1935. Of the remaining nine, 56% said they felt least friendly toward the German government, 28% said they felt least friendly toward the German people. Next in order of unpopularity came Japan, Italy, Russia. Overwhelming winners in a vote on "most friendly" feeling was the nation with which America is most likely to ally herself in a future war: Great Britain.

●

Basuto girl, Northern Transvaal

★

SOUTH AFRICA
LAND OF COLORFUL CONTRASTS

A Mountain Pass in the Zwarte Bergen Range

THE famous "Garden Route" of South Africa includes Mossel Bay, a quaint Indian Ocean resort — glorious Montagu Pass, the "Wilderness" (an unusual name for a region of transcendent beauty), picturesque Knysna, and George, called the "prettiest village on the face of the earth."

By rail or motor, the "Garden Route" is one of the world's rarest scenic treats — gem-like villages that make one long to live there, towering mountains, primeval forests.

South Africa abounds in beauty and marvelous sightseeing, travel is comfortable, the climate delightful, and the people are charmingly hospitable.

And there's a wonderful plus attraction this fall — the big Empire Exhibition at Johannesburg, the "Golden City" — celebrating its Golden Jubilee and the marvelous progress of South Africa — Sept. 15, 1936-Jan. 15, 1937.

Detailed information from all leading travel and tourist agencies

[1936]

"Aw please, mother—can't we go on the STREET CAR?"

There's a "new" kind of transportation on our city streets today

ABOUT thirty years ago, the thrills of streetcar riding were crowded out of youthful favor by the automobile. But they're showing strong signs of a comeback today. It's old stuff to go downtown in the family car — but gosh! wouldn't it be fun to go in that big, shiny, low-slung trolley! It travels along so smooth and nice you can hardly hear it coming — picks up and "goes places" like a sport roadster.

And talk about four wheel brakes...!

It is a far cry from the "Toonervilles" of yesterday to the modern streamline electric cars and trolley coaches. This new-day *electric* equipment is evidence of the "public-be-pleased" attitude of modern street-transit management. It combines speed and mobility with the clean, quiet smoothness of electricity itself.

To make such equipment possible, car builders called upon Westinghouse engineers to solve many technical problems. On a large proportion of the new cars, the motors, control apparatus and braking systems are Westinghouse-built. The street railway industry is thus one of many through which Westinghouse serves the public indirectly, besides its direct services to homes, farms, offices and factories everywhere.

Westinghouse
The name that means everything in electricity

[1937]

SOAP AND WATER

Traditional foes of dirt are the partners Soap and Water. But sometimes these allies fight with each other. Let's look . . .

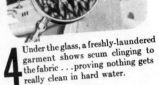

1 Lady steps in bath, hoping to find cleanliness. When she gets out . . .

2 there is a line of dirty scum around the tub. That scum is not dirt from her body. It is the result of chemical reaction between soap and minerals present in the "hard" water.

3 This same scum coats her whole body. Rinsing can't remove it. It clogs pores...makes skin dry and itchy . . . causes irritation.

4 Under the glass, a freshly-laundered garment shows scum clinging to the fabric . . . proving nothing gets really clean in hard water.

5 How different is a bath in conditioned water! Soap whips up into rich, bubbly lather . . . then rinses off completely . . . leaving body relaxed, skin velvety.

6 No matter what your present water supply, it can be conditioned . . . *automatically* . . . right in your own home. Permutit equipment is connected into your supply pipe. Provision can also be made to remove dirt, iron, bad taste and odor, as well as softening all the water that you use. Permutit water softeners cost only 2c a day to operate, return their cost through savings in soap, in plumbing repairs, and in housework. Priceless comfort, health and beauty are thrown in, free of charge!

Find out about conditioned water. Authorized Permutit dealers everywhere. Send for the free booklet, "The Magic of Wonder-Soft Water," filled with interesting information.

Permutit *Water Conditioning*

DISTRIBUTED EXCLUSIVELY BY AUTHORIZED DEALERS

Crime takes a tumble in Evansville

60% more arrests…17% fewer crimes, since 2-way radio was put on the police force…

During the six months after Western Electric police radio was adopted, that was the record in Evansville, Indiana.

With Western Electric 2-way radio, patrol cars may reach the scene of crime even before the get-away. Cars report results instantly to headquarters; ask for and receive further instructions.

Western Electric radio equipment is dependable—backed by 54 years of Bell telephone making.

Ask your police department if your town has radio protection.

GRAYBAR ELECTRIC — DISTRIBUTORS

"Calling all cars"

Western Electric
Leaders in Sound-Transmission Apparatus

[1936]

WAR!
Says BOAKE CARTER

Philco News Commentator
in the
TIME*liest* book of the year

"BLACK SHIRT BLACK SKIN"
$1.50

The Story behind the Story of the Italo-Ethiopian feud.

More thrilling than fiction!

EVERYWHERE BOOKS ARE SOLD or DIRECT FROM THE PUBLISHERS BY USING COUPON BELOW

THE TELEGRAPH PRESS   T-923
Harrisburg, Pennsylvania

Please send me postpaid "BLACK SHIRT BLACK SKIN" for which I enclose (check, money order) for $1.50.

PRINT NAME AND ADDRESS PLAINLY

Name_____
Address_____
City_____

[1935]

Love
as burning as Sahara's Sands

From Ouida's romantic novel of the French Foreign Legion, flashes this glorious spectacle-drama of men's heroism and women's devotion, enacted by one of the greatest casts the screen has ever seen.

UNDER TWO FLAGS

starring
Ronald COLMAN
(Beau Geste)

featuring
Claudette COLBERT
(It Happened One Night)

VICTOR McLAGLEN
(The Informer)

ROSALIND RUSSELL
(Rendezvous)

with GREGORY RATOFF • NIGEL BRUCE • C. HENRY GORDON • HERBERT MUNDIN

AND A CAST OF 10,000

a DARRYL F. ZANUCK 20th CENTURY PRODUCTION
(Les Miserables . . House of Rothschild)

Presented by Joseph M. Schenck
Directed by Frank Lloyd *(Cavalcade . . Mutiny on the Bounty)*
Associate Producer Raymond Griffith • Based on the novel by Ouida

20th CENTURY FOX

[1936]

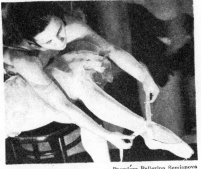

RITZ GOES TO A PICNIC

There they go. This is the second package of Ritz our hungry sun-bathers have consumed. And competition for the rest of these taste-teasing crackers is keen.

Let this be a lesson! When you go picnicking take plenty of Ritz. They add such a zest to salad, cheese and spreads that a basket lunch tastes like a banquet.

Reward to the winner. The young lady behind the screen has just given her husky opponent a severe trouncing. The gallery pays tribute by offering Ritz—her favorite cracker. And is the defeated gentleman unhappy? No! For in one minute he's going to get a long, cold beverage and plenty of Ritz for himself. He knows (just as all America does) that nothing tastes so good with all drinks, as golden, nut-like Ritz.

Three's never a crowd—when the third party is Ritz! To paraphrase Mr. Khayyam —"a summer sun, a box of Ritz and thou" —is fun enough for any young man. These "give me another" crackers are good companions for any summer outing.

FREE! A fascinating book "50 Delicious Desserts"—with delectable, easy-to-make recipes that will brighten up any menu. Write National Biscuit Company, 449 West 14th Street, Dept. 82, New York.

THE SEAL OF PERFECT BAKING *Ritz is a product of* NATIONAL BISCUIT COMPANY

[1937]

Johnny Farrell

Tells How His Deep Sleep Secret Helps
Win Golf Tournaments
THE NIGHT BEFORE

JOHNNY FARRELL, whose phenomenally accurate putting has made him one of the greatest golfers of his time, says:—

"Golf isn't a game of strength, but rather one of perfect *control*, requiring keen judgment plus *precision*. You learn these things by endless practice during the day—but you *keep* them by sound, regular sleep at night. That's why I say that many of the most important tournaments I ever played were really *won the night before*—with the help of *Ovaltine*.

"It was when I was under unusual tension during a tournament that I first began taking *Ovaltine* to help me get to sleep. It worked like a charm and has been a regular standby with me ever since. Because steady nerves and a cool head in the morning can make all the difference between WIN or LOSE in golf—or anything else."

Thousands of People in All Walks of Life are Now Adopting This Deep Sleep Secret—for Clear-eyed "Morning Freshness" and Energetic Days

HERE'S that new "sleep insurance" idea so many people are following nowadays:—a cup of hot *Ovaltine* taken every night before getting into bed.

They take this *protecting* food-drink not merely to avoid nerve-wracking tossing and turning at night. But, more importantly, for the clear-eyed, energetic days that follow sound and *restful* sleep!

For of all the things that influence our lives, nothing is more vital than sleep! Loss of it can lead to shaky nerves—to sluggish bodies and *minds!*

On the other hand, many of the most important business and social "victories" are won in advance—as the result of deep, refreshing sleep *the night before*.

Physicians will tell you this is so. And more and more people are coming to realize it every day. That's why the Ovaltine "sleep insurance" idea has spread so rapidly among people in all walks of life.

How Ovaltine Acts

(1) *Ovaltine* is *not* a medicine. Helps the body relax normally. Relieves that feeling of "inner tension" in a purely *natural* way.

(2) It provides certain food elements needed to prevent muscular and nervous irritability that, according to some authorities, may cause night-time tossing.

Also important—*Ovaltine* helps replenish worn-out muscle, nerve and body cells during sleep, and furnishes "protective" food factors:—minerals, proteins and Vitamins A, B, D, and G.

That's why so many people awaken more completely *refreshed* after a night of "*Ovaltine* sleep." Not "dopey" as after taking drugs. But wide awake and vital—alert and "on their toes." They *get MORE out of sleep!*

So—for sleep that really *rests* you—get acquainted with *Ovaltine*. You simply mix it with milk. For sale everywhere.

NOTE: Ovaltine was originated in Switzerland, now made in the U. S. A. Created as a restorative food for convalescents, it is used in 57 countries today. Doctors approve it. And over 1,700 hospitals serve it in America alone!

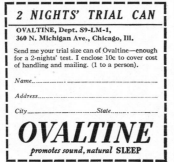

41% OF PEOPLE UNREFRESHED UPON AWAKENING!

In an investigation reported in a medical magazine, 41% of the people questioned said they felt unrefreshed on arising—indicating that they did not get the *maximum* benefit out of their sleep.

In a 3-year scientific sleep study, it was found that taking Ovaltine regularly at bedtime tended to cut down tossing and turning and give a feeling of being "better rested" in the morning.

---

2 NIGHTS' TRIAL CAN

OVALTINE, Dept. S9-LM-1,
360 N. Michigan Ave., Chicago, Ill.

Send me your trial size can of Ovaltine—enough for a 2-nights' test. I enclose 10c to cover cost of handling and mailing. (1 to a person).

Name.....................................

Address.................................

City....................State............

OVALTINE
promotes sound, natural SLEEP

[1939]

Slumber American en route to Europe

SAIL AMERICAN – FOR THE COMFORTS, THE LUXURIES, SO TYPICALLY AMERICAN

IT'S in a big room, this big, deep, real bed equipped with Simmons Beautyrest mattress. Adjoining is the modern bathroom (shower and toilet). Thick-pile carpet covers the floor. Several soft chairs mutely invite. An attractive room, a luxurious room, *an American room*

But back to this real, American bed. The sort of bed you really *slumber* in. With lots of room for comfortable turnings and stretching . . . and lots of soft depth to ease away tiredness.

In a way this modern American bed is typical of all things offered you on your own American ships...extra comfort, extra luxury, extra good times...all in keeping with the American standard of living. Roosevelt Steamship Company, Inc., Main Office, No. 1 Broadway, New York. Offices and agents everywhere. *Your travel agent knows the Manhattan and Washington. Ask him about the great value they offer!*

UNITED STATES LINES

Continental Can Announces
BEER

A-h-h-h

Continental

in CAP SEALED CANS

BEER

USE ANY BOTTLE OPENER

Tastes better • Easy to open
Protected from light
No deposit • No empties to return
Cools quicker • Takes up less space
No danger of breakage
Sanitary—used once—thrown away
Holds 12 fluid ounces same as bottle
Drink right from can if you wish

Now you're going to know what fine beer really ought to taste like—right in your own home or anywhere.

A brand-new container makes it possible . . . a special can designed by Continental Can Company after long research. This can is sealed with a cap and opens just like a bottle.

There are many reasons why you will prefer beer in this handy new container. But the chief reason is that it tastes better.

Why is this?

Because the can permits faster pasteurization. Because it keeps out flavor-robbing light. And because Continental's special lining retains the brewery goodness unchanged.

At present we can't make these cans fast enough to keep up with demand. But before long you should be able to enjoy your favorite beer in this new and better container. Watch for it, ask for it—and you'll thank us.

NOTICE TO BREWERS

Brewers have been pleased to learn that Continental's cap sealed can may be run on present bottling lines with very little change in equipment. Full details on request.

Can Company

**NEW YORK
CHICAGO SAN FRANCISCO**

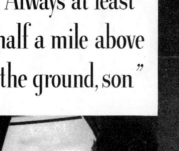

"How high? Always at least half a mile above the ground, son"

Son: How can you tell how high we're flying, dad?

Dad: Why, I can't, but I just asked the stewardess. She told me it's United Air Lines' strict policy, now, to fly half a mile or more above the ground over all their routes.

Son: It sure lets you have a swell view!

Dad: Yes, but that's not why they fly high, son. It's for greater safety. And besides, the air is usually a good deal smoother up here. Your mother was just saying what a comfortable ride we're having . . .

DO YOU KNOW ABOUT THESE REMARKABLE NEW DEVELOPMENTS IN AIR TRAVEL?

 **You fly at least ½ mile above terrain** all the way. It is now United's rigid policy to fly at least ½ mile above the ground. United was first to install *in every plane* a barograph which records the altitude automatically, providing an official record of every trip.

Pilots are paid for their judgment in NOT flying, too. If weather looks doubtful, United's pilots need not hesitate to cancel a trip. *Only United* guarantees pilots' salaries regardless of hours flown, at least $650 a month. Thus they are compensated for using caution.

 A constant flow of weather facts gives United a clear, up-to-the-minute picture of conditions all along the route—at every level up to 20,000 feet. Pilot and dispatcher, both expert meteorologists, study this data before agreeing on a plan of flight.

Your plane has TWICE the power and cruising range needed. United's Mainliners can fly 1500 miles non-stop—double their longest scheduled flight. And they can *climb two miles* in the air with only one of their twin engines in use.

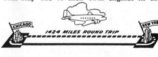

CHICAGO · *1424 MILES ROUND TRIP* · NEW YORK

Next time you travel, "fly high" in a United Mainliner! NEW YORK-CHICAGO . . . *the shortest No. 1 route; 6 flights daily.* NEW YORK TO LOS ANGELES, SAN FRANCISCO, SEATTLE . . . *two de luxe coast-to-coast sleeper flights nightly, including the world-famous "Continental"—also a scenic daylight flight. Only United's "Main Line" airway links the East with all California and Northwest cities.*

UNITED AIR LINES

THE "MAIN LINE" AIRWAY—A YEAR 'ROUND ROUTE

SLEEP — OVERNIGHT — COAST·TO·COAST

Fly the Favorable Southern Route

When you Fly, overnight, Coast-to-Coast on American Airlines, you sleep as you are accustomed to—clothes off and in bed.

Only "American" has Flagship Sleeper Planes; large, comfortable berths and separate dressing rooms for men and women. These giant Flagships are the most spacious and luxurious planes in the United States. Specially designed and built—with longest-flying range—for transcontinental travel.

Delicious meals are served aloft *at no charge*, on tables with real china, silverware and linen. After dinner you relax in your big, deep, lounge chair; read, play bridge, or move about and visit with friends—and then to bed, for a night's Sleep. That's Flying "First-Class"!

Only "American" flies the favorable *Southern* Transcontinental Route, that gets you away from winter quicker. Two convenient daily flights. No changing planes.

The AMERICAN MERCURY Flagship—New York to Los Angeles OVERNIGHT—3 stops only—Memphis, Dallas, Tucson.

The SOUTHERNER Flagship—New York to Los Angeles OVERNIGHT—4 stops only—Memphis, Ft. Worth, El Paso, Phoenix.

This winter is the time to go to the Sun Country of the Southwest and Southern California. Let "American" help you plan your trip. Get descriptive booklet, "The Sun Country." Write American Airlines, Inc., Chicago, Ill.

AMERICAN
AIRLINES INC.

[1936]

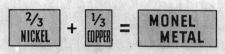
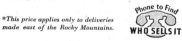

"*That's* *either an Orchestra or a* LABYRINTH RADIO"

This realistic reproduction is due largely to Stromberg-Carlson's exclusive development — the Acoustical Labyrinth. It brings you face to face for the first time with radio which has but a *single voice!* The *rear* voice of the speaker is no longer left to boom and reverberate within the cabinet. These unwanted tones are led off, silently and scientifically. The *front* voice of the speaker remains free to recreate the rich harmony of sound which is radio—without interference from any direction.

But tone is not all which finds new perfection in the 1937 Stromberg-Carlsons. There are new conveniences in Dials...in Tri-Focal Tuning...Indexed Control Knobs...Beam Power Tubes...Carpinchoe Leather Speakers ... and in the Free-floating Phonograph Pick-up, all in addition to the new *actuality* of tone which again proves, "There is nothing finer than a Stromberg-Carlson."

Stromberg-Carlsons range in price from $49.95 to $985. (Slightly higher in Southeastern States and West of the Mississippi.) Booklet "How to Choose a Radio," may be obtained from authorized dealers listed in your classified telephone directory or by mailing coupon.

NO. 140-L TRIPLE RANGE, Walnut finish. Equipped with Labyrinth. Price . . . **$149.50**

NO. 130-H TRIPLE RANGE, Walnut finish. Price, **$74.50** Other table models in Rosewood and in Walnut.

Stromberg-Carlson

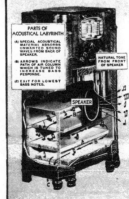

PARTS OF Acoustical Labyrinth

(A) SPECIAL ACOUSTICAL MATERIAL ABSORBS UNWANTED SOUND WAVES FROM BACK OF SPEAKER.

(B) ARROWS INDICATE PATH OF AIR COLUMN WHICH IS TUNED TO INCREASE BASS RESPONSE.

(C) EXIT FOR LOWEST BASS NOTES.

NATURAL TONE FROM FRONT OF SPEAKER

SPEAKER

LABYRINTH RADIO

The long, winding passageway of the Acoustical Labyrinth takes the place of the usual box-like cavity in the cabinet which is the source of the exaggerated boom in low tones. It gives you deeper bass notes, with a new fidelity and increases the volume capacity and accuracy of the loud speaker. Labyrinth shown in No. 145-L.

Stromberg-Carlson Telephone Mfg. Co.
143 Carlson Road, Rochester, N. Y.

Send illustrated booklet "How to Choose a Radio."

Name...

Street...

City............................State............

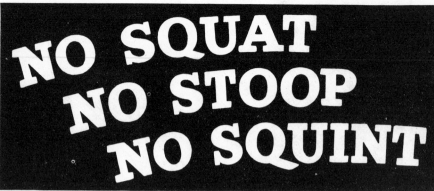

NO SQUAT
NO STOOP
NO SQUINT

She's not tuning in the morning setting-up exercises. She just hasn't heard about Philco "NO SQUAT" Tuning!

Not exactly a picture of grace . . but give the lady time. She'll soon be enjoying Philco "NO STOOP" Tuning!

No need to strain *your* eyes to tune a radio! Not when you can buy a Philco 116 Double-X with "NO SQUINT" Tuning!

Philco makes a complete line of Automatic Tuning Models with the Inclined Control Panel. Your present radio may be traded in as part payment or you can buy a Double-X Philco for as little as $7.95 down and $1.00 a week. Ask your Philco dealer about this Special Philco-Commercial Credit Company Plan.

Tune easily . . . gracefully . . . speedily . . . accurately . . . with Philco Automatic Tuning on the new Philco Inclined Control Panel

Instantly, silently, precisely . . Philco Automatic Tuning brings in any of your favorite stations. No waiting . . no buzzing. A glance at the Inclined Control Panel . . a flick of your fingers . . there's your station! Faultless, rapid-fire, time-tested Automatic Tuning . . plus the new ease and convenience of the Inclined Control Panel. No hesitation when you want a station with Philco!

But there's far more than speed and convenience to the complete story of the Philco 116 Double-X. There's Philco High-Fidelity . . double the tonal range of ordinary radios. There's the Philco Foreign Tuning System that doubles the foreign short-wave stations you can hear and enjoy. And fifteen tubes and five tuning ranges bring all that's interesting in the air right into your home!

Here's the radio that makes dreams come true . . the radio that has everything and does everything . . the 1938 Philco 116 Double-X.

PHILCO
A Musical Instrument of Quality

Be sure to ask your Dealer to show you the new Automatic Tuning Philcos with Inclined Control Panel

[1937]

404

Saratoga...

THE *Spa* THAT WAS *Inevitable*

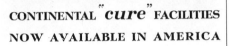

CONTINENTAL *"cure"* FACILITIES
NOW AVAILABLE IN AMERICA

To take a Spa "cure" is not new. It is centuries old among the Continentals; generations old among Americans. But to "cure" in America, in the continental manner, was never possible until the New Saratoga Spa was opened last year.

Complete in details and facilities, this great new Spa presents health advantages never before obtainable. Whether you come for treatment of a chronic ailment or for a "restoration cure" you will have reason to sing the praises of *The Spa that was Inevitable.*

Illustrated booklet and rates on request. Address: The Director, Saratoga Spa, 640 Saratoga Springs, N. Y.

Nature's
Own Correctives
for Acidity

Intermingled with tennis courts, golf course, bridle paths, swimming pool and magnificent Georgian buildings, geysers spout their rare mineral waters throughout the Park.

The "cures" themselves are dependent upon the health-giving properties of these waters —which are both taken internally and applied externally.

Geyser, Hathorn and Coesa waters are bottled at the springs and made available through grocers and druggists in eastern United States. Order some today.

[1936]

THE NEW
SARATOGA SPA

OWNED AND OPERATED BY 🛡 THE STATE OF NEW YORK

U. S. ARCHITECTS PRESENT 1⊙1 SMALL,

The architectural profession has given to THE ARCHITECTURAL FORUM an extraordinary demonstration of its skill in the creation of small houses. The result is a publishing event of unprecedented importance to everyone with a stake in land or building, to everyone who owns a home or ever hopes to. Two bulging issues of THE FORUM will contain more pictures, plans and solid facts about small houses than have ever before been assembled in book or magazine form. The data cover all sections of the U. S. Every type from Early American to New American. Landscaping, flat roofs, pitched roofs. Wood, brick, concrete, stucco, steel. Sleeping porches. Sun terraces. Street front garages. Today's bath and kitchen. Air Conditioning. Insulation. Fireproofing. Termite prevention. Cost saving.

THE OCTOBER ISSUE. Planning and design. Every house presented in two pages of photographs, plans and detailed information. Costs in the majority of cases. Complete specifications (with trade names) in all cases. This 300 page issue comes off the presses October 1st. Use coupon on opposite page to get a copy.

It is physically impossible for THE FORUM's staff of experts to produce the second part of this encyclopedic treatment of the small house without a month's interval. Thus the Planning and Design material appears in October, the Structural and Engineering material in December.

THE DECEMBER ISSUE. All the worthy new methods of house building in photographs, text and special drawings. Also, in compact, understandable form, the new developments in materials, air conditioning, heating, lighting and all other service considerations in the small house.

84 . DEMONSTRATION HOUSE, LOS ANGELES, "TIMES"

Showing the growing tendency in California residential architecture to combine features of modern and traditional design. Not unlike the typical ranch house with its long lines and sloping roof, this house takes on new character through the use of horizontal rows of casements, and of thin metal members for the lattice over the entrance terrace. The plan provides living and sleeping quarters separated without loss of convenience. The one bath is accessible from any part of the house. A dining terrace and a porch furnish outdoor living spaces, privacy being obtained by screens of translucent glass. The interiors carry out the scheme of combining old and new motives; the walls of the living room, hall and dining room are covered with large sheets of wood veneer, while the bedroom is treated in a more conventional manner. This and other houses in this issue should dispel the notion that houses to be modern must be white boxes with flat roofs.

CONSTRUCTION OUTLINE

FOUNDATION
Walls and piers—reinforced concrete. Riverside Portland Cement Co.
FRAME CONSTRUCTION
Entire frame steel—standard rolled sections Columbia Steel Co. Fabrication Unitype Builders, Inc., Los Angeles. Frame electrically welded.
MASONRY CONSTRUCTION
Terrace walls and chimneys. Same brick and mortar as for exterior veneer.
Face Brick—Roman Brick—Gladding McBean & Co.
EXTERIOR SURFACE
Brick veneer specially manufactured small roman brick light coral color manufactured by Gladding McBean & Co. and Los Angeles Brick Co. Mortar by California Moba Cement Co.

ROOF
Tile on Sheathing—Entire roof of shingle tile on 1⅜" wood sheathing and is special white overglazed tile by Gladding McBean & Co. Sheathing is 1¼" T & G Oregon Pine by E. J. Stanton Lumber Co.
Gutters ⎫ Galvanized Iron—"ARM-
Flashings ⎬ CO"— American Rolling
Down Spouts ⎭ Mill Co.
Composition sheathing
paper—Two thicknesses "Flintco" furnished by Pioneer Roofing Co., subsidiary of Johns-Manville Co.
DOOR AND WINDOW FRAMES
Casement—Windows all steel casements by Druwhit Metal Products Co., Los Angeles, as were French Doors.
Doors and frames

(exterior)—Main entrance and service only exterior doors of wood. All interior doors wood by E. J. Stanton Mfg. Co.
Garage Doors—Garage door also by Stanton hung on "Over-the-Top" door equipment by Frantz Mfg. Co.
PORCHES
Brick Floor—Only entrance terrace paved with brick same as used for exterior veneer.
Tile Floor—Dining terrace and living room terrace quarry tile by Alhambra Kilns, Los Angeles.
GLASS
"Penn-Vernon," by Pittsburgh Plate Glass Co.
EXTERIOR PAINT
All paint and stain by General Paint Corp.

These two pages are reductions of a typical presentation from the October issue. Picture not a few but 300 pages just as exciting, just as informative as these. Every house selected for its excellence by The Forum's editors. Every house built recently. Every condition of site,

TERRACE—Design for outdoor living by Gordon B. Kaufmann. Young America— and old—wants a place in the sun. The house of today, with its sheltered terrace on the ground or roof, is the answer.

ANSWERS THESE QUESTIONS

What is a modern home? Where is the best place for a garage? Is a separate dining room necessary? Can provisions for guests be handled without an extra room? Is a central hall outmoded? What about built-in furniture? Is landscaping a luxury or a necessity? How many closets, and where? Are corner windows practical? Can the stairs be outdoors? Does air conditioning eliminate a fireplace? What is functional planning? Prefabrication, myth or reality? What is glass brick? Are flat roofs practical in snow belts? The only questions unanswered are the ones FORUM editors haven't thought of.

HIGHEST PRICED HOUSE $20,000 — LOWEST $982

AIRFLOW CHRYSLER EIGHT SIX-PASSENGER SEDAN, $1345*

WHY!

Why the Airflow Chrysler is different . . . and why you should ride in one before you buy any car!

Why it's safer. In an Airflow Chrysler, you ride *inside* the frame. Strong steel girders run from end to end of the car . . . above, below, and on all sides. Frame and body are inseparably welded into a single unit. This construction is not only the strongest ever devised . . . it also contributes to the steadiness of the car on the road. For further reassurance, you have Chrysler's famous hydraulic brakes . . . tested, proved, and perfected by over 12 years' experience . . . and Lifeguard tubes to end blow-out worry.

Why it rides better. The Floating Ride of the Airflow Chrysler is a basic result of Airflow design . . . is possible only with Airflow design. With the engine far forward, passengers cradled close to the center of balance, the rate of spring action is slowed and lengthened to an almost imperceptible glide. No sudden jolts . . . no jars . . . no tiring little jiggles and bumps. The only way to appreciate the enormous difference between this ride and all other rides is to get into an Airflow and head for the worst roads you know about.

[1936]

Airflow **CHRYSLER**

TOMORROW'S CAR TODAY

Why it's roomier. In designing the Airflow Chrysler to slip through the air, Chrysler engineers created a car with perfect aerodynamic contours. This correct streamline design places the greatest width of the car where it is also most advantageous to the passengers. The result is the first car to give six adult passengers real room to ride without crushing . . . seats as wide and deep as divans . . . leg-room, head-room, elbow-room . . . room to stretch out and relax . . . the greatest comfort ever built into a motor car.

Why it gives more lasting value. The Airflow Chrysler gives you a whole new standard of values . . . comforts, safeguards, and economies that all cars must come to sooner or later. The trend toward this better type of transportation is perfectly clear. Yet you can enjoy it today in an Airflow Chrysler at no greater investment than for cars which may quickly become out-of-date in design and value.

Before you buy any car at any price, you owe it to yourself to ride in an Airflow Chrysler. Your Chrysler dealer will gladly arrange a trip which will show you all of the delightful advantages of Airflow design. You can't appreciate these things by looking at the car . . . you must get into the car and ride!

☆ CHRYSLER SIX . . . 93 horsepower, 118-inch wheelbase, $760 and up.

☆ DE LUXE EIGHT . . . 105 and 110 horsepower, 121 and 133-inch wheelbase, $925 and up.

☆ AIRFLOW EIGHT . . . 115 horsepower, 123-inch wheelbase. All models, $1345.

☆ AIRFLOW IMPERIAL . . . 130 horsepower, 128-inch wheelbase. All models, $1475.

☆ AIRFLOW CUSTOM IMPERIAL . . . 130 horsepower, 137-inch wheelbase, $2475 and up.

Automatic Overdrive is standard on Airflow Imperial. Available on all 1936 Chryslers at slight additional cost.

*All prices list at factory, Detroit; special equipment extra.

Ask for the Official Chrysler Motors-Commercial Credit Company Time Payment plan. Available through all Chrysler Dealers.

New SUPER-CHARGED Models.

Again Auburn leads the way to more gracious living, with a New 150 horse-power SUPER-CHARGED Speedster—each car certified at a speed secured after being *run in* and tested, and *each car* carrying its own plate showing a maximum speed of over One Hundred miles per hour. There are few places where you can drive One Hundred miles per hour, but it means added dependability, as the engine will be loafing at "60." You, who want your car to mean more than mere transportation, are invited to see, drive and compare the truly fine 1935 Auburns. Prices, considering the outstanding values, are remarkably low, as they start as low as $695 and up, at factory.

Auburn Automobile Co., Auburn, Ind.
Division of Cord Corporation

New 1935

AVBVRN

QUESTION: Will service costs be low on the new $980 Packard?

ANSWER: Yes, and you can prove it <u>before</u> you buy the car.

PACKARD 120

For every $1.00 you would spend for service on the PACKARD 120, you would have to spend for:

CAR "A"	· ·	$1.24
CAR "B"	· ·	1.09
CAR "C"	· ·	1.06

PACKARD 120

For every $1.00 worth of new parts in the PACKARD 120, the same parts for three leading cars in this price class would cost:

CAR "A"	· ·	$1.10
CAR "B"	· ·	1.09
CAR "C"	· ·	1.02

BEFORE you drive a single mile in the new Packard 120, you can establish this important fact:

Its service costs will not be higher than service costs on other cars in its price field. This is a definite Packard policy. And you can verify it by making a direct comparison of costs on other cars in the Packard 120 price range.

Actually, such a comparison shows that Packard's service costs are frequently *lower* than those of other cars.

The charts at the left show such a comparison for three of the leading cars at or near the price of the Packard 120. These figures are an average of all common repair operations, and an average of all most commonly used parts. No comparison of figures, however, will give you the chief reasons why the Packard 120 is an economical car to operate.

The way Packard builds this car, the long experience in fine-car manufacture that is back of it, the better materials that are in it, and the newest, most precise manufacturing methods in the industry, have combined to reduce service needs far below anything you have ever experienced.

Packard has spent millions of dollars to make the new Packard 120 a car you can afford to purchase—*and a car you can afford to operate.*

ASK THE MAN WHO OWNS ONE

PACKARD 120
$980 to $1095

List prices at factory—standard accessory group extra

In a stock Studebaker...over *railway ties*...Luther Johnson raced the *Dixie Flyer!*

and rear seat passengers get convincing evidence of Studebaker's inimitable Miracle Ride

AS LOW AS $695 AT THE FACTORY

YOU might not care to volunteer to make a trip like this yourself. But you wouldn't need to worry a moment. You would be riding in a Miracle Ride Studebaker. And it doesn't take a driver anywhere near as expert as Luther Johnson to prove that this finest Studebaker ever built has the greatest combination of restful riding, sure footedness and obedient handling ever offered in any car.

On a stretch of C. & E. I. double track near Momence, Illinois, Johnson, veteran of the international speedways, paced the Dixie Flyer, famous Chicago-Florida train, with nothing better than "washboard" railroad ties for his roadway. And the way that Miracle Ride Studebaker "took it" and came through with flying colors is the talk of the whole automobile world.

You can purchase one of these new Studebaker Champions now at sharply reduced delivered prices—in fact, some models cost only a few dollars more than the very lowest priced cars.

Dictator $695, Commander $925, President $1245. Base prices at the factory, special equipment extra.

THE TAPE MEASURE TELLS YOU STUDEBAKERS ARE ROOMIER   You get an excess of elbow room, shoulder room, leg room and head room in all the new Studebakers. Measure and see.

THEY PUSH STUDEBAKERS OFF CLIFFS TO PROVE THEY'RE SOUNDLY BUILT

—and the famed steel-reinforced-by-steel Studebaker construction doesn't disappoint. Studebaker safety is matched by exceptional comfort, roominess and operating economy.

LISTEN TO RICHARD HIMBER AND HIS STUDEBAKER CHAMPIONS ON THE AIR TWICE A WEEK—NBC Chain every Monday, Columbia Chain every Friday.

ALL MODELS HAVE HYDRAULIC BRAKES

And they're *compound* hydraulic brakes—a 1935 Studebaker advancement. You stop swiftly, smoothly and in a straight line—and with new precision steering the car always goes where you point it.

Miracle Ride STUDEBAKER CHAMPIONS

[1935]

411

First showing of the new
CORD

at
New York and Los Angeles
Automobile Shows this week

YOUR NAME AND ADDRESS
WILL BRING COMPLETE SPECIFICATIONS

AUBURN AUTOMOBILE CO.
AUBURN, INDIANA

[1935]

Half the gas*...
twice the Smartness

NOTE THE WIDTH • NOTE THE ROOM

THE SURPRISE CAR OF THE YEAR!

✻ One motorist says: "Before I bought my Willys, I generally purchased 15 gallons of gas each week. Now I buy only seven."

✻ A salesman writes: "Recently I drove with three in the car, a 76-mile trip on exactly two gallons of gas."

✻ A son writes: "I've saved enough money on my Willys to buy mother a refrigerator and completely outfit my car with a new radio, a hot-water heater, and special seat covers."

✻ A credit manager says: "When I changed to Willys, I cut my driving expense . . . and in this manner am saving enough out of my mileage allowance to pay for the car."

up to 35 miles per gallon

Lowest priced full-size car — safety all-steel body and top.

Here's the New Willys—the car people have wanted for years.

All eyes follow as it passes . . . Its FULL-SIZE width and cleverly designed interiors mark a new era in USABLE space . . . Its spirited performance captures the imagination of modern youth . . . But most important is *low operating cost.* Willys makes it possible for motorists to save their hard-earned money.

Up to 35 miles on a gallon of gas! Just like cutting the cost of gas in half. Only four quarts of oil to buy when you change. Up to 40,000 miles on a set of tires. Lowest depreciation. Lowest taxes and insurance. Lowest down payment and monthly payments. In fact, with savings you will find Willys can *pay for itself* within 35,000 miles.

The brilliant beauty and exclusive economy of the New Willys are matched by the great safety provided by all-steel body and top, extra large brakes, safety glass, low center of gravity, fender lights and highly responsive operation and control. Willys-Overland Motors, Inc., Toledo, Ohio.

$395 *list, Standard Coupe, F. O. B. factory, Toledo—other models higher. Prices and specifications subject to change without notice.*

The New WILLYS

[1936]

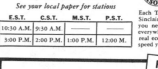

HYDRA-MATIC DRIVE!

NO GEARS TO SHIFT...
NO CLUTCH TO PRESS!

NO CLUTCH PEDAL

1940's ONE BIG
ENGINEERING ADVANCEMENT

FOR YEARS it's been coming and now it's *here*—a car without a clutch pedal...a car that shifts for itself...a car that reduces driving to its absolute essentials! It's the 1940 Oldsmobile with Hydra-Matic Drive—the world's simplest, easiest car to operate. Oldsmobile's new Hydra-Matic Drive is a combination of liquid coupling and fully automatic transmission. It steps up performance to thrilling new highs...gives a smoother, quieter flow of power...and definitely improves gasoline mileage. It's optional on all Olds models for 1940—the Sixty, Seventy and Custom 8 Cruiser—at an extra cost of only $57. Visit your Oldsmobile dealer and try it—for the driving thrill of your life!

ALL SHIFTING IS AUTOMATIC!
You simply set the control lever in "Hi," step on the accelerator and the car runs through four forward speed-ranges softly, smoothly—entirely *automatically*. You can drive all day without shifting!

YOU CAN'T STALL THE ENGINE!
Oldsmobile proves it by this spectacular, specially arranged test—driving a car up a steep flight of steps, letting it come to a stop and holding it motionless by pressure on the accelerator only!

ALL YOU DO TO DRIVE IS

1 — STEER   SHIFT   2 — STEP ON IT   DE-CLUTCH   3 — STOP

Offered Only in
OLDSMOBILE

AMERICA'S BIGGEST MONEY'S WORTH

BIGGER AND **BETTER** IN *Everything!*

[1939]

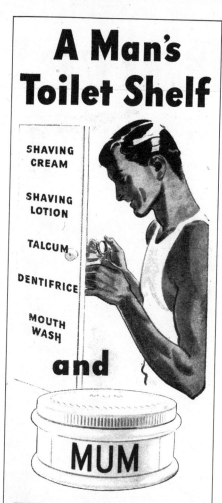

"That's not your only offense, mister"

—and then the copper told him . . . told him what his best friends had never had the heart to tell him. It simply stunned Hartley . . . now he understood why people deliberately dodged him . . . why business acquaintances always sat as far as possible away from him and cut his calls to a minimum. Then and there he resolved that never again would he be guilty of an offensive breath.

* * *

The insidious thing about halitosis (unpleasant breath) is that you yourself never know when you have it. And since the subject is so delicate, even your best friends won't tell you.

Due to conditions frequently existing even in normal mouths, everyone is bound to have an offensive breath at some time or other. Fermentation of tiny bits of food is one of its principal causes.

Fortunately this condition yields to the regular use of Listerine as a mouth wash and gargle. For Listerine, possessing marked antiseptic and deodorant qualities, halts food fermentation in the mouth, overcomes disagreeable odors, and leaves the breath sweet, fresh, and clean.

Keep a bottle of Listerine handy in home and office. Get into the delightful habit of using it morning and night, and between times before business and social engagements. *Lambert Pharmacal Company, St. Louis, Mo.*

[1936]

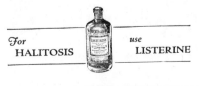

For **HALITOSIS** use **LISTERINE**

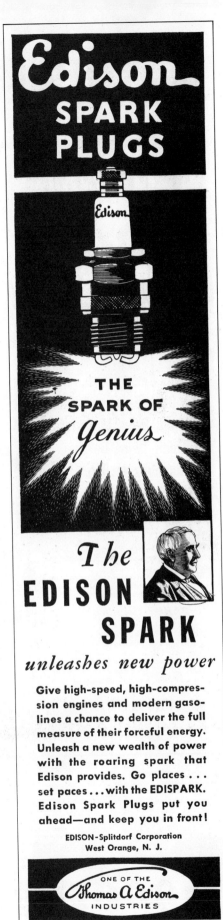

Edison SPARK PLUGS

THE SPARK OF *Genius*

The EDISON SPARK

unleashes new power

Give high-speed, high-compression engines and modern gasolines a chance to deliver the full measure of their forceful energy. Unleash a new wealth of power with the roaring spark that Edison provides. Go places . . . set paces . . . with the EDISPARK. Edison Spark Plugs put you ahead—and keep you in front!

EDISON-Splitdorf Corporation
West Orange, N. J.

ONE OF THE
Thomas A. Edison INDUSTRIES

[1936]

A TRUE STORY BY ZANE GREY

HE WAS RIDING ON DYNAMITE AND NEVER KNEW IT UNTIL...

"...This Close Shave," says Zane Grey, Famous Author, "Should Make Motorists Think Twice Before Gambling on Tires"

THERE WAS one thing that Edward Zachary of Hartford, Connecticut, looked forward to—and that was his regular week-end spin out into the wide-open spaces.

Nothing suited him better than to open the throttle and "get away from it all." Not that he was a reckless driver. On the contrary, Ed Zachary was plenty strict when it came to observing traffic rules.

But there is one motoring mishap that the best of drivers cannot forecast. And it caught Mr. Zachary completely off guard.

BANG! Then What?

He was whizzing along at a good clip. He had the North Ford Road practically to himself when BANG! Quicker than a Texas Ranger could draw a gun, the right front tire blew out. An uncontrollable drag yanked the car smack alongside of a guardrail. Flying wheels mowed down fence posts. Seconds seemed hours before the wildest ride Mr. Zachary ever had came to a sudden halt. It took plenty of starch out of him and he's now a sadder but wiser motorist. And he'll tell the world that it pays to think twice before taking chances on tires.

The cards may be stacked against you when you gamble on tires. Today's streamlined cars and faster driving conditions call for a *special* tire.

Many of the blow-outs you hear and read about are due to the terrific heat generated *inside* of all tires by today's high speed driving. This heat may cause rubber and fabric to sepa-

The right front tire blew out. Flying wheels mowed down fence posts.

Thousands of motorists are killed or injured every year when blow-outs throw cars out of control. Many of these blow-outs are due to heat generated inside of all tires by today's high speeds.

rate. And if it does, an invisible blister forms. Bigger and BIGGER it grows until, sooner or later, BANG! you have a blow-out. Where you might land, what you might hit, nobody knows.

The Goodrich Safety Silvertown is just the kind of a tire you need to give you *real* protection against blow-outs like this. It's the *only* tire with the Life-Saver Golden Ply. This life-saving invention is a layer of *special* rubber and full-floating cords, scientifically treated to resist the treacherous blowout-causing heat generated *inside* all tires by today's higher speeds. By resisting this heat, these

Golden Ply Silvertowns give you, and everyone that rides with you, *real* protection against those high-speed blow-outs.

Edward Zachary has no desire to go through the mental anguish of another blow-out. From now on you'll find his car equipped with Silvertowns. For your own peace of mind—for the protection of your family and friends make *your next set of tires* Golden Ply Silvertowns. You pay no price premium for these life-saving tires and you'll find them on sale at Goodrich Silvertown Stores and Goodrich dealers everywhere.

Zane Grey.

HEAT CAUSES BLOW-OUTS. PROTECT YOURSELF AGAINST THOSE BLOW-OUTS WITH THIS HEAT-RESISTING GOLDEN PLY

Goodrich SAFETY Silvertown
With Life-Saver Golden Ply Blow-Out Protection

YOUR CAR'S NO NUDIST

The sooner you dress your car with Simoniz, the better! Simoniz is indispensable for preserving the life and beauty of all automobile finishes.

Only Simoniz contains the certain secret ingredient, which keeps lacquers and enamels from getting dull, bleached, and eventually ruined by the weather, dirt, and ultra-violet rays. So, it's no wonder millions of motorists insist on Simoniz, and on the wonderful, easy-to-use Simoniz Kleener. Be wise! Get these world-famous products, and Simoniz your car now!

MOTORISTS WISE
SIMONIZ

SIMONIZ **KLEENER**
MOTORISTS WISE

SIMONIZ
TRADE MARK REG. U. S. PAT. OFF. AND FOREIGN COUNTRIES

[1937]

SQUIRM IF YOU MUST...

But You Mustn't

YOU'RE ALWAYS AT EASE
IN Y-FRONT Shorts

TRADE MARK REG.

You're sure to do the wrong thing—sooner or later—if you're a victim of bunchy, binding underwear. You can stand just so much discomfort—and then *bang* goes the water glass as you struggle for freedom.

You're always at ease in Coopers Masculinized Underwear—whether dancing or sitting or pulling a romantic oar in summer moonlight. There's plenty of *give* for outdoor athletics—snug, trim fit for perfect grooming. And comfortable, restful support! Y-Fronts by Coopers fit throughout and put an end to squirming.

Look at the picture, at the left, of the famous Coopers Jockey short with the Y-Front construction. You can *see* at a glance why they're so comfortable—why the man in Y-Fronts never squirms.

The ingenious Y-Front by Coopers gives you snug, comfortable support in any position. No bunching, no binding, no buttons. Varied lengths: Jockey (illustrated), very brief; above the knee; knee; calf; and ankle. Shirts—sleeveless or short sleeve. The garment 50 cents and up at your favorite men's store.

Your dealer has varied lengths for your selection

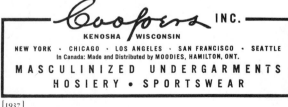

Coopers INC.

KENOSHA WISCONSIN

NEW YORK · CHICAGO · LOS ANGELES · SAN FRANCISCO · SEATTLE
In Canada: Made and Distributed by MOODIES, HAMILTON, ONT.

MASCULINIZED UNDERGARMENTS
HOSIERY · SPORTSWEAR

[1937]

"A Mile! I could walk fifty in shoes as *flexible* as these"

Swing along in Bostonians with the Flexmore* Process. An exclusive construction insures ease in every springy stride without a single sacrifice to looks. Rugged, handsome, built for active men in Luggage Calf—Bostonians' new, smart leather for Fall. At leading men's apparel and shoe shops, $6.50 to $8.50. Bostonian Foot Savers, $10.00.

*Registered U. S. Patent Office

Bostonians
SHOES FOR MEN
BUILT WITH THE FLEXMORE PROCESS

[1935]

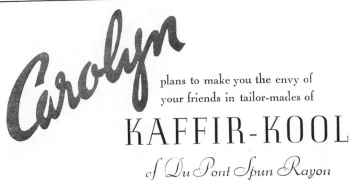

Carolyn

plans to make you the envy of your friends in tailor-mades of

KAFFIR-KOOL
of DuPont Spun Rayon

IT'S AQUA SEC'd

to resist water spotting and perspiration stains

Let the sun shine and the temperature rise. You won't lose your immaculate, crisp appearance if you wear one of these Carolyn Suits. For KAFFIR-KOOL, the newest lightweight suiting, is a miracle of breeziness that you can enjoy from late Spring through hottest Summer. It has been VITALIZED...a process which makes the garment highly resistant to wrinkles. In eight new blended pastels. Sizes 10 to 20..... $14⁹⁵

STYLED BY SWANSDOWN

KAFFIR-KOOL is an exclusive
fabric by SAMUEL J. ARONSOHN, Inc.

He spends plenty for clothes
– but he always looks a mess

Don't let a sagging stomach spoil your appearance when it's so easy to keep trim – athletic with THE BRACER

HE'S DONE his best to look neat, but even the finest tailor — the most expensive suit can't hide that bulging waistline. No matter how much care he gives to his clothes, sagging stomach muscles spoil the effect — he still looks messy!

Why let this happen to you? It's easy to get that trim, youthful look — easy to have a firm, flat waistline! Just slip into The Bracer!

The Bracer is an amazing new-type supporter belt that gives complete support — controls that wandering waistline. Scientifically tailored for perfect fit and absolute comfort, The Bracer is knitted from two-way stretch "Lastex" yarn with four small flexible ribs to prevent rolling and with an exclusive fly-front supporter. Has no buttons or buckles and the supporter type leg strap is always comfortable.

But that's not all! The Bracer can be laundered again and again without shrinking or losing elasticity. Seams are impregnated with live rubber — cannot loosen or pull out.

A Bauer & Black product, The Bracer is the result of the same scientific care that has made Bauer & Black famous for medical and surgical supplies and has made them the world's largest manufacturers of athletic supporters. When you buy The Bracer you know it is made with the greatest care under the most sanitary conditions.

Try The Bracer now. Get several — have a clean one always on hand. You'll look younger, feel better, too! The Bracer can be purchased at department, drug, haberdashery and sporting goods stores.

BEFORE — Sagging stomach muscles make you feel tired — make you look old.

AFTER — The minute you put The Bracer on you look better — feel better.

THE ONLY SUPPORTER BELT WITH THIS EXCLUSIVE FLY-FRONT

No other supporter belt offers you the comfort and convenience you get with The Bracer. The exclusive *fly-front* is a feature that will be welcomed by every man. It means you can wear The Bracer all day without removing. Be sure you get The Bracer!

THE BRACER

If your dealer cannot supply you with The Bracer, simply fill out and mail this coupon with a check or money order. Price $2.00 (Canada $2.75).

BAUER & BLACK, Dept. A-25, 2500 So. Dearborn St., Chicago, Ill.
(In Canada, Station K, Toronto)

I am enclosing check or money order for_____.

Please send me_____ Bracers. My waist measurement is_____

Name_____

Address_____

City_____ State_____

My dealer's name and address is_____

[1937]

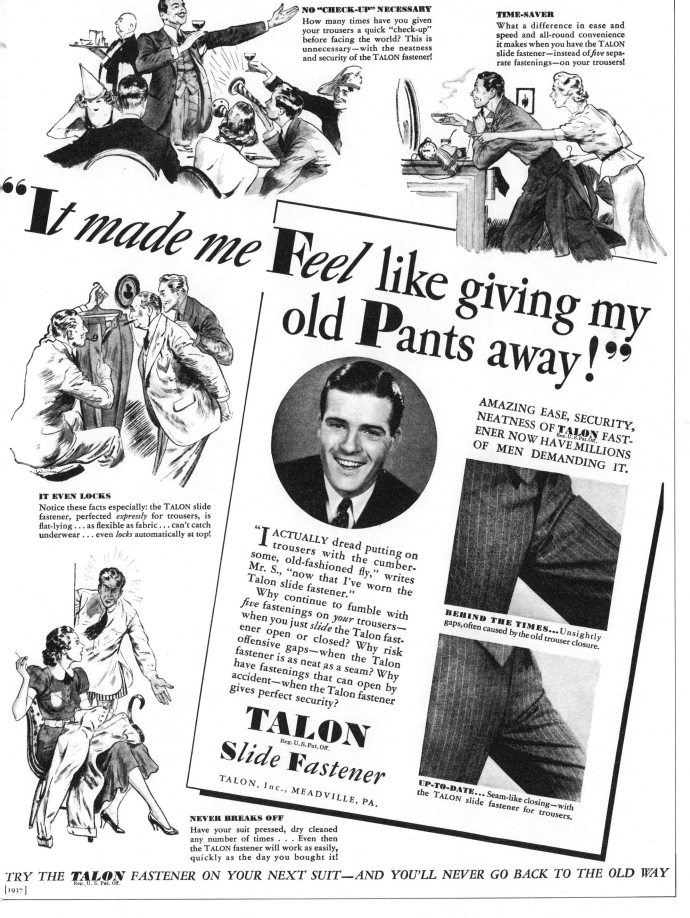

NO "CHECK-UP" NECESSARY

How many times have you given your trousers a quick "check-up" before facing the world? This is unnecessary—with the neatness and security of the TALON fastener!

TIME-SAVER

What a difference in ease and speed and all-round convenience it makes when you have the TALON slide fastener—instead of *five* separate fastenings—on your trousers!

"It made me Feel like giving my old Pants away!"

IT EVEN LOCKS

Notice these facts especially: the TALON slide fastener, perfected *expressly* for trousers, is flat-lying . . . as flexible as fabric . . . can't catch underwear . . . even *locks* automatically at top!

AMAZING EASE, SECURITY, NEATNESS OF TALON *Reg. U.S. Pat. Off.* **FASTENER NOW HAVE MILLIONS OF MEN DEMANDING IT.**

"I ACTUALLY dread putting on trousers with the cumbersome, old-fashioned *fly*," writes Mr. S., "now that I've worn the Talon slide fastener."

Why continue to fumble with *five* fastenings on *your* trousers—when you just *slide* the Talon fastener open or closed? Why risk offensive gaps—when the Talon fastener is as neat as a seam? Why have fastenings that can open by accident—when the Talon fastener gives perfect security?

TALON
Reg. U.S. Pat. Off.
Slide Fastener

TALON, Inc., MEADVILLE, PA.

BEHIND THE TIMES . . . Unsightly gaps, often caused by the old trouser closure.

UP-TO-DATE . . . Seam-like closing—with the TALON slide fastener for trousers.

NEVER BREAKS OFF

Have your suit pressed, dry cleaned any number of times . . . Even then the TALON fastener will work as easily, quickly as the day you bought it!

TRY THE **TALON** *Reg. U.S. Pat. Off.* *FASTENER ON YOUR NEXT SUIT—AND YOU'LL NEVER GO BACK TO THE OLD WAY*

[1937]

423

"You ought to <u>hate</u> yourself for spanking that child!"

Peggy shows Bill the modern way to bring up their child

1. BILL: You keep out of this, Peggy...I've got to make this boy listen to reason!

PEGGY: You're certainly going about it in a funny way.

2. BILL: Don't you worry—he'll take that stuff if I have to hold his nose to do it.

PEGGY: That's going from bad to worse. Don't you know that using force on a child can shock his entire nervous system?

3. BILL: Who said so?

PEGGY: The doctor! Where do you think I've been all morning! I told him about our struggles in getting Junior to take a laxative. The doctor absolutely "put his foot down" on force.

4. PEGGY: Then I asked him about giving Junior some of the laxative you take, and again he said NO. He said an adult's laxative can be too strong for a tot. So he recommended a modern laxative made especially for children.

5. BILL: Is there such a thing?

PEGGY: Certainly! Fletcher's Castoria. There isn't a harmful ingredient in it. It's mild, yet surprisingly thorough. It won't form a habit or cause any griping cramps. And it's *SAFE!*

6. BILL: He certainly takes it easy enough.

PEGGY: I'll say he does! Even the taste of Fletcher's Castoria is made especially for children. They love it. I don't see how any home can get along without it!

Chas H. Fletcher **CASTORIA**

The modern—SAFE—laxative made especially for children

[1939]

424

The survivors
were shaved with
Schick *Shavers*

MANY of the passengers and crew of the ill-fated "Hindenburg" whose faces were burned were shaved with Schick Shavers during their stay in the hospital.

So badly burned were they that there was a thick crust of tissue on their faces through which their beards grew. It was quite impossible to use a blade to shave them.

But the Schick Shaver glided gently and painlessly over the injured skin, removing the hair at the scarred surface.

MORE HOSPITALS ARE USING SCHICK SHAVERS

Each day's mail brings us stories of the use of Schick Shavers under extraordinary conditions. Men with skin troubles, patients confined to their beds, men with broken right arms or injured hands, blind men and those partially paralyzed—it is an amazing list and an overwhelming trib-

ute to the Schick Shaver which is changing the shaving habits of the world.

HOW MUCH BETTER FOR A NORMAL FACE!

The Schick Shaver, continuously and exclusively used, permits nature to discard the skin calloused and toughened by ordinary methods of shaving. In its place comes a new, more youthful-looking and softer skin easier to shave quickly and closely.

FIRST—AND STILL THE LEADER

Twenty years' thought and mechanical genius created the Schick *and the methods of making it.* We know of no mechanical shaver that shaves more quickly, more closely or with greater comfort. Six years' experience and a million-and-a-half users should convince you that Schick is the best and most economical way to shave with "no blades— no lather—no chance to cut yourself."

ASK A SCHICK DEALER TODAY

$15
AC & DC

Any authorized Schick dealer will demonstrate the shaver, and show you how easily you can learn to shave either immediately or in the number of days necessary to bring your skin into perfect condition for Schick shaving.

SCHICK DRY SHAVER, INC., STAMFORD, CONN.
Western Distributor: Edises, Inc., San Francisco
In Canada: Henry Birks & Sons, Ltd., and other leading stores

SCHICK ⬤ SHAVER

[1937]

426

Because "the office couldn't spare him"

THIS MAN has received many a warning from his body that all was not well with him.

And he has been given many a scolding by family and friends because of his do-nothing attitude. "I know, I know," he has replied, "but I haven't time to be sick. The office can't spare me. Fellow has to be on his toes every minute these days."

Here you see the result—the man who had to be "on his toes" lies flat on his back. And the office will *have* to manage without him. The bitter truth is that the office will manage without him even if he never recovers.

Cases like this have become almost common these past few years. Any number of people whose health has pleaded for attention, have been "too busy" to do anything about it. They have had the rather peculiar notion that it is a display of weakness to admit being sick.

That, of course, is utter nonsense. If you have had warnings that something is wrong, the only intelligent thing to do is to see your physician. Those warnings may or may not indicate a serious disorder—your physician can tell. If they do, he can start you on the road to a cure or betterment of the condition. On the other hand, if these warnings indicate only some minor disturbance, aggravated perhaps by worry, he can set your mind at rest and institute whatever corrective measures may be needed.

There's no good reason to stay away from the doctor—there is every good reason to go to him. And the sooner you go, the less likely it is that you will have to endure the possible serious consequences of neglect.

[1935]

428

AFTER THE

Linit Luxury Bath

⌐FEEL YOUR SKIN!

Lovely women everywhere have enjoyed the soft, satiny smooth skin the Linit Beauty Bath imparts. There is both beauty and soothing body refreshment in a Linit bath. Dissolve half a package or more in a tub of warm water. Bathe with your favorite soap. You will be amazed that so luxurious a bath can be so simply prepared and so economical.

THE BATHWAY TO A SOFT, SMOOTH SKIN

[1937]

My adventure with the invisible

by Lowell Thomas, *World Traveler—Radio Commentator*

MACHINES chattered around me, a bewildering complexity of mechanism endowed with superhuman faculties of precision. They had cost millions of dollars—years of thought and research. As I stood on the fifth floor of the Gillette factory in Boston I reflected: "Imagine this prodigious assembling of technological perfection, just to make a blade."

My guide corrected me, saying: "That isn't what we are turning out here. We are all collaborating here to produce a perfect edge. And that, actually and positively, is a thing that you *cannot see*."

I was to learn he was right. My guide took me upstairs and introduced me to a technician who presided over an amazing instrument. The pet gadget of the blond young modern Merlin from M. I. T. is a "sharpness comparer." Within its mysterious interior an adaptation of the weird usefulness of the photo-electric eye detects to an uncanny degree of accuracy whether that precious edge comes up to Gillette standards of sharpness.

There I realized that what my guide had told me was true. The perfect edge is perfectly invisible. It can be measured only with light-waves!

In my wanderings around the globe this is just about the most astounding spectacle I have observed in modern industry. I mean all this mighty, elaborately mechanized organization engaged in producing the unseeable.

Electric furnaces in which coils of steel are hardened and tempered, furnaces that look like long, miniature tunnels. Inside they are 1500 degrees hot, outside they are so cool you can rest your hands upon them. Diamonds from the fields of Kimberley or Brazil that play their part in the testing machines. Microscopes with a 3000-power magnifying capacity. Cathode ray oscillographs that far outstrip man's poor faculties of perception or accuracy.

And all for what? To turn out something too fine for the human eye to perceive—to produce a shaving edge of incomparable keenness. The doctors of physics, the draughtsmen in the designing room, the toolmakers in the machine shop are constantly experimenting, to produce an even sharper, smoother-shaving edge—and it's difficult for me to imagine that today's Gillette blade could be improved upon. I know—I've tried them all—in all parts of the world.

So in view of what I've seen and experienced, I can't imagine how any shaver could select a blade other than Gillette.

Here are the facts about razor blades. Why let anyone deprive you of shaving comfort by selling you a substitute! Ask for Gillette Blades and be sure to get them.

GILLETTE SAFETY RAZOR COMPANY, BOSTON, MASS.

[1936]

Life's Greatest Thrill

FOR BOYS 6 TO 60...

LIONEL TRAINS

Look what they now do by Electric Remote Control

WANT TO LOAD A COAL CAR? I'LL DO IT: PRESS BUTTON AND I'LL FILL IT TO THE BRIM!

I WHISTLE WHILE I WORK— LOUD & LONG, OR SHORT & SHARP

WOO-oo-Woo-

HERE'S A NEAT TRICK, PRESS THAT BUTTON AND WE'LL UNCOUPLE — ELECTRICALLY!

I CAN TILT... ELECTRICALLY, AND ROLL THE LOGS

TOUCH BUTTON...PRESTO... CAR TILTS, UNLOADING COAL WHEREVER YOU SAY

SIDE OF CAR LIFTS—BARRELS TUMBLE OUT

BUILT BY LIONEL

Everything Real Trains Do Lionel Trains Will Duplicate

First time ever . . . captured and reproduced in miniature by Lionel . . . the whole exciting drama of real railroading! Model freight cars loading, tilting and unloading — electrically. Cars coupling and uncoupling — at the touch of a button. Locomotive whistles shrieking. Signals flashing. Bells ringing. Something happening every second! This story is this year's biggest Christmas news. Told with complete details in the 1939 Catalog. For a free copy, clip coupon below.

★ ★ ★

FOR ANY SPACE! AT ANY PRICE!

Now, space is no longer a problem . . . every father and son can enjoy hobby railroading . . . for Lionel now builds "00" Gauge scale models so small you can operate them on the top of an ordinary bridge table. It's the ideal size for city apartments. And cost can no longer be a factor either, for there are complete Lionel train outfits, with transformers, for as little as $7.95.

THE LIONEL CORPORATION, Dept. AL
15 East 26th Street, New York, N. Y.
Please send me a FREE copy of the new, full-color, 1939 Lionel Catalog and Railroad Planning Book.

Name_____

Address_____

City_____ State_____

FREE! SEND NO MONEY!

Coupon at the right entitles parents to a free copy of the 1939 full-color 52-page Lionel Catalog. Clip, fill in, mail today.

[1939]

1940-1944

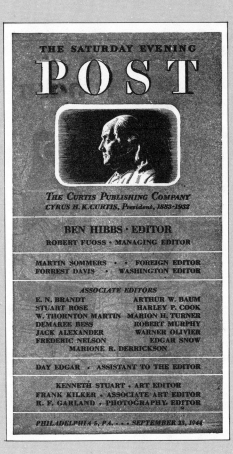

THE SATURDAY EVENING

POST

THE CURTIS PUBLISHING COMPANY
CYRUS H. K. CURTIS, President, 1883-1933

BEN HIBBS · EDITOR
ROBERT FUOSS · MANAGING EDITOR

MARTIN SOMMERS · · FOREIGN EDITOR
FORREST DAVIS · WASHINGTON EDITOR

ASSOCIATE EDITORS
E. N. BRANDT   ARTHUR W. BAUM
STUART ROSE   HARLEY P. COOK
W. THORNTON MARTIN   MARION H. TURNER
DEMAREE BESS   ROBERT MURPHY
JACK ALEXANDER   WARNER OLIVIER
FREDERIC NELSON   EDGAR SNOW
            MARIONE R. DERRICKSON

DAY EDGAR · ASSISTANT TO THE EDITOR

KENNETH STUART · ART EDITOR
FRANK KILKER · ASSOCIATE ART EDITOR
R. F. GARLAND · PHOTOGRAPHY EDITOR

PHILADELPHIA 5, PA. · · · SEPTEMBER 23, 1944

The Price of Freedom is High

THOSE who have lost sons or husbands in this war inevitably resent statements that the casualties are "only" a fraction of what some extravagantly pessimistic people predicted they would be. In the homes which have been darkened by the death of a soldier, or which have welcomed back the shattered remnants of vigorous youth, the burden of war's tragedy is little lightened by assurances that it might have been worse.

Already there is a heavy toll of sacrifice. On almost any street you pick can be found a home already visited by bereavement. There will be many more before the final accounting. Nevertheless, there are grounds for hope that the awful price will not be as great as many believed. The June invasion of France cost the United States 69,526 casualties, including 11,026 killed, as against the "half million casualties" freely predicted in certain quarters at home. The soldier in England who said to a visitor, "I don't mind going over there, but I don't want to be counted out in advance," is at least vindicated by the result.

There is no cause for overconfidence. Undoubtedly there will be other Tarawas and Saipans in the Pacific. But the over-all result so far makes it plain that the business of landing in enemy countries, preparatory to rolling ahead in a 1944 adaptation of the 1940 blitzkrieg, was accomplished with less loss of human life than even the most hopeful prophets believed was possible. For that fact, which in no way lightens the sorrows of the victims of war's grim lottery, we can all be grateful.

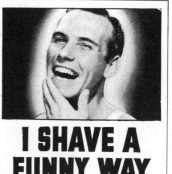

How Defense Needs have been met and Ford Quality improved

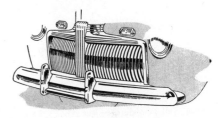

As DEFENSE PRODUCTION has gained pace, many people have wondered about its effect on 1942 cars. Would shortages of some materials force substitutes into the motor car? Would buyers get less quality for their money this year? For our part at Ford, we are glad to say that defense requirements have been met in full without a single reduction in the goodness of the car mechanically—and with many real improvements in its beauty, comfort and performance. Some new materials have replaced old ones, generally at greater cost to us. In every case, the new is equal to or better than the old. Here are instances of what we have done . . .

Steel Stampings for Die-Castings

Exterior parts like radiator grilles, and mechanical parts like generators and starter end plates, are now made from steel stampings instead of die-castings, without affecting their usefulness or appearance. This has freed large amounts of zinc, aluminum and other defense-needed materials.

Plastics Replace Metal for Interior Trim

Molybdenum Replaces Nickel

We have been developing plastics for a long time at Ford. The value of this is now apparent. The wider use of plastics this year in instrument panel, radio grille, door handles and other interior trim has released large quantities of zinc formerly used in metal die-castings, as well as nickel and chromium formerly used in plating bright metal parts. The new plastic parts are lighter in weight, fully as serviceable, and very attractive in appearance.

Nickel is important not only in the finish of plated metal but in improving the toughness of steel. In defense production it is used in the manufacture of aviation engine parts and armor plate. Ford valves, transmission gears, shafts, and other parts formerly containing nickel, are now alloyed with molybdenum and chromium. For the purpose, these parts are as good as or better than those replaced.

Some Results in Defense Metals Saved

Based on present conditions, here are some examples of how new materials and methods in the 1942 Ford are helping relieve defense "shortages." Figures show the *cut* in use this year of the materials named:

Primary (*new*) Aluminum has been cut out 100% . . . Secondary (*re-melted*) Aluminum has been cut down 70% . . . Nickel has been cut down by 90.7% . . . Magnesium, cut out almost entirely, is down 98.7% . . . Zinc has been reduced by 37.5% . . . Copper, Tin, Lead, and Tungsten cut down in varying amounts from 5.2% to 81%.

America's Most Modern 6 . . . America's Lowest-priced 8

"LOOKS LIKE THE HONEYMOON'S OVER!___"

MINNIE: She used to fix herself up cute's a kitten, but look at her now!

MATTIE: *I think her dress just kinda shrunk a little, Minnie.*

MINNIE: Well, bein' dumb is just as bad as bein' careless! She should of looked for a "Sanforized" label.

MATTIE: *Now, Minnie . . . no matter what they tell you about a wash dress, the fit always changes some.*

MINNIE: Not if it has a "Sanforized" tag on it! The tag says the fabric won't shrink more'n a teeny 1%, and that's too little to change the fit at all!

MATTIE: *Merciful days! Where on earth do you find dresses like that?*

MINNIE: You can get 'em from a dollar or two on up, in all kinds of materials and styles. Just look for the "Sanforized" label and you're safe. I ought to tell her so.

MATTIE: *Well, Minnie, the way your voice carries, you already have!*

↓ "THOSE OLD CATS"

BRIDE: Handing out advice about the kind of clothes I ought to buy!

Just wait until I tell Bill what they said behind my back!

BRIDE: Did you ever hear of a label called "Sanforized," Bill?

HUSBAND: Sure! I wouldn't buy a shirt without it. Shirts marked "Sanforized" never shrink out of fit. And what's more . . .

. . . they have shorts and pajamas labeled "Sanforized" now, in all styles and prices. And . . . er . . . women's dresses, too!

BRIDE: Guess everybody's smart except me. But wait 'til tomorrow!

INSIST ON a "Sanforized" label when buying other cotton, linen, or spun rayon washables . . . children's clothes, uniforms, slacks and work clothes, slip-cover and curtain materials. It's the way to be safe!

SANFORIZED
REG. U. S. PAT. OFF.

Insist on this trade-mark when buying a **Compressive-Shrunk** fabric. It signifies that the residual shrinkage will be less than 1% conforming to tests and standards established and supervised by the owner of the trade-mark.

FOR PERMANENT FIT... LOOK FOR THE "SANFORIZED" LABEL

[1941]

LOCAL WOMAN
SERIOUSLY HURT
Struck by car while
crossing street

Landsdale, Jan. 12—Struck by an
automobile as she was crossing
Hammond Street...
...22, of 10... Street was seriously
injured here today. She was rushed
in an ambulance...
...here she in... ...hospital

CLAIM NO.
12741
Policyholder liable.
Investigate claimant's
injuries today.

"WHAT HAVE I DONE?" I GASPED

*Like you, W. B. M. had a perfect driving
record until that morning last January*

"I was parking my car when suddenly I heard an
agonized cry. 'What have I done?' I gasped. Then with
horror I realized my car had struck a young woman.

"It was my first accident and in the moments which
followed I was dazed and bewildered. A crowd col-
lected. One man pointed at me and shouted, 'Why don't
you look where you're going? It was all your fault.
You'll pay plenty for this.' Then an ambulance arrived.

"Later, when I reported the accident to Liberty
Mutual, a great weight was lifted from my mind. The
claims man asked careful but friendly questions about
the accident and assured me that I had full protection
under my Liberty Mutual policy. Then he went to work
—found and interviewed witnesses, forgot no detail,
stayed on the job until the case was settled—out of
court.

"My accident gave me a brand-new slant on car insurance. Years ago, I chose Liberty Mutual as my company mainly because of the dividend savings. And I
have received cash dividends every year, reducing the

cost of my protection by one fifth. More recently I have
also benefited from reductions in car insurance rates
in this state, and from discounts due to my good driving
record. But Liberty Mutual did more than save me
money. They're my 'Friend on the Highway.' When I
needed help most, a Liberty Mutual man was on the
spot to protect me from loss and worry."

This story is typical of the preferred service enjoyed
by more than 200,000 other responsible car owners who

are protected by Liberty Mutual. If you should have an
accident, skilled investigators and adjusters are immediately available to protect your interests, to relieve
you of worry, to act as "Your Friend on the Highway."

Don't buy or renew your car insurance until you read
the free booklet offered below. It tells how careful
drivers are securing full protection and a friendly insurance service at lower cost, explains how you can qualify,
describes our convenient deferred payment plan. Mail
the coupon today—no obligation.

LIBERTY MUTUAL
INSURANCE COMPANY
BOSTON

Your Friend on the Highway

[1941]

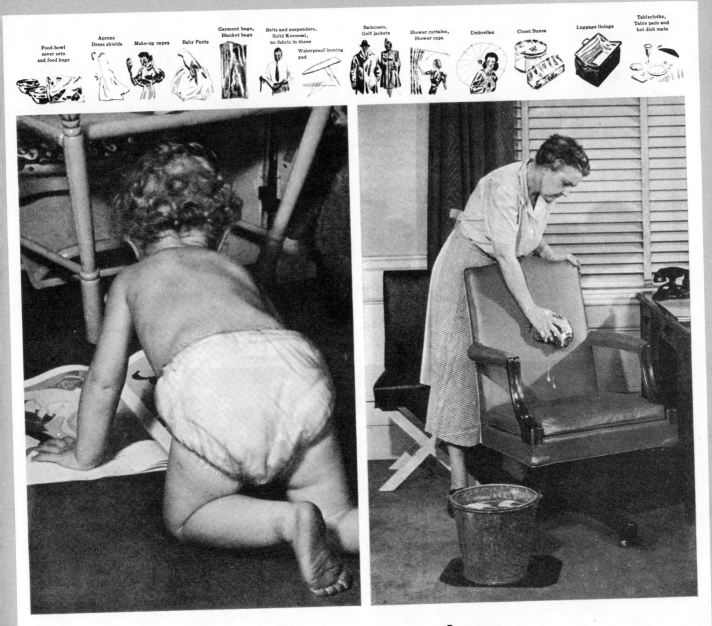

Food-bowl cover sets and food bags | Aprons Dress shields | Make-up capes | Baby Pants | Garment bags, Blanket bags | Belts and suspenders. Solid Koroseal, no fabric in these | Waterproof ironing pad | Raincoats, Golf jackets | Shower curtains, Shower caps | Umbrellas | Closet Boxes | Luggage linings | Tablecloths, Table pads and hot dish mats

For seat coverings—
the new material is Koroseal

Even if you have a Koroseal raincoat, shower curtain, garment bag — you haven't seen anything yet!

Moistureproof pants so soft they make it comfortable to be a baby are all ready for postwar arrivals. They're as smooth as a rose petal and yet they're made of three hard materials — limestone, coke and salt. They're Koroseal by B. F. Goodrich.

Koroseal is the new material with a hundred uses waiting for it as soon as its war needs are met. It is waterproof, is not hardened by sun, nor harmed even by strong acids, stays flexible, can be washed off just by a damp cloth,

Koroseal—Reg. T. M.

and is not affected by air or age for years. It can be made in any color and form, in any degree of hardness, in strands or tubes or sheets. It can be used as a coating on cloth or paper.

Koroseal upholstery fabric for porches and lawns will be rainproof because it cannot absorb water and will not get hard nor crack. It's ideal indoors, too — it wears better than leather or cloth, does not scuff, and can always be kept clean and fresh because it can be washed easily.

Koroseal resists hard wear and rough use so well that it will make longer-lasting luggage, shoe soles, camping equipment. Because it resists oils and greases, Koroseal is ideal for food packaging, automobile upholstery, work clothes. Koroseal strands can be woven into window screens that never corrode, braided into flexible, longer-lasting suspenders and belts, woven into women's hats that stay fresh and crisp in a rainstorm.

For industry, Koroseal hose will handle oils and greases, Koroseal tanks will hold even those acids used in chrome plating which no other commercial tank lining can stand, Koroseal gaskets will not get brittle even in

extreme cold—and new uses are being discovered almost every day.

Before the war Koroseal was used chiefly for articles like those across the top of this page. After the war they will all be back in your stores, plus the scores of new things of Koroseal which B. F. Goodrich research has developed. *The B. F. Goodrich Company, Koroseal Division, Akron, Ohio.*

Koroseal

BY

B.F. Goodrich

[1944]

You
feel like
dancing
in

Air Step

THE SHOE WITH THE MAGIC SOLE

Dress from Nicole de Paris, Inc., New York. Simply tailored in pale blue lamé, lovely for late afternoon. Shoes by Air Step.

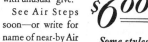

The designed-in, hidden comfort of Air Steps is the Magic Sole—thousands of tiny air cells form a soft, resilient cushion that absorbs jolts to feet and jars to nerves when you walk.

The Air Step look is one of lightness—the Air Step styling is handled with a light touch —and the Air Step feel is "I'm light on my feet."

Air Step shoes are designed with a definite woman in mind. Smartly conservative in taste. Well aware that a good line in a shoe is the making of a pretty foot. Intent on the kind of quality that lasts as long as the shoes themselves.

For these women Air Step offers a light and feminine handling of good style—with a plus of light and cushiony comfort in its Magic Sole that keeps you "Fresh at Five." Another new comfort is a wonderfully pliable, hand-flexed sole—with unusual "give."

See Air Steps soon—or write for name of near-by Air Step Store. BROWN SHOE COMPANY, St. Louis.

$6⁰⁰

Some styles $6⁵⁰

Higher Denver West

WHIRL—(shoe shown on record above) beautifully simple gabardine—swirled with patent.

SPICE—a little classic, so smooth, so chic with everything.

TAM—with a huge round button to give it a gay, new look.

SHELTON—for your tailored moments. Airy perforations for coolness.

SKIPPER—"sassy" little shoe with bold cable stitching.

WELTON—new idea —appliqué of patent leather on crushed kid.

PHILCO
brings you a new kind of Radio-Phonograph !

NO NEEDLES TO CHANGE

RECORDS LAST TEN TIMES LONGER

GLORIOUS NEW PURITY OF TONE

PHILCO 255T. The finest table model radio money can buy. 9-tube circuit gives amazing performance and tone. New kind of Overseas Wave-Band. Eight Electric Push Buttons. Lovely Inclined Panel walnut cabinet. *Only $5.95 down.*

PHILCO-Transitone PT-87. The All-Year, Indoor-Outdoor Portable, plays either on long-life battery or any house current. Convenient to move from room to room or play outdoors. Exclusive Philco features give matchless performance where ordinary portables fail. *Only $19.95 complete.*

PHILCO-Transitone PT-2. AC-DC. Finest tone quality ever achieved in a compact. New 6-inch Oval Speaker. Beam Power output. Improved Built-In Loop Aerial. Illuminated Horizontal Dial. Smart, streamline plastic cabinet in walnut shade. *A sensational value, only $12.95.*

PHILCO 280X Radio Console. Radio's champion value! New 8-tube circuit doubles selectivity, reduces noise and interference by 5 to 1. New kind of Overseas Wave-Band brings in Europe 5 times stronger and clearer. New Built-In American and Overseas Aerial System. 8 Electric Push Buttons. Large walnut cabinet. *Yours for only $6.95 down.*

Plays any Phonograph Record on a "BEAM OF LIGHT"!
NEW TILT-FRONT CABINET... *No lid to raise...no unhandy compartment!*

The new Philco "*Beam of Light*" Radio-Phonograph is the new sensation of the radio world! Lovers of recorded music everywhere have hailed it as the first basic improvement in record reproduction since the phonograph was invented. Based on *modern* scientific discoveries, it brings you new delights in radio and recorded music which you enjoy for the first time ... and *only in a Philco!*

It's needless, now, to change needles, to put up with surface noise and record wear, to fuss with lids, doors and clumsy compartments. In the new Philco Photo-Electric Radio-Phonograph, a rounded jewel floats over the records and *reflects* the music on a *beam of light* from a tiny mirror to a photo-electric cell. The scraping needle is gone

... no needles to change. Record wear and surface noise are reduced by 10 to 1. And you hear new overtones of beauty, released from your records for the first time!

Only Philco gives you the Tilt-Front cabinet. No lid to lift, no need to remove decorations, no unhandy compartment. Simply tilt forward the grille, place your records and tilt it back again!

HOME RECORDING is optional equipment with every Philco Photo-Electric Radio-Phonograph. Make your own records at home; record family voices and events, radio programs, etc.

PHILCO 608P Radio Phonograph, *illustrated above,* brings you these new Philco achievements at a popular price. Powerful 9-tube circuit, Automatic Record Changer, American and Foreign radio reception. Hand-rubbed Walnut cabinet. *Only $12.95 down.*

[1941]

440

TWO just made for YOU !

NEW
CHEVROLET
Fleetline
AEROSEDAN

NEW
CHEVROLET
Fleetline
SPORTMASTER

IT PAYS TO BUY THE LEADER AND GET THE LEADING BUY

DESIGNED TO LEAD IN STYLING

Chevrolet alone of all low-priced cars has new "Leader Line" Styling, distinctive new "Door-Action" Fenders and new Fleetline Body by Fisher with No Draft Ventilation.

DESIGNED TO LEAD IN PERFORMANCE

Chevrolet alone combines a powerful, thoroughly proved Valve-in-Head "Victory" Engine, Safe-T-Special Hydraulic Brakes, Unitized Knee-Action Ride, and Extra-Easy Vacuum-Power Shift at no extra cost.

DESIGNED TO LEAD IN ECONOMY

Chevrolet is the most economical of all the largest-selling low-priced cars from the all-round standpoint of gas, oil and upkeep.

They're cars of custom quality...the newest of all "Torpedo" models . . . each outstandingly beautiful, and designed to carry six passengers . . . each engineered to bring you an unequaled combination of performance and economy . . . each built to gratify your desire for a car that is distinctive without being expensive.

CHEVROLET MOTOR DIVISION, *General Motors Sales Corporation*, DETROIT, MICHIGAN

THE FINEST CHEVROLET OF ALL TIME

[1941]

441

A Look at Plymouth is a Look Ahead

Advanced Engineering creates a big, low-slung, powerful car— now 95 H.P.— with new driving economy.

Here's a first-class investment in value and long life— Plymouth's Finest! It's low, long, wide—more powerful *and* more economical—a finer car in *every* way.

Plymouth gives you the greatest power of "All 3" low-priced cars. And because the big, eager engine purrs along with fewer revolutions per mile, you save gas and oil!

The low-slung design that everyone admires also gives Plymouth a sure-footed, road-hugging stability—new ease of handling!

Forward-looking engineering gives you the safety of Safeguard Wheels, the long-term savings of an Oil Bath Air Cleaner, Oil Filter, Superfinished engine parts, Coil Springs!

Plymouth Builds Great Cars! A look at Plymouth's Finest is a look ahead...to invest in it is to buy wisely. All prices and specifications subject to change without notice. Plymouth Division of Chrysler Corporation.

TUNE IN MAJOR BOWES, THURS., C. B. S. NETWORK.

PRODUCTS OF CHRYSLER CORPORATION

Army Tanks • Anti-Aircraft Guns • Aircraft Parts • Army Vehicles • Passenger Cars • Trucks • Marine and Industrial Engines • Diesel Engines • Oilite Bearings • Airtemp Heating and Air Conditioning Equipment.

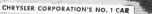

CHRYSLER CORPORATION'S NO. 1 CAR

*Buy Wisely_* BUY PLYMOUTH
THE CAR THAT STANDS UP BEST

[1941]

Illustrated: Packard One-Twenty Business Coupe, $1038* (white sidewall tires extra)

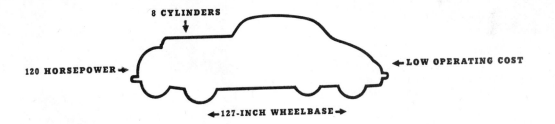

8 CYLINDERS

120 HORSEPOWER →

← LOW OPERATING COST

← 127-INCH WHEELBASE →

Choose a car as you choose a friend!

NO other eight we know of has such winning ways. No other eight has quite the same ability to make warm and loyal friends.

This, because the Packard 120's unique qualities parallel those which men instinctively seek in the lasting friendships they make. Qualities to be admired and esteemed. For your car, like a friend, must win your complete confidence.

And recognition of this crops up in your *first* chat with the *first* member of the One-Twenty's loyal family you meet. He will pull out all the stops in his praises of this great Packard's stunning appearance, flashing pick-up, and the luxurious feel of "riding on air" which its *extra length* provides.

And he will tell you tall but *true* tales of the mileage his car spins from gasoline and oil. If he has had his car long enough for any of the commoner service operations—he will confide happily that One-Twenty service charges are right in line with those of *much smaller and cheaper cars!*

Such enthusiasm is worth looking into, so drive this Packard 120 *yourself!* Note its eager answer to your half-formed wish. Its stirring tempo when you give it the gun . . . its "sixth sense" in its noiseless drift through traffic. And when you've done all this, compare this truly fine car with *any other eight!* Chances are dollars to dimes, on the record of 1940, you'll choose a Packard One-Twenty!

PACKARD 120
$1038

AND UP. Packard 110, $867 and up. Packard 120, $1038 and up. Packard Super-8 160, $1524 and up. Packard Custom Super-8 180, $2243 to $6300. *All prices delivered in Detroit, State taxes extra.

ASK THE MAN WHO OWNS ONE

[1940]

ON THE AIR AND EVERYWHERE, IT'S—

CALL FOR PHILIP MORRIS

YOU CAN'T HELP INHALING—BUT

YOU CAN HELP YOUR THROAT!

IT'S a fact — all smokers sometimes inhale. More smoke reaches delicate nose and throat passages. And *chances* of irritation *increase!* But now look *at the findings* of eminent doctors who <u>compared</u> five leading brands of cigarettes... and report that:

IN STRIKING CONTRAST TO PHILIP MORRIS — IRRITANT EFFECTS OF THE FOUR OTHER LEADING BRANDS AVERAGED THREE TIMES AS HIGH — AND LASTED MORE THAN FIVE TIMES AS LONG!

Some inhaling goes with smoking... but worry about throat irritation need *not* go with inhaling. <u>Change now</u> to Philip Morris — for pleasure *without penalties. Why wait?*

Finer Pleasure PLUS Real Protection

AMERICA'S FINEST CIGARETTE

[1941]

Van Raalte GLOVES

"BECAUSE YOU LOVE NICE THINGS"

STOCKINGS · UNDERTHINGS · GLOVES

VAN RAALTE · 417 FIFTH AVENUE · NEW YORK CITY

[1941]

[1941]

[1944]

Trim that

Bulging Waistline

with the
BAUER & BLACK
Bracer
SUPPORTER BELT

●Take a look at your waistline! Can you boast the trim, athletic, well-groomed appearance you'd *like* to have?

If you have a bulge . . . even a *little* one . . . it may be hurting your appearance, and having an effect *even on how you feel.* That added girth can destroy the fit of your clothes . . . make you look older. And when you *look* that way . . often you *feel* that way, too.

To regain those clean cut lines, *brace up* . . . with the Bracer! This exclusive Bauer & Black supporter-belt has these distinctive features. Knit of "Lastex" yarn—has *two way stretch.* No roll—four removable stays at top. Soft, roomy, fly-front pouch. Tailored to fit. For extra support, extra coolness, you'll like the Bracer Royal—costs slightly more. At department, drug, men's apparel and surgical stores everywhere.

If your dealer cannot supply you, simply fill out and mail the coupon with a check or money order. Bracer—$2.00. (In Canada $2.75); Bracer Royal—$3.00. (Canada $3.50)

1941]

What *Do* men want anyway?

THE GIRL: I'm easy to look at...my figure's certainly okay, but—why doesn't a man ever *tell* me I'm wonderful?

US: They *would,* my dear...if you'd only learn the real secret of personal daintiness...the secret of bathing body odor away, the *feminine* way!

THE GIRL: The *feminine* way? What feminine way? I always thought a soap that removes body odor effectively *had* to have that strong, "mannish" smell!

US: Not *this* one, darling...here's a truly gentle, truly feminine soap that leaves you alluringly scented... and daily use actually stops all body odor! Here, try it...

US: It's today's specially-made Cashmere Bouquet Soap, and its rich, fragrant lather will positively bathe away every last trace of body odor *instantly.*

THE GIRL: It's marvelous, it's true! Look at those creamy suds...and that *perfume*—mmm—smells like $20-an-ounce!

US: That, you'll be happy to know, is the famous "fragrance men love"! And we repeat, not even the strongest "mannish" soap can get rid of perspiration better than complexion-gentle Cashmere Bouquet!

THE GIRL: Hope I feel as full of oomph tomorrow as I do tonight...there's a certain Someone I'm going to "accidentally" meet on the beach!

THE GIRL: My goodness gracious, I never *heard* so many pretty speeches! Does Cashmere Bouquet guarantee compliments like this *all* the time?

US: You attract the compliments, dear girl ...Cashmere Bouquet just insures your perfection in the close-ups by guarding your daintiness!

THE GIRL: B-but, my feminine instinct tells me the *next* pretty speech I hear is going to be a proposal!

US: Well, good luck! You'll hear it if you remember the lucky secret of Cashmere Bouquet Soap!

Stay dainty each day...
with Cashmere Bouquet
THE SOAP WITH THE FRAGRANCE MEN LOVE

Lend $3, get $4—Buy more *War Bonds*

[1943]

AMERICA MUST SAVE MORE FUEL THIS WINTER . . !

★ **Say Government Authorities** ★

Another winter of war for America finds the heating problem even more acute than last year. All the heat-saving measures you've ever used are again necessary. And you'll be wise to discover new ones. For the greater comfort of your family and as an important contribution to the war effort, every bit of heat must be carefully conserved.

HEAT-SAVING HINTS EVERYONE CAN FOLLOW—

Close doors quickly when you enter or leave the house. Put a rug against bedroom doors at night. When ventilating rooms, turn off heat and close doors to keep cold air out of other parts of the house. Close fireplace damper. Keep heating plant and heat pipes free from soot.

30% of all heat loss goes out the windows

By proper use of your cloth window shades you can reduce heat loss through glass panes by as much as one-third and thus save up to 10% on fuel. Scientific tests conducted by the Armour Research Foundation have convincingly proved this fact. A drawn shade creates an insulating dead air space between the shade and the pane.

USE YOUR CLOTH WINDOW SHADES THIS WAY

DURING THE DAY...
Draw shades to sills in all rooms not being used

DURING THE DAY...
Draw shades at least half way in rooms being used

AT NIGHT...
Draw shades to sills in all rooms

PULL DOWN YOUR SHADES save up to 10% on fuel !

FREE HELP—get this interesting booklet on helpful wartime uses of cloth window shades. Ask your dealer or write Window Shade Institute, 60 E. 42nd St., New York, 17, N. Y.

Sponsored by THE CHAS. W. BRENEMAN CO.—THE COLUMBIA MILLS, INC.—STEWART HARTSHORN COMPANY—ILLINOIS SHADE CLOTH CORPORATION—INTERSTATE SHADE CLOTH COMPANY—LAPSLEY INTERSTATE SHADE CLOTH COMPANY—McMASTER-REILLY SHADE CLOTH COMPANY—OSWEGO SHADE CLOTH COMPANY—WM. VOLKER & COMPANY—THE WESTERN SHADE CLOTH COMPANY

[1943]

"Just 30 extra seconds and I'm *Fragrantly Dainty* for hours"

450

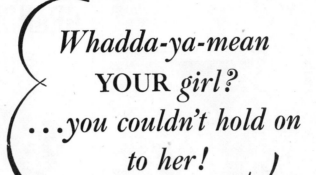

Whadda-ya-mean YOUR girl? ...you couldn't hold on to her!

T HAT'S what Red shot at Tommy as the two glared hotly at each other before the girls got them away ... and it was a poser for Tommy. He blamed his break with Polly on everything but the simple truth itself ... the very thing* that Polly would not tolerate and which he himself never suspected.

It's Unforgivable

Few things can equal a case of halitosis* (bad breath) as a monkey-wrench in the wheels of romance. It's the offense unforgivable in either a man or a woman. Unfortunately, anyone may suffer from it at some time or other. The worst of it is, you yourself may be guilty without even realizing it—and your best friends won't tell you.

But why take long risks? Why offend needlessly? There's an easy, simple, delightful precaution against halitosis—Listerine Antiseptic used as a mouth rinse. Fastidious people use it every morning and every night, and between times before business and social engagements.

Halts Fermentation

Some cases of halitosis are due to systemic conditions, but most cases, say some authorities, are due to the fermentation of tiny food particles in the mouth. Listerine Antiseptic quickly halts such fermentation, then overcomes the odors it causes. The breath quickly becomes sweeter, fresher, purer, less likely to offend.

If you want to appear at your best, if you want others to like you, get into the cleanly habit of using Listerine Antiseptic every morning and night. It pays.

LAMBERT PHARMACAL COMPANY, St. Louis, Mo.

LISTERINE

Leaves the breath sweeter, purer ... use it before every business and social engagement

WILL YOU HELP HIM
COME BACK_*Alive?*

MAYBE you never thought of War Bonds — as *life-savers* — and yet that's exactly what they are.

Look at a War Bond . . .

A piece of paper. Weighs a tenth of an ounce, maybe. Printed in black and green ink.

Read it. You'll see the interest you get from it—$4 from every $3 you invest, as it pays you $25 for $18.75 in ten years.

Signed by the Secretary of the Treasury of the United States, and backed by the power and good faith of the world's mightiest nation.

But there are some things it *won't* tell you. Things that come from *your* heart. More important than interest. More important than security.

LIVES! Of clean, smiling American boys. Hundreds of thousands of them.

Their lives depend upon bullets for the rifles they fire . . . shells for the cannon to blast Jap landing barges . . . bombs that drop from soaring planes . . . tanks that roar to the attack . . . great ships . . . submarines.

Supplied in abundance—and on time—they spell the difference between life and death—between Victory and defeat.

That is why it is up to us—here—now—every day—to buy War Bonds not only as an investment in our own future security—but as an investment in human lives today.

Think of *that* when you think of War Bonds. Buy them regularly—every pay-day—with 10% of your income—as a minimum goal.

And you, too, will help him come back —ALIVE!

FACTS ABOUT WAR BONDS

1. War Bonds cost $18.75 for which you receive $25 in 10 years — or $4 for every $3.

2. War Bonds are the world's *safest* investment—guaranteed by the United States Government.

3. War Bonds can be made out in 1 name or 2, as co-owners.

4. War Bonds *cannot* go down in value. If they are lost, the Government will issue new ones.

5. War Bonds can be cashed in, in case of necessity, after 60 days.

6. War Bonds begin to accrue interest after one year.

Keep on Buying War Bonds

[1943]

GRANDMA CALLED IT SINFU

IN MY DAY we women couldn't do much about those bristles on the manly chin that scraped like sin. But nowadays any woman's a fool to put up with one of those human porcupines. Which reminds me, my dear, Margie has picked the most delightful young man — always so well groomed—he must shave twice a day—yet his skin's never the least bit irritated looking. It's what Margie calls a Barbasol Face.

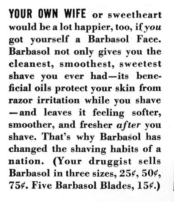

YOUR OWN WIFE or sweetheart would be a lot happier, too, if *you* got yourself a Barbasol Face. Barbasol not only gives you the cleanest, smoothest, sweetest shave you ever had—its beneficial oils protect your skin from razor irritation while you shave —and leaves it feeling softer, smoother, and fresher *after* you shave. That's why Barbasol has changed the shaving habits of a nation. (Your druggist sells Barbasol in three sizes, 25¢, 50¢, 75¢. Five Barbasol Blades, 15¢.)

Barbasol

For modern shaving—
No Brush—No Lather—No Rub-in

[1940]

"Look! There's a man under my bed!"

"THAT'S BILL. He's my husband. I've put him to work fixing that loose bed spring that just tore one of my precious Cannon Percale Sheets. It won't happen again!

"Now that it's wartime, sheets just *have* to be Methuselahs! The government wants all of us to make *everything we have* last longer—so we won't need to buy more, unnecessarily. That's plain waste!

"And it's awfully easy to make sheets last and last. Why, a home-economics expert told me that if women took the best possible care of sheets, they'd probably last *twice as long*. The sheets would, I mean. So I've learned a whole bag of tricks that mean long life to a sheet!"

My common-sense sheet-savers.

"I make sure nothing about the beds can catch and tear my sheets. (Now that one sheet's been torn!) I lift sheets off gently instead of yanking them. And the minute I spot a rip or worn place, I scurry for my mending basket!"

My washday wiles.

"I'm a clock-watcher—15 minutes for soaking

sheets; 5 to 8 minutes of washing in the machine. Then plenty of rinses to get every smitch of soap out. And *then* I pray for sunshine—my favorite bleach!"

My hints for hanging.

"I fold my sheets hem to hem, and clothespin 'em with the fold hanging over about a foot. If it's windy, I hang them in a sheltered spot where they won't flap too much."

My ironing ideas.

"I don't use too hot an iron—that causes 'hidden scorch'—death on sheets! I never bear down directly on the folds. Before I put my sheets away, I make sure they're bone-dry so they won't mildew. And I use 'em round-robin style—taking fresh sheets from the *bottom* of the pile every time—to equalize wear."

My tip-off when you must buy sheets.

"Of course, you won't buy unless you're in desperate need! But when your linen-cupboard is

really bare, remember this: smooth, dreamy-soft Cannon Percales cost just about the same as heavy-duty muslin. And there are 25% more threads to the inch in Cannon Percales than in the best muslin—wonderful for wear!

"And Cannon Percales save money if you send your wash out at average pound laundry rates—because percale's lighter. Easier to do at home too!"

My best words of advice.

"Don't buy sheets unless you honestly have to! If you *do*, be sure to pick a name you can trust for all the things you can't see for yourself in a sheet. Take the Cannon name—you've seen it on those wonderful Cannon Towels! It's every bit as dependable on sheets!

"One last reminder. Whether you buy new Cannon Percale Sheets or own some already—resolve to add *years* to their life by proper care!"

Cannon also makes an economy muslin sheet— well-constructed, long-wearing—a splendid value!

Cannon Percale Sheets

TRADE MARK
CANNON

Made by the makers of Cannon Towels and Hosiery

[1943]

First-Class Fighting Man

BACK of the American soldier is a tradition of valor that extends unbroken from Lexington and Saratoga to the mountains of Batan. Give him training and equipment and you can trust him to lick anything that moves on feet or wheels or wings.

The United States Army has a secret weapon . . . secret only because it can never be comprehended by dictator nations. *It is an army of free Americans*, willingly serving the land that made them free.

Today your country needs this spirit in its fighting men as never before. Here is *your* opportunity. Men 18 and 19 years old, with keenness, enthusiasm and daring, are especially desired. Thousands of patriotic young men are entering the Army through voluntary enlistment and the Selective Service System, and you can be one of them, sharing the comradeship and the splendid training of Army life. On the ground or in the air, there's a place where you are needed, *now*.

Call at the nearest Army Recruiting Station and get full details on how you can best serve your country.

VOLUNTEERS WANTED FOR PARACHUTE DUTY

Qualified men may now enlist direct from civilian life for service with the Army's parachute troops. Volunteers must be from 18 to 30 years old, alert, active, aggressive fighters, with strength and endurance. You can obtain full information from your local Army Recruiting Officers.

U. S. ARMY RECRUITING SERVICE

Visit or write the nearest U. S. Army Recruiting Station or write to: "The Commanding General," of the Corps Area nearest you:

First Corps Area................................Boston, Mass.
Second Corps Area............Governors Island, N. Y.
Third Corps Area............................Baltimore, Md.
Fourth Corps Area................................Atlanta, Ga.

Fifth Corps Area......Fort Hayes, Columbus, Ohio
Sixth Corps Area....................................Chicago, Ill.
Seventh Corps Area............................Omaha, Nebr.
Eighth Corps Area......Fort Sam Houston, Texas
Ninth Corps Area, Presidio of San Francisco, Calif.

Or write to:
Enlisted Division, E-4, A.G.O., Washington, D. C.

[1942]

"I'd rather be with them— than waiting for them"

I'll admit there's a funny lump in my throat . . . But here I am, loaded with my overseas pack. Climbing up the side of the biggest boat I've ever seen—*and glad of it*.

Glad I said "good-by" to civilian life months ago—and went into the WAC. Went through all the training and on to active duty.

For, as a Wac, I'm *really* working for victory. Sharing the hard part of war. And the glory that will come.

I'd rather be *with* them—in the Army . . .

Than waiting back home—thinking up things to make the time go by—listening to the news— wondering when it'll all be over.

Yes, I'm in the Army and on my way—and I'm glad to the bottom of my heart!

• • •

For complete information about the Women's Army Corps, go to your nearest U.S. Army Recruiting Station. Or mail the coupon below.

Good soldiers...

THE **WAC**

WOMEN'S ARMY CORPS

[1944]

Native of Toronto, lovely Margaret Knight has been uprooted from home soil to act as private secretary to the Wing Commander of the R.A.F. Delegation, Washington, D. C. Questioned about her lovely skin, Margaret confided, "My complexion would be only 'so-so' without Woodbury Soap. Yet friends tell me my skin is like creamy velvet."

"Prettiest Canadian War Worker in the U.S."

She keeps her complexion sparkling with a Woodbury Facial Cocktail

1. "Pressure of work leaves little time for beauty frills," says Margaret. "After a long and grimy day, I take a Woodbury Facial Cocktail to bring back clear, fresh sparkle."

2. "That veil of dirt and stale make-up is soon dissolved. I just pat a rich, silky lather of Woodbury Soap over my face. Then take a cold, clear rinse." Try this true *skin* soap.

3. "Homesick? Not with so many of our boys about," says Margaret. Her beauty soap, gentle Woodbury, contains a costly ingredient for mildness. Helps cope with clogged pores.

4. Use Woodbury Soap to cleanse your skin of dirt which may coarsen pores. Made of pure oils, quick to lather. Let Woodbury bring you *"The Skin You Love to Touch."* Only 10¢.

★ BUY WAR BONDS AND STAMPS ★

[1943]

456

HOW YOU CAN HELP WIN THE WAR!

NOT ALL OF US CAN SHOULDER A GUN OR MAKE A PLANE, BUT ALL OF US CAN DO SOMETHING TO BACK UP THE BOYS AT THE FRONT. BELIEVING THAT EVERYONE, YOUNG AND OLD, IS ANXIOUS TO KNOW WHAT TO DO, THE MENNEN COMPANY VOLUNTARILY SUBORDINATES ITS OWN ADVERTISING TO FURTHER CIVILIAN WAR EFFORTS. HERE ARE A FEW WAYS YOU CAN HELP—

RENT SPARE ROOMS TO WAR WORKERS. INADEQUATE HOUSING IS HAMPERING PRODUCTION IN MANY AREAS. PHONE OR WRITE PERSONNEL DIRECTORS OF PLANTS IN YOUR VICINITY.

CARRY PARCELS TO SAVE GASOLINE, OIL, TIRES, AND MANPOWER ON DELIVERY TRUCKS — YOU'LL BE HELPING TO DELIVER MORE BOMBS ON THE ENEMY.

GIVE A LIFT TO OTHERS. IT COSTS NO MORE TO CARRY SEVERAL PEOPLE - AND SAVES PRECIOUS TIME AND TIRES. WORK OUT A "SHARE-THE-CAR" PLAN WITH NEIGHBORS AND FELLOW WORKERS.

NOTHING TOO GOOD FOR OUR BOYS! ALL BRANCHES OF THE ARMED SERVICES ARE USING LARGE QUANTITIES OF MENNEN SHAVE PRODUCTS TO MAKE LIFE A LITTLE EASIER FOR OUR FIGHTING MEN. DON'T BLAME YOUR DRUGGIST IF HE HAPPENS TO BE TEMPORARILY OUT OF YOUR FAVORITE MENNEN SHAVE PRODUCTS.

Post this page on bulletin boards of offices, plants, schools, churches, clubs, etc.

SAVE EMPTY TUBES FROM SHAVE CREAM, TOOTHPASTE, ETC. THEY HAVE A HIGH CONTENT OF BADLY NEEDED TIN. LEAVE THEM WITH YOUR DRUGGIST WHO WILL FORWARD THEM TO A CENTRAL DEPOT.

3-STEP MENNEN SHAVE

GROW VEGETABLES IN YOUR OWN BACK YARD FOR YOUR FAMILY. START A COMMUNITY-GARDEN MOVEMENT TO MAKE VACANT GROUND PRODUCE. THIS WILL RELEASE FOOD FOR OUR FORCES AND ALLIES.

① **WHISKERS OFF!**
Mennen Brushless. It's the fastest-growing Brushless. In tubes or glass jars.
Lather, plain or Menthol-iced (best-seller of its kind).

② **FACE PEPPED-UP!**
Skin Bracer — America's best-selling shave lotion. Cools, refreshes. Everyone likes its manly odor.

③ **PERFECT FINISH!**
Talcum for Men. Neutral tint, doesn't show. Most popular men's talcum.

The Mennen Co., Newark, N. J., San Francisco, Toronto

1942]

DO YOUR BEST ... AND *Be at your Best*

THESE are simple obligations, to our country, to our men at the front, and to ourselves.

No matter what your job—housewife, office employee, war worker—give it all you've got : : : do your best all of the time.

That means keeping strong, keeping healthy: This job's going to take every bit of stamina we can muster. And health is your greatest asset.

But as you work, don't forget to play. Play is the great equalizer. Make it part of your life also. Step forth. Go places. Meet people. Cultivate old friends and make new ones—lots of them. And try to be at your best always. Look your neatest. Be your sweetest. Swap a smile for a tear. Trade a laugh for a frown. Don't let down. Keep smiling. Keep going. That's the way the boys at the front would like it:

As a safe, efficient household antiseptic for use in a thousand little emergencies, Listerine Antiseptic has stood pre-eminent for more than half a century. In the later years it has established a truly impressive test record against America's No. 1 health problem, the ordinary cold, and its frequent attribute, sore throat.

It is hardly necessary to add that, because of its germicidal action which halts bacterial fermentation in the mouth, Listerine Antiseptic is the social standby of millions who do not wish to offend needlessly in the matter of halitosis (unpleasant breath) when not of systemic origin.

LAMBERT PHARMACAL COMPANY, *St. Louis, Mo:*

LISTERINE ANTISEPTIC

for Oral Hygiene

ATTENTION PLEASE: If you haven't tried Listerine Tooth Paste you're missing something!

[1943]

Idle words make busy subs!

1. IN MAINE A SHIPYARD WORKER SPOKE WITHOUT MUCH THOUGHT...(THE SHIP!).

2. IN FLORIDA A WAITER OVERHEARD SOME CARELESS TALK...(THE PORT!).

3. IN NEW YORK A SAILOR'S FRIEND GOT CONFIDENTIAL...(THE DATE!).

4. IN MICHIGAN AN OFFICE WORKER MADE A TOO-GOOD GUESS...(THE CARGO!).

5. AND A U-BOAT CAPTAIN EARNED AN IRON CROSS.

OFFICIAL U. S. NAVY PHOTO—I. N. P.

Remember, the enemy gathers most of its information in small quantities—little scraps of our careless talk—that can be pieced together into knowledge useful to them and dangerous to us. Help beat them with silence. Let our tanks do our talking.

Stetson "Whippet"...bound edge, medium brim and a fine, medium tapered shape to the crown. Rich felt made light and springy by the exclusive Stetson Vita-Felt* process...$10.

*REG. U. S. PAT. OFF.

Keep it under your STETSON

MEAT

is matériel of War!

SWIFT'S WARTIME POLICY— *We will cooperate to the fullest extent with the U. S. Government to help win the war. We will do everything possible to safeguard the high quality of our products. Despite wartime difficulties, we will make every effort to distribute available civilian supplies to insure a fair share for all consumers all over the U. S.*

[1943]

IN ON ONE WHEEL
FROM "POWDER PUFF LANE"

Through a Hail of Flak on an Italian run known as "Powder Puff Lane," came the Marauder bomber "Shark" . . . its structure weakened from nose to tail . . . its fuselage riddled . . . its right motor badly hit . . . the hydraulic lines controlling its landing gear and brakes knocked out. But, with expert handling, its gallant pilot brought it in safely without injury to a single member of its crew. Reports of these heroic actions are a constant spur to us to keep on building our best. This we are doing with high-precision, large-scale production of fuselage sections for these Marauder bombers, wings for Helldivers and important components for Wright Cyclone engines.

OVER the continent of Europe they roar—these American fliers—ruling the air, carrying ceaseless and merciless attack to the enemy. No tribute can over-praise their courage, skill and daring.

Here at Hudson, we are maintaining the highest of standards in building for these sky heroes —for the ships that fight below them and for the armies that move behind them.

We are glad that we have been able to bring to

Buy U. S. War Savings
Stamps and Bonds

the task the long experience of this company in building automobiles that could "take it"— as well as an organization trained in mass production, schooled in high precision, and used to hard-hitting teamwork.

We are glad, too, that on another important front—the home front, Hudson distributors and dealers are playing their part so well—servicing a great army of Hudson owners, helping keep 'em rolling until Victory.

THEY HAVE TO BE BUILT RIGHT

Aviation Division Awarded Army-Navy "E" for High Achievement in War Production.

ARMY E NAVY

HUDSON
MOTOR CAR COMPANY
DETROIT 14, MICHIGAN
34 Years of Engineering Leadership

To Land Our Fighting Men on Enemy Shores—Hudson is building large numbers of husky Hudson Invader engines, power plants for Allied landing boats, which are pouring by the thousand from American shipyards. They are vital to successful invasion, and they "have to be built right." To this job, we bring the engineering and manufacturing experience that produced a generation of famous Hudson automobile motors.

Down Went 32 Jap Fliers! Oerlikon 20-mm. guns built in the U. S. Naval Ordnance Plant operated by Hudson were among the U. S. battleship batteries that shot down 32 of 35 Jap Zeros in less than 30 minutes, in a recent South Pacific action. By their combat record, these guns have proved themselves the answer to the dive bomber menace to ships at sea.

OUR PLANTS ARE DEDICATED TO WAR PRODUCTION...OUR DEALERS TO MAINTAINING WAR TRANSPORTATION!

[1944]

462

The story behind the Boeing Superfortress

Remember back to January, 1940? The war in Europe was not yet five months old and war with Japan still two years away, but the U. S. Army Air Forces even then determined they must have an airplane *that would carry a heavier bomb load farther, faster and higher* than any the world had ever known.

Leading aircraft companies were invited to submit designs.

In February, thirty days before Hitler invaded the Low Countries, the Army issued a supplement, radically increasing its specifications. Those new requirements made the design problems still more difficult. But Boeing — with its unequaled background of 4-engine experience in building such planes as the Flying Fortress, the Stratoliner and transocean Clippers — was in the best position to solve them.

Wind-tunnel tests of the Boeing model so impressed the Army that Boeing was authorized to build three experimental airplanes. And then — even before the first of these had been completed and flight tested — the Air Forces decided that *this* was the world's number one bomber! Quantity production was ordered — *one of the greatest manufacturing programs ever put behind any weapon of war.* This program eventually included the Bell and Martin plants as well as three Boeing plants and literally hundreds of sub-contractors.

This placed a tremendous responsibility upon Boeing, not only in successfully engineering the design but also in getting it into production.

A master plan had to be created . . . factories built . . . new tools designed . . . co-ordination of production arranged in all participating plants.

So sound was the basic design that not one major change had to be made when actual flight tests got under way.

And approximately a year and a half later the first production models were bombing Japan.

Superfortresses are taking their place along with the famous Flying Fortresses in Boeing's effort to provide the Army's great bombing crews with the best possible airplanes to accomplish their hazardous and important missions.

[1944]

DESIGNERS OF THE FLYING FORTRESS • THE NEW B-29 SUPERFORTRESS • THE STRATOLINER • TRANSOCEAN CLIPPERS   **BOEING**

Of course...
you may marry!

When you join the WAC you're really taking the first exciting step toward a new career—a career that may lead to a better post-war position, financial security . . . even romance and marriage!

Of course Wacs may marry while in the service. And the Women's Army Corps places no restrictions on *whom* you marry, Army man, Navy man, Marine or civilian. You'll find Wac life—not easy—but full, rich, satisfying. Get the full details about training, pay, promotion, opportunities. Apply at any U. S. Army Recruiting Station or mail coupon below.

YOUR COUNTRY NEEDS YOU
JOIN THE WAC NOW

IT'S GETTING DARK . . . very dark . . .
and quiet. Funny . . . when you get it . . . the one with your name on it . . . after so
many have missed . . . not much time now . . . to think . . . tired . . . damn
tired . . . sleepy . . . eyes don't seem to stay open . . . yeah . . . funny . . . when you get it . . .
how your mind clears . . . then travels . . . back there . . . to home . . . to mom . . . and
dad . . . and Mary . . . gee . . . Mary was swell . . . the way she stood there when I left . . . proud
and brave . . . and I kissed her . . . and said . . . "I'll be back . . . keep waitin' for me" . . . but
I guess not . . . not now. Wonder if they really know back there . . . what this is like . . . to die
. . . for something you believe in . . . wonder if there's anything to this talk of discontent
back home . . . and complaining . . . because a few things are taken away . . . little things
that don't mean much . . . wonder if they're all really in there slugging . . . so too
many of us won't have to die like this . . . when all we want in the world is just to
live . . . back home . . . where it's free . . . and a guy can be something and get
somewhere . . . and not be kicked around. Gee . . . I hope they know in time . . .
if I could just be sure . . . it wouldn't be so tough leaving . . . leaving the others
to finish this job . . . the others . . . thinking of life back home . . . after the hell is over with . . .
and just wanting to settle down quietly somewhere . . . and go to work . . . and have faith
in things and people . . . and breathe free air again. It's getting dark . . . and gee
I wish I knew . . . for the rest of the gang . . . whether the folks back home really know
what it's like . . . to die . . . for something you believe in . . . tired . . . damn tired
. . . if I could just be sure . . . it wouldn't be so tough leaving . . .

★   ★   ★   ★

This is one of a series of advertisements suggested by actual letters from men at the front who have seen their comrades die.

"It is a struggle for maintaining in the world that form and
substance of government whose
leading object is to elevate the
condition of men—to lift artificial
weights from all shoulders; to clear
the paths of laudable pursuits for all;
to afford all an unfettered start and
a fair chance in the race of life."

A Lincoln

The Saturday Evening
POST

[1943]

Getting along with relatives
by
BOB HOPE

1. It doesn't take any special talents to get along with relatives... just a little Commando Training. Of course, almost everyone has trouble with relatives—especially their in-laws ...in-law, that's an outlaw who gets in by marriage. It's not so bad with relatives who are born into your family, though. As a matter of fact, we get along fine with an uncle who is borne in every Saturday night.

2. Always join in the children's games. This makes you popular with your nephews and nieces. It also gives your wife a wonderful chance to practice her first aid training. Naturally, everyone knows the best first aid to brighter, cleaner teeth is Pepsodent. No wonder it's Number One with men in the Service!

3. Feed the folks well. You'll find most relatives have fierce appetites. In fact, at our house we make it a point to count the children after every meal. I'll never forget the time we counted in a strange kid. We knew he was strange because he didn't know that Pepsodent—and only Pepsodent—contains Irium.

4. Be kind to rich uncles. You can never tell when one might leave you a fortune. Of course, mine never did. He just left me a copy of Esquire. But I only read the ads anyway...especially the ones that say "Pepsodent with Irium loosens the film you can feel on your teeth...uncovers the natural brightness of your smile."

5. Don't let their wrangling get on your nerves. I wouldn't say my relatives were noisy...but I do enjoy my quiet vacations as a riveter in the shipyards. There's only one thing my family won't argue about, and that is if you use Pepsodent twice a day, you'll have brighter teeth in a hurry.

Only Pepsodent contains Irium

How PEPSODENT with IRIUM uncovers brighter teeth

Film on teeth collects stains, makes teeth look dingy—hides the true brightness of your smile.

This film-coated mirror illustrates how smiles look when commonplace methods don't clean film away.

But look what Irium does to that film! It loosens and floats it away, leaves the surface clean and bright.

That's how Pepsodent with Irium uncovers the natural cheery brightness of your smile . . . safely, gently.

Lend $3, get $4—Buy more War Bonds

[1943]

466

Yes—your job is waiting for you, Soldier!

HERE ARE SOCONY-VACUUM'S ANSWERS TO YOUR QUESTIONS:

FROM MANY SOURCES comes word that the things America's fighting men worry about most in their spare moments are the years lost from their jobs during one of the most productive periods of their lives... their place in the world after the fighting is over.

That is the reason for this Statement of Policy from the Socony-Vacuum Oil Company. Socony-Vacuum's 4406 regular employees now in military service have nothing to worry about so far as their post-war jobs are concerned.

WE WANT YOU BACK! Before the war, we considered the group of Socony-Vacuum employees now in the Armed Forces as an important part of our strong future manpower. We still do. It won't be a question of "making a place" for you. Socony-Vacuum will welcome you!

THERE WILL BE JOBS! Socony-Vacuum is not waiting until the end of the war to make provisions for rehiring returning servicemen. All Socony-Vacuum divisions are now planning complete post-war organizations . . . based on *conservative* estimates of post-war volume. These surveys indicate that there will be many more openings than the number of employees now on "leave of absence" with the Armed Forces.

YOU HAVEN'T STOOD STILL just because you've been away from your job at Socony-Vacuum! Many of you have acquired new skills. Many *more* have gained maturity and ability to handle men from your training, your travels, your experiences in the Armed Forces. *All of this will be taken into consideration in assigning you to a job.*

OPPORTUNITY WILL BE GREAT! We believe that the petroleum industry—and Socony-Vacuum in particular—will offer a splendid future to returning servicemen. There will be great opportunities for capable men with Socony-Vacuum—and with the thousands of independent dealers who market Socony-Vacuum products. We want our part of the "pick of the nation's manpower" to return to us. We are sure they do, too!

SOCONY-VACUUM OIL CO., INC.

and Affiliates: Magnolia Petroleum Co., General Petroleum Corp. of Calif.

Mobilgas
SOCONY-VACUUM

Makers of Mobilgas, Mobiloil
and more than 200 other
petroleum products for peace and war!

[1944]

A is for Ample

[1943]

468

Imagine Fibber McGee and Molly...

on TELEVISION

brought to you by N B C

Yes, on NBC Television that crowded closet at Wistful Vista—the foibles of lovable Fibber and the trials of patient Molly, for instance—could all become real visual experiences . . . experiences for you to *watch* as well as hear.

Think what television programs originating in studios of the National Broadcasting Company . . . such programs as the top-notch sound radio which has won NBC the distinction of America's most popular network . . . will add to home entertainment!

Already, plans—within the limitations imposed by wartime—have been placed in operation by NBC . . . plans which with the co-operation of business and government will result in extensive NBC tele-

vision networks . . . chains spreading from Eastern, Mid-Western and Western centers . . . gradually providing television after the war, to all of the nation.

Moderate-priced television receivers will provide your home with sight and sound programs consistent with the highest standards of NBC . . . offer the most popular of the shows in this new, vastly improved field of entertainment. Look forward to other great NBC accomplishments such as FM, noise-free reception . . . faithfulness of tone reproduction.

* * *

Look to NBC to lead in these new branches of broadcasting by the same wide margin that now makes it *"The Network Most People Listen to Most."*

National Broadcasting Company

America's No. 1 Network

A Service of Radio
Corporation of America

1945-1950

VOL. XXXII NO. 22   NOVEMBER 22, 1948

Newsweek
Registered U. S. Patent Office

The Magazine of News Significance

Trivia

The fancy new uniforms of the Waves
have started a woman's war in the Penta-
gon. Wacs won't be permitted a more attractive uniform until the present supply,
estimated to last another year, is exhausted. And the Wafs can't design a
separate Air Force uniform until the
Army disposes of the Wac issue . . .

The best news in the world!

"HOMEWARD BOUND" TELEGRAMS are coming every day to thousands of American homes, speeded by special Western Union services for returning veterans.

● Even before his foot touches the gangplank, his first "homeward bound" telegram is on its way . . . rushed ahead by the Western Union man who meets the boat.

At reception centers, telegraph officials are alerted. By debarkation time Western Union is ready. All is set for a jubilant exchange of telegrams between reception centers and thousands of happy homes. Soon, a battery of Teleprinters is flashing a flood of the gladdest words ever written. . . . *He's coming home!*

Whatever the hour, whatever the problem...soldiers, sailors and marines are getting all possible help from Western Union, ably and generously assisted by the military authorities.

And looking ahead, recent Western Union developments in automatic telegraphy and electronics foreshadow a new era in the transmission of good news.

[1946]

AND WELL LIVE HAPPILY EVER AFTER...

"I know it will be just the way your letters describe it to me . . . the life we'll live in the house we'll build when you come home . . .

"A bright, sunny house that's a blend of old and new, with a white-shuttered door and a picket fence around a world all our own . . .

"A garden where you can dig while sunshine warms you through and through . . . and you're alive right down to your fingertips to the sound and touch and scent of Spring . . .

"And a kitchen for me that's *full* of magical things. A wonderful new electric range (the kind they're planning now) that starts coffee perking and biscuits browning before we wake up . . . and cooks our dinners while we're away.

"A refrigerator that's big and roomy with a zone of cold for every kind of food we keep . . . with glistening shelves full of good things to eat . . . thick lamb chops and ice cold milk, all kinds of cheese, butter and eggs and greens, spangled with dew behind crystal doors.

"And still another fabulous chest will make our kitchen complete . . . a home freezer we'll dip into all winter for peaches, cherries, juicy asparagus, ice cream and all kinds of meat . . .

"Oh, it's easy to see how happy we'll be . . . when our days are filled with the peace of being together in our very own home . . . forever and ever."

•   •   •

Here, at Kelvinator, we pledge you this. When our war job is done—all our strength, all our new skills born of war, will be turned to production for peace.

That means that Kelvinator will build more and finer refrigerators, electric ranges, home freezers and electric water heaters to make the kitchens of America the truly enchanted places they can be.

This will be our part in the building of a greater, a happier nation. For we believe all of us owe to those who have fought to preserve it, a strong, vital and growing America—where all men and women will have the chance to make their dreams come true.

This booklet, "Kelvinator in the Home of Your Dreams," with pictures and floor plans for six modern low-cost homes, together with details of their exciting new postwar kitchens designed for easy living, is offered to home planners without cost. See your Kelvinator retailer or drop a post card to Dept. 7-C, Kelvinator, Detroit 32, Michigan.

HEART of your postwar kitchen . . . the Kelvinator electrical appliances: the new Kelvinator Refrigerator . . . the new Kelvinator Electric Range . . . the new Kelvinator Electric Water Heater . . . and the new Kelvinator Home Freezer that keeps foods at flavor peak indefinitely!

A NEW RADIO HIT SHOW!
TUNE IN "THE ANDREWS SISTERS" AND GUEST STARS
SUNDAYS 4:30 P. M. E. W. T. BLUE NETWORK

Kelvinator
of NASH-KELVINATOR CORPORATION
Refrigerators, Home Freezers, Electric Ranges, Electric Water Heaters, Beverage Coolers, Ice Cream Cabinets, Frozen Food Merchandisers, Commercial Refrigerating Units.

[1945]

WHAT
DODGE
IS GOING TO DO

★

Again and again, from one end of the country to the other, the question is continuously asked — "What's Dodge going to do?"

The same question has been asked down the thirty years since the days of John and Horace Dodge at every turning point in the history of the motor car, —"*What's Dodge going to do?*"

Today's answer is — Dodge is starting production on the finest passenger car in its history. *It is not an experimental car*. It is as sound and certain a product as thirty years of leadership experience can make it.

If you know the immediate background of these new cars, you will recall that fully Certified Public Tests established for the last pre-war Dodge cars a public record in economy and performance that remains unchallenged to this day.

If you pause to think again, you will recall that Dodge All-Fluid Drive was an abrupt turning point in the technical development of all cars, giving an entirely new quality of automobile driving and performance.

The new Dodge will continue this brilliant advance. The styling of the new car will be in smart keeping with the fluid smoothness of its performance. Tests have already shown that in economy it will be another record breaker.

DODGE

Division of Chrysler Corporation

New Thursday Night Program! The Music of Andre Kostelanetz with the most Popular Stars of the Musical World, Thursdays CBS, 9 P. M., E. Y. T.

[1945]

"Imagine! All this for 5¢ a day!"

She's getting along fine! Because she has the finest of care . . . a nice room at the hospital, best doctor in town, efficient nurse, *everything* that modern medical science can provide.

And all of it costs her just $15 a year, actually less than 5¢ a day!

You see, before she had her accident, this smart housewife got Hartford "Medical Reimbursement" accident insurance.

Here's What Your 5¢ Will Buy

With this low cost policy, you get up to $500 to pay hospital, nursing, doctor's and other medical expenses in case of accidental injury. IN ADDITION, you get special allowances up to $162.50 for specified dislocations, fractures, etc. IN ADDITION, you get substantial benefits ranging from $1,250 to $5,000 for loss of a hand, a foot, eyes, etc.

More than half of all accidental injuries occur in the home, so every housewife needs this protection. Get yours *before* you have an accident! See your Hartford agent or your insurance broker . . . this very day.

[1945]

is America poor?

You can answer that question by studying these facts . . .

43% OF AMERICA'S HOMES lack private bath or shower. That means approximately 18,000,000 families do not have what is considered a basic necessity of American good living. In addition, there are 14,000,000 homes which are without flush toilet facilities; surveys show that 9,800,000 homes have only three rooms or less.

31% OF AMERICA'S HOMES lack running water. In short, more than 10,700,000 dwelling units are not equipped with modern plumbing facilities. And that's not all: over 9,000,000 homes in the United States have no refrigeration; 19,800,000 homes do not have the warmth and comfort of a central heating system.

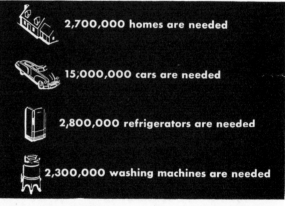

2,700,000 homes are needed

15,000,000 cars are needed

2,800,000 refrigerators are needed

2,300,000 washing machines are needed

21% OF AMERICA'S HOMES lack electricity. It is estimated that more than 8,000,000 families do not enjoy the modern convenience of electric light and power. Right now there is also an accumulated need for appliances which use electricity: 2,800,000 refrigerators, 2,300,000 washing machines, 750,000 electric ranges.

MOST OF AMERICA today lacks consumer goods. The accumulated demand for automobiles, homes, appliances, as illustrated in the diagram above, is in addition to the estimated need for basic necessities. It far exceeds the expectations of 1946 production; it offers a challenging opportunity to the manufacturers of America.

How Can America Get What It Needs?

The answer is *more production!* No matter what America's needs may be, they can be met by the efficient use of production machines. By producing more, prices will be lowered and demand will be increased because more people are able to buy. Remember: America's industrial output of goods per man-hour rises at the rate of 50% every ten years; a man's productivity is no longer measured by the clock, but rather by the capacity and efficiency of the machine he operates. This is the formula for more jobs, high wages, high standards of living. It's the formula that keeps America *busy!* Now is the time for manufacturers to start replacing high cost, obsolescent tools with modern, new machine tools which make possible the low costs, low prices, high wages everybody wants.

KEARNEY & TRECKER
CORPORATION
MILWAUKEE 14, WISCONSIN
Milwaukee Machine Tools
BETTER PRODUCTS . . . BETTER EARNINGS
SPRING FROM BETTER MACHINE TOOLS

[1946]

Hey! I'm Miss America!

"**T**HE newspapers? They're nuts! Every year they tell you Miss America's tall. Miss America's willowy. She's got 36 inches here. 25 inches there. She's—a typographical error, that's what! *I'm* Miss America. And here's figures to prove it.

"I'm 5 feet 4 in platform soles. Sorta petite, that is. Hips? I got 39 inches of 'em. Waistline? Well, let's not mention it. But I'm the national average, see. The *real* Miss America. So watch it, fellas— they've been foisting an impostor on you!"

Like the lady says, it's easy to be led astray by slightly wishful figures. Which is all very well, where the form divine's concerned— but it simply won't do in more mundane affairs. *Business* affairs, for instance. That's where figures must be accurate, impartial, up-to-the-minute— no beautiful illusions allowed!

FOR these very reasons, today's business management relies to such a great extent on Comptometer adding-calculating machines. They know Comptometer turns out *accurate* figures— faster—for less money. And they know it's versatile, too—a speedy means of solving *every sort* of problem in office production.

The Comptometer, made only by Felt & Tarrant Manufacturing Co., Chicago, is sold exclusively by its Comptometer Division, 1731 North Paulina Street, Chicago 22, Illinois.

Comptometer REG. U. S. PAT. OFF.
ADDING-CALCULATING MACHINES

N. W. AYER & SON
[1947]

477

It's fun to grow old when you have no money worries

How to get a retirement income of $200 a month as long as you live

This morning, as Peg and I were walking down to the beach, our mailman handed me the white envelope we get every month. "That check comes regular as clockwork, doesn't it, Sam?" I said. "Yes, sir," he grinned, "and you're mighty lucky—to be retired and enjoying life on an income. It must be fun to grow old ... with no money worries!"

Later on, lying out in the sun, relaxed and enjoying the warm salt breeze, I thought how right he was. "It *is* fun," I said to Peg, "and it's all thanks to you!" For I give Peg credit. Frankly, if it hadn't been for her, I'd be back at the office right now, grubbing away for my pay check. You see, until I was about forty, I never dreamed I'd ever be able to retire on an income.

But one day Peg cornered me with a pencil and paper. She'd written down my yearly salary and multiplied it by twenty. *That's how much money you're going to make in the next twenty years*, she said. And I whistled! For, even if I never got another raise—it ran up to a six-figure total. A fortune! (Add up your own salary for the next twenty years. You'll be amazed.)

In the next twenty years, Peg pointed out, I'd *spend* that money as fast as I'd make it. We'd *never* been able to save much before. So most likely we'd just fritter it away having a good time.

It was shortly afterwards that I discovered the Phoenix Mutual Retirement Income Plan. It was just what we needed. With it, I could use part of my present salary to buy me a retirement income later. In twenty years, when I reached 60, Peg and I would get a monthly check for $200 guaranteed for life. More than that, the Plan provided life insurance—protecting my family until I reached retirement age.

Not long after, I qualified for my Phoenix Mutual Plan. And now, twenty years later, that plan is paying *me*. Each month, every month, as long as we live, Peg and I will get a check for $200. We're free to do just as we please. Yes, our

mailman put it right. Growing old *is* fun, when you have *no money worries*.

Send for Free Booklet

This story is typical. Assuming you start at a young enough age, you can plan to have an income of $100 to $200 a month or more—starting at age 55, 60, 65 or older. Send the coupon and receive, by mail and without charge, a booklet which tells about Phoenix Mutual Plans and how to qualify for them. Similar plans are available for women. Don't delay. Send for your copy now.

How do you look to a Hero?

Like a Rhinoceros? ... Thick-Skin doesn't need any little hints about meeting veterans. Not *him*, he Knows How To Handle Men. Forget about vets needing rest before they go back to work, he says. Just yell, "What's wrong with *you*, Soldier? Get up! Get to work! Be a man!" A few hours in a foxhole would be *so* good for the Rhinoceros.

... a Lion? Most civilians are pretty modest about what they've done. But not the Lion. He practically won the war with his Victory Garden alone. And the bonds he bought ... ! Veterans begin to wonder if maybe draft dodgers didn't have the right idea.

... a Ferret? She'll get The Details if it kills her ... or the officer. And the gorier the details, the better. Doctors may spend months helping a soldier forget a bad battle experience. The Ferret can bring it all back in minutes.

... a Fox? Veterans want to feel proud of the people they fought for. But it's hard to be proud of the Fox. He's done pretty well in this war and he doesn't mind telling you about it. "Know those lots I bought in 1937? Well ..." Veterans who saw land traded for lives don't enjoy this kind of talk.

... a Crocodile? Her tears flow like wine when she sees a wounded service man. And her sympathy flows over him like carbolic acid. She turns a high-powered spotlight on a veteran's disability. No better morale-wrecker exists.

• • •

Prepared by the War Advertising Council, Inc. in Cooperation with the Office of War Information and the Retraining and Reemployment Administration.

Or Star-spangled Citizens! They see the returned veteran as an able, capable citizen. They're proud of him, anxious to help. They weep no tears over him, ask no questions, listen when he talks—they make him think, "Boy! What a wonderful country!" Most of us are like them ... *let's help the rest to be like them too!*

 This stands for honorable service—Remember ... the man or woman who wears this button has been honorably discharged from our armed forces.

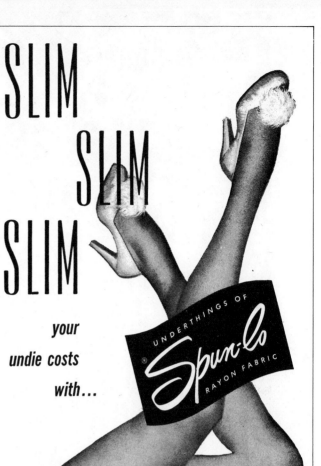

Movie Wins Court Verdict

San Francisco, May 18 — (Associated Press) Howard Hughes' movie "The Outlaw", featuring Buxom Jane Russell, was cleared of indecency charges by a municipal jury yesterday.

("The Outlaw" was closed by the San Francisco Police, April 28.)

In the instructions to the jury, Judge Twain Michelsen said as follows:

"We have seen Jane Russell. She is an attractive specimen of American womanhood. God made her what she is.

"There are some fanatical persons who object to Miss Russell in a low-necked blouse. The scene is in the desert -- hardly a place for woolens or furs.

"Life is sordid and obscene to those who find it so," the judge pointed out.

Some of the women in the courtroom hissed indignantly.

[1946]

like it...
but the Public does!

In its first week, "The Outlaw" has broken every attendance record ever established by any motion picture or theatrical production ever shown in any theatre in the history of San Francisco!

"The Outlaw" has exceeded all previous records by the astounding margin of 51,193 persons!

BEAUTY TAKES A BOW

When you see those new cars with Body by Fisher—you'll be quick to say that beauty takes a bow. They are truly beautiful.

It's easy to see that the Fisher Body organization has come out of the war with its skill and craftsmanship at a new peak.

So when you have the pleasure of selecting a new car again, there's one thing to remember —be sure that it carries the emblem of Body by Fisher.

It stands today, as it has stood for more than 37 years, as the sure sign of a better automobile. It means that all the skills inherent in the Fisher Body organization have now been combined to bring you greater beauty, to give you greater comfort and safety.

Body by Fisher

BETTER BY FAR

Fisher Body Craftsman's Guild Model-Building Competition—8 university scholarships, 624 other awards for boys 12 years of age and older. Enroll now! Guild Headquarters: General Motors Bldg., Detroit 2, Michigan.

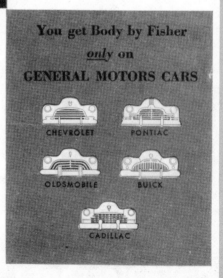

You get Body by Fisher *only* on GENERAL MOTORS CARS

CHEVROLET PONTIAC
OLDSMOBILE BUICK
CADILLAC

[1945]

KAISER and FRAZER SERVICE
Available Everywhere!

When you buy a KAISER or a FRAZER car, you do so with the satisfying assurance that you will find carefully selected dealers, with factory-approved service facilities, *wherever you go*. What is more, each dealer carries a well-maintained stock of genuine factory parts, to serve you and save you time in any emergency. As a member of *one of the four largest automobile dealer organizations in the world*, your KAISER and FRAZER dealer has made *service to owners* one of his foremost responsibilities. And he is prepared, with equipment, personnel and convenient location, to carry out the obligation he has assumed. You will find too, that he is well qualified to render competent service on *other* makes of cars. Look for the K-F service sign whenever your car requires expert attention.

WHEREVER YOU GO!

**BORDER TO BORDER
—COAST TO COAST!**

One of the four largest dealer organizations in the world stands ready to serve your needs. Large dots on above map indicate location of distributors and parts warehouses. Small dots represent K-F dealers offering genuine factory parts and service in every state of the Union.

KAISER-FRAZER CORPORATION • WILLOW RUN, MICHIGAN

[1947]

Hudson Custom Commodore Sedan pictured in the luxuriously modern Hotel Statler, Washington, D. C.

Here's a long look ahead—
the modern design for '49
new *Hudson*

Illustrated above—Interior, Hudson Commodore Club Coupe, typical of the roomy, luxurious interiors in all New Hudsons.

TRY AUTOMATIC GEAR SHIFTING in forward speeds as provided by Hudson's Drive-Master transmission—by far the easiest of all ways to drive. You can accelerate as long and as fast as you like in pick-up gear, then lift your toe momentarily, and you're in high. The shift into high comes *only* when you are ready! Button control on the instrument panel provides instant change to conventional driving if ever desired. Drive-Master transmission is optional on all New Hudsons at small extra cost.

HUDSON FLOORS are recessed down within the frame (shown in red above), full-height seats are lowered, so you get more than ample head room in this car with the new, lower center of gravity.

YOU RIDE DOWN within a base frame (shown in red above), and rear seats are positioned ahead of the rear wheels so that full body width becomes available for wonderfully roomy seats—four inches wider than the car is high. Box-section steel girders encircle and protect the passenger compartment.

You can see and drive it today—the new Hudson with the "step-down" design that is years ahead of the parade—the design that provides streamlined beauty, roominess, comfort, riding qualities and safety available in no other type of automobile!

O NLY once in a blue moon does a car step so far out ahead that it is a *protected investment* in motor-car value. You are invited to see just such a car—the New Hudson with "The modern design for '49"—and for years to come!

Here is truly streamlined beauty—a stunning combination of free-flowing, low-built lines that develop naturally out of a recessed floor which is the key to a basically new and exclusive design principle.* The New Hudson is the only car you step *down* into.

The development of a "step-down" zone in an exclusive, all steel Monobilt body-and-frame† permits Hudson to build the *lowest car on the highway*—only five feet from ground to top— while maintaining *more* interior head room than in any mass-produced car built today!

But no amount of just looking at this gorgeous

*This new design principle is fully explained in an illustrated booklet available without charge at the nearest Hudson dealer's.
†Trade-mark and patents pending.

streamlined beauty—as inviting as it is—can equal the thrill of a Hudson ride!

Hudson has a hug-the-road way of going on every conceivable kind of highway. Once you see how this car takes even the sharpest curves, it will just naturally spoil you for any other type of automobile!

This remarkable ride is largely due to the fact that the New Hudson provides the lowest center of gravity in any American stock car— yet road clearance is ample! *It is a widely recognized fact that the lower to the ground a car can be built, the more stability it will have and the safer it will be.*

You sense a delightful conformity to the road the minute you begin to ride, and this stability, plus the protection of riding encircled by a sturdy box-section steel frame, gives you a grand feeling of safe well-being. This feeling is further enhanced by the ease with which this car is operated, and the restful quiet with which Hudson glides along—thanks to the superb sound control engineered into this advanced automobile!

We cordially invite you to investigate and drive the car with "The modern design for '49". The nearest Hudson dealer will make it possible for you to discover for yourself the many advantages of Hudson's fabulous "step-down" design. Hudson Motor Car Company, Detroit 14.

Eight body styles in Super Series and Commodore Custom Series. Your choice, 121 h.p. all-new Super-Six or 128 h.p. masterful Super-Eight engine. Super-Cushion tires. Ten rich body colors. Two special colors or five two-tone combinations—white sidewall tires—at extra cost.

THE ONLY CAR YOU STEP DOWN INTO

Nothing

could be finer

LINCOLN CONTINENTAL CABRIOLET FOR 1946

Lincoln   DIVISION OF FORD MOTOR COMPANY

[1946]

Luxurious interior of the beautiful Plymouth Special De Luxe 4-Door Sedan. Insert is the newly designed, richly grained instrument panel.

the car that likes to be compared

Inside and out...

PLYMOUTH BUILDS GREAT CARS

The instant you step through the wide-opening doors of the new Plymouth, you are taken with the interior roominess and richness of appointments. You relax in chair-height seats that are wider and deeper from front to back.

The new instrument panel, with its richly grained finish, groups gauges for easy reading. By simply turning a key, you turn on the ignition, start the engine, put the automatic choke in operation—all at once! Whether you choose pile fabric or rich broadcloth, you get smart, long-wearing upholstery materials that harmonize with body colors. The luxury of the entire ensemble is highlighted with gleaming chrome and plastic.

But it's not just on its face value that the new Plymouth likes to be compared. Drive this great new car and discover for yourself its greater power and safety, its luxurious riding comfort, its amazing ease of handling. Compare this drive . . . and let the ride decide!

PLYMOUTH Division of CHRYSLER CORPORATION, Detroit 31, Mich.

White sidewall tires, chrome wheel covers, rear fender scuff guards optional at extra cost.

[1949]

486

Jewels by Cartier

Cadillac

White Sidewall Tires available at extra cost.

FOR SPARKLING BEAUTY of style, for perfection of taste in every detail of design, the 1949 Cadillac stands alone among motor cars. But this is hardly a new experience for Cadillac. Every car which has ever borne this distinguished name has, in its time, set the world's standard for automotive beauty. . . . The truly unique story of the 1949 Cadillac is a story of performance — performance which extends the world's conception of what an automobile can do. In large measure, this wholly new idea of motor car performance is the result of Cadillac's remarkable new power plant — a V-type, high-compression engine of completely new design. The effortless flow of power from this new engine is so silken smooth at any speed, so silent, so eagerly responsive in every driving situation that most people — even those who have driven it many, many miles — can compare it only to automatic propulsion. . . . We feel the 1949 Cadillac represents such a significant advance in motoring that anyone planning to buy any new car owes it to himself to see and examine this wonderful automobile. It affords an entirely new basis upon which to judge motor car value.

★ CADILLAC MOTOR CAR DIVISION ★ GENERAL MOTORS CORPORATION ★

[1949]

"He'll get there first? . . . over my dead body!"

Maybe you're right, son . . . it happens every day. Every *minute*, in fact . . . that's the frightful smash-up record on our highways.

And yet it's so easy to keep out of trouble, if you'll remember two things.

First, that *accidents don't always happen to the other fellow.* So drive carefully!

Secondly, that *you're exposed to a wide range of risks* every time you drive. Hartford's modern Automobile Insurance protects you against them. Just consider the following examples of the broad protection this low cost coverage offers you:

You can't win a law suit

If it goes against you, you may lose everything. If you "win," you'll still lose heavily in time, worry, expense. Hartford Automobile Damage Suit Insurance takes this load off your shoulders.

Don't forget this "debt of honor"

If members of your family or other people in your car are injured, you'd like to pay for their medical care. For as little as $3 a year in most places, your Hartford policy will pay medical expenses for your guests, your family, yourself—up to $250 per person. Larger amounts at small additional cost.

This won't do your car any good

Gas and oil fires are tough! Hartford Comprehensive Automobile Insurance protects your car from loss by fire and many other causes of damage, and by *theft*, too.

Do your children drive other cars?

The Damage Suit policy covering your own car can be extended to include your children when driving other cars. A dollar or so spent for this additional protection may save a loss of thousands.

Who pays for collision damage to your car?

Hartford does . . . if you've been thoughtful enough to invest a few extra dollars in Hartford Collision Insurance.

[1946]

Hartford Insurance

Hartford Fire Insurance Company . Hartford Accident and Indemnity Company
Hartford Live Stock Insurance Company

Writing practically all forms of insurance except personal life insurance • • *Hartford 15, Conn.*

EXTRA FEATURES that surprise and delight you!

Only on the new Boeing Stratocruiser do you find them ALL!

NO EAR POPPING! Going up in an elevator only 15 stories above street level you experience more ear pressure than you do in the twin-deck Stratocruiser at 15,000 feet! It's the world's most completely altitude-conditioned airplane.

LIKE SITTING ON A CLOUD! Petite blonde or 200-pounder— you'll find Stratocruiser seats just right for *you!* Thousands of engineering hours went into design of these soft, deep, reclining seats. Foam rubber and special shock mountings eliminate vibration. At your finger tips are controls for individual reading light, attendant call button and seat reclining adjustment.

SMELLS GOOD! The air inside the Stratocruiser is purer than the air you breathe at home! Odorless, draftless, smokeless, it's filtered and completely changed every 90 seconds! In winter cold or summer heat the air-conditioned Stratocruiser is equally comfortable—in the air or on the ground.

PLENTY OF ROOM! The ladies' powder room and men's dressing room each accommodates six comfortably. They have dressing tables, big mirrors, dental lavatories and *hot and cold running water*. 110-volt current for electrical appliances.

WHO'S HUNGRY? On this 340-mile-an-hour luxury liner, oven-hot meals to delight a gourmet are served on *individual tables at your seat*. Coffee, fresh-made in the plane's galley—plus iced drinks and snacks from the lower-deck service bar.

TAKE A WALK? Stroll along the Stratocruiser's wide aisle. Go down the spiral stairs and enjoy yourself in *the cozy lower-deck lounge*—your club car in the sky.

BOEING
S T R A T O C R U I S E R

Boeing is building fleets of Stratocruisers for these forward-looking airlines:

AMERICAN OVERSEAS AIRLINES
UNITED AIR LINES
BRITISH OVERSEAS AIRWAYS CORPORATION
PAN AMERICAN WORLD AIRWAYS
NORTHWEST AIRLINES

For the Air Force, the B-50 Superfortress, B-47 Stratojet and C-97 Stratofreighter.

[1949]

490

High in a comfortable sky—a bridge game in the Boeing Stratocruiser's main cabin

The Stratocruiser—fastest, finest transport in the air

Trumps in air travel

Gracious modern living reaches a climax in Boeing's great new Stratocruisers. Never before have passengers enjoyed such complete comfort in the air—or such distance-devouring speed. In the time it takes to play a rubber of bridge, whole states flash below!

The entire interior of the two-deck Stratocruiser is air and altitude conditioned. Fresh air circulates under constant temperature control. Comfortable, normal atmospheric pressure even at 25,000 feet; complete comfort during climb and descent.

Boeing introduced the first pressurized airliner—the Stratoliner—in 1938. During the war the B-29 Superfortress was the only military aircraft similarly conditioned for crew comfort and wellbeing. From this background Boeing will soon bring you—in the Stratocruiser—altitude-conditioned air-travel comfort and pleasure unparalleled by any other transport.

For airline operators, the Stratocruiser, because of its utility and advanced design, offers maximum earning capacity—lowest operating cost. For their passengers— greater speed, comfort, reliability. "Built by Boeing," it's built to lead.

BOEING

[1946]

New Coach for CINDERELLA!

New York Central's New Cars Play Fairy Godmother To Travel Budgets

I felt like Cinderella when I found I'd have to plan my holiday trip on a shoestring!

But I felt like a Princess when I saw my gleaming new air-conditioned coach, with its huge windows and smart interior done by a famous designer.

Reserved for her Highness is the way I felt about the wonderful, soft reclining seat reserved for me at no extra charge on this luxurious New York Central coach streamliner.

The Lounge was Palatial. It had a deep-cushioned divan for smoking and chatting. And there was a real dressing table with lighted mirror and all the latest fixings!

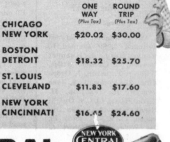

"Look at these LOW COACH FARES!"

	ONE WAY (Plus Tax)	ROUND TRIP (Plus Tax)
CHICAGO NEW YORK	$20.02	$30.00
BOSTON DETROIT	$18.32	$25.70
ST. LOUIS CLEVELAND	$11.83	$17.60
NEW YORK CINCINNATI	$16.^5	$24.60

Coming!
CARS ENOUGH FOR 52 NEW STREAMLINERS TO UNDERLINE THE *NEW* IN ...

NEW YORK CENTRAL
The *Scenic* Water Level Route

"...and <u>I</u> gave the junk man our coal shovel!"

"I FINALLY got so fed up with tending the furnace that I went on a shovel strike. George got the point, we got Timken Oil Heat, and I *personally* gave the junk man our coal shovel."

You can start next heating season with clean, comfortable Timken Silent Automatic Oil Heat *if you see your Timken Dealer right NOW!*

It costs so little for this perfect home comfort. Owner records prove that Timken Wall-Flame Oil Burners use *up to 25% less fuel than ordinary oil burners*—and save money over hand-firing in Spring and Fall.

Some of the reasons for this exceptional economy are shown below. With such simple, modern design, it's no wonder that, over the years, Timken has become "The Accepted Standard" for quality, economy and dependability.

Your Timken Dealer is now receiving shipments of new and improved Timken Oil Burning Equipment for installation in old and new homes. See the yellow pages of your phone book for his name and address. Phone him now—for a lifetime of heating happiness.

TIMKEN SILENT AUTOMATIC DIVISION OF THE TIMKEN-DETROIT AXLE CO., DETROIT 32, MICH.

TIMKEN
Silent Automatic
HEAT

OIL BURNERS • AIR CONDITIONING OIL FURNACES
OIL BOILERS • OIL BURNING WATER HEATERS

The Accepted **HEAT** *Standard*

1 **The Timken Wall-flame** is a quiet, drifting flame that blankets the walls of your furnace or boiler. Other oil burners shoot a blowtorch flame into ashpit, waste heat up the chimney.

2 **The fuel-thrifty** Timken chrome-steel flame-rim vaporizes the oil completely . . . burns the air-oil mixture cleanly and *completely*. Gets all the heat out of the new fuel oils.

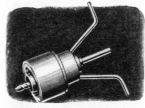

3 **Timken Wall-Flame** Oil Burners have only one moving part . . . and it is *simple as a spinning top*. Moreover, this famous burner is so automatic it even lubricates itself!

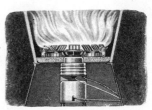

4 **A Timken** can be custom-built into your *present* heating plant, or you may select one of the new Oilfurnace models which will soon be available. Installation requires only a few hours.

[1946]

493

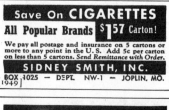

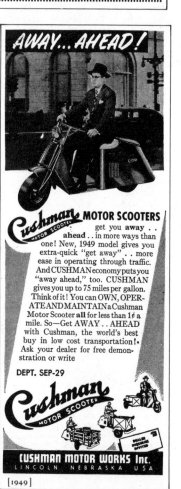

494

THE COMPLETE ANSWER to WINTER COMFORT

1-A Good Heating System

2-Then Add ≋

How many millions of families have bought homes that looked beautiful—only to find out later that they couldn't keep warm in winter! Far too often home owners have installed gadgets that appeal to the eye and have skimped on the heating system.

If your house is one of the hard-to-heat variety, there is relief in sight! Minneapolis-Honeywell has invented an entirely different type of heat control that is bringing "comfort unlimited" to thousands of homes throughout the nation. This remarkable control system is called Moduflow. Moduflow operates on an entirely different principle from the ordinary on-and-off control system. It furnishes heat *continuously* at whatever temperature is required to maintain comfort in any kind of weather. Moduflow eliminates the drafts and "shiver spots" caused by intermittent heat supply, and prevents wasteful overheating.

Best of all, Moduflow can be easily and inexpensively installed *right now* on practically any type of automatic central heating plant. You don't have to wait until you remodel or build a new home. In fact, you don't even have to shut down your heating plant to install Moduflow control. Mail the coupon today for the interesting booklet "Comfort Unlimited" that tells more about Moduflow.

A GOOD HEATING SYSTEM + MODUFLOW
= COMFORT UNLIMITED

MODUFLOW
the new HONEYWELL heating control system

FREE!

MINNEAPOLIS-HONEYWELL REGULATOR COMPANY, MINNEAPOLIS 8, MINNESOTA . . . CANADIAN PLANT: TORONTO 12, ONTARIO.

1947]

MODERN HOMES
$18 per MONTH RENT!

How would you like to live in one of these attractive modern homes, nestled deep in the hills of West Virginia, for only $18 per month rent?

Well, if you were a Bituminous Coal miner, you might be able to do so! For that is the average monthly rental of these handsome little homes built by a coal-mining company to house its employees.

Not all coal miners, of course, live in homes as fine and new as those you see pictured above. But these are typical of the best, and they do illustrate how coal operators and miners, in increasing numbers, are meeting the problems of housing, sanitation, recreation, and other aspects of community living.

Today, about two-thirds—over 260,000—of the nation's Bituminous Coal miners own their homes or rent from private landlords; the remaining one-third live in company-owned houses...at a national average rental of $11.50 per month!

MODERN WORKING CONDITIONS have also come a long way—thanks to the mechanization program sponsored by the country's progressive coal operators. Nowadays, more than 90% of all Bituminous Coal mined underground is mechanically cut, and more than 50% is mechanically loaded. Only about 5% is mined by pick and shovel.

As a result, America's Bituminous Coal mines are the most productive—and pay the best wages—on earth. The miners' average pay in recent months has exceeded $60 for a work week of less than 43 hours, including travel time. And thousands of coal miners earn steadily from $90 to $100 a week.

BITUMINOUS COAL
BITUMINOUS COAL INSTITUTE
Washington, D. C.
Affiliate of NATIONAL COAL ASSOCIATION

BITUMINOUS COAL . . . LIGHTS THE WAY . . . FUELS THE FIRES . . . POWERS THE PROGRESS OF AMERICA

[1947]

Garbage nuisance ended by new kitchen appliance that shreds food waste and washes it down the drain.

Picture your home—rid forever of garbage.

Picture your family—safer, healthier because you've banished the garbage can, breeder of germs and disease.

Picture the ease, convenience and cleanliness—with all food waste disposed of *electrically*, right down the sink drain.

Make yours the most modern, most sanitary of kitchens. Install the amazing General Electric Disposall*—and forget you ever heard of garbage!

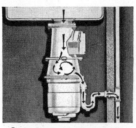

1. A simple appliance, hiding under and fitting most any sink. The Disposall has capacity enough for an average family's food waste from any one meal.

2. Once all food waste, even rinds and bones, is scraped into drain, you lock protecting sink drain cover. Clean, flushing water enters opening in cover!

3. Disposall starts automatically as cold water is turned on. Food waste is shredded into tiny particles, flushed into sewer or septic tank. The Disposall works with either sewer or septic tank.

4. Drains are kept clean by the Disposall's swirling action. Food waste that would have become garbage is disposed of—forgotten. This is the modern, easy, sanitary way!

5. We can hear you now, agreeing with other Disposall users who say: "It's one kitchen appliance I'd never give up." "So clean . . . so sanitary." "Great invention!"

DISPOSALL

DISPOSALL MEANS GOOD-BY TO GARBAGE AUTOMATICALLY!

*General Electric's registered trademark for its food-waste appliance.

For the perfect laborsaving combination, the Disposall can be teamed up with a General Electric Dishwasher in a complete Electric Sink! General Electric Company, Bridgeport 2, Conn.

[1948]

GENERAL ELECTRIC

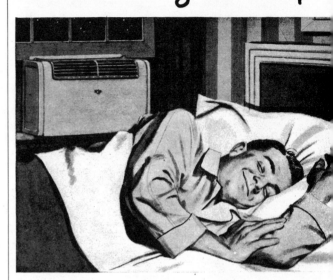

The Windsor Imperial combines the finest Radio-Phonograph Magnavox ever built with Magnascope—the new excellence in television. Radio-Phonograph, $895. Bookcase Television Receiver, $750.

Perfection in home entertainment

FOUR HOURS of continuous music from one loading of the new LP records...plus MAGNASCOPE TELEVISION which may be added to your Magnavox at any time

MAGNAVOX brings you a great new instrument for home entertainment. This is the first radio-phonograph to play both the new LP (long-playing) and standard 78 rpm records *automatically*. Further, Magnascope television which brings sharper, clearer pictures without glare or eyestrain may be had now or added later.

Only magnificent Magnavox radio-phonographs and television receivers offer you a wide choice of traditional and modern cabinets. And as you would expect, there is no truer, more flawless AM-FM and world-wide Short Wave reception.

Record-playing's greatest innovation in twenty years is yours with Magnavox. You enjoy a full evening of continuous recorded music with one loading of the new Duomatic Changer. In all models from $375 to $895; other furniture models from $179.50. Television receivers from $299.50 to $750. Write for brochure. The Magnavox Co., Dept. 220, 2175 Bueter Road, Fort Wayne 4, Indiana.

Prices subject to change without notice.

the magnificent Magnavox radio-phonograph + television

The Windsor Imperial Radio-Phonograph.

The Modular Television Receiver correlated with Magnavox Cosmopolitan AM-FM Radio-Phonograph.

[1948]

New RCA Theatre Television System projects 15 x 20 foot pictures of television programs.

Giant size Television—"shot from a Barrel!"

You've seen television. Now you'll see it in its finest form—giant projections of special events, transmitted *only* to theatres on private wires or radio beams to make movie-going *better than ever!*

Success of the system comes from a remarkable RCA kinescope, and something new in projection lenses. The kinescope, developed at RCA Laboratories, is in principle the same as the one on which you see regular telecasts. But it is *small*—only a few inches in diameter—and produces images

of high brilliance. These are magnified to 15 x 20 feet by a "Schmidt-type" lens system like those used in the finest astronomical telescopes.

Because of its size and shape, the new projector is referred to by engineers as the "barrel." It's already going into theatres, where you'll be seeing giant television—shot from a barrel.

* * *

See the latest wonders of radio, television, and electronics at RCA Exhibition Hall, 36 West 49th St., N. Y. Admission is free. Radio Corporation of America, Radio City, New York.

The same research laboratories which developed RCA's new theatre television system also give you big, brilliant pictures on 1951 RCA Victor home receivers.

RADIO CORPORATION *of* AMERICA

World Leader in Radio—First in Television

[1950]

No more broken-up Beethoven

Enjoy the world's greatest music <u>without interruption</u> on Columbia ⓛⓟ Records

Hear music as the composer wrote it! Uninterrupted! Each movement complete . . . without a single pause not planned by the composer himself. Up to 50 minutes of music on 2 sides of a single Columbia Long Playing Microgroove Record! Up to 4 hours of continuous music on automatic changers! Just as important is the wonderful Columbia LP tone quality! An advance made possible by new Microgroove recording techniques . . . noiseless nonbreakable surfaces . . . and "professional" 33⅓ rpm speed! Great music has been recorded at Columbia on original masters of full range and undistorted quality *since 1939*. This foresight not only gives you America's largest catalog of high fidelity recordings, but it means sensational savings as well.

Now available on LP . . . America's largest catalog of high fidelity recordings featuring the world's great orchestras, conductors, and soloists . . . Complete Operas, Symphonies, Concerti, Musical Comedy Scores, Popular Music and Children's Records.

COLUMBIA
ⓛⓟ MICROGROOVE
RECORDS

ⓛⓟ the <u>Ultimate</u> in Recorded Music . . .

the finest phonograph record

ever manufactured

"Columbia," "Masterworks" and ⓒ Trade Marks Reg. U. S. Pat. Off. Marcas Registradas ⓛⓟ Trade Mark

Here's how THE ALDRICH FAMILY enjoys

America's Grandest Entertainment

House Jameson (Sam Aldrich) of the famous "Aldrich Family" over NBC network Thursday evenings.

Model 814

GE DAYLIGHT TELEVISION

Extra bright, extra clear for extra enjoyment in undarkened rooms. G-E automatic clarifier for sharper pictures. Large 12½" tube, biggest daylight picture yet! All active channels. Mahogany veneered cabinet. Model 814. *General Electric Co., Electronics Park, Syracuse, N.Y.*

Performance-Engineered at Electronics Park

Model 119M

G-E Console Radio-Phonograph

G-E Electronic Reproducer for incomparable record reproduction. Superb standard radio. Compact mahogany veneered lowboy. *Slight extra charge for built-in LP record player — for the new, long-playing records.* G-E Television $325* to $2100.* Installation, service contract extra. G-E Radios $19.95* to $499.50* *Prices slightly higher West and South — subject to change without notice.*

You can put your confidence in —

GENERAL GE ELECTRIC

[1949]

"Madame X" was the code name, during research and development, for an entirely new system of recorded music . . . perfected by RCA.

The remarkable background of "Madame X"

Now the identity of "Madame X," the *unknown* in a long search for tone perfection, has been revealed. From this quest emerges a completely integrated record-playing *system* —records and automatic player—the first to be entirely free of distortion to the trained musical ear . . .

The research began 11 years ago at RCA Laboratories. First, basic factors were determined—minimum diameters, at different speeds, of the groove spiral in the record—beyond which distortion would occur; size of stylus to be used;

desired length of playing time. From these came the mathematical answer to the record's *speed*—45 turns a minute— and to the record's size, only 6⅞ inches in diameter.

With this speed and size, engineers could guarantee 5⅓ minutes of distortion-free performance, and the finest quality record in RCA Victor history!

The record itself is non-breakable vinyl plastic, wafer-thin. *Yet it plays as long as a conventional 12-inch record.* The new RCA Victor automatic record changer accommodates up to 10 of the new records—1 hour and 40 minutes of

playing time—and can be attached to almost any radio, phonograph, or television combination.

Not only records are free of surface noise and distortion—the record player eliminates faulty operation, noise, and cumbersome size. Records are changed quickly, quietly . . . RCA Victor will continue to supply 78 rpm instruments and records.

This far-reaching advance is one of hundreds which have grown from RCA research. Such leadership adds *value beyond price* to any product or service of RCA and RCA Victor.

 RADIO CORPORATION of AMERICA
World Leader in Radio — First in Television

[1949]

507

For shows that are first in their fields...

Listen to
ABC
AMERICAN BROADCASTING COMPANY

VARIETY

DRAMA

Theatre Guild on the Air
Radio's most distinguished dramatic program—broadcasts of outstanding stage hits starring world-famous players—on ABC every Sunday night from 10:00 to 11:00 EST. Above, Walter Huston as he appeared recently in a Theatre Guild on the Air production. (U. S. Steel)

Bing Crosby Show
Now Bing Crosby joins the galaxy of ABC stars! The one-and-only Bing—and a big assortment of famous guests—in a brand new, top-notch variety show. On all ABC stations Wednesday nights from 10:00 to 10:30 in the East, 9:00 to 9:30 in all other time zones. (Philco)

NEWS

Walter Winchell
The nation stays home to hear Walter Winchell—first in the field of news broadcasting—as he raps out his news reports and gossip about the world and the people in it. On ABC, 9:00 p. m., EST, Sundays. (Jergens)

OPERA

Metropolitan Opera
First in the field of great music, ABC brings you the entire season of Saturday afternoon operas direct from the stage of the Metropolitan Opera House, together with opera news and discussions by noted musical authorities. Series begins Saturday, Nov. 16, at 2 p. m., EST. (The Texas Company)

SPORTS

Cavalcade of Sports
Major sports events such as the National Open Golf Tournament and the Louis-Conn fight—which drew the biggest audience of any commercial radio program in history—are broadcast exclusively by ABC. And there's always a good fight Friday nights at 10:00 EST on your ABC station. (Gillette)

EACH YEAR the American Broadcasting Company tries to give its millions of listeners the best of as many different kinds of radio programs as possible.

The *Theatre Guild on the Air*, for example, is now acclaimed by millions as radio's outstanding dramatic program. The *Metropolitan Opera* and the *Boston Symphony* have helped build ABC's reputation for great music. Among discussion programs dealing with national affairs, *America's Town Meeting of the Air* is the nation's most consistent winner of top awards. And now, with Bing Crosby's return to the air, ABC adds still another program to its list of number-one shows.

Whether you prefer music or mystery, quiz shows or comedy, you can depend on your local American Broadcasting Company station for radio entertainment at its best. That, plus the fact that ABC gives *all* sides of *all* the news, is why so many millions of families from coast to coast are setting their radio dials on ABC stations today.

Leading advertisers buy time on ABC

Eversharp, Philco, Swift, Sterling Drug, U. S. Steel, General Mills, Westinghouse, Kellogg, Quaker Oats, Jergens, Bristol-Myers, Procter & Gamble—all outstanding American businesses—are among the great companies now advertising via the American Broadcasting Company. The reason: ABC reaches all the people who live in 22,000,000 radio homes—at economical rates that make possible a low cost per thousand listeners. *If you are an advertiser, remember: a good ABC time period bought today means a valuable franchise for years to come.*

American Broadcasting Company
A NETWORK OF 216 RADIO STATIONS SERVING AMERICA

[1946]

HE GAVE HER THE AIR...
and was it frigid!

THERE HE WAS . . . that wonderful boy she met last night at the hotel dance! Suzanne uncorked her most glamorous smile, batted her most luscious lashes. No recognition. She waved her shapeliest arm, "yoo-hoo-ed" her most musical "yoo-hoo." No response. All of a sudden it dawned on her that he was deliberately giving her the air . . . *and was it frigid!* She hadn't the foggiest notion why he should snub her so.

Your breath may be beyond suspicion most of the time. And then, when you want to be at your best, you can be guilty of halitosis (unpleasant breath) . . . *without realizing it.*

You Can't Always Tell

If you're smart, you won't fail to guard against offending this way. You'll use Listerine Antiseptic, the *extra-careful* precaution that so many rely on.

Listerine Antiseptic is no mere makeshift of momentary effectiveness. Its wonderful cleansing, freshening effect is a *continuing* effect . . . helps keep the breath sweet and agreeable . . . not for seconds . . . not for minutes . . . but for hours, usually!

Never Omit It

Get in the habit of using Listerine Antiseptic night and morning and never, never omit it before any date where you want to be at your best.

While some cases of halitosis are of systemic origin, most cases, say some authorities, are due to the bacterial fermentation of tiny food particles clinging to mouth surfaces. Listerine Antiseptic quickly halts such fermentation, then overcomes the odors fermentation causes. LAMBERT PHARMACAL CO., *St. Louis, Mo.*

Before any date... **LISTERINE ANTISEPTIC** the extra-careful precaution against Bad Breath

---

VACATIONING? Take Listerine Antiseptic along—Because of safe germicidal action, it is an efficient first-aid in cases of minor cuts, scratches and abrasions. By the way, it helps take the sting out of mosquito bites.

[1949]

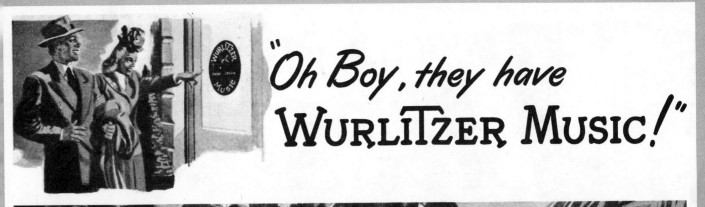

"Oh Boy, they have WURLITZER MUSIC!"

America's favorite nickel's worth of fun

All over America today, people in search of good entertainment at a reasonable price are learning to look for the Wurlitzer *Sign of the Musical Note.*

There you find Wurlitzer Music . . . 24 of the latest tunes played by the greatest bands in the land . . . for only a nickel a number. Pick your favorites from a musical menu of sweet numbers, jazz classics, hill billy hits, waltzes, fox trots, polkas.

You'll go home humming their haunting melodies, higher in spirit, happier at heart for having spent a pleasant musical interlude by spending only a few small coins. That's why Wurlitzer Music is nationally known as *America's Favorite Nickel's Worth of Fun.* The Rudolph Wurlitzer Company, North Tonawanda, New York.

[1946]

The *Sign of the Musical Note* identifies places where you can have fun playing a Wurlitzer.

WURLITZER PHONOGRAPH MUSIC

THE NAME THAT MEANS *Music* TO MILLIONS

The music of Wurlitzer pianos, accordions, electronic organs, and juke boxes is heard " 'round the world." Wurlitzer is America's largest manufacturer of pianos all produced under one name . . . also America's largest, best known manufacturer of juke boxes and accordions.

513

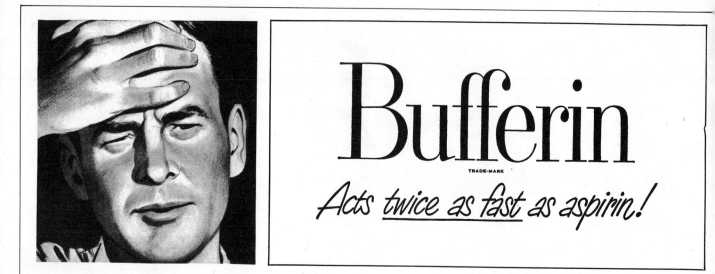

Bufferin

TRADE-MARK

Acts twice as fast as aspirin!

New product for fast pain relief <u>doesn't disagree with you!</u>

No tablet or powder can give you relief from pain until the pain-relieving ingredients enter the blood stream. No tablet or powder can *enter* the blood stream until the Pyloric valve (the trap door of the stomach) opens. Bufferin opens the trap door, gets *into* the blood stream *twice as fast* as aspirin, acts *twice as fast* to relieve pain.

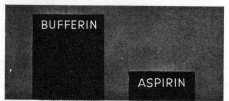

Clinical studies prove that Bufferin starts relieving pain *twice as fast* as aspirin. 20 minutes after taking Bufferin, people had *twice the amount* of pain-relieving ingredients in the blood stream as those who took aspirin. *And Bufferin won't upset your stomach,* because Bufferin is antacid, actually *protects* your stomach from aspirin irritation.

Ask your physician or dentist about Bufferin. Get Bufferin from your druggist. Carry the 12-tablet, pocket-size package. Keep the economical 36- or 100-tablet package in your home medicine chest. Bufferin is also available in Canada.

[1950]

Here's how Bufferin acts <u>twice as fast</u> as aspirin

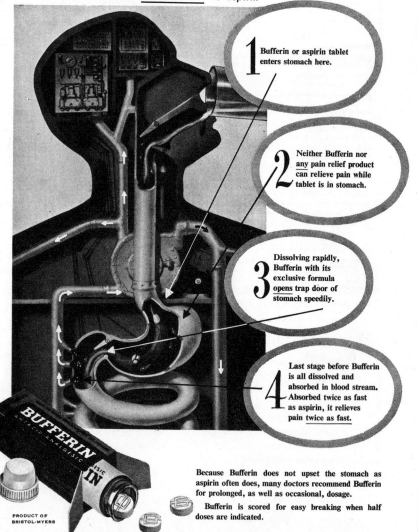

1 Bufferin or aspirin tablet enters stomach here.

2 Neither Bufferin nor any pain relief product can relieve pain while tablet is in stomach.

3 Dissolving rapidly, Bufferin with its exclusive formula opens trap door of stomach speedily.

4 Last stage before Bufferin is all dissolved and absorbed in blood stream. Absorbed twice as fast as aspirin, it relieves pain twice as fast.

PRODUCT OF
BRISTOL-MYERS

Because Bufferin does not upset the stomach as aspirin often does, many doctors recommend Bufferin for prolonged, as well as occasional, dosage.

Bufferin is scored for easy breaking when half doses are indicated.

IF YOU SUFFER FROM **ARTHRITIS** OR **RHEUMATISM**, ASK YOUR PHYSICIAN ABOUT BUFFERIN

[1945]

BE PROTECTED

Elliott Springs, president
of The Springs Cotton Mills,
says he is prepared to make
everything shown in the picture.

During the war, The Springs Cotton Mills was called upon to develop a crease-proof cotton fabric. It was used with great success as a backing for maps, photographs, and other valuable assets. This fabric has now been further perfected and made available to the torso-twister trade.

After a convention, a clam-bake, or a day in the Penta-gon Building, you need not eat off the mantel if you have your foundation covered with SPRINGMAID *POKER* woven of combed yarns 37″ wide, 152 x 68 count, in tearose, white, nude, and black, light and medium gauge. If you bruise easily, you can face the future confidently with the SPRINGMAID trademark.

SPRINGS MILLS

200 Church Street • New York 13, New York

Chicago   Dallas   Los Angeles

Coming soon . . . SPRINGMAID *sheets, pillowcases, diapers, broadcloth, poplins and tubings.*

[1948]

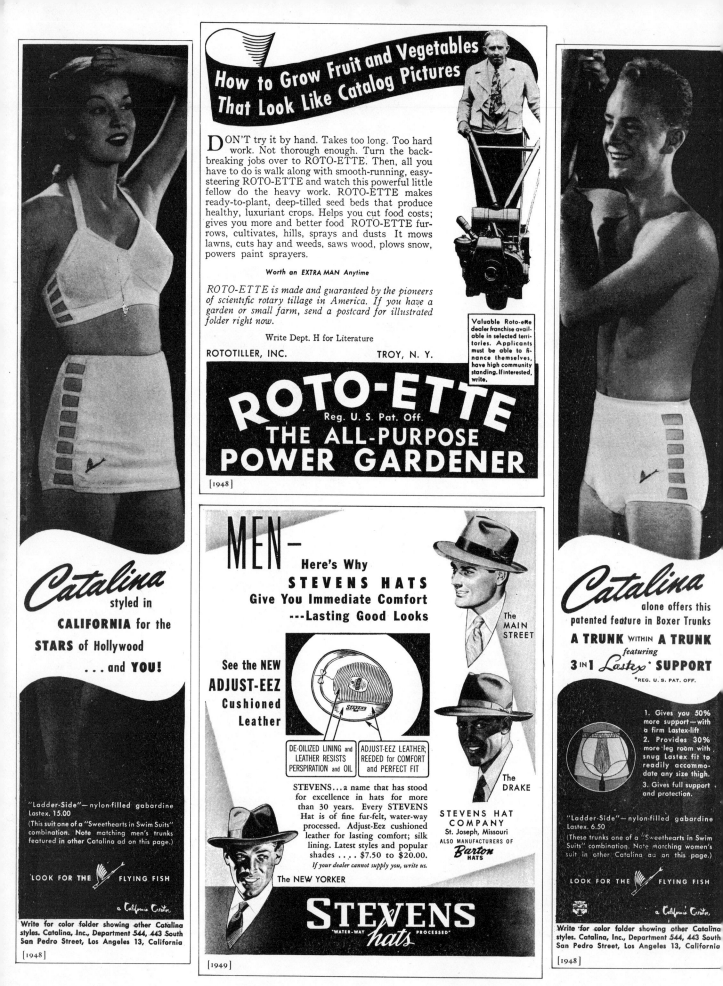

518

[1950]

The great new protein cereal
that helps you have
a fine

CORN
SOYA

SO YUM
YUM
YUM

No other well-known
cereal, hot or cold, is
so rich in protein—
the master body-
builder.

"Your Initial" Silverware Offer on Package! Set of
4 luxurious, famous-make teaspoons (gift-
quality plate) with your own personal initial, for only one Corn-Soya box top and 75¢

[1950]

body

ENJOY KELLOGG'S CORN-SOYA, THE TOASTY-TASTING CEREAL WITH THE HIGH PROTEIN FACTOR

"Can this be possible?" you ask yourself. "A cereal that can help me have a fine body?"

It's not only possible. It's here. It's Corn-Soya. It's life itself in cereal form. Sure, it has B vitamins. Sure, it has iron. Sure, it gives you energy . . . and tastes just wonderful. All that you expect from Kellogg's new cereal.

But here in Kellogg's Corn-Soya is the stuff that rippling muscles are made of . . . fine firm flesh . . . growth and staying power. This is the cereal that's really rich in protein—complete, high-quality protein, when served with milk. This is the cereal with "muscles." The cereal that has what it takes to build a fine body.

The Kellogg Company created Corn-Soya. In years to come, its benefits can be measured in the fine bodies of men and women who are boys and girls today. It can help *you* have a fine body now.

Kellogg's CORN SOYA

THE CEREAL WITH "MUSCLES"

"Cut the struttin'— this ain't Ladies' Day!"

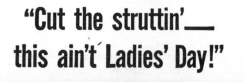

HIT: Can I help how this knit-for-fit Munsingwear glorifies even *my* manly figure? Clings as snug as a bug in a rug...and twice as comfortable! But say, how come you still stick to a Unionsuit?

RUN: Well, the way Munsingwear knits this slick one-piece job it has plenty of give and freedom...*plus* being light, cool and absorbent. Couldn't *want* better protection against a draft between innings.

HIT: O.K., but what us active young moderns go for is Munsingwear's famous "STRETCHY-SEAT."* What a pleasure when I crouch for fast ones...because it stretches with every move. So does this matching "T"-Shirt!

RUN: No error there, slugger...I'll admit "STRETCHY-SEAT"* won't creep, crawl or bind. But *I'm* gonna bank on this good old Unionsuit. However you see the play, we're *both* safe with Munsingwear!

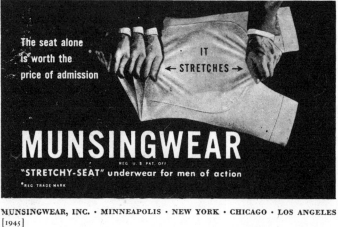

The seat alone is worth the price of admission

IT ← STRETCHES →

MUNSINGWEAR
REG. U. S. PAT. OFF.

"STRETCHY-SEAT" underwear for men of action

*REG TRADE MARK

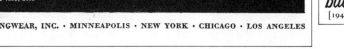

MUNSINGWEAR, INC. · MINNEAPOLIS · NEW YORK · CHICAGO · LOS ANGELES

[1945]

Trailer Living ... surges in popularity.

Increasing trailer parks offer a new profit opportunity

Carefully-engineered insulation, ventilation and heating systems shield you comfortably from the sun's hottest rays or winter's iciest blasts.

Comfortably furnished homes-on-wheels and thousands of woodsy, friendly trailer parks are attracting more and more families who enjoy this closer-to-nature way of life

Charming living rooms, separate bedrooms and modern kitchens make living or vacationing in a trailer coach pleasant, easy and economical.

Increasing thousands find the smart built-in furniture and other appointments styled by decorators create the warmth and completeness they've always wanted in a home. Even the newest shower and toilet facilities are available. Its mobile feature enables you to take your accommodations anywhere.

Send for the free illustrated 72-page book describing America's finest trailer coaches. Address T.C.M.A., Dept. P-59, Civic Opera Bldg., Chicago 6, Illinois.

You'll find a network of modern T.C.M.A.-approved trailer parks everywhere. Many are architect-planned. Recreational developments frequently even include swimming pools or beaches.

More parks are being built throughout the nation as thousands are finding them highly profitable business opportunities. T.C.M.A. will give you guidance in starting or improving a trailer park, even to free architect's plans and other professional advice. Write for "Planning a Profitable Trailer Park". Address: Trailer Parks, T.C.M.A., Dept. P-59, Civic Opera Bldg., Chicago 6, Illinois.

 Trailer Coach Manufacturers Assn.

THE TCMA SYMBOL DISTINGUISHES THE <u>BEST</u> TRAILER COACHES AND THE <u>BEST</u> TRAILER PARKS

PLATT • PRAIRIE SCHOONER • RICHARDSON • ROYCRAFT • SCHULT • SILVER DOME • SPARTAN AIRCRAFT • SPORTSMAN-COLONIAL • STEWART • STREAMLITE • SUPERIOR • SUPREME • TERRA CRUISER
TINI HOME • TRANSCONTINENTAL • TRAVELITE • TRAVELMASTER • TRAVELO • TROTWOOD • UNIVERSAL • VAGABOND • VINDALE • WALCO • WHITLEY • ZIMMER • ALL STATES • AMERICAN • CASTLE
COLUMBIA • CONTINENTAL • DUO • ELCAR • EMPIRE • GENERAL • GLIDER • HOWARD • INDIAN • INGLIS-SCHULT • IRONWOOD • KIT • KOZY COACH • LA SALLE • LIBERTY • LIGHTHOUSE • LUXOR
MAIN-LINE • MAJESTIC • MODERN • NATIONAL • OVERLAND • PACEMAKER • PALACE • PAN AMERICAN • PEERLESS

[1946]

52